Evangelical
Missiological
Society
Series

no. 22

The

MISSIONARY FAMILY

Other Books in the EMS Series

No. 1   *Scripture and Strategy: The Use of the Bible in Postmodern Church and Mission*, David Hesselgrave

No. 2   *Christianity and the Religions: A Biblical Theology of World Religions*, Edward Rommen and Harold Netland

No. 3   *Spiritual Power and Missions: Raising the Issues*, Edward Rommen

No. 4   *Missiology and the Social Sciences: Contributions, Cautions, and the Conclusions*, Edward Rommen and Gary Corwin

No. 5   *The Holy Spirit and Mission Dynamics*, Douglas McConnell

No. 6   *Reaching the Resistant: Barriers and Bridges for Mission*, Dudley Woodberry

No. 7   *Teaching Them Obedience in All Things: Equipping for the 21st Century*, Edgar Elliston

No. 8   *Working Together With God to Shape the New Millennium: Opportunities and Limitations*, Kenneth Mulholland and Gary Corwin

No. 9   *Caring for the Harvest Force in the New Millennium*, Tom Steffen and Douglas Pennoyer

No. 10 *Between Past and Future: Evangelical Mission Entering the Twenty-first Century*, Jonathan Bonk

No. 11 *Christian Witness in Pluralistic Contexts in the Twenty-first Century*, Enoch Wan

No. 12 *The Centrality of Christ in Contemporary Missions*, Mike Barnett and Michael Pocock

No. 13 *Contextualization and Syncretism: Navigating Cultural Currents*, Gailyn Van Rheenen

No. 14 *Business as Mission: From Impoverished to Empowered*, Tom Steffen and Mike Barnett

No. 15 *Missions in Contexts of Violence*, Keith Eitel

No. 16 *Effective Engagement in Short-Term Missions: Doing it Right!* Robert J. Priest

No. 17 *Missions from the Majority World: Progress, Challenges, and Case Studies*, Enoch Wan and Michael Pocock

No. 18 *Serving Jesus with Integrity: Ethics and Accountability in Mission*, Dwight P. Baker and Douglas Hayward

No. 19 *Reflecting God's Glory Together: Diversity in Evangelical Mission*, A. Scott Moreau and Beth Snodderly

No. 20 *Reaching the City: Reflections on Urban Mission for the Twenty-first Century*, Gary Fujino, Timothy R. Sisk, and Tereso C. Casiño

No. 21 *Missionary Methods: Research, Reflections, and Realities*, Craig Ott and J. D. Payne

ABOUT EMS
WWW.EMSWEB.ORG

The Evangelical Missiological Society is a professional organization with more than 350 members comprised of missiologists, mission administrators, teachers, pastors with strategic missiological interests, and students of missiology. EMS exists to advance the cause of world evangelization. We do this through study and evaluation of mission concepts and strategies from a biblical perspective with a view to commending sound mission theory and practice to churches, mission agencies, and schools of missionary training around the world. We hold an annual national conference and eight regional meetings held throughout the United States and Canada.

Evangelical
Missiological
Society
Series

no. **22**

DWIGHT P. BAKER & ROBERT J. PRIEST

EDITORS

The

MISSIONARY FAMILY

WITNESS · CONCERNS · CARE

WILLIAM CAREY
LIBRARY

Published by William Carey Library
1605 E. Elizabeth Street
Pasadena, CA 91104 |www.missionbooks.org

Aidan Lewis, editor
Hugh Pindur, graphic designer
Rose Lee-Norman, indexer

William Carey Library is a ministry of the
U.S. Center for World Mission
Pasadena, CA | www.uscwm.org
Printed in the United States of America

18 17 16 15 14   5 4 3 2 1 BP1000

Library of Congress Cataloging-in-Publication Data

The missionary family : witness, concerns, care / editors, Dwight P. Baker and Robert J. Priest.
    pages cm. -- (Evangelical Missiological Society series ; no. 18)
    Includes bibliographical references and index.
    ISBN 978-0-87808-044-1 -- ISBN 0-87808-044-9
    1. Missionaries--Family relationships. 2. Sex crimes--Religious aspects--Christianity. I. Baker, Dwight P., editor of compilation.
    BV2063.M5645 2014
    266.0085--dc23
                    2014016730

CONTENTS

Introduction
Dwight P. Baker xi

PART ONE: Families in Mission

INTRODUCTION: Families in Mission
Robert J. Priest 3

1   Walter and Ingrid Trobisch and a Missiology of "Couple Power"
    Anneke Stasson 5

2   Experiencing Risk: Missionary Families in Dangerous Places
    Donald Grigorenko and Margaret Grigorenko 25

3   The Family and Missions: Reflections from the Life of a U.S.
    Missionary
    Jerry Rankin 45

4   Caring for the Parents of Missionaries: A Case Study of Global Bible
    Translators
    Sunny Hong 60

5   The "Family Problem": Challenges in Balancing Maternity and
    Mission in Nineteenth-Century Equatorial Africa
    Mary Carol Cloutier 79

6   William Carey's Vision for Missionary Families
    Andrew D. McFarland 98

PART TWO: Responding to MK Sexual Abuse and to Reports of Abuse
Based on Recovered Memories

INTRODUCTION: Responding to MK Sexual Abuse and to Reports
of Abuse Based on Recovered Memories
Robert J. Priest 119

7   Getting It Right, Healing the Wrong: Legal Issues in Protecting
     Children and Organizations from Child Sexual Abuse
     Theresa Lynn Sidebotham 122

8   Out of the Past: Assessing Historical Reports of Sexual Abuse
     Philip Jenkins 143

9   Recovered Memories and Accusations of Sexual Abuse: A Review of
     Scientific Research Relevant to Missionary Contexts
     David R. Dunaetz 163

10   Malleability of Memory: Evaluating Testimony and Accusations
     within the Mission Community
     Raymond Phinney 182

PART THREE: Forum on Sexual Orientation and Mission: An Evangelical
Discussion

     INTRODUCTION: Forum on Sexual Orientation and Mission: An
     Evangelical Discussion
     Dwight P. Baker 205

11   Gay and Lesbian Christians: Framing Questions and Clarifying
     the Debate about a Place in Church and Mission for Evangelical
     LGBTQ Youth
     Sherwood G. Lingenfelter 208

12   Lingenfelter Raises Questions Other Than Those He Has Stated
     Andrew J. B. Cameron 231

13   Same-Sex Relationships: Toward an Old Testament Orientation
     M. Daniel Carroll R. 236

14   Urgent Question, but with Marked Reservations
     Graham A. Cole 241

15   Asking the Bible for Answers to Questions It Does Not Ask
     John Goldingay 244

16 Experience at the Heart of the Matter
    Joshua W. Jipp 247

17 The Church's Definitive Teaching
    Stanton L. Jones 251

18 The Impact of Contemporary Trends in Sexuality on Mission
    Agencies
    Phillip Marshall 256

19 A Complex Multilevel Issue
    Craig Ott 260

20 Exploring Conversations on Same-Sex Attraction
    Jenell Paris 264

21 Breaking the Evangelical Silence on Sex—with Clarity
    Kersten Bayt Priest 268

22 Additional Questions
    Steven C. Roy 273

23 Widening the Field of Vision
    Michael A. Rynkiewich 277

24 The View from a University President's Office
    David Wright 281

25 Tensions between *"What Should Be"* and *"What Is"*: A Response
    Sherwood G. Lingenfelter 285

    Bibliography 294

    Contributors 317

    General Index 323

    Scripture Index 333

INTRODUCTION

DWIGHT P. BAKER

The title of this book, *The Missionary Family: Witness, Concerns, Care*, points to a feature—the missionary family—often considered to be a distinctive of the Protestant missionary movement. Within Protestantism the image of the missionary family has perhaps a prominence in the popular imagination comparable to that of the monks and nuns of the long-enduring missionary orders within Catholicism. Married missionaries for Protestants and celibate missioners for Roman Catholics are recognizable as the modes favored by these two branches of Christianity in organizing themselves for mission. Within the Orthodox churches, monks and monasteries have not been the sole means of missional outreach, but they have played a significant if not predominant role. One thinks, for example, of the monks and monasteries that carried the faith eastward into the steppes and taiga as the Russian empire pushed eastward.

Over the course of the past two and a quarter centuries, the presence of families has been a central factor in enabling, configuring, and restricting Protestant missionary outreach. Not that families were absent from the somewhat sparse ranks of Protestant missionaries before the time when William Carey somewhat bumptiously, it would seem, led his family to India, where he would launch an illustrious missionary career. But the practicality of involving wives and children in missions was a point of contention. Hard on the heels of Carey's publication of his *Enquiry into the Obligations of Christians to Use Means for the Conversion of the Heathens* (1792) came Melvill Horne's 1794 printing of *Letters on Missions, Addressed to the Protestant Ministers of the British Churches*. Sales of Carey's volume languished; Horne's book received a hearing and continued to be updated with new editions issued over several decades. In his book, Carey urged strenuously for Christians to become engaged in missions and developed a proposal for how to go about them. Horne concurred with the call to mission outreach, but had reservations about the means, if that were to involve sending missionary families abroad. He thought the idea less than expedient.

Horne wrote in Letter Six that an essential component of "a call to Missions is a freedom from such ties as exclude the engagement," that is, freedom from responsibilities that would preclude engaging in missions, among which he counted "domestic" or "ministerial" obligations. He questioned "the propriety of married men and fathers of families engaging in missions," stating, "Generally speaking I do not think it advisable." Though he held back from advocating an outright ban on having married men serve as missionaries, he raised a number of considerations that weighed against the idea. Clearly for him the male was the missionary; a wife and children, if any, were ancillary. Men on their own could travel and labor more readily if unimpeded by domestic obligations. It would be unchristian, Horne opined, to "divorce" a wife "by leaving her behind" for the sake of becoming a missionary, and resorting to the "force" of "conjugal authority" would be foredoomed. A wife might be persuadable, Horne conceded, but clearly for him should a wife and children accompany the missionary, they would do so as the family of the missionary, not as a missionary family or a family in mission.[1]

Protestantism has not been, certainly, without its eunuchs for Christ and the Gospel's sake, that is, those who have felt a singular call of God upon them to remain unmarried so as to engage in the spread of the Gospel in settings of danger or hardship that foreclosed the opportunity of marriage or rendered it inadvisable. But marriage, entailing families laboring together in mission, has more commonly been the mode and even an ideal for Protestant missionaries.[2] Whereas for Paul the right to marry may have been a question and a decision to be weighed (1 Cor. 9:5), for Protestant missionaries it has largely been an assumption. When Jim Elliot in the mid-twentieth century decided that the demands and dangers of the task to which he was committed—that of carrying the Gospel to previously unreached tribes in the Amazon jungle—required that he and those who envisioned joining with him remain celibate, he upset his own and others' contemplated marriage plans. His later decision to marry Betty Howard after all (had he received a revised call? come to a deeper understanding of God's will?) served to release the pent-up inclinations to marry held by several of his missionary colaborers.[3]

THE FAMILY IN MISSION

From the decision to be families in mission flowed a host of endlessly fascinating entailments, some virtually unique to missionary families. Many revolve around missionary children—their role, their status, their education, their settlement (where *is* home?), their stories and life contributions. Missionaries may have resided locally, but they did so consciously as extensions of their sending countries. Rare was the missionary, man or woman, who married locally.[4] Many died in-country, but most expected to return to their home countries upon retirement and, unlike William Carey, did so if they lived to retirement age. In the meantime their presence created a liminal social space and they served a catalytic function. But the gifts they presented—and they offered many, religious and spiritual, educational, social, medical, occupational, material—and the labor they exerted were not carried out with a view to the benefit of their children and grandchildren in the way that an immigrant's lifework would be.[5]

The chapters found in part 1 interact with some of the breadth and complexity bound up with "the family in mission"—sickness and health, danger and discernment, risk taking and personal growth, concern for the well-being of missionary children and for the care of the parents of missionaries, issues of calling and ministry of both husband and wife and of a role for the children, and the effort to build something wider and stronger than nuclear families embarking on their own in mission.

MISSION BOARDING SCHOOLS, MK SEXUAL ABUSE, AND "RECOVERED MEMORIES"

The entailments of long-term residence without immigrating were of considerable import, one facet of which is treated in part 2. Precisely because missionaries were not immigrants, the education of their children, for example, was problematic in ways that the education of immigrants' children would not have been. The children may be born *here*, but they must be educated so that they will be equipped to enter life *there*, back home. Precisely because missionary families were not immigrant families investing their children as well as themselves in the future of the country to which they had come, mission boarding schools came into existence, and with them the tragedies of Mamou Alliance Academy and others.[6] Not everyone's experience in mission schools was a travesty on Christian grace, certainly—and by no means do all reports or accusations of abuse center on boarding situations. But inside and outside school settings far too many missionary children were sacrificed on the altar of advancing "the work."[7]

Existentially, psychologically, and sociologically fraught terrain—isolated islands of a pseudo-elsewhere surrounded by a sea of otherness—these mission primary and secondary educational establishments were closer than the home country but too distant for effective parental contact, informedness, or oversight. Children in their most vulnerable years were left—abandoned?—to the mercy and grace or malignity of whoever happened to be assigned to be in charge of them.

Not everyone's experience of the mission boarding schools was equally traumatic by any means. Many dedicated servants of Christ served as teachers, administrators, and staff at mission boarding schools. See, for example, the range of appraisals and assessments of their boarding school experience offered by missionary children in *Far above the Plain*.[8] Too often, however, the schools served as fertile seedbeds for a large share of today's bitter harvest of stories of child abuse, sexual and otherwise, in mission settings. Some real, some imagined, some magnified by childhood's sense of utter dependence and vulnerability stripped of parental defenses, some enlarged through the accreting power of memory: not all accusations of abuse have equal validity, though they supply the fuel for much current tension, including litigation, confronting mission agencies. Wounds incurred and wrongs suffered are, to the extent possible, matters to be redressed. In any case accusations made, whether well-founded or not, are indices of persons in need to whom grace and care in some appropriate form need to be extended.

To sort out the factual from the confabulated in today's morass of accusations of abuse is a task beyond herculean. This is especially the case with accusations brought on the basis of memories alleged to have been blocked or repressed and then recovered, sometimes decades later. Memories said to be recovered during therapy or in support group settings are particularly pliable. Persons making accusations may have experienced damage, but whether of the exact sort alleged or at the hands of the persons accused has real-life consequences for the lives, ministries, reputations, and well-being of other persons who frequently are ill-positioned or, being dead, unable to defend themselves.

The boarding schools may largely be gone, but the issues surrounding the education of missionary children remain vitally current, as studies of Korean missionary families show.[9] Concerns raised about abuse and constraints at mission boarding schools led to the closing of a number of the schools and helpful reforms at others. But accusations of sexual abuse based on "recovered memories" continue to haunt mission organizations, including evangelical missions. The four chapters of part 2 are of great service to mission agencies by placing this cluster of issues in historical, psychological, legal, and practical context.

FORUM ON SEXUAL ORIENTATION AND MISSION: AN EVANGELICAL DISCUSSION

Part 3 of this year's volume introduces an innovation in the annual Evangelical Missiological Society Series by creating an evangelical forum for discussion centered on a single highly significant issue for mission studies and practice. The forum is patterned after the practice found in *Current Anthropology* in which all major articles are accompanied by critique in the same issue supplied by selected scholars from around the world, to which the author of the article then responds.

Nearly two years ago the editors invited Sherwood Lingenfelter—provost and professor of anthropology first at Biola University and then at Fuller Theological Seminary, anthropological and missiological consultant to Wycliffe/SIL for nearly four decades (along with his wife, Judith), and parent to his daughter, Jennifer, a lesbian—to speak at the 2013 annual EMS meeting in Dallas on homosexuality/same-sex attraction as a missiological issue. Lingenfelter brought much—personal involvement, anthropological expertise, lifelong biblical engagement, concern for missional outreach, and a focus on ministry to the real living person standing in front of one—to this assignment. He presented the material first to the North Central regional EMS in April 2013, revising the paper he had written both before and after that meeting. His paper was further revised for the annual meeting in September

2013. Lingenfelter's presentation there was both well attended and well received, earning numerous expressions of appreciation from mission leaders.

Once Lingenfelter's final revision was received, the editors asked a number of evangelical scholars representing a variety of fields, disciplines, and professional roles to engage with it. Their responses follow chapter 11. It will immediately be seen that they took the assignment seriously. Lingenfelter receives the final word, both responding to their comments and taking the discussion further.

The editors, along with Sherwood Lingenfelter and the discussants, offer this forum with the prayer that it will serve as an opening and basis for ongoing missiological conversation about an urgent and timely topic.

NOTES

1. For convenience the quoted words are taken from Melvill Horne, *A Collection of Letters Relative to Foreign Missions* (Andover [Mass.]: Ware, 1810), 32–33, https://archive.org /details/acollectionlett00horngoog.

2. Dana L. Robert, "The 'Christian Home' as a Cornerstone of Anglo-American Missionary Thought and Practice," in *Converting Colonialism: Visions and Realities in Mission History, 1706–1914*, edited by Dana L. Robert (Grand Rapids: Eerdmans, 2008), 134–65.

3. James Elliot, *The Journals of Jim Elliot*, ed. Elisabeth Elliot (Old Tappen, N.J.: Revell, 1978); Olive Fleming Liefeld, *Unfolding Destinies: The Untold Story of Peter Fleming and the Auca*, ed. Verne Becker (Grand Rapids: Zondervan, 1990).

4. The missionary career of one who did marry locally, George Leslie Mackay, who ministered in Formosa, now Taiwan, at the end of the nineteenth century, was uncommonly fruitful.

5. For the story of one immigrant family in the United States, see William Form, *On the Shoulders of Immigrants: A Family Portrait* (Columbus, Ohio: North Star Press, 1999).

6. Wess Stafford, *Too Small to Ignore: Why the Least of These Matters Most*, with Dean Merrill (Colorado Springs, Colo.: WaterBrook Press, 2007).

7. Dan Harrison, *Strongest in the Broken Places: A Story of Spiritual Recovery*, ed. Maria Henderson (Downers Grove, Ill.: InterVarsity Press, 1990).

8. Paul Asbury Seaman et al., *Far above the Plain* (Pasadena, Calif.: William Carey Library, 1996).

9. Jonathan J. Bonk, ed., *Family Accountability in Missions: Korean and Western Case Studies* (New Haven, Conn.: OMSC Publications, 2013).

PART ONE

FAMILIES IN MISSION

INTRODUCTION

FAMILIES IN MISSION

ROBERT J. PRIEST

While the Roman Catholic Church sent exclusively unmarried missionaries abroad, from the time of William Carey, Protestant churches have sent out married missionary couples as well as singles. These missionary couples had children. On the one hand this step involved unique challenges, burdens, and risks. But it also brought strengths. Married missionary couples often have greater social access than single missionaries. The husband has access to male relationships and settings, and the wife to female relationships and settings. And they model not only the piety of the individual life, but also of a Christian marriage and home. This modeling has often been invaluable for both evangelism and discipleship. Not infrequently missionaries' own children acquired missionary commitments as well as linguistic and cultural competencies that contributed to their parents' ministries. Missionary children have often become a second generation of missionaries with better cultural and linguistic understandings than their parents.

In the first chapter of this book, Anneke Stasson reviews the ministry of Walter and Ingrid Trobisch, whose influential writings about courtship and marriage were read by many tens of thousands of African Christians. The Trobisches, like many missionaries before them, placed their own marriage and family life on display as part of missionary witness and discipleship. Not surprisingly, this sometimes involved a measure of ethnocentrism. More seriously, as judged by Stasson and by their own children, their ministry also had parental weaknesses that missionaries today should work to avoid.

In the next chapter Donald and Margaret Grigorenko point out that the Apostle Paul reported having faced many dangers (2 Cor. 11:26) and that missionaries today do so no less. Paul faced those dangers as a single missionary, not as a husband and father accompanied by a family. The Grigorenkos, themselves long-term missionaries in Nepal, report on their fascinating research into the risks that contemporary missionary families face around the world today, with particular attention given to the experience of children. They consider risk theologically and provide guidance on wise risk management.

Out of long missionary experience Jerry Rankin writes personally about the place of family in missions. He stresses the importance of both the husband and wife having a sense of personal calling to missionary service, with husband and wife sharing in responsibilities of home and family, and with children being involved in the ministry.

Missionaries also were raised within families. What are the responsibilities of missionaries to their parents? In her case study, Sunny Hong considers the parents of Korean missionaries. These elderly parents often had only one or two children. They commonly invested heavily in their children's education and counted on their children's support and filial piety in old age. Apart from support by their children, many Korean parents experience relative poverty in old age. Hong provides a fascinating look at how Chinese and Korean missionaries with Wycliffe Bible Translators are attempting to address this situation wisely as itself a part of Christian mission.

Finally, Mary Cloutier and Andrew McFarland examine missionary family life in earlier eras of mission history, both the positive vision for what the missionary family ought to be and do, and the suffering and risk that earlier missionary families routinely faced. McFarland treats the well-known case of William Carey and his family, while Mary Cloutier focuses on missionaries with whom most readers may not be familiar. But both chapters help to provide historical perspective on the part played by families engaged in mission.

1

WALTER AND INGRID TROBISCH AND A MISSIOLOGY OF "COUPLE POWER"

ANNEKE STASSON

Walter and Ingrid Trobisch were Lutheran missionaries in Cameroon, West Africa, in the 1950s and 1960s. Walter was German and Ingrid, American. In 1962 Walter wrote *I Loved a Girl*, a book about sexual and marital issues in Africa that ended up being translated into over seventy languages.[1] *I Loved a Girl* established the Trobisches as authorities on love, sex, and marriage, and they went on to lead marriage seminars around the world.

The story of the Trobisches' marriage and ministry illustrates an important tradition in Protestant mission theory—namely, the missiology of the Christian home. Although the Christian home has traditionally been the domain of women missionaries, the Trobisches' missiology of "couple power" blurred the boundaries between men's work and women's work. Both spouses spoke in public, both wrote books, and, at least initially, both took care of the children.

Through historical analysis of the Trobisches' books, correspondence, and diaries, this chapter will argue that while the Trobisches' joint involvement in mission was integral to their own sense of vocational fulfillment, it also took a toll on their children. The chapter will give a fairly critical portrayal of the Trobisches' family life, but it does so with the understanding that this is exactly the kind of thing that the Trobisches themselves did in their marriage seminars. They often used their own mistakes to teach others. This was part of the way they sought to deepen their own couple power and to deepen the couple power of those who sought counsel from them. It is hoped that the Trobisches' story might shed light on the ongoing conversation among mission scholars and practitioners about how to achieve a fruitful work-family balance on the mission field.

MARITAL PARTNERSHIP IN TCHOLLIRÉ, CAMEROON, 1953–56

The Trobisches' first years as missionaries in Tcholliré were also their first years of married life. Consequently, they were learning what it meant to be missionaries at the same time that they were learning what it meant to be husband and wife. As they worked at learning the local language, they also learned what all spouses learn—namely, to express their needs and to meet the needs of the other. As they ran a dispensary, they also learned how to accommodate one another and to forgive. As they taught people how to read, they also continued to get to know each other. Walter told Ingrid about growing up in Leipzig, one of the most cultured cities in Europe. She told him about life in the Missouri Ozarks with nine brothers and sisters.

Besides sharing stories with each other, the Trobisches also came up with other strategies for coping with the loneliness of life in the mission field. For example, they reserved Friday night as "game night." They would wind up their record player, play one of the three records they owned, and create space for relaxation and enjoyment. The mail typically came on Fridays, so this added to the joy of the evening.[2] They also made sure their home was a place where they could feel comfortable and refreshed after the challenges of the day. As Ingrid wrote in her autobiography, "Walter and I found it important to have a neat and tastefully furnished home in which we could relax after . . . exhausting mornings. Our two rooms, with the beautiful picture on the wall, the fresh vase of flowers, and even the brightly decorated table, helped to restore us."[3]

In their efforts to cultivate marital intimacy and keep a neat and orderly home, the Trobisches were doing what generations of missionary couples in rural Africa had done before them. Historian Dana Robert has observed that missionary attention to cultivating an exemplary marriage and home life is itself a distinct missionary strategy. This missiology of the Christian home, she argues, has been a "cornerstone of Anglo-American missionary thought and practice."[4] Nineteenth-century missionary societies felt that it was good for indigenous peoples to view the interactions between husband and wife and between parents and children in a healthy Christian home. In the words of American Board Secretary Rufus Anderson in 1836, "The heathen should have an opportunity of seeing Christian families."[5] Therefore, missionary societies began sending out more married couples than they previously had done. Gradually, sending married couples to the field became a hallmark of evangelical Protestant mission.

Couples developed various ways of handling the division of labor that came with married life on the mission field. Some couples worked alongside each other, translating the Bible into the local language and traversing the countryside to evangelize.[6] Other couples maintained the gender roles that were popular in their home countries, whereby men occupied the public sphere and women the private sphere. Among these couples, some found the Victorian gender roles completely acceptable. Although they faced struggles peculiar to their roles, each viewed the sacrifices as part of his or her missionary commitment.[7] Other couples who held to Victorian gender roles on the mission field found them oppressive. Many women, particularly, grew frustrated when domestic duties made it difficult for them to engage in the mission work for which they had originally come to the field.[8]

For their part, Walter and Ingrid did not operate under strictly divided gender roles in their early mission career. While they did some gender-specific work, such as Walter's preaching and Ingrid's attending at births, they shared most of the duties of their mission life. They both taught, handed out medical supplies from their dispensary, and went on evangelistic trips to the surrounding area. Because they shared so many of their missionary duties, they developed a highly satisfying sense of marital partnership.

In 1955 Ingrid gave birth to their first child, Katrine. As with many missionary mothers before her, Ingrid found that the women of Tchollíré opened up to her in a new way after she became a mother.[9] The women observed with interest the way little Katrine grew healthy and strong. They also saw how Walter shared the duties of carrying the child. The women then questioned Ingrid about these things. Walter's favorite response, when accused of being unmanly by carrying a child, was to say, "Before the baby was born madame carried the baby; now monsieur can carry it."[10] Both he and Ingrid were pleased when some of the men in the village decided that they, too, could carry around their little ones.

As soon as Walter and Ingrid discovered that Walter's carrying baby Katrine was a lesson on marital partnership for their observing neighbors, they made a point of having him carry the baby often. This process, by which unintentional actions become infused with theological significance, has a long and fruitful history. Making daily life into "object lessons" has been a classic strategy for missionary wives.[11] In fact, it has given them a deeper sense of integration between their domestic and mission work.

Around the time when Katrine was born, one of the new Christians in Tcholliré took a second wife. Perplexed, Walter asked the man, "Don't you love your wife?" The man replied that he took a second wife precisely *because* he loved his first wife. She was pregnant with their first child, and since couples were to abstain from sexual relations until the child was two or three years old, he took a second wife. For him, respecting the sexual taboo and taking another wife to satisfy his sexual urges was a way of respecting his first wife. The Trobisches learned that in many traditional African societies, women tended to abstain from sex during pregnancy and lactation, lest the semen poison the child.[12] They decided then that one way of fighting polygamy was to teach people about human anatomy in order to show that it was not possible for the semen to come into contact with the child.[13]

Another problem the Trobisches encountered, however, was that couples in Tcholliré used this sexual taboo during lactation to space out the birth of their children. If a mother got pregnant while she was nursing an infant, her milk might be reduced and the newborn child might starve. This is likely why the idea developed that semen could poison a child. In their eagerness to correct mistaken biological knowledge and fight polygamy, it is doubtful that the Trobisches recognized how the sexual taboo during lactation actually protected the newborn child. What they did recognize was that in order for monogamy to become a more feasible option, couples would have to be given alternative methods of birth control.[14] The only method of natural family planning available at the time was the rhythm method, but in later years the Trobisches would teach couples in Africa about the more effective symptothermal method of natural family planning.

For both Walter and Ingrid, teaching about fertility became what they would later call "an open door for missions."[15] Children were an integral part of African society, so couples in Tcholliré who were struggling to get pregnant welcomed the fertility information the Trobisches offered.[16] For their part, the Trobisches hoped this interest would lead to interest in Christian faith.

However, conversion was not their sole aim in teaching about fertility. They also believed that helping couples manage their fertility was, itself, part of their responsibility as missionaries. Genesis 2:24 called for husband and wife to "cleave to" or be united to each other.[17] So enabling couples to "cleave" was, in the Trobisches' eyes, an important Christian aim. Natural family planning helped couples achieve or avoid pregnancy as each couple desired, and this strengthened marriages. Fertility awareness allowed couples to resume sexual relations much sooner than the traditional two years, and this, the Trobisches believed, also served to enhance marital satisfaction.

Walter and Ingrid garnered many of their ideas about marriage from their Swiss marriage counselor, Theodor Bovet. During the 1950s one of the most popular conceptions of marriage in German Lutheran circles was that it was a way of enacting the divine order of creation. Because God made man before he made woman, man was to rule over woman in church, society, and marriage.[18] Bovet's understanding of marriage was incompatible with this view; he emphasized that marriage was a companionship. As the Trobisches talked with couples in Tchirolé about natural family planning and developed their own ideas on marital partnership, they were influenced more deeply by Bovet's teaching than by the idea of marriage as a divine order of creation. Their preference for the companionship view of marriage over the hierarchical view was reinforced by their observations of the division of labor in Tchirolé.

For the Trobisches the division of labor they found in Tchirolé was unjust, leaving women "completely overburdened." Walter wrote:

From 6 a.m. to 3 p.m. they [the women in Tchirolé] weeded their gardens, sometimes with a baby on their back. Then they had to fetch wood and water, take care of the children, prepare the food, which included pounding the grain, grinding and sifting it, a process that takes two hours time. Meanwhile the husband was already waiting impatiently for his evening meal, after which he demanded sexual union, in some cases even repeatedly. No wonder that those women often urged their husbands to take second and third wives. They looked at polygamy as a possibility to take once in a while a "vacation from marriage."[19]

Walter and Ingrid grew deeply concerned about the way in which traditional African gender roles seemed to prevent women from enjoying marriage. They noticed that men seemed to love their siblings more than they did their wives. Later, an African pastor would explain to them that in traditional African society, "a man's wife is like an ambassador from a foreign tribe. He never trusts her as he does his blood brothers and sisters."[20]

The Trobisches began to feel that putting their own marriage on display was the best way of proclaiming the Gospel.[21] They had found that people had difficulty believing in Jesus as a loving person. They wondered if this was because love was usually reserved for blood relations. Ingrid said, "The fact that Walter and I could live together in love and harmony in our family was perhaps the first way that they could believe [in Jesus]."[22] Just as natural family planning had proven to be a relevant topic, the Trobisches believed that discussing the division of labor and putting their own marriage on display would be "an open door for missions" and a way to improve marital relationships in Tchollire.

Their description of the unequal distribution of labor in Tchollire corresponds to Ester Boserup's findings from the 1970s. In her description of "male and female farming systems," she argued that

in very sparsely populated regions where shifting cultivation is used, men do little farm work, the women doing most. In somewhat more densely populated regions where the agricultural system is that of extensive plough cultivation, women do little farm work and men do much more. Finally in the regions of intensive cultivation or irrigated land, both men and women must put hard work into agriculture in order to earn enough to support a family.[23]

Boserup also described the correlation between "female farming systems" and polygyny: "In regions where shifting cultivation predominates and the major part of agricultural work is done by women . . . we can expect to find a high incidence of polygamy (polygyny), and bride wealth being paid by the future husband or his family. The women are hard-working and have only a limited right of support from their husbands."[24] During the mid-twentieth century, Boserup was a leader among modernist, second-wave feminists whose research aimed to empower women in developing nations. These Western feminists significantly shaped international development programs sponsored by the United Nations and other international aid organizations. Although the Trobisches preferred to think of their marriage counseling work in Africa primarily as a biblically-inspired mission, it is likely that they were also aware of and influenced by the modernist development project.[25]

There was, however, a key difference between the approaches of mid-twentieth-century missionaries like the Trobisches and second-wave feminists like Boserup. While both were concerned with improving life for women in developing nations, second-wave feminists like Boserup tended to focus on programs that would improve women's access to power and resources. Missionaries, on the other hand, usually focused on efforts at reform for *both* men and women. Remember that Walter's carrying around the baby was a lesson for both women and men in Tcholliré. During the 1960s and 1970s, as the Trobisches wrote family life books for Africa, they addressed both men and women as they challenged traditional African conceptions of gender. In many ways, their actual focus was on men, hoping to show how a biblical conception of personhood challenged African conceptions of gendered identity.[26]

It is important to note that both the Trobisches' observations of gender roles in Tcholliré and the observations of many second-wave feminists such as Boserup were based more on their own conceptions of proper gender relations than on the actual testimonies of African couples themselves. When Walter surmised that African women were overburdened and African men were demanding, he was not making reference to conversations he had had with individual couples in Tcholliré. Rather, he was interpreting spousal relations in Tcholliré through the lens of Bovet's theology of marriage, which was written with mid-twentieth-century Europeans in mind. Throughout the Trobisches' years in Africa they maintained that they were arguing for a "Christian" view of marriage, but in reality their view of marriage was strongly marked by Western biases and could not therefore be called simply "Christian." Their stress on the partnership of husband and wife was as much a product of changes in the economic structure of Western society as it was a commentary on Genesis 2:24.

Moreover, in their initial assessment of African gender roles, the Trobisches were guilty of what postcolonial scholars have called "silencing" non-Western women.[27] By advocating a new vision of marriage, the Trobisches were essentially saying that they knew what was best for African women. And as postcolonial critics have so effectively pointed out, this has been the classic stance of the colonialist oppressor.[28]

In their eagerness to fix what they considered cultural patriarchy and oppression, the missionary couple was also blind to some of the ways in which the traditional life may have appealed to African women. For example, the Trobisches depicted child rearing, housework, and sex as exhausting, but sociologist Sylvia Moena has highlighted the ability of African women to integrate their multiple tasks in a satisfying manner. She has argued that women's "roles as wives and mothers were easily accommodated" with the work they did "for the survival and subsistence of their families."[29] Moena goes so far as to say that women's roles were empowering in the Western feminist sense of the word. With the coming of industrialization and men's leaving home to work in cities, African women "practically ran their communities without the help, guidance, and support of their male counterparts. Through this they became independent and resourceful, learning to depend on themselves or on each other."[30]

Were the women of Tchollíré oppressed, as the Trobisches thought, or were they empowered, as Moena suggests? Since we do not have the words of the Tchollíré women themselves, it is impossible to answer this question conclusively. It is important to recognize that the Trobisches were indeed guilty of some of the same colonialist tendencies that plagued other missionaries and expatriates of the day. For example, they tended to stereotype the "other" and thereby to miss some of the subtleties of marital life in Tchollíré. They, however, were not alone in thinking that the division of labor and the state of marriage present in Africa discriminated against women. During the late 1950s, several congresses of African women advocated major changes to African marital customs.[31] Thus the Trobisches' stance on African marriage was not simply a colonialist perspective.

Historian Cheryl Johnson-Odim has drawn attention to the way in which many West African cultures have "simultaneously oppressed, venerated, and feared women." Her perspective is helpful: "Women . . . derived a certain autonomy and status from their roles as cultivators, traders, artisans, and providers of other marketplace services. Yet there is a discrepancy . . . in the autonomous ways women behaved collectively and in women's obeisance as daughters-in-law and especially as wives. Women are far more subordinated to men privately than publicly."[32] Since the Trobisches were more interested in the private lives of women, it is not surprising that they picked up on the ways in which women in West Africa might feel oppressed by their cultural traditions. And since Moena was more interested in the public lives of women, it is not surprising that she highlighted women's autonomy and freedom.

EXEMPLIFYING A MISSIOLOGY OF THE CHRISTIAN HOME

The Trobisches' mission work in Tcholliré demonstrates several of the key features of a missiology of the Christian home.

- This missiology involves women missionaries and is concerned with the lives of women in the mission context.
- The marital partnership and home life of the missionary couple is considered an essential part of the mission.
- Couples put their marriage and family life on display for people around them.
- This missiology is holistic, but it also has the potential to be ethnocentric. The potential is always present for missionaries concerned with home and family life to overemphasize their own culture's way of doing things and to fail to acknowledge the extent to which they are spreading cultural ideas that are not necessarily Christian.

DEVELOPING A MISSIOLOGY OF COUPLE POWER

Though the Trobisches endeavored to build a missiology of couple power, they did not consciously develop this concept while they were missionaries in Tcholliré in the 1950s. Rather, it was an idea they developed later, after they had left Africa and moved to Austria. Nevertheless, it is helpful to think of their earlier life through the lens of their later theology of couple power.

Ingrid defined couple power as "the multiplied power of two whole people joined as man and wife. Two people together can do more than two separately, especially when they know that as man and woman they have been created in the image of God. Together they mirror His image to the world."[33] Ingrid said that her passion in life was to release couple power: "I knew in the depths of my soul that, for both men and women, a committed marriage to one's best friend is a wonderful source of wellbeing and a firm foundation for healthy family life. Instead of watching couples bail water out of a sinking marriage boat, I felt a strong need to help men and women find new ways to repair the leaks that were causing them to sink." The Trobisches did not believe that everyone should be married; they did not believe that married couples were somehow better than single people. But they did think that marriage had been designed by God with some deeply redemptive and missiological purposes.

The Trobisches' vision of couple power was based on Genesis 2:24 (KJV): "Therefore shall a man leave his father and his mother, and shall cleave unto his wife: and they shall be one flesh." At the heart of their message was the idea that the husband and wife should be equal partners. The acts of leaving, cleaving, and becoming one flesh were acts that should be done by both partners. These acts would result in couple power. Couple power was about the sense of intimacy and security that would be present for the couple that had learned to leave their family of origin, cleave to each other, and become one flesh, in terms not only of sharing physical intimacy but of sharing everything—finances, possessions, hopes, and fears.[34] For the Trobisches, couple power was not just about building up a solid marriage. It was about using one's marriage to bless others. As has been noted, this idea that the Christian home has deep missiological potential is a thread that has run throughout the history of Protestant mission.

There is a major way, however, in which the Trobisches' idea of couple power departed from missiological tradition. In the nineteenth and early twentieth centuries, the home was viewed as the sphere of the woman, who created a warm, hospitable environment in which she could nurture and support her husband, who worked in the public sphere.[35] Historically, the separate spheres model of the Christian home has given women a role in mission work, but it has also kept women from doing some of the other work that many of them wanted to do, such as public preaching and teaching. The Trobisches' missiology of couple power represented a different model of the Christian home, one that gave both men and women responsibilities for maintaining the home and that also validated women as full participants in the public sphere of mission. For example, when Ingrid was asked about the Navigators, a campus ministry group, she said that many of the Navigators glorified the husband's work but kept the wife back home. "They had not yet learned the essence of couple power," Ingrid explained.[36]

On their furlough in 1958 Walter preached about the importance of having fathers be in the home for significant periods of time, rather than only involved in their public work outside the home. "Can it be right for a man to spend almost every evening away from his family? Most of our Christian homes are just motels where people gas up, get some food and sleep, and then go again. Do you think a needy soul would seek out such a family motel as a place to unburden his heart? Christ cannot use such homes for his strategy."[37]

During the three years the Trobisches spent in Tcholliré, they had worked together in mission both inside the home and outside it. This led to a highly satisfying sense of marital partnership. That changed, however, when they took their next post at Libamba.

DISINTEGRATION OF COUPLE POWER IN LIBAMBA, CAMEROON, 1957–63

The Trobisches were not able to live up to their own ideal of couple power during their six years in Libamba. Walter served as chaplain and professor of German at Cameroon Christian College in Libamba. The Trobisches wrote in a letter to their friends that because Walter had to teach in French and had only a "modest knowledge of French" he sometimes had "to work harder than his students, especially if it [came] to translating Goethe and Schiller into French."[38] It was not unusual for Walter to rise before dawn and stay up until midnight to finish his work.[39] In addition to his teaching responsibilities, Walter and the other faculty members had to do such things as supervise meal times and help in the kitchen and business office.[40] Needless to say, Walter was very busy.

Ingrid was also quite busy. When they arrived at Libamba in 1957, the Trobisches had two children, Katrine and Daniel. By 1961 they had five children. Ingrid would later testify that the years of having young children were "among the happiest in my life," but there were certainly days when she did not feel so cheery and optimistic.[41] Probably her most difficult time came in July of 1962, when Walter was gone for nine weeks teaching in Tanzania.[42] After a month, Ingrid wrote in her journal: "I've been struggling to keep sane and even-tempered surrounded as I am by my five children—Ruth just 10 months up to Kathy not quite seven. Often I've failed miserably and would like to do nothing quite as much as sit down in a desolate corner and weep."[43] With five children Ingrid found the rainy season especially difficult. Lonely and fed up with being housebound due to rain, she wrote, "There are . . . days (today for example) when I wish it would be evening before we even eat breakfast."[44] Mealtimes were the most difficult. Ingrid wrote to Walter, "I just wish you could . . . live through an hour here about supper-time. I don't know whether to scream or laugh when things get too involved with the children. I usually end up doing some of both."[45]

There is no doubt that Ingrid loved her children, but in reading her diaries from the period, one cannot help but think that both Ingrid and Walter would have been better served by a different division of labor. Walter suffered from a nervous breakdown during the summer of 1962. He was simply overwhelmed by the workload at Libamba. And Ingrid's journal is filled with entries that give the impression that she was having a hard time subsuming her missionary fervor in domestic duties. During their years at Libamba she still felt a call to public missionary work, but she had no time to devote to it. At one point she did teach a course at Libamba, but in general she had to give up her public mission work in order to raise her children and provide "a haven of rest for my busy husband."[46]

Had they stayed in Tcholliré rather than moving to Libamba, the Trobisches might have been able to maintain the more equitable division of labor that they had initially established there. They might have been able to work out an arrangement that would have allowed Ingrid to continue to share in the public mission work and Walter to take his turn caring for the children. In her autobiography Ingrid reflected that although as a child Walter had "observed that the care of infants was predominantly the mother's domain . . . he was never one to be trapped into acting a certain way if it didn't make sense."[47] Had they stayed in Tcholliré, it might not have made sense for Ingrid to take over the sole care of home and children. In Libamba, however, it did make sense. The children needed care, and Walter's job took so much time that it was not possible for him to be involved in their daily care. That task fell to Ingrid, and it so consumed her that she rarely took part in school-related activities.

Ultimately, Ingrid realized that she would be a much happier woman and a better wife and mother if she were able to "have a creative project of my own."[48] In 1961 she did embark on a creative project, and it was a project that gave her great joy and helped her feel as though she could again fulfill a bit of her public missionary vocation. For a long time she had wanted to write the story of her father and his missionary work. In 1961 she wrote to the publisher Harper & Row to see if they would be interested in the story. The publisher told her to send a sample chapter and an outline, which she did. A few weeks later she received a letter from Harper, offering her a contract and inviting her to come to New York City to discuss the book. Ingrid was ecstatic.

FAILURE OF COUPLE POWER IN AUSTRIA, 1963–79

Although neither Walter nor Ingrid realized it at the time, Ingrid's book contract marked a turning point in their missionary career. In the late 1960s and the 1970s, writing, rather than evangelism or college teaching, became their primary ministry. In 1963 the Trobisches left Libamba to go on furlough. They never returned to live in Africa. Rather, they settled in Austria and devoted themselves to developing marriage-counseling literature for Africa. Walter also took a job with the Lutheran World Federation, which required him to make two trips to Africa each year to conduct marriage seminars. As often as they could arrange care for the children, Ingrid accompanied Walter. This working together and publicly presenting as a couple was one of the significant contributions they made to Christian home missiology. Presenting as a couple gave much weight to their message about marital partnership. People would often tell them that their *message* was not revolutionary; what was revolutionary was that they were publicly embodying that message.

There was, however, a serious problem with the Trobisches' decision to present their message as a couple. It meant that they both had to leave their children periodically for a span of weeks. To the children, it seemed that their parents were always just getting back from a trip or just about to leave. Their son Stephen remarked later that when he was a child "it was one of the hardest things for me to see [Father] and Mother leave. . . . I can well remember how [Father] asked me once what would make me happy. I said, 'The coming back home.'" Walter's response was not exactly comforting: "How can you come back home if you have not been away from home?"[49]

The Trobisches did feel bad about leaving their children. Ingrid wrote in a letter that they "would not dare [to do it] if it were only for adventure's sake."[50] In talking to their children, however, one wonders whether they made the right decision, for their son David believes that "Walter and Ingrid were great marriage counselors but they failed their children."[51] According to David, all of the children—but especially Katrine, the oldest—felt abandoned. This is likely because while the Trobisches were in Libamba they did as most missionaries of their generation did and dutifully sent six-year-old Katrine to the missionary boarding school four hundred miles away. She was there for a year and a half, only coming home over the summer and at Christmas. Ingrid wrote in her journal that it was an "unnatural situation" to have children that young living away from home.[52] However, at that point it was hard for her to conceive of doing otherwise.

The Trobisches' ministry also took a toll on Stephen, whose feelings of abandonment probably go back to 1963. That was the year the Trobisches left Libamba. They developed a complex plan for transporting the family out of Africa that would also allow both Walter and Ingrid to do some missionary business of their own. Ingrid had been invited to New York to discuss the terms of her book contract. Walter had been invited to be a keynote speaker at an All-Africa family life seminar in what was then Rhodesia. So in January, while Walter prepared for the conference, Ingrid flew to Germany with their three youngest children (the two oldest children were at the missionary boarding school in Ngaoundéré, Cameroon). Ingrid left four-year-old David with Walter's mother and took three-year-old Stephen to stay with another family. Taking two-year-old Ruth with her, she then flew to New York to discuss her book with Harper & Row. Finally, she flew to Missouri, where she hoped to finish her book at her mother's house.

The Trobisches had planned to reunite as a family in Germany in May.[53] "But then everything went wrong."[54] Little Stephen cried for two weeks straight after Ingrid left. Rosemarie, the mother who was caring for him, broke her arm. Rosemarie's husband wrote to Ingrid to say Rosemarie could no longer take care of Stephen; Ingrid would have to return to retrieve him.[55] But Ingrid had just had an operation and could not travel.[56] Stephen could not go to stay with Walter's mother because she had the flu. So Stephen was taken to an orphanage in the Black Forest.[57] As Ingrid wrote in a letter to friends, "What a paradox—Walter lecturing on Christian family life at the All-Africa Conference in Rhodesia and I trying to write a story which would be a testimony of how one family lived out their Christian faith—and our own little family had to pay the price."[58]

In many ways, Ingrid, at least, was simply following in the footsteps of her father when she put mission before family. Her father felt such a strong missionary call that in 1943 he left his wife and their ten children in order to travel as a missionary to Africa. He died of malaria soon after getting there. The Trobisches' friend Ruth Nyquist believes that Ingrid never really recovered from "her experience as a child of missionaries."[59] According to Ruth, Ingrid "admitted to a distant relationship with her mother and idealized her father" who left the family to go to Africa. Sadly, it seems that rather than correcting some of her parents' mistakes, Ingrid and Walter perpetuated them.

The Trobisches' friend Ruth also offers insight into Walter's personality and his overemphasis on his missionary vocation, to the detriment of family life. The Trobisches often visited with Ruth and her husband, Jim, while they were in the United States. Ruth remembers that on most occasions, Walter was "so ministry-focused that he talked with Jim not seeming to notice any of the rest of our family." This is exactly how the Trobisch children likely experienced their father. One would have hoped that Walter's work-heavy experience at Libamba would have made him eager to achieve a more sane work-family balance once they moved to Austria. Instead, Walter continued to work just as hard. He did take time away from his work occasionally to take the children on hikes or teach them to ski, but his usual routine was to begin work around 4:00 a.m. He would stop for breakfast, then head back to work, often not stopping again until dinner.[60] And then he would be back to work. One of his friends remembers that when he ran into Walter on the road or in town, Walter often did not even recognize him because he was so engrossed in his own thoughts.[61] One can imagine that when Walter paused his work for breakfast or dinner, he was not always the best conversation partner with Ingrid or his children.

As the children began to grow up, Walter eventually came to the realization that he had not been present enough with them when they were young. On a visit to the United States in 1979, the Trobisches stayed with their friends Ruth and Jim. Ruth remembers that Walter was incredibly different on that visit from the way he had been on previous visits. He shared with Ruth and Jim his concern over his teenage children. He was far less obsessed with his own work and far more interested in Ruth and Jim's family. Ruth said, "He cupped the face of our little Kathy in his hands and talked so beautifully with her—it was like a benediction. Wow! I thought, this is a new Walter whom God is going to use mightily."

But Walter was never able to develop a healthier work-family balance. Two weeks after returning to Austria in 1979, he died tragically of a heart attack.

CONCLUSION

Early in the Trobisches' life together, they did a commendable job of balancing familial responsibilities and vocational aspirations. They truly embodied their own missiology of couple power, a missiology that represented a radical development within the Christian home missiological tradition. Their own work-family balance, however, collapsed with the addition of more children and the move to a less family-friendly work environment. Once they moved to Austria, their efforts to regain a satisfying sense of partnership outside the home led to problems within the home.

Had Walter lived longer, he might have written a book about work-family balance, incorporating some of the lessons he learned late in life. It has been the aim of this chapter to do what Walter could not, to take some of the Trobisches' family history and offer it to mission scholars and practitioners who are contemplating the division of labor on the mission field. Many women today want to continue working part-time after they have children. Many men want to cut back so as to be able to spend more time with their children. How might the missionary community enable them to do this? Might it be possible for both spouses to share a position, so that both can work part-time and care for the children part-time? Ultimately, how can the missionary community foster the ability of both fathers and mothers to feel fulfilled in their work as missionaries without sacrificing their ability to be good parents?

NOTES

1. Melvin Arnold to Ingrid Trobisch, June 13, 1969, Ingrid Trobisch Papers, David Trobisch Residence, Springfield, Illinois.

2. Ingrid Hult Trobisch, interview by Robert Shuster, September 27, 1988, audiotape, Collection 400, Billy Graham Center Archives (hereafter BGCA), Wheaton College.

3. Ingrid Trobisch Youngdale and Katrine Stewart, *On My Way Home* (Bolivar, Mo.: Quiet Waters Publications, 2002), 137.

4. Dana L. Robert, "The 'Christian Home' as a Cornerstone of Anglo-American Missionary Thought and Practice," in *Converting Colonialism: Visions and Realities in Mission History, 1706–1914*, ed. Dana L. Robert (Grand Rapids: Eerdmans, 2008), 134–165.

5. Rufus Anderson, "Introductory Essay on the Marriage of Missionaries," in William Ellis, *Memoir of Mrs. Mary Mercy Ellis, Wife of Rev. William Ellis, Missionary to the South Seas* (Boston: Crocker & Brewster, 1836), xi.

6. Dana Robert calls Ann Judson an example of this "activistic" type of missionary wife. "In addition to childbirth and care and running a household in a foreign country, she did evangelistic work, ran a small school, and was a pioneer Bible translator in two languages" (Dana L. Robert, *American Women in Mission: A Social History of Their Thought and Practice* [Macon, Ga.: Mercer Univ. Press, 1997], 45).

7. Robert and Mary Moffat are an example of this type of missionary couple. Their son John remembered his mother saying that while she did not "take a prominent part in direct missionary work, it was her satisfaction to provide for the temporal wants of a servant of Christ who was doing this work; and she felt—what was true—that he [Robert] never would have been the missionary he was but for her care of him" (John S. Moffat, *The Lives of Robert and Mary Moffat*, 12th ed. [London: T. Fisher Unwin, 1925], 304).

8. See Patricia Grimshaw, *Paths of Duty: American Missionary Wives in Nineteenth-Century Hawaii* (Honolulu: Univ. of Hawaii Press, 1989); Jane Hunter, *The Gospel of Gentility: American Women Missionaries in Turn-of-the-Century China* (New Haven: Yale Univ. Press, 1984).

9. Ingrid Hult Trobisch, *On Our Way Rejoicing* (New York: Harper & Row, 1964), 160.

10. Ingrid Hult Trobisch, interview by Shuster, BGCA.

11. Robert, *American Women in Mission*, 65.

12. This observation is confirmed in Masamba Ma Mpolo, "Polygamy in Pastoral Perspectives," in *Families in Transition*, ed. Masamba Ma Mpolo and Cécile de Sweemer (Geneva: WCC Publications, 1987), 104–5; John S. Mbiti, *African Religions and Philosophy* (New York: Praeger, 1970), 111.

13. Ingrid Hult Trobisch, interview by Shuster, BGCA.

14. Although the Trobisches saw the biological reasons behind polygamy as paramount causes of the practice, scholars have cited several other factors as more significant causes

of polygamy, such as "tribal stability . . . inter-tribal peace . . . [and] the extension of the individual's kinship range" (Henri Ngoa, "Qu'est-ce que la Polygamie Négro-Africaine?" *Flambeau* 42 [1975]: 12). According to Mpolo, a wife's barrenness and inheriting the wife of a deceased brother were two of "the most frequent" cultural reasons for polygamy (Mpolo, "Polygamy in Pastoral Perspectives," 101). And according to Oheneba-Sakyi and Takyi, polygamy could also increase one's status, create more workers for the fields, and allow the wives to share household work (Yaw Oheneba-Sakyi and Baffour K. Takyi, "Introduction to the Study of African Families: A Framework for Analysis," in *African Families at the Turn of the Twenty-First Century*, ed. Yaw Oheneba-Sakyi and Baffour K. Takyi [Westport, Conn.: Praeger, 2006], 12).

15. Walter Trobisch, *My Journey Homeward* (Ann Arbor, Mich.: Servant Books, 1986), 63.

16. Oheneba-Sakyi and Takyi, "Introduction to the Study of African Families: A Framework for Analysis," 12.

17. "Therefore shall a man leave his father and his mother, and shall cleave unto his wife: and they shall be one flesh" (Gen. 2:24 KJV).

18. See Fritz Zerbst, *The Office of Woman in the Church: A Study in Practical Theology* (St. Louis: Concordia Pub. House, 1955).

19. Walter Trobisch, "The Discrimination of Women," Box 12, Folder 39, Walter Trobisch Collection, Evangelical Lutheran Church in America Archives, Elk Grove Village, Ill.

20. Ingrid Hult Trobisch, interview by Shuster, BGCA. For confirmation of this tendency in African relations, see Denise Paulme, ed., *Women of Tropical Africa* (Berkeley: Univ. of California Press, 1960), 3–4; William J. Goode, *World Revolution and Family Patterns* (New York: Free Press, 1963), 190.

21. This is a classic strategy in the history of Christian mission; see Robert, "The 'Christian Home' as a Cornerstone of Anglo-American Missionary Thought and Practice," 153–54.

22. Ingrid Hult Trobisch, interview by Shuster, BGCA.

23. Ester Boserup, *Woman's Role in Economic Development* (London: Earthscan, 1970), 35.

24. Ibid., 50. Jack Goody has also described the correlation between "female farming systems" and polygyny. See Jack Goody and S. J. Tambiah, *Bridewealth and Dowry* (Cambridge: Cambridge Univ. Press, 1973); Jack Goody, *Production and Reproduction: A Comparative Study of the Domestic Domain* (Cambridge: Cambridge Univ. Press, 1976).

25. I am indebted to Kersten Priest for this observation.

26. For example, see Walter Trobisch, *I Loved a Girl* (New York: Harper & Row, 1965); *A Baby Just Now* (Kehl/Rhein, West Germany: Editions Trobisch, 1969); *My Wife Made Me a Polygamist* (Kehl/Rhein, West Germany: Editions Trobisch, 1971); *Love Is a Feeling to Be Learned* (Kehl/Rhein, West Germany: Editions Trobisch, 1971); *I Married You* (New York: Harper & Row, 1971); and Ingrid Trobisch, *The Joy of Being a Woman . . . and What a Man Can Do* (San Francisco: Harper & Row, 1975).

27. Leela Gandhi, *Postcolonial Theory* (New York: Columbia Univ. Press, 1998), 89. See Trinh T. Minh-ha, *Woman, Native, Other* (Bloomington: Indiana Univ. Press, 1989); Chandra Talpade Mohanty, "Under Western Eyes: Feminist Scholarship and Colonial Discourse," in *Colonial Discourse and Postcolonial Theory: A Reader*, ed. Patrick Williams and Laura Chrisman (New York: Columbia Univ. Press, 1994), 196–220; Gayatri Chakravorty Spivak, "French Feminism in an International Frame," in *In Other Worlds: Essays in Cultural Politics*, ed. Gayatri Chakravorty Spivak (New York: Routledge, 1988), 134–53. Gandhi, however, argues that the above critics "paradoxically re-invest the 'third-world woman' with the very iconicity they set out to contest" (88).

28. In a famous essay, Spivak gives the example of Western attempts to abolish Hindu *sati*: "'The abolition of this rite by the British has been generally understood as a case of 'White men saving brown women from brown men.'" She concludes that this understanding of *sati* is inadequate. See Gayatri Chakravorty Spivak, "Can the Subaltern Speak?," in *The Post-colonial Studies Reader*, ed. Bill Ashcroft, Gareth Griffiths, and Helen Tiffin (New York: Routledge, 2006), 33.

29. Sylvia N. Moena, "Family Life in Soweto, Gauteng, South Africa," in Oheneba-Sakyi and Takyi, 262.

30. Ibid.

31. Sister Marie André du Sacré Cœur, *The House Stands Firm: Family Life in West Africa* (Milwaukee: Bruce Pub. Co., 1962), 230–31.

32. Cheryl Johnson-Odim, "Actions Louder Than Words: The Historical Task of Defining Feminist Consciousness in Colonial West Africa," in *Nation, Empire, Colony: Historicizing Gender and Race*, ed. Ruth Roach Pierson and Nupur Chaudhuri (Bloomington: Indiana Univ. Press, 1998), 79.

33. Youngdale and Stewart, *On My Way Home*, 163.

34. Walter Trobisch, *The Complete Works of Walter Trobisch* (Downers Grove, Ill.: InterVarsity Press, 1987), 383.

35. See Leonore Davidoff and Catherine Hall, *Family Fortunes: Men and Women of the English Middle Class, 1780–1850* (Chicago: Univ. of Chicago Press, 1987).

36. Ingrid Hult Trobisch, interview by Shuster, BGCA. I want to thank Kersten Priest for the observation that the Trobisches were actually "unbending gender" within marriage before that idea had been coined by third-wave feminists in the 1990s. See Joan Williams, *Unbending Gender: Why Family and Work Conflict and What to Do about It* (New York: Oxford Univ. Press, 2001).

37. Trobisch, *Complete Works of Walter Trobisch*, 742–43.

38. Walter and Ingrid Trobisch to friends, June 1956, Ingrid Trobisch Papers.

39. Walter and Ingrid Trobisch to friends, March 1961, Ingrid Trobisch Papers.

40. According to David Gelzer, "Help was needed in the two dining halls, especially when the bread, baked by a local baker, did not arrive in time for breakfast, or failed to come altogether, or cockroaches, in the flour, were kneaded into the dough and baked! We were needed to calm the angry students deprived, once more, of their breakfast!" E-mail to author, 31 August 2010.

41. Youngdale and Stewart, *On My Way Home*, 108.

42. Ingrid to coworkers, December 8, 1962, Ingrid Trobisch Papers.

43. Ingrid Trobisch, Journal, July 20, 1962, Ingrid Trobisch Papers.

44. Ingrid Trobisch to Walter and Mutti, July 22, 1962, Ingrid Trobisch Papers.

45. Ibid.

46. Youngdale and Stewart, *On My Way Home*, 121.

47. Ibid., 108.

48. Ingrid Trobisch, Journal, June 11, [no year], Ingrid Trobisch Papers.

49. Trobisch, *My Journey Homeward*, 114.

50. Walter and Ingrid Trobisch to friends, November 1969, Ingrid Trobisch Papers.

51. David Trobisch, interview by author, Springfield, Mo., September 4, 2010.

52. Ingrid Trobisch, Journal, September 6, 1962, Ingrid Trobisch Papers.

53. Ingrid Trobisch to friends, May 20, 1963, Ingrid Trobisch Papers.

54. Walter Trobisch and David Trobisch, *The Adventures of Pumpelhoober in Africa, America, and Germany* (St. Louis: Concordia, 1971), 47.

55. [No name] to Ingrid Trobisch, February 15, 1963, Ingrid Trobisch Papers.

56. Ingrid Trobisch to friends, May 20, 1963, Ingrid Trobisch Papers.

57. Trobisch and Trobisch, *The Adventures of Pumpelhoober*, 47.

58. Ingrid Trobisch to friends, May 20, 1963, Ingrid Trobisch Papers. In the years to come, Ingrid and Walter would more fully realize the myriad ways in which their own children continually paid the price of their missionary endeavors. They made an effort to make it up to the children. For example, in the summer of 1968 they "cancelled all speaking appointments and invitations" so that they could spend the whole summer with their children. Despite efforts like these, at least a few of the Trobisches' children feel that their parents' mission work compromised their ability to be good parents. Walter and Ingrid Trobisch to friends, November 1968, Ingrid Trobisch Papers; David Trobisch, interview by author.

59. Ruth Nyquist, e-mail to author, December 20, 2010.

60. Linde Danzer, interview by author, Minneapolis, Minn., August 18, 2012.

61. Hans-Joachim Heil, e-mail to author, November 22, 2011.

2

EXPERIENCING RISK:
Missionary Families in Dangerous Places

DONALD GRIGORENKO AND MARGARET GRIGORENKO

The cover story of the Spring 2011 issue of *Multnomah* magazine told of the experiences of a missionary family of four serving in the far northwest corner of Nepal. The article caught our attention because, having served in Nepal, we were familiar with that part of the country, one of the most remote, least developed, and least reached with the Gospel. The family featured in the article transparently shared the hardships they had endured in their attempts to carry the Gospel to a remote village at 8,200 feet in the mountains. They had had a rough go of it.

The following issue of the magazine brought further surprise. The opening paragraph of the Letters to the Editor read, "No past issue has elicited the number of letters and emails from readers the way the Spring 2011 issue did. The strong words of caution and support from readers regarding the cover story 'Aliens' provide much for all to consider. —eds." Letters alternated between extremes of praise for this family's willingness to sacrifice for the cause of the Gospel and outrage for flagrant abuse of their children. The sparks the article cast off ignited our interest in exploring contemporary missionary families' experience of risk and danger.

Mission ministry has always been risky business. Jesus stated that it would be. Paul faced "dangers from rivers, dangers from robbers, dangers from my countrymen, dangers from the Gentiles, dangers in the city, dangers in the wilderness, dangers on the sea, dangers among false brethren" (2 Cor. 11:26). Today the church has a growing list of missionary martyrs and those who suffer as missionaries.

Missionary training and mission publications have not ignored the topic of risk. We recall reading Mabel Williamson's book *Have We No Rights?* as missionary candidates. Williamson's third chapter begins with a quotation from the *Overseas Manual* of the China Inland Mission:

> [Missionaries] must count the cost, and be prepared to live lives of privation, of toil, and perhaps of loneliness and danger. They will need to trust God to meet their need in sickness as well as in health, since it may sometimes be impossible to secure expert medical aid. But, if they are faithful servants, they will find in Christ and in His Word fullness, a meetness, preciousness, a joy and strength, that will far outweigh any sacrifice they may be called upon to make for Him.[1]

In this chapter we explore the minds of missionaries who serve with their families in risky places, particularly looking at the experience of missionary families, including children, that face danger where they serve. We are looking at responses to questions such as: What risks do you face? How have you responded to them? What considerations did you take into account before coming to this ministry? What considerations have informed your decision to stay in or leave this ministry? How do your children factor into these considerations?

We are not alone in considering the issue of risk and danger. Recent publications such as the Evangelical Missiological Society's *Missions in Contexts of Violence* and the World Evangelical Alliance's *Sorrow and Blood: Christian Mission in Contexts of Suffering, Persecution, and Martyrdom* have examined related topics.[2] Laura Mae Gardner's chapter "Missionary Families," in the latter book, is especially relevant to this study.[3]

In the present work, Mary Cloutier's chapter documents the health risks faced by missionary families in equatorial Africa in the mid-nineteenth century.[4] Her study provides a rich description of how missionaries processed risk and loss, as well as the attitudes of Christians in the United States toward the decision to take a family to Africa. Cloutier's account demonstrates that many of the struggles missionary families face today in deciding what is best for the mission effort and for the health of their families have a long history.

Others who work in cross-cultural contexts that present risk have also carried out instructive studies to guide social science researchers working in areas of danger. Nancy Howell addresses a number of hazards, including human hostility, accident, and disease.[5] Both Jeffery Sluka and June Nash look at risks posed to anthropologists who work in contexts of conflict and violence.[6] Although these authors focus on anthropologists doing fieldwork in risky places and not on missionaries doing ministry, our research has benefited from the suggestions they offer for managing or at least mitigating danger.

Statistical analyses of various types and levels of risks as encountered in different countries of the world can be found on the websites of the World Health Organization and LeDuc Media. The records the World Health Organization maintains are reliable and are standardized for cross-cultural comparisons.[7] The LeDuc Media website offers statistical comparisons of categories of risk by country and region of the world.[8]

METHOD

The data, findings, and recommendations that follow arise from a study of missionary families and risk that we conducted in 2012–13. For the study we utilized a qualitative design that allowed the findings to arise from the data.[9] Utilizing ethnographic methods of interviewing, we started with open-ended questions and then followed up responses by encouraging respondents to expand upon the topic based upon their lived experiences. After sifting the accumulated information from the interview data, we considered allied literature to create case-based knowledge that has implications for application.

The concern of our study was broad: families and risk. We did not differentiate between categories of risk or seek to isolate risk arising from the missionary's Christian identity, the missionary's national identity, or factors related to neither of these. Further, we did not deal with the threat of persecution per se. Rather, our research focused on how missionary families perceive and process risks and dangers of various kinds.

For us as researchers, the topic had more than merely academic interest; we ourselves served as missionaries in the country of Nepal from 1987 to 1996 with our four children, who were ages one, three, five, and seven when we arrived. During those years we experienced serious illness, traffic accidents, and revolution.

We conducted nine interviews with fourteen missionaries who are working or have worked in risky environments and whose children were with them on the mission field. Six interviews involved husband-wife couples who were interviewed together, and the remaining two were missionary husbands who were interviewed individually without participation of their wives. Table 2.1 summarizes the demographics of the participants.

DEMOGRAPHIC BREAKDOWN

Interview participants by family	
Number of families	8
Interview participants by gender	
Male	8
Female	6
Interview participants by age	
Years of age	48–59
Size of family	
Children accompanying parents	Number of families
1 child	1
2 children	4
3 children	2
4 children	1
Length of missionary service in risky areas	
Years	9–20
Interview participants by geographic region	
Africa	2
Central Asia	5
South Asia	6
East Asia	1

Table 2.1
Demographics of interview participants

The ethnographic interviews took place in person and by telephone over a period of eight months. All interviews were transcribed and analyzed, looking for themes and using discourse analysis.[10] Names and places in the interviews have been masked to protect the identities of the missionaries.

FINDINGS

When asked what they considered to be substantial risks, respondents spoke of travel, disease, poisonous snakes, earthquakes, robbery, kidnapping, IEDs, rockets, terrorist attacks, and nuclear war. Travel received frequent mention as a risk. One missionary in South Asia said, "The biggest cause of mortality among missionaries is car accidents." Statistics show that road fatalities are higher in many nations where missionaries serve than in the United States. In 2012, India averaged 22 traffic deaths per hour compared to 4 traffic deaths per hour for the United States. Adjusted for their difference in population size—India's population is four times that of the United States—the Indian fatality rate of 18.7 fatalities per 100,000 people is 1.375 times that of the United States (13.9 per 100,000). Eritrea has the highest rate of fatalities at 48.4 per 100,000.[11] The risk is not just that missionaries might be killed or injured on the road, but also that they might hit others in chaotic traffic. One respondent related that two different co-workers had hit children who had run in front of their vehicles, and one of those children had died.

In many fields sickness is an ongoing risk. Medical missionaries have a heightened understanding of serious medical dangers. One physician who watched his son suffer with pneumonia shared that "in my job I watch people die fairly often. I know exactly what it looks like, and my son could die in this circumstance." Treatment is often unavailable or a plane flight away, and so missionary families can be faced with situations where "there is nothing else that can be done."

For our participants, violence most often topped the list. Sometimes that violence was directed at foreign workers and Christians specifically. Missionaries, however, also found themselves the victims of violence simply because they were are at the wrong place at the wrong time. One participant shared that he had had two close calls with IEDs. He was not targeted but happened to be traveling nearby when they exploded. Others shared experiences of colleagues who were attacked and executed. One of the more traumatic experiences for the remaining missionaries was kidnapping. With these various dangers, four strands related to missionary families serving in risky places emerged from the data: risk in relation to children, defining risk, theological reflections on risk, and strategies for managing risk.

CHILDREN IN DANGEROUS PLACES

Taking children to dangerous places is a matter about which many people have strong opinions, both for and against. Consequently, missionaries are often placed on the defensive. As they spoke about experiences their children had undergone while living in places of accented risk, they stated that at times they felt the need to defend their decision to minister in risky locations since supporters believed that the experience was overwhelmingly negative for children. Though they were realistic about the risks to their children, they also believed that growing up under difficult circumstances was beneficial in certain ways.

Benefits

Missionaries contrasted the lives of their children to the more secure and comfortable lifestyle of American families. Being in difficult environments, they indicated, caused the family to live and work as a more cohesive unit, and going through crisis situations only cemented those relationships. Further, the children were forced to evaluate what was important to a greater degree than when they were surrounded by affluence. One missionary mother whose family had been evacuated during a civil war stated, "I think for our kids, through the war, when you go through difficult times with people, you've been in it together. And for our kids to have also been a part of something that's been a struggle or difficult, it develops character in them. The easy life is not the best life."

The missionary parents spoke of their children as being compassionate, with a strong sense of justice. For these children the evil of the world is tangible and concrete, a lived reality and not a news item. They see firsthand the power of Christ to transform the life of a person or community, made more vivid when life and death are an ugly part of their own experience. "You know, our kids have seen little babies, after a raid, with their heads blown off. And little hurt boys, castrated. Horrors. I don't think it has hurt our kids. I think it really has given them clarity. There is evil in the world. And you cannot stand by, cannot be neutral."

The benefits were also stated in terms of adventure. Families enjoyed the challenge of living on the edge—not for thrills, but to see the Gospel advance in difficult places. Families shared the challenge of overcoming obstacles and living in places where life was not easy. They were living a compelling, directed life, one with a strong sense of purpose. "This is a crazy journey that we're called on, but life is good. The mission life is a tiger by the tail and you don't know where it's going to take you. But there's always adventure." Children as well as parents considered this vibrant, sometimes crazy, out-of-control lifestyle to be fulfilling, and parents reported that their children were the most resistant to leaving when circumstances demanded it. "The situations that our children went through, the bomb close to their house, and yet, they were the last ones that wanted to leave. . . . They said they would not have anything different about their growing up years."

Challenges

Along with the benefits, missionary children face unique challenges, such as moving frequently. Living in risky areas means that families have to be prepared to make changes, move quickly, and sometimes evacuate for periods of time. When it is unwise or too dangerous for the families to stay in one area of the country, they move to a different location. One family that had survived two terrorist attacks returned to their home country for a time and then spent additional time in a more stable country before returning to their place of ministry. "It's interesting that the one thing that our children say was the hardest, out of the whole experience, was the moving."

Risky conditions also force children to grow up. Missionary kids at times have to deal with weighty issues that are outside the experience of many children in the United States. Some were put under great pressure to act in mature roles and make decisions that would have a strong impact on the well-being of their family members. In some locations children received training by crisis counseling agencies to prepare them for circumstances such as being attacked or having their parents kidnapped or imprisoned. Others lived through attacks, were evacuated, or received counseling after harrowing events. One poignant story described a case in which the missionary father was in the United States for a meeting when a tribal raid occurred. The mother, who was at home with her fourteen-year-old son and a younger daughter, called her husband at the time of the attack. The family's oldest son had earlier gone out for a motorcycle ride. The father explained to us,

I'm in [the United States], my family is under attack, [my wife] is home and my eldest son is out, possibly being picked up, so I say to [my wife], put [our second son] on the phone. He is fourteen or fifteen and I said, "[Son,] don't tell your mom this, but if they pick up [your older brother], they will try to use [him] to get into the house." The windows are barred, the doors have quarter-inch plate, and I said, "You've gotta promise me that you won't open that door, no matter what they are doing to [your brother]."

Finally, some of the missionary children had difficulty integrating back into Western culture when, for various reasons, they returned to their country of origin. They expressed frustration at the way people complained about things that seemed insignificant or petty. One missionary stated, "I can think of experiences each one of my kids had that indicated a deep sense of right and wrong. [They had] clarity about things that our culture in America seeks to muddle. It drives them crazy. It makes them bitter, like my twenty-six-year-old daughter. She has a sense of justice that her peers don't have."

THE FROG IN THE POT

Most people, when they imagine the lives of missionary families who live in risky places, think primarily of the dangers. When the missionaries themselves were interviewed, however, they indicated that they rarely thought about the risks. One missionary stated that they were "frogs in a pot" and did not notice that the temperature of the water was rising. Another stated, "There are a lot of days of just rowing the boat," with little thought given to risk.

For the missionaries the concept of risk is fluid, not a concrete construct. Depending on a number of factors, something may or may not be perceived as risky. In defining risk within the context of their ministries, respondents identified the long list of possible risks that were enumerated above, but their explanations consistently spoke of risk on a continuum, recognizing that they were living in an inherently unsafe, fallen world. They indicated that when they were questioned directly, they could identify risks within their environment, but that on a day-to-day basis those things did not often enter their conscious thinking as risks. Once they had become familiar and commonplace, risks were managed and became part of life. Thus, perceptions of risk were tied to things that were unusual, out of the ordinary, or unfamiliar—that is, specific situations or activities that could potentially be dangerous, rather than to things that clearly posed a recognizable threat.

Missionary families manage risk by becoming familiar with their context, developing cultural competence, building close relationships in their communities, and becoming fluent in the local language.[12] Participants in the study told stories of new missionaries who ended up leaving the field because they were unable to manage the uncertainties that resulted from not understanding the local social practices. Many informants indicated that situations can become risky when missionaries are unaware of cultural expectations and cues: they are unable to "read" the situation or they inadvertently miscommunicate their intentions.[13] Missionary families may put themselves into situations where they face various types of risk because of their ignorance of the environment—natural, political, or interpersonal. Several informants indicated that only after living among the nationals and learning the nuances of language and communication—including gestures, facial expressions, and their associated social implications—were they able to effectively manage risks. One missionary put it this way: "We've lived there a long time, so we know the people around us. I don't perceive risk to a fault. I'm so comfortable in my neighborhood, and I know the people. I have a place I can go, a local home, and I speak the language. And so I don't feel as 'at risk' as other people might feel. Because I can get myself out of situations, I know when I need to escape."

Thinking ahead and being prepared for potential emergencies was also a method missionary families used to manage risks. This preparation ranged from simple strategies such as having family members immunized for diseases that were prevalent in the area, to more extensive strategies such as consulting with crisis management experts and State Department personnel in formulating crisis management plans. In recent years, mission agencies have required missionaries to develop crisis management plans and have appointed security officers on many of their fields. One missionary who was serving as the security officer for his field said,

[Our] organization has well developed security policies, [and] what we've found is when people ask us, we say, "Here's how we do our risk assessment. Here's how we look at it, here's how we use objective markers," and we list all those things. Then we say, "Also, we feel we're acting in obedience to God's call in our lives. We do have responsibility to take care of our children and each other. We do not think doing something foolish and unwise would be right. This is the way we think is wise." However, at the end of the day, we have a certain level of risk acceptance that may be different from what others do, but we feel that is what God has called us to do.

Politically volatile situations present particular difficulties in managing risks for missionary families. Informants indicated that they frequently try to maintain political neutrality in situations such as civil disturbances or areas of fighting; however, in many situations the combatants identified them as being on one side or the other, since in their minds no neutrality was allowed. Simply because of their nationality, skin color, relationships, or the assistance that they had offered to some nationals, foreigners were perceived to be implicated politically. "Whether or not you take sides, those actively involved in the situation are going to define whose side they think you are on. They will act toward you on the basis of this definition, regardless of your professions of neutrality."[14]

Missionaries expressed that they managed risk in much the way anyone manages the risk of a busy street. In any city in the United States, crowds walk along sidewalks bordering streets with fast-moving traffic. The walker is familiar with the situation and manages the danger. So missionaries in dangerous places take precautions, and those who tend to stay on the field long term learn to cope with manageable risks without much conscious thought. They become competent not only in the language, but also in the social, legal, and political practices of those around them. They come to recognize the social roles that they play within their context and work within the social boundaries and relational networks that those roles create. Multiple respondents indicated that many things that supporters considered to be risks were "manageable." They all, however, also recognized that situations exist that are simply unpredictable and therefore unmanageable.

DEVELOPING A THEOLOGY OF RISK AND SUFFERING

The reality of pain and suffering in the places where the missionaries in our study serve has required them to reflect theologically and to consider how that theology plays out "on the ground" in their own contexts. Informants reported a disconnect between the way that Americans and others in the West consider the missionary task and the way that they as missionaries view their task. At the center of this disconnect is a theology of suffering. Our study participants lamented that American evangelicals, on the whole, do not acknowledge the place of pain and suffering in a believer's discipleship and service. Further, American Christians unconsciously promote an ideal of a comfortable, pain-free, and worry-free existence. For missionaries in risky places, that kind of unbiblical idealism is not only wrong; it simply does not work. New missionaries who carry such a perspective with them to risky places will quickly leave.

One missionary explained what he believes lies behind the Western church's resistance to placing families in risky places and why many missionaries who do go to risky places do not stay.

> There's no theology of suffering. There's no belief that suffering is almost the norm throughout Christian history. So a prosperity gospel bleeds over unintentionally and unconsciously. But we talk a lot about a theology of suffering out there. What does this mean? You've got ten of your colleagues dead. If you don't have a theology of suffering, you're not going to last.

A theology of risk and suffering will include at least four essential elements. First, and a critical theological point, is that God allows pain and suffering. In a fallen world, the expectation should be that we will suffer—because of our own sin, because of the sins of others, and because we live in a fallen world. "We believe that we're called to the poor and suffering. Not just the poor, but the suffering. There's tremendous suffering in [our country], almost unbelievable. It's just part of everyday life for the vast majority of people."

Second, missionaries must come to terms with the fact that presenting the Gospel and seeing people come to faith may actually *bring on* suffering and pain. The Gospel commonly presented in the West focuses on the benefits and pleasures of making a commitment to follow Jesus. In many contexts, the same decision may put a new believer and that person's family in grave danger. Therefore, missionaries must come to a biblically grounded belief that faith in Jesus is worth any kind of suffering, even death. One respondent stated:

> Our belief is that bad things really can happen to us. There's no promise that we will be physically safe at all times. There's a promise that even

if we're killed, that is not the worst thing, and then everything will ultimately be redeemed, but there's no promise that we will not get sick. We can still get malaria or dysentery and all those things. We're just as vulnerable to a 7.62 millimeter bullet as anybody else, [or to] an explosion.

We've seen God protect us at times and we praise him for it, but we've also seen times when God has not protected. And there are times when we've felt protected and other people have died. We're also working with people who, if they come to faith, risk terrible persecution or death. I know of someone who has been murdered for his faith. He refused to deny the faith and they killed him.

How can we then say to them, "Yes, come to faith in Christ. Become a believer. Everything will be fine." It's not fine. They will know of people who have died, who have been driven out of their families. I know people who can't buy bread in the local bakeries. If we are going to say to them, "You need to follow Jesus anyway; this is the most important thing to do. This is more important than death and life. Nothing can separate you from the love of God," I've got to be able to face that [reality, also].

Third, things are not fine, we cannot make them fine, and that may lead to our own suffering. In coming to this recognition, missionaries have to come to recognize the implications of this belief for their families. If they preach that the love of Christ is worth dying for and then leave as soon as there is any risk, their actions will teach that their message is not true or that their faith is not the same kind of faith that they are asking of the local believers.

We can leave. We can go on holiday. We make everyone get out once a year. They [the local people] can't leave, and if they can, they don't want to come back. So they have to go through the everyday danger, the sickness, the killing—two million people killed. The various wars. And our belief is that, first of all, we're called to be there incarnationally representing Jesus Christ.

Missionaries expressed the conviction that families are part of that incarnation, for families are the context of life in every part of the world.

And what about children in those countries who are exposed to risks every day without Christ? Children are the context of our ministry, and our family should share the same risks as the people we go to reach. If you asked anyone in our [local] church why they gave the Gospel a hearing, they will say it is because we never saw a family like yours. We never saw a marriage like yours. We never saw children that respected their parents and respected all the elders in the community. And it was you. Your family is the context from which you preach the Gospel.

A theology that produces a commitment to live as families in risky places also leads missionaries to face the possibility that their families could suffer or die. Most of the missionaries whom we interviewed expressed the conviction that being willing to deal with the reality of dying was a critical part of the process that missionary families must go through before they will be able to witness effectively or even to stay in risky locations.

Fourth, missionaries recognize there is redemptive power in seeing God work through pain, suffering, and even death. In several cases the missionaries described how God had used a crisis to "shake up" ingrained patterns of thinking—for both missionaries and locals—which allowed revival. Sometimes revival occurred rapidly and sometimes it came years later, but there is evidence that God has a redemptive purpose for allowing suffering. In the case of a terrorist attack on his children's school, a father said, "The attack caused revival in the school, major revival. You know how Christian schools can be sometimes. They go downhill and it's not cool to be a Christian, and that's where the school was at the time. This completely turned it around." In another case, a civil war became the occasion for the planting of a church in an unreached area. "We arrived in a very risky situation where people had not heard of Jesus before. They had a bit of [Christian] literature that had been sent around, but now there's a church of 200 baptized believers up there. The joy is worth the sorrow."

DRAWING LINES IN THE SAND

Missionaries in dangerous places talked with us about the considerations that enter into a decision to remain in or leave their place of service. We talked with families who had left as well as those who had stayed but who had had other families on their teams that did leave because of the dangers. Different families, it became clear, had different "lines in the sand." Some families had a higher practical, spiritual, or emotional tolerance for risk than did other families. Often it came down to what risks a family was willing to live with. But for many interviewees the line of decision was negotiable. In other words, setting a predetermined limit would cause a family to reconsider their continuing presence in a risky location, but a decision to leave once that limit was reached was not automatic. Having crossed a predetermined threshold would raise the question of leaving, but in some cases a new threshold would be established and the family would stay. In other cases the limit would be respected and the family would leave.

In cases where there was a threshold, that threshold could be determined by the missionary's sending agency, by the missionary team, by the missionary family, or by a combination of the three. Usually, there was also consultation with government agencies such as the U.S. State Department or other area, possibly interagency, security teams. One respondent stated, "If we have missionaries that have been on the field a long time [and] have a track record, we have confidence in their judgment. We will allow them to make that decision to stay or not, to determine their own threshold." What our interviews made clear, however, was that deciding whether to stay or not was not an individual decision. One security advisor for his agency and others stated, "We believe very strongly that without good accountability there is no good security. There are things I can be overridden on. My family can be sent out, even if *I think* it's okay to be here. That's one of the keys to remaining in a high risk [place]; there has to be accountability. Without that it's every man doing what's right in his own eyes, and it falls apart very quickly."

A point does come when missionary families feel they should leave. When this happens, the challenge is for both the remaining mission team and the departing family to deal with the situation appropriately. Missionaries we interviewed indicated that the remaining team should respond supportively: "We have a hard and fast policy that when an individual or family feels uncomfortable or feels they need to go, we support that 100 percent." It is important that team members do not pressure families to stay in violation of the families' threshold.

Those who did leave were reported as later responding in different ways. Some who left were comfortable with their decision and comfortable with the decisions of those who stayed. Others were uncomfortable with teammates who did not leave and even condemned them for staying. "I've been surprised at how angry some people [who have left] have gotten, saying, 'You shouldn't be here at all. Everyone leave, it's irresponsible.'"

We asked respondents when a missionary family should leave. Responses to this question were instructive. Risks can escalate so much that virtually all a missionary family is doing is managing risk. Seemingly, little else is accomplished. In an environment of chaos or continuous lockdown, study participants asked, "What's the point of staying?" More personally, the cumulative effects of stress from living with constant danger to the family mount up. Increased uncertainty after a series of attacks or other ongoing dangers adds to the stress. "Who's going to be next?" A missionary can become consumed with "what ifs" and the various possibilities to the point that he or she becomes unproductive in ministry. The tension can be exacerbated when the risky situation is related to the vocational practices that allow the missionary access to the country. For example, one family listed the accumulation of risks experienced within one year: physical illness, a kidnapping, hostility from business partners after the firing of workers for embezzlement, interrogation by the local tax officials, and the natural death of a colleague followed by the murder of another colleague. The respondent explained:

> So with all these things, once she was shot . . . the whole Christian community was getting together every single day just to discuss security concerns. I was part of those meetings and it was obvious to everyone that maybe it's time to take families out of here. But in conjunction with the burnout that I was feeling . . . [our son] approached us, saying, "I wonder if it's time that we should go." It was the combination of all those things that just kind of drove us to finally make the decision.

Further, the *presence* of a missionary in a dangerous context in itself can pose risks to others and can bring a family to decide that it is time to leave. National colleagues, both believers and unbelievers, can be put at significant risk by the presence of the missionary. And in the event of abduction, there are risks taken by an extraction team and the real possibility that some will be killed in a rescue attempt. With a family, wives and children may become targets for kidnapping, or family members may be used for negative propaganda when one member of the family is kidnapped, injured, or killed. The missionary family is not an isolate functioning alone. The missionary's presence and actions have an impact on others, whether it is recognized or not. "What I do can get everybody else kicked out or pulled out."

Most missionaries in difficult places have points at which they *want* to leave. They do not *like* being where they are. At times they are afraid for themselves, their families, and their fellow laborers. On these occasions the missionary must discipline his or her emotions and wisely assess whether or not to stay, remembering that part of a strategy of living and even thriving in high-risk contexts is accepting risk. One missionary shared the words of a veteran missionary who worked in a dangerous country: "Make up your mind. You might get killed. Deal with it and then move on. And don't live in fear all the time."

CONCLUSION

One of the key insights that surfaced from the interviews was the recognition that adequate information and preparation will enable families to manage many of the risks that arise through living in a cross-cultural context. Studying about potential dangers in order to prevent, manage, or respond to risks appropriately must begin before the family leaves for the field. Missionary families should be taught about cultural norms and taboos as a way of protecting themselves from getting into dangerous situations unnecessarily or from giving social cues that would put them at risk. Newer missionaries should utilize experienced residents as resources and should listen to advice.[15] Most long-term missionaries, however, acknowledge that without extended time in a locale, a thorough mastery of the local language, and a network of trustworthy "sponsors" in the community who can inform missionaries about local practices, it is very difficult to recognize and intuitively respond to risky situations. These friends, with varying degrees of standing and recognition among the local populace, frequently protected or "ran interference" for missionary families until they had developed culturally appropriate practices.

Developing a biblically grounded theological perspective is a second dimension of preparation related to risk and suffering. At the top of Gardner's list of things "helpful to prepare missionaries for intense hardship" is the need to "formulate your own theology of suffering."[16] For missionaries to be able to interpret the suffering that they and others experience and to express a theological understanding of it is critical.

The wisdom of making contingency plans for foreseeable dangers was a third element that stood out. Contingency planning includes appointing a security consultant and training members of a team on how to respond to dangerous situations. In places of ongoing danger, such as political conflict, constant reevaluation of the risks and use of multiple sources to gather information is imperative. Jeffrey Sluka advises, "Make a continuing effort to define and redefine risks and dangers in light of actual experiences, and work to reduce such dangers by improving old methods and developing new ones as your network of contacts and degree of experience expand over time."[17]

Fourth, being proactive by taking steps to deescalate tensions is also important. Missionaries need to know local laws and to avoid breaking them. They must evaluate their actions lest they exacerbate risk related to the ministry or interpersonal relations, and they must carefully consider alternative options so that their practices will be culturally appropriate and avoid giving offense. Sometimes it is necessary to address misconceptions that locals may have about a missionary's identity or reasons for serving in a particular locale. Sluka observes, "It is not enough to not be a threat. . . . Act in such a way as to *be seen* as not a threat."[18]

Fifth, missionaries need to be flexible when ministering in risky places with a family. The presence of both adults and children (of varying ages) creates additional considerations as to what, where, and when ministry can occur. Often the families we interviewed saw benefit from having their children live and minister with them in risky places. At other times, however, families found it necessary to change their original plans for ministry and for some or all of the family to leave their location of ministry, either temporarily or permanently. In discussing marriage in 1 Corinthians 7:29–34, Paul indicates that single men and women—because they do not have responsibility for a spouse—have wider freedom to devote themselves to the Lord's affairs. By extension, a married person may have responsibility for children, which could limit his or her potential service to the Lord. This principle should be given appropriate consideration in decisions about where families should go or whether they should remain for ministry. Paul's admonition indicates that it may be wise for singles to serve in certain places where families cannot productively minister because of the physical and emotional demands.

Finally, though careful education about and preparation for risky situations is prudent and sensible, missionaries and sending bodies must recognize that not all risk is predictable or controllable. Sluka's comment, "Danger is not a purely 'technical' problem and is never totally manageable," applies to missionaries, also.[19] One respondent said, "You're not always safe in God's arms." For many of the missionaries that we interviewed, safety was not the objective of missionary service any more than safety is the final objective of a rescue team carrying out a mission. These missionaries were not suggesting that they sought out danger. As missionary parents they cared deeply about their children, and stories they told of when their children were in danger brought us to tears. They were aware of both the benefits and the challenges that their selected lifestyle held for their children. They conducted their ministry as safely as possible. Yet safety was not their chief goal—not for themselves as parents and not for their children.

Informing members of congregations is also necessary. In interacting with supporters and supporting churches, mission sending agencies—as well as missionaries themselves—must address the realities that face families serving in risky locations. Misconceptions that confuse the perceived need for missionary children always to be "safe" with their being "comfortable" must be corrected. Lack of information about either the nature of the ministry or the actual level of risk involved (as opposed to what may be communicated by U.S. media) can play a part in creating negative relations between Christians in home countries and missionary families. One interviewee observed that "Americans have a hard time believing that God can lead into [dangerous] situations." The missionaries expressed the importance of passing on their vision for ministry along with a vision for how families can serve in productive ways so as to solicit backing and prayer support for their work. "In the American church, we pray for security and success, and we need to pray for faithfulness and endurance." The missionaries saw a need for Christians in the United States to recognize the inherently risky nature of cross-cultural ministry in the twenty-first century. As one informant said,

> I think we're going to start seeing security issues come up anywhere we are working, not just in what we call the hard places. I think everywhere is in danger of becoming a hard place and missionaries are going to face threats. We can either get out of the mission business

or we can develop the theology of why we do what we do and deal with the security issues.

The ongoing challenge for missionary families, their sending bodies, and their supporters will be to use wisdom in order to avoid unnecessarily or gratuitously putting children and families at risk—for example, by sending them uninformed or unprepared to their place of ministry—but at the same time to demonstrate courage and conviction in backing dedicated families in their vision to take the Gospel to difficult places and unreached peoples.

NOTES

1. Mabel Williamson, *Have We No Rights? A Frank Discussion of the "Rights" of Missionaries* (Chicago: Moody Press, 1957), 23.

2. Keith E. Eitel, ed., *Missions in the Contexts of Violence* (Pasadena, Calif.: William Carey Library, 2008); William D. Taylor, Antonia van der Meer, and Reg Reimer, eds., *Sorrow and Blood: Christian Mission in the Contexts of Suffering, Persecution, and Martyrdom* (Pasadena, Calif.: William Carey Library, 2012).

3. Laura Mae Gardner, "Missionary Families," in *Sorrow and Blood*, ed. Taylor, van der Meer, and Reimer, 369–73.

4. Mary Cloutier, "The 'Family Problem': Challenges in Balancing Maternity and Mission in Nineteenth-Century Equatorial Africa," see chapter 1 in this volume.

5. Nancy Howell, *Surviving Fieldwork: A Report of the Advisory Panel on Health and Safety in Fieldwork, American Anthropological Association* (Washington, D.C.: American Anthropological Association, 1990).

6. Jeffrey A. Sluka, "Reflections on Managing Danger in Fieldwork: Dangerous Anthropology in Belfast," in *Ethnographic Fieldwork: An Anthropological Reader*, ed. Antonius C. G. M. Robben and Jeffrey A. Sluka (Malden, Mass.: Blackwell, 2007), 259–69; June Nash, "Ethnology in a Revolutionary Setting," in *Ethnographic Fieldwork*, ed. Robben and Sluka, 223–32.

7. World Health Organization, www.who.int/countries/en.

8. LeDuc Media, www.worldlifeexpectancy.com.

9. Barney G. Glaser and Anselm Strauss, *The Discovery of Grounded Theory: Strategies for Qualitative Research* (Chicago: Aldine Publishing Company, 1967).

10. Quotations given in the following text that are not otherwise attributed come from our interview transcriptions.

11. World Health Organization, http://apps.who.int/gho/data/node.main.A997?lang=en.

12. Gardner, "Missionary Families," 370.

13. Nancy Howell, *Surviving Fieldwork*, 238. Howell, addressing the risk of rape, describes how women unfamiliar with the culture may be "unaware of the signals of challenge and deference with which local women protect themselves" and so put themselves at risk.

14. Sluka, "Reflections on Managing Danger in Fieldwork, 266.

15. Gardner, "Missionary Families," 370.

16. Ibid.

17. Sluka, "Reflections on Managing Danger in Fieldwork," 268.

18. Ibid., 264.

19. Ibid., 269.

3

THE FAMILY AND MISSIONS:
Reflections from the Life
of a U.S. Missionary

JERRY RANKIN

We were preparing to leave for our initial term as missionaries in Indonesia with our two children, ages ten months and two years old. As we visited churches prior to our departure, we encountered a surprising question. More than once people asked us, "You are not taking the children with you, are you?" Somewhat shocked, we would reply quite confidently that, yes, we were taking the children, and then offer an explanation of our conviction that the family was instituted by God and was, indeed, a part of his divine plan for our missionary calling.

My amusement at that distorted and provincial perspective on missionary service, however, was challenged when my own children prepared to leave for the field. I was serving as president of the International Mission Board when my son was appointed for service in East Asia and came through orientation. Being in a communication role, he spent an additional six-month internship working with our staff, which gave us quality time with our two grandsons, ages one and three. Our emotional bonding was strong, and it was all I could do to refrain from asking, "You are not going to take the kids, are you?" as we took them to the airport.

We need, all of us, to be reminded that the family was the first and foundational institution established by God, and it has always been an intrinsic element in the fulfillment of his kingdom mission.

In May 2001 Gracie and Martin Burnham, missionaries with New Tribes Mission in the Philippines, were captured by the Abu Sayyaf terrorist group and held hostage for thirteen months. Multiple efforts to respond to the hostage-takers' demands and to negotiate their release failed. While the mission agency, with its no ransom policy, attempted to coordinate the crisis management, communication became conflicted and confusing as families, churches, and both the United States and Philippine governments sought to influence and manipulate the negotiations. Martin subsequently died during a military attack on the terrorists. Later, in a debriefing with leaders of mission agencies seeking to learn from this tragedy, Gracie expressed a profound insight. She said, "You need to realize there are multiple stakeholders. You, as the missionary sending agency, would like to think that you are in charge, but there are also families, churches, and governments. All of them are in the Bible, but you guys [speaking of mission leaders] aren't there!"

BIBLICAL BACKGROUND

To acknowledge the weight of Gracie Burnham's statement does not imply that modern-day mission modalities do not have a biblical role. God has, however, clearly established families, churches, and governments as divinely ordained entities for the well-being of society and the fulfillment of his mission. Adam and Eve, and their offspring, were intended to have dominion over the earth. They were to "be fruitful and multiply, and fill the earth and subdue it" (Gen. 1:28). What they failed to accomplish literally, we have been called to fulfill spiritually.

Abraham's call involved a whole family lineage: Isaac, Jacob, and the nation of Israel. He did not personally see the nations blessed and a heritage that numbered beyond the stars in the sky. The successive generations of patriarchs represented that perpetual covenant with God that would eventually expand to the Gentiles and all the nations of the world. As Israel became a people on mission to tell of God's "salvation from day to day" and to "declare his glory among the nations, his marvelous works among all the peoples" (Ps. 96:2–3), more than being a nation they were a family on mission.

Families today need to realize, even as God reminded his family of Israel, that "it is too light a thing that you should be my servant to raise up the tribes of Jacob and to restore the survivors of Israel; I will give you as a light to the nations, that my salvation may reach to the end of the earth" (Isa. 49:6). Mission agencies and organizations have a significant role in facilitating the sending and support of missionaries, but the calling and responsibility from God for the witness of families to extend to the nations is unique. They do not have God's permission to focus simply on their own welfare and concerns.

GAINING PERSPECTIVE

I am not the first or the last to have aspired to be like Paul. Having felt a passion to reach the nations, my youthful zeal reasoned it would be much better to remain single and unencumbered by a family in storming the strongholds of lostness. It did not take long, however, for me and others to realize the value of a helpmeet, a partner and lover for mutual support and encouragement. And with a wife come children and increased family responsibilities, creating a tension with the mission task. This inclination toward marriage is not to disparage the multitude of singles who do go to the mission field and embrace a celibate lifestyle in making the Gospel known. Whether married or single, each missionary will find that personal needs are sometimes in apparent conflict with total devotion to the work.

Many families, however, succumb to the consuming demands of keeping the family fed, the children cheerful, their helpers happy, pastors appeased, and siblings safe, secure, and sane in an environment where germs are rampant and sanitation nonexistent. Being both the "P" and the "T" of PTA is not easy when homeschooling kids in multiple grades, communicating with supporting churches, and providing a comfortable home far from the amenities of America. Without skillful discipline and time management, the needs of one's family can leave very little time for frontline, cross-cultural ministry and witness.

Having served many years as a field director and then as a mission executive, I readily acknowledge the multiple challenges and potential problems that families bring to the missionary role. The initial stress of language learning and cross-cultural adjustments leaves families reeling as they deal with the loss of a comfortable environment and disruption of family routines. The children no longer have their friends and support group, and they struggle to cope with being not only a minority but also an oddity in a foreign culture. The needs of a husband and wife are exacerbated, with both expecting more from their spouse than can be provided in terms of understanding, encouragement, and affection. The self-imposed pressure that each feels to get on with the ministry assignment, though not yet equipped and competent in language or understanding of new worldviews, overwhelms emotions with anxiety, insecurity, self-doubts, and impatience. Trying to meet the needs of one's family becomes an imposition that conflicts with the higher priorities of evangelism and of responding to the ubiquitous needs of an impoverished population in which one is suddenly immersed.

On the field I never got used to the funerals. Accidents claim the lives of missionaries as readily as others, and disease is no respecter of persons. But the burden and cost of obedience to the missionary call is stretched to the limit when a child is buried in foreign soil. During our own tenure on the field, the saddest experiences were when the ten-year-old child of a colleague died of leukemia and when on two different occasions missionary children were killed in motor scooter accidents. I will never forget the grief when a fourteen-year-old girl, a friend the same age as my own daughter, was asphyxiated and died due to a malfunctioning water heater, or when I stood behind two small caskets of five- and seven-year-old siblings who were killed in a traffic accident. The dangers and health risks are real.

Why would parents carry their children to a place where safety is uncertain and lives will be put in jeopardy? It does not make sense to those who make their own comfort and security their highest priority. But to those who prioritize the glory of God among the nations and consider disobedience to God's call not an option, the mission of God requires putting not only one's life on the altar but that of one's family as well.[1]

MAKING A BEGINNING

When we finally finished language study and arrived at our assignment among an unreached people group in a remote area of East Java, all we wanted to do was to engage in the task of proclaiming Christ, probing and witnessing in the villages to discover pockets of response and start churches. Our family, however, began to break out with staphylococcus infections that caused boils all over our bodies. After advising us first to wash our clothes and bed sheets, then to burn our clothes and bed sheets, medical advisers decided the infection probably came from our water supply and was draining through our lymph systems.

One night as our two-year-old son was sitting between my wife and me at dinner, we noticed a red streak running from a boil on his forehead to his eye. Sensing that this was dangerous, we drove five hours to our mission hospital. By the time we arrived his head was swollen as the infection drained into his brain. Antibiotics were administered. We were told, two days later after he was out of danger, that if we had not come to the hospital when we did, he likely would have died. Since we were at the hospital, we were given overdue physical examinations and unexpectedly discovered that my wife needed immediate surgery. After her extended recovery we finally returned home, only for both my wife and me to contract dengue fever. Nothing could be done to alleviate the symptoms, so we suffered extreme fever and excruciating headaches for the next ten days. It was our first Christmas, but neither of us was well enough for decorating, buying gifts, or indulging our children in the usual holiday festivities.

The day after Christmas we received a phone call from our mission office in Jakarta informing us that my wife's parents had been in an automobile accident, her father had been killed, and her mother was in critical condition. We could never have imagined feeling so forlorn and forsaken. Why were we experiencing such debilitating adversity when all we wanted to do was serve the Lord and witness to the lost around us? Why did not God put a hedge of protection around us so we could freely devote ourselves to our mission calling?

All that we experienced that first term, however, pales in comparison to the tragedies that many missionary families go through. We had to learn, as do others sooner or later, the sufficiencies of God's grace. When plans go awry, trials intensify, and suffering seems to be the course of life, the tendency is to succumb to discouragement and decide, "We don't have to put up with this." Many give up and return home, forsaking the call and leaving a lost community without a witness. Families are not exempt from suffering. Missionaries must learn that they have ventured into Satan's territory and he will do whatever he can to thwart their efforts to infringe on his dominions of darkness. Missionaries are most vulnerable when the necessary sacrifices and unavoidable suffering touches their family. Those who persevere and are found faithful must come to the place, usually through trying and adverse circumstances, of discovering that God is faithful, his grace is sufficient, and the promises of his Word are sure.

STRENGTH OF MISSIONARY MARRIAGES

Another negative impact on families and missions is the baggage that modern young couples take with them to the field—not their trunks and crates of material possessions, but their background of broken homes, abuse, and absence of healthy models of parenting. Some couples have never had the privilege of seeing parents in a loving, selfless relationship. Many have spent their younger years being bounced around among separated parents, living with siblings from the previous marriage of a step-parent, or being raised by grandparents. They are trophies of grace in finding the Lord and in answering his call to missions, but they have meager practical experience in a normal home life, especially one in which Christ is exalted and love characterizes relationships.

For new missionary couples coming from the United States, each spouse is likely to have had his or her own role and job and circle of friends. An active lifestyle, and even the demanding schedule of church programs, kept them busy, with each carrying out fulfilling responsibilities, especially during seminary and stateside church-related ministries. Husbands and wives presume upon their relationship, assuming that communication and all else are fine until they get to the field. There they no longer have their familiar, fulfilling activities and support groups at church and work and in the neighborhood. Isolated and remote, they struggle with communication and mutual needs that are not being met. Children often become the victims of stressed-out parents and their lack of patience and sensitivity in situations in which the whole family is simply struggling for survival.

Dennis Rainey, president of Family Life Today, an affiliate of Campus Crusade for Christ, now Cru, approached a group of mission executives in 2006, concerned that family breakdowns among missionaries had been a detriment to fulfilling the Great Commission. Each mission organization had had experience in dealing with attrition due to stress, unmet family needs, and even moral lapses. Subsequent research, however, revealed that family structures on the mission field were unusually strong. What Rainey's research showed was that "husbands and wives were applying themselves to sound biblical principles and intentionally working to provide mutual support to each other and giving priority to spiritual and emotional needs. Although the challenges [of marriage and family life] were real and often severe, [these] trials were being used as building blocks to strengthen the family bonding and appropriate strength and guidance from God."[2]

My own organization, the International Mission Board, maintains a relatively low attrition rate of 4–5 percent annually. Factors contributing to that low rate include thorough screening and training of missionaries prior to their departure for the field. Also, a team of member care professionals is deployed in every region to be available for counseling before problems escalate to the point at which people must be brought home. Reports from member care staff reflect three basic elements that have been shown to be essential in nurturing strong family structures on the mission field.

Both husbands and wives testify to a personal call to missionary service. We believe in a complementarian principle of a wife being in submission to her husband as the head of the home in line with Ephesians 5:22–33. For a wife to go to the mission field out of obligation to follow and support her husband, however, without any sense of personal call, seldom works. Only a deep conviction of a personal call and obedience to God can sustain one through the difficulties and challenges of the mission field.

The strongest families on the mission field are those in which there are shared roles of home and ministry. Some wives are exceptions, being content to focus on caring for the home and family while the husband busies himself in ministry. But the wife who has a call herself and lives in the midst of pervasive lostness will have a desire and need to be involved in witness and ministry as well. To be denied that opportunity results in frustration and lack of fulfillment. But for her to be engaged in her own ministry opportunities requires that her husband share in the responsibilities of the home and child care.

My role as a church planter required me to be out among the people, itinerating among the villages each day. I would arrange to be at home at least one afternoon and evening each week in order for my wife to lead a ladies' Bible study and teach an English class. I would teach our children the first hour each morning to allow my wife a leisurely quiet time and added margin for preparing homeschooling lessons for the day. The family was often engaged with me in village ministries.

Finally, it is important to involve the children in ministry. Missionary kids (MKs) need to understand what their parents are doing and why they left the United States to live in a sometimes remote cross-cultural environment. Many families have made the mistake of trying to shelter their children from exposure to and immersion in the culture. Their primary friends are other Western expatriates. They never develop relationships with local children or learn the local language. If they live in an urban area, they can usually indulge in the amenities of McDonalds and Pizza Hut, and they may participate in American sports at an international school. But if the children do not develop a level of comfort in the culture, the strain on the family will threaten long-term tenure and effectiveness. Certainly there are MKs who have adjustment problems and have returned to the home country bitter and scarred, but invariably their parents have exhibited negative attitudes toward the people and culture.

Children hear when their parents complain and criticize the way things are done, as well as when they attack missionary colleagues. They register if their parents are constantly focused on the inconveniences to which they are subjected or on the incompetence of local officials. If the parents complain about the heat, the dirt, and traffic congestion, the children, not surprisingly, often develop similar attitudes and become resentful. But when children are led to pray for lost neighbors and when they accompany parents in sharing the Gospel, they develop a burden for a world that needs Christ—and they come to consider it a privilege to be chosen by God to live cross-culturally in order for people to be introduced to Jesus.

Life on the mission field, however, does confront families with unique challenges. It is evident that there are ill-adjusted children and former TCKs (third-culture kids) who struggle with their identity into adulthood. Adolescents are exasperated in trying to understand the provincialism and materialistic values of stateside peers and long to return "home" to their familiar culture abroad. A number of MKs return to the United States for college not knowing where home really is. They usually excel academically but find themselves challenged socially. But when the family life is strong, the parents are fulfilled, and spiritual life is nurtured, the family is an asset in fulfilling the mission of God.

THE FAMILY IS AN ASSET TO CROSS-CULTURAL WITNESS

In the Muslim society in which our family served, I could approach men. But as I followed up pockets of potential response in the neighborhoods and villages, I had little access to the women and children unless my wife accompanied me. When our children were with us, the doors of hospitality were flung wide open as the whole community embraced us and were receptive to hearing our message. We did not exploit our children, but they enjoyed the adventure of going with Dad. They discerned the uniqueness and challenges of each village and became acquainted with the leaders we were discipling.

Problems did arise, however, when they were younger and were not discreet in their witness. The parents of our children's Muslim playmates objected when their children were told that they were going to hell because they did not believe in Jesus! Missionary friends in Nigeria told about explaining to their two daughters why they had come to live among the people of Africa: it was because the local people did not know that Jesus was God's Son. Later they heard their daughters, aged three and five, leaning out the window shouting to the crowds passing in front of their house, "Jesus is God's Son! Jesus is God's Son!"

The family is an asset to the mission task, not just because children in growing up observe a model of Gospel proclamation and learn to distribute evangelistic materials, but because living as a missionary family within a cross-cultural community is in itself an incarnational witness. When—in contrast to practices in the host culture—people observe a wife being honored and respected in a loving relationship, the family's way of life testifies to the difference Christ makes. When people see disciplined and respectful children being kind to each other and to others, the witness may be "passive" but it makes an impression. God calls families to his mission task because of the powerful testimony of Christ's love lived out at the practical level of day-to-day family life.

THE MISSION FIELD IS AN ASSET TO THE SPIRITUAL NURTURE OF THE FAMILY

Although life on the mission field is always busy, usually the pressures of secular entertainment and activities that infringe on quality family time in the United States are absent. Our children did not have a full schedule of band practice, soccer games, swim meets, and Little League baseball, along with a weekly calendar of church-related organizations. Some would see them as having been deprived, but they were able to travel the world, become fluent in multiple languages, and avoid the self-centered provincialism that infects so many monocultural young people. As we traveled back to the United States for periodic furloughs, our children expressed concern about being able to understand and relate to their U.S. schoolmates. I asked them to consider how many of their classmates would have ridden a sea turtle in Indonesia, an elephant in India, and a camel in Israel during the previous month as they had done!

Being on the mission field without television and a plethora of activities enabled us to maintain quality family time that contributed to nurturing our children's spiritual development. In Deuteronomy 6:5 we are commanded to love God with all our heart and soul. The following verses exhort us: "Keep these words that I am commanding you today in your heart. Recite them to your children and talk about them when you are at home and when you are away, when you lie down and when you rise."

The quality and consistency of our time together as a family, without a lot of distractions, nurtured in our children a love for God and a desire to serve him. It afforded us, as missionary parents, an opportunity to model what it meant to follow the Lord in obedience. Several years ago I wrote a book of devotional reflections on the Psalms that was the product of a lifetime of meditating on these inspiring passages.[3] Since the reflections were initially written for the benefit of my children and grandchildren, when they were published I asked my son to write the foreword. The following is an excerpt from what he wrote:

> I was about five years old when I received from my parents a children's illustrated Bible for Christmas. It was the version many children received at a young age—a thick hardcover with colorful pictures

interspersed throughout that illustrated the Bible stories: Noah and the ark, Jonah and the whale, David conquering Goliath, and the pictures of a smiling Jesus surrounded by children.

It was with this Bible that I learned all the books of the Old and New Testaments and began to learn about the stories contained within. I remember the encouragement my parents gave me about the importance of spending time every day in personal Bible reading. I loved that Bible; it sits on a shelf in my home today, marked with awkward scrawling of a child just learning to write. Some additional artwork can be found in the inside covers and throughout the pages as well, most certainly the doodles of a restless child in church.

As a child I was usually one of the first ones up in the mornings. It was during these cool, tropical mornings in Indonesia that I received a visual imprint that taught me more than I ever could have learned from a book or verbal lesson. Tip-toeing quietly out of my room, I would make my way through our house to a back corner where my dad had his office set up. His desk, which still sits in his house today, was a large wooden carved desk with deep drawers and pull-out center console that smelled of ink and paper. It contained all sorts of treasures with which curious little boys love to tinker when their dads aren't around. But in the quiet of the morning, I could be assured that my dad would be sitting at that desk, his Bible open before him and his hands clasped beneath his chin. His expression—to a child—was furrowed and weighty. I knew this was not a time to crawl under the desk and play.

In his responsibilities as a church planter in Indonesia with the (then) Foreign Mission Board, he would travel to villages all over East Java preaching, teaching and training national leaders. As I grew older, I came to understand what was transpiring during those solemn times in the morning. These were moments that were foundational to my father's life. This was his fuel. He drew his strength and inspiration from the pages of the Scriptures, and his meditations and times of prayer and petition were for people I didn't even know and for burdens I couldn't even begin to grasp at my young age. Many times I would retreat back to my favorite corner in my room with my own Bible. I did this because this is what I saw my father doing.[4]

My later move into a regional leadership position entailed our family's relocation from our isolated assignment to a more central location. We subsequently left Indonesia to live in Bangkok, Thailand. In between these moves came a year of furlough in the United States. As a result of these relocations our daughter attended a different school for each of her four years of high school, a very difficult and undesirable consequence. As we were visiting with her during her first year of college, she began to reflect on the challenges of never being able to settle into long-term friendships and how difficult it was to break into established cliques as a new student each year. Tears began to flow as she spoke of the loneliness and constant adjustment to a new school during her teenage years. It broke my heart. I was sobbing as she spoke of the hurt and scars from our moves. I blurted out through my own tears, "I am sorry; I am so sorry." She reached out, put her hand on mine, and said, "It's all right, Daddy; you had to do what God was calling you to do. The moves were difficult for all of us, but through it I learned what obedience was, and that it always has a cost." Today she is faithfully serving with her family among Muslims in Central Asia, obedient to the call to go to the edge despite the cost and hardship.

Psalm 78:3–4 refers to all the mighty wonders of God experienced in the history of Israel and their understanding of his instructions regarding "things that we have heard and known, that our ancestors have told us. We will not hide them from their children; we will tell to the coming generation the glorious deeds of the Lord, and his might, and the wonders that he has done." Children on the mission field do not just hear stories and secondhand reports of what God has done; they get to see it, experience it, and live it. Our children celebrated the joy of seeing Muslims miraculously come to faith in Jesus Christ and prayed for them as they experienced harassment and rejection by their families and community. The Muslim call to prayer five times a day reminded them of the spiritual darkness around them and enhanced their motivation to pray for Indonesians and our work among them, even at a young age. Our family Bible reading stimulated questions and discussion that led them to an incredible understanding of God's Word and its application to their lives.

Too often the spiritual training and nurturing of children is a task relinquished to Sunday School and the church youth group. Testimonies of God's marvelous works are secondhand stories rather than something the children see in their parents' lives and ministry. Missionary kids may return to their home country not knowing the latest pop stars or the television sitcoms that are the current rage, but they usually know the Bible and the reality of God's power and grace.

THE FAMILY IS AN ASSET TO MOBILIZING SUBSEQUENT GENERATIONS

At a recent reunion of our missionary colleagues, most now retired, reports and updates on families revealed that twenty-five children, now adults, from our generation of Indonesian missionaries are now serving as career missionaries around the world. I have noticed, in conducting missionary appointment services over the years, that a significant portion of those responding to God's call are former missionary kids. Before being appointed, they undergo thorough scrutiny regarding their call. Have they not been able to adjust to U.S. culture or to find their niche in the West? Are they motivated by a desire to return "home" to the culture in which they grew up and with which they are most familiar? While MKs' broadened worldview cannot be discounted and they will always be more at home where they have spent most of their lives, it is only natural that they would follow in the steps of their parents.

They have seen the darkness of people seeking God through the futile means of their traditional religious practices. They have observed multitudes dying without hope of a life after death, not because they rejected Jesus Christ but because they have never heard the Gospel. They have seen and contemplated the passion and sacrifice of their parents for extending the kingdom of God among unreached peoples and unevangelized villages. It is understandable that they would measure the call of God to the nations as being far superior to pursuing the American dream of success and prosperity.

We must acknowledge the reality of missionary kids who have floundered and have never discovered where they belong or found their purpose in life. Many MKs struggle with identification problems and feel deprived in having been subjected to an austere lifestyle and limited social outlets in a foreign culture. Some are in counseling or estranged from their parents. But those are the exception. As an Asian who grew up in America once observed, "Trees with two tap roots are the strongest trees." With roots in two cultures, missionary kids excel in academia and distinguish themselves in the sciences, entrepreneurial businesses, and foreign service, as well as in various areas of ministry. Family structure, the model of their parents serving the Lord, and the intentional involving of children in ministry and witness make it understandable that they would follow in the footsteps of their parents. The International Mission Board commonly sees third- and fourth-generation missionaries serving with our agency, or three and four siblings deployed in missionary assignments. The call may not be inevitable, but the family on the mission field is an asset for mobilizing subsequent generations of missionaries.

LOOKING BACK

Several years ago I had the privilege of participating in a retirement recognition for Tom and Gloria Thurman, who had served for thirty-one years in Bangladesh. Gloria's sister remarked, "The Great Commission takes on an altogether new perspective when your family becomes missionaries. When you pray, 'God bless the missionaries,' you are praying for someone's brother or sister, son or daughter. The strange, hard-to-pronounce names of far-away people groups become familiar and personal." She went on to say that she discovered that missionaries make poor decisions. "When war broke out and the family had to cower in the hallway under a mattress during an air attack, they should have come home, but they didn't. When their boys were born with respiratory difficulties, they should have come home, but they didn't. When Gloria contracted leprosy, they should have come home, but they didn't."

In a subsequent testimony Tom reflected on the challenges and difficulties throughout their tenure of service and why they did not come home. "We have experienced many circumstances we would not have chosen during these thirty-one years in Bangladesh—earthquakes, floods, cyclones, tidal waves in which hundreds of thousands were killed, drought and famine, three robberies, four broken bones, 291 country-wide strikes that paralyzed the economy and restricted travel, 186 flat tires, struggle with a difficult language, frequent electrical blackouts sometimes for days, leprosy, hepatitis, and one stabbing. But we have nothing but gratitude and praise that one day God tapped us on the shoulder and said, 'I have a place for you.' We came because of the lost millions of this land. We walked with him and our joy has been full." It is not surprising that the Thurmans' two boys are faithfully serving the Lord in Christian ministry.

One missionary parent of missionaries expressed it beautifully:

As my own two children went through the appointment process to become international missionaries, I found myself sifting through special, heart-treasured memories of their childhood and adolescent years. Specific incidents through which God affirmed His work in my children's lives resulted in their embracing His heart for the peoples of the world. My faith was strengthened and a deep abiding peace concerning their future began to emerge as I recalled God's word to Jeremiah: "Before I formed you in the womb I knew you; before you were born I sanctified you; I ordained you a prophet to the nations" (Jeremiah 1:5).[5]

In 3 John 4 the apostle testifies, "I have no greater joy than this, to hear that my children are walking in the truth." Missionary parents might add that they have no greater joy than to see their children and grandchildren fulfilling the mission to which they had been called.

To sum up, we can affirm wholeheartedly that the family is not an albatross, inflicting burdens and inhibiting effective missionary service. The family is a strategic part of God's plan to enhance missionaries' cross-cultural witness, to nurture children in a deeper walk with God and understanding of his will, and to sustain the legacy of the missionary call to subsequent generations.

NOTES

1. See Donald Grigorenko and Margaret Grigorenko, "Experiencing Risk: Missionary Families in Dangerous Places," pp. 27–46, in this volume.
2. Dennis Rainey, "Missionary Marriages" (unpublished manuscript, February 2007).
3. Jerry Rankin, *In the Secret Place* (Nashville, Tenn.: B&H Publishing, 2009).
4. Russell Rankin, "Foreword," in ibid., ix–x.
5. Terri Willis, ed., *Parents as Partners* (Richmond, Va.: International Mission Board, 2003), 1.

4

CARING FOR THE PARENTS OF MISSIONARIES:
A Case Study of Global Bible Translators

SUNNY HONG

Discussions of missionary care usually focus on maintaining missionaries' physical, emotional, psychological, and spiritual health, as well as on caring for the needs of missionary children (MKs). In the West, caring for the parents of missionaries is not usually part of the discussion. Parental care ministry, however, is a pertinent issue in Korea, because the smallest separable unit in Korean society is the family, not the individual.[1] Using the parental care ministry (PCM) of Global Bible Translators (GBT), this chapter examines the missiological implications of PCM. The value Korean society has placed historically on honoring parents, under the influence of Confucianism, and the effects of social changes currently under way are important background for understanding both Korean society today and the value of PCM.[2]

CONFUCIANISM IN KOREA

With the founding of the Yi Dynasty (1392–1910), Korea adopted Confucianism as its governing philosophy and moral principle. "Confucius identified five proper relationships in society: subject to king; son to father; younger brother to elder brother; wife to husband; and friend to friend."[3] This philosophy—so concerned with maintaining proper order, precedence, and balance in these relationships—continues today to define relationships in many aspects of Korean society.

The relationship between parents and children is expressed in Korea as *hyo*, or filial piety. Although the basic principle of hyo is obedience to parents, it means more than just obedience. Hyo includes the socially acceptable behavior of a child, which reflects the good teaching of his parents. To speak of someone as "a fatherless child" is an insult, for it means that the child does not behave properly and is a useless person. Behavior here indicates not only a person's actions but also and even more his or her character. Koreans do not separate behavior from character, because behavior is the outcome of character. When a child behaves well, his parents receive honor; the successes of children bring honor to their parents.

One aspect of hyo, to care for aged parents, is illustrated by the Chinese character for filial piety (孝), which means that a son (子) carries his elderly parents (老). Rather than expressing their love verbally, Koreans honor and love their parents by actions, such as providing financial support, giving gifts, or looking after parents' needs. Korean folklore includes a story about a daughter who sacrifices her life so her blind father can gain his vision. In Korea she is highly praised as embodying the concept of hyo. When an official in a high position during the Yi dynasty resigned from his work in order to fulfill his filial duty, the king was not able to object to the resignation.[4] Of the five relationships of Confucian teaching, hyo is regarded as having the highest value. Hyo is spoken of as *chun-yul*, literally "a principle from heaven," which implies that it is the most important value in human relationships.[5]

Confucian teaching holds that once an ancestor dies, the ancestor becomes a god to be revered. For this reason, rituals for a deceased ancestor are particularly closely observed in Confucianism. "Filial piety while the parents are alive is a virtue, but after death it is religion. . . . Then a funeral must be the contact point between the rules of life and religion. . . . Ancestral rites are religious ceremonies to express filial piety and a funeral is the most important part."[6] Even with the lessening of Confucianism as a religion in Korea, it is still significant for understanding how hyo plays out in Korean society. And even though Korean society has changed through modernization, Confucian teachings are still foundational to much of the way Korean society operates.

CHANGES IN KOREAN SOCIETY

Traditionally, the eldest son receives a greater inheritance than his siblings. In return he takes care of his elderly parents by residing with them and providing for their needs after retirement. As Korean society has changed to have less commitment to hyo, elderly people have shown a growing tendency to take responsibility for their own retirement. Today some elderly people believe they will be a burden on their children if they need to rely on them financially after retiring. Many elderly parents in Korea, however, do continue to rely on their children financially.

Changing Factors

Increasing modernization has brought several changes to Korea. First, life expectancy has increased greatly, from 61.9 years in 1970 to 81.2 in 2010.[7] Only 3.1 percent of the population was age 65 or older in 1970; this increased to 11.8 percent in 2012.[8] Due to increased longevity, children are supporting their parents many additional years. Second, Koreans have fewer children on whom they can rely after retirement. In 1970 the fertility rate was 4.53; by 2010 it had dropped to 1.22 children per Korean woman.[9] In comparison, the 2010 fertility rate for the United States was 1.9.[10] Due to the low fertility rate, the average size of a family declined from 5.7 persons in 1960 to 2.69 in 2011; therefore, Korean parents have fewer children to rely on following retirement.[11] Third, Korea's pension program is inadequate. When it began in 1988, the program covered only about 20 percent of the workers. The assumption when the Korean government initiated the pension policy was that children would provide financial help because of hyo. The effect was that the pension program was incapable of making retired people financially independent.[12] Even though it now covers every worker, not many people have accumulated enough funds to be financially self-sufficient following retirement.[13] According to 2012 statistics, "31.8% of the aged population received a public pension . . . 40.2% of the aged population regarded 'financial difficulty' as the hardest problem . . . and 59% of the population aged 55 to 79 wanted to have a job."[14]

Fourth, Korean parents are known for their sacrificial love for their children and enthusiasm for their children's education. National statistics show that 13.4 percent of household income was spent on education in 2012.[15] The proportion of educational expenses relative to household income has not changed since 1984 and is very high compared to other countries.[16] Parents not only feel obligated to provide a good education for their children, but also feel responsible for their children's success in life. They continue to provide all they can for their children instead of saving funds for their own retirement.

For these reasons, most elderly parents in Korea will rely on their children financially after retirement.

Taking Care of Parents as an Aspect of Hyo

In 2005 Keong-Suk Park and his colleagues reported on the attitudes of middle-aged adults and the elderly regarding care for parents.

> Middle-aged adults were asked the question, "What do you think about children taking care of their elderly parents?" In response to this question, 39.2% of adult children responded that this activity was to be "taken for granted or treated as a duty." Similarly, the survey instrument for the elderly sample asked, "Who do you think is most responsible for old age security?" In response to this question, only 35.6% of the elderly parents emphasized that this responsibility was primarily that of the family or the children.[17]

Children can assist their parents in two major ways: through coresidence and providing financial help. Coresidence has decreased over the years, but is still a widespread way of helping elderly parents. In 2011 Erin Hye-Won Kim and Philip Cook estimated

> that 41.5 per cent of elderly Koreans lived with a child; that among those who had at least one child, 42.5 per cent were co-resident; and that among elderly people who lived with a child and had at least two children including a son, 52.6 per cent were co-resident with the first son. It is clear that the first son still plays a bigger role than any of his siblings in providing co-residence.[18]

Even though coresidence has decreased over the years, in Korea it still plays a major role as a way for elderly parents to receive economic support as well as emotional and physical support from their children. The eldest son is expected to be the main provider for his elderly parents.

In accord with the concept of hyo, working children provide financial support for their elderly parents. Kim and Cook report that "child-to-parent financial transfers seem crucial to an average elderly Korean's income, accounting for 26.3 per cent of the total."[19] Though Korean children continue to play an important role in providing financial help for their elderly parents, the pressure of influences coming from the West (such as urbanization and modernization) has led to a significant decline in the previous system of parents being supported by their children.[20]

Alarming statistics indicate that Korea is the most suicide-prone country in the world; in 2010 an average of 42.6 people took their own lives each day. This suicide rate—roughly double that of Hungary (23.3) or Japan (21.2)— has made Korea the leading country in suicides within the Organisation of Economic Co-operation and Development (OECD) for eight consecutive years.[21] Persons intentionally taking their own lives range in age from youth to senior citizens. In 2000 the number of people over age 65 who committed suicide was 1,161; that figure rose to 4,378 in 2010, the highest suicide rate among senior citizens in the developed world.[22] According to Korean government statistics, people over age 65 commit suicide because of sickness or disability (39.8 percent), economic hardship (35.1 percent), loneliness (12.9 percent), a problem with a significant other (4.8 percent), family issues (4.3 percent), and job issues (1 percent).[23] People who are economically affluent can get better medical treatment. Therefore, sickness or disability is at least partially related to economic hardship. *Chosumilbo* reports astonishing figures: "The poverty rate among elderly Koreans is 45 percent, the highest in the OECD, where the average is 13.5 percent. Nearly half of all senior citizens in Korea are living in poverty."[24] As the traditional Korean concept of hyo has faded—coupled with insufficient pensions and inadequate financial support from children—the result has been an increase in the number of suicides among elderly Koreans who feel abandoned, mainly by their children but also by the Korean government.

THE PCM OF GLOBAL BIBLE TRANSLATORS

In February 2013 Global Bible Translators, established in 1985, had 202 members and 20 associate members working in twenty-eight countries. As a partner organization of Wycliffe Global Alliance, GBT's members are involved in translation of the Bible and related work.[25]

Founding of GBT's Parental Care Ministry

In 1997 while Luke Yoon was working overseas with GBT, his co-worker travelled to Korea and visited Luke's mother. The visit was a big encouragement to her. That inspired him to start a parental care ministry (PCM) for GBT members, because its members on the field were very concerned about their parents in Korea. When he became GBT's director of personnel, he invited Philip and Okja Kahng to consider launching the new PCM for GBT. Philip had served for three years in Papua New Guinea as a computer technician and Okja as manager of the SIL PNG guesthouse. The Kahngs began the PCM in 2004 while based in the United States, visiting Korea for the work. John and Esther Lee, who served as dorm parents at Faith Academy in the Philippines for seven years, moved to Korea in 2012 to join the PCM. Both the Kahngs and the Lees are Korean Americans.[26]

In February 2013 there were 195 parental units, of whom 73 were widowed; they ranged in age from early 50s to late 90s. More than two-thirds were Christians; at least 20 percent were nonbelievers. Most of the parents resided in various parts of Korea, though some lived overseas. Predominantly the parents who lived in Seoul and Kyungki province were believers; a higher proportion of the nonbelieving parents lived in other parts of the country. The people who lived in Seoul and Kyungki province were also asssumed to be more economically affluent than people who lived in other parts of the country.

Focuses of Parental Care Ministry

As PCM workers, the Kahngs and the Lees have worked to build relationships with the parents of GBT missionaries. Building relationships with the parents of missionaries, comforting them, encouraging them to make field visits, visiting the sick, and attending funeral services have been given special focus in this ministry.

Building relationships with parents of missionaries. The PCM workers' primary ministry to missionary parents has been one of relating to them. In the early years when the PCM workers called, most parents were reluctant to receive phone calls from a stranger. When parents are against having their children become missionaries, the beginning of the relationship is usually difficult, for the parents reject the PCM workers, also.[27] The PCM workers found it easier to relate to Christian parents.

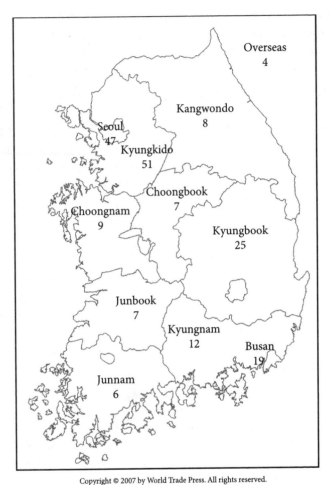

Map 4.1
Parents of South Korean missionaries by province

From early on, the workers made it a practice to listen to the parents, which helped them to release their anger. Parents around the world want their children to do well. Korean parents work exceptionally hard to provide their children with a good education. Most GBT members graduated from good universities and had the potential to get well-paying jobs. Parents whose children became missionaries and left Korea without a paid position felt betrayed. Some parents felt an emotional separation from their children and were disappointed that they had gone so far away. Even some Christian parents were against having their children become missionaries. They were hurt, having lost hope of getting their reward back. In the ordinary course of life, not only do parents receive economic help from their children, but also having a good story to share with their friends about their child's success is a means of saving "face." Having their children destroy their hopes and dreams has led some parents to build up *han* (sorrow, sense of loss, or resentment). Han develops "as a result of permanent frustration, repressed anger, evasions, remorse and the inability to change the situations."[28] Listening to what parents have to say about the wishes and dreams they had for their children is at times a way to let them release their han, even though they cannot change the course of their children's lives.

Comforting parents. As the relationship builds and as parents' hearts are opened, PCM workers are able to begin to comfort them. Major concerns parents have are how their children's needs will be met, how they will handle living overseas, and what they will eat. The parents need information and reassurance. The PCM workers try to explain the field situations so that parents will have peace about their children being so far away. Many parents do not understand their children's ministry. Nonbelieving parents simply think that their children are involved in doing good works and are unable to grasp the spiritual aspect of the work. Unfortunately, missionaries often share only positive details of their life and ministry with their parents. Shielding their parents in this way arises predominantly from the influence of hyo: they do not want their parents worrying about them. The PCM workers help parents become proud of their children, who are involved in expanding God's kingdom, or at least help them to acknowledge that their children are doing good works for others, something that not everyone is willing to do. Parents then become more eager to tell their friends about the good works their children are doing.

Encouraging field visits. PCM workers encourage Christian parents to visit the field where their children are working. Most parents who visit the field come back with a better understanding of their children's situation. They are less anxious about their children and are able to pray more specifically for their children's ministry and the country where they serve. Some parents express a desire to go back to the field to help in any way they can.

Visiting the sick. Parents who are sick receive special attention from PCM workers, who visit those in the hospital, pass along prayer requests through the GBT prayer network, and make sure to follow up with the parents by calling or revisiting them.

Attending funeral services. Thirty-three parents of GBT members died during the years 2004–12. PCM workers attended funeral services for all thirty-three parents. When children come back to Korea after the death of a parent, PCM workers accompany them to the grave site.

When a missionary dies, the official relationship between GBT and the missionary ends. PCM workers, however, continue to care for the parents of deceased missionaries. Three GBT missionaries died during the years 2008–10. PCM workers visit the grave sites of the missionaries on each anniversary and send annual gifts to their parents just as they do to the parents of living GBT members.

Methods Used in Parental Care Ministry

As means of extending a ministry of parental care, PCM workers call by telephone, send personalized cards and letters, visit, host gatherings, and send gifts. At the twentieth anniversary of GBT they also extended special recognition to the parents of missionaries.

Phone calls. Parents receive a phone call, generally from the Kahngs, once every two months. If PCM workers call more often they find that parents feel uneasy about the frequency of the calls. When a parent is sick, however, the Kahngs call more frequently. When they make an international phone call from the United States, parents are even more appreciative. The Lees have found, however, that many parents do not listen carefully to what is being said on the phone if a relationship has not yet been fully established.

After working with missionary parents for nine years, the Kahngs have seen attitudes change. From being distant, cold, and even opposed to what their children are doing, parents have become more warm, supportive, and involved with their children's ministry. The Kahngs feel validated and fulfilled in their role when they hear parents say, "Our day was brightened by your phone call."

Sometimes parents contact the Kahngs to find out about their children's safety if they have not heard from their children for a while or if the country where their children work is experiencing a natural disaster or political turmoil. The Kahngs reassure parents that GBT will contact them if something happens to their children.

Personalized cards and letters. When the Lees began working with PCM in 2012, they sent two personalized handwritten cards to the parents in an attempt to build relationships with them. The cards became a good excuse for the Lees to call parents and initiate conversations. As they got to know parents better, they followed up with personal letters of encouragement to each of them.

Visitation. Before visiting parents, PCM workers phone to inquire. When they receive a positive response, they schedule a visit. They avoid mealtimes to lessen the burden on the parents. In Korean culture, a host provides a meal or sometimes offers money for travel expenses in appreciation of a visit from a teacher or pastor. When the Kahngs visit, some parents feel obligated to provide funds for their travel. If they sense this, they do not visit the home. Some parents are reticent to show outsiders how they live because their home is humble or they are embarrassed by their physical limitations. In the years since the inception of the PCM, the Kahngs have yet to meet about thirty of the missionaries' parents. PCM workers value visitations because in them real relationships can be developed. Sometimes during a visit parents will ask the PCM workers to stay overnight; such invitations indicate that a deep relationship has formed.

Gatherings. When visiting a major city where many parents live, the PCM workers host a meeting. Through such gatherings, they encourage parents to meet other parents and to build new friendships to talk about their children.

Sending gifts. Gift giving is a part of Korean culture. GBT sends gifts to parents twice a year: on Parents Day and Christmas. Most of the gifts are practical things such as gloves, umbrellas, GBT calendars, blankets, scarves, and snack items. Sending gifts is another means of honoring parents in a culturally relevant way.

Recognition of parents at the twentieth anniversary of GBT. When GBT celebrated its twentieth anniversary in 2004, the parents of missionaries were invited for a special gathering at which they were recognized. They were presented with gifts and a few parents shared their testimonies. This event was the first time that the parents had gathered, and it formed the beginning of the PCM.

Fruits of Parental Care Ministry

The PCM's consistency over the nine years, 2004–13, has borne fruit. From it have come a prayer movement and the salvation of parents, as well as financial and practical help.

Prayer. By custom in the traditional Korean belief system, a mother would rise early in the morning, get her heart ready, and pray to a god who controls heaven and earth for the well-being of her family members or for any other pertinent desires. The Kahngs encourage those parents who are not believers to pray to the God their children serve rather than praying to a god who controls the heavens and earth.

One of the fruits of PCM is the prayer meetings some Christian parents have started in Seoul, Daeku, and Busan to pray for their children's ministry. They meet seven times a year, though as parents weaken with age the number of participants has slowly decreased due to deaths and physical limitations. Younger parents, busy with church involvement, often do not come to the parental prayer meetings. Some parents, however, who live in places where there are no parental prayer meetings join GBT's regional monthly prayer meeting.

Salvation of parents. Over the years 2004–13, five nonbelieving parents started attending church as an outcome of PCM. At least one parent was assured of his salvation. This fruit has come even though PCM workers have not focused on sharing the Gospel with nonbelieving parents; they have placed their emphasis first on building relationships, a challenging endeavor due to the difficulty of maintaining long-distance relationships.

Financial and practical support. As parents understand more about their children's ministry, some well-off parents are led to help their children and GBT financially. The past decade in Korea, as people have had fewer children, has seen a social trend in which parents focus their attention solely on their children. When the children decide to become missionaries, their parents take care of the grandchildren while their children are in missionary training.

Some parents even consider moving to the field to raise their grandchildren and give other practical help.

PARENTAL CARE MINISTRY BEYOND GBT

In Korea other mission agencies, such as Global Missions Pioneers and Hope, also engage in PCM. Wycliffe organizations in Asia seek to care for missionary parents in various ways. Wycliffe Hong Kong, for example, allocates US$200 per member per month to support parents. If a husband and wife are both members, then US$400 is set aside for the parents' allowance. That amount, while not large, is intended to show respect. Home staff visit parents after Chinese New Year's Day to show their respect, and parents are invited to attend special occasions in their honor. Through all of these activities, Wycliffe Hong Kong wants to communicate to the parents that their children care for them.

Wycliffe Singapore includes about US$400 per month for each member as a parents' allowance. Given on behalf of the children, this amount is a token honoring the parents, and it is not considered insignificant. The former director of Wycliffe Taiwan, who served from 2006 to 2012, visited all of Wycliffe Taiwan's parents of missionaries and gave them gifts during the Chinese New Year and Moon festivals. He did this on behalf of all Wycliffe Taiwan missionaries working overseas, to do filial piety. The visits comforted not only the parents but also the missionaries.

Wycliffe Japan sends out Christmas and summer greeting cards to their missionaries' parents to show appreciation for their sacrifice, support, and understanding. In Japan, during natural disasters Wycliffe Japan checks to see whether or not the parents of their missionaries are safe. If parents are severely affected by a natural disaster or are critically ill and would welcome a visit from Wycliffe Japan, people on staff visit them. If a missionary dies and the funeral is being held in the field, Wycliffe Japan staff accompany the parents to the field.

Singapore has the lowest fertility rate (0.79) in the world; Taiwan and Hong Kong (1.11) are third; while Korea, at 1.22, has the world's sixth lowest fertility rate. Since parents have fewer children to depend on for support after retirement, more demand financially is placed on each child in countries strongly influenced by Confucianism. This Confucian influence may account for Wycliffe Singapore and Wycliffe Hong Kong's factoring in of some financial support for parents. Doing so reflects cultural and social expectations in those countries.

All of these steps taken by Asian Wycliffe affilitates have been made a part of the organizations' formal institutional practice. Wycliffe USA, with different cultural expectations, has not as an organization instituted PCM.

MISSIOLOGICAL IMPLICATIONS

PCM provides a way to share the Gospel with nonbelieving parents, initiates a prayer movement among missionaries' parents, helps the local churches to be more missional, provides a way to honor missionaries' parents in culturally appropriate ways, and promotes a more holistic approach to the missionary family unit.

Sharing the Gospel with Nonbelieving Parents

As of February 2013, seventeen parents of GBT missionaries had clearly been identified as nonbelievers because of their children's prayer requests for their parents' salvation. In addition, at least forty people have not identified their faith and so are potentially nonbelievers. During the first nine years of PCM, five nonbelieving parents started attending church. Sadly, one mother confessed that she tried attending church, but could not continue because the church was too foreign to her.

Christianity's short history in Korea, just over one hundred years, may be a reason why many who become missionaries are first-generation Christians and why 20 percent of their parents are still nonbelievers. That their parents are nonbelievers is a spiritual burden for these missionaries.[29] Extending care ministry to parents of missionaries has brought to light a special group to be reached with the Gospel. As parents come to know the Lord, their children's burden will be reduced and the parents will be able to offer spiritual support to their children.

As greater numbers of missionaries are sent out from Majority World countries during the twenty-first century, it can be assumed that more first-generation Christians will become missionaries than ever before.[30] Reaching out to missionary parents is, therefore, a vital ministry both for bringing the Gospel to a unique group and for undergirding the ministry of missionaries.

Initiating a New Prayer Movement

Even though attendance at the parental prayer meetings has decreased in recent years, as parents understand more about the situation on the mission field they can pray at home for their children's ministry. Their prayers are not bound by their physical weakness. Through PCM more people like Hannah (1 Sam. 1:10–28), Anna (Luke 2:36–38), and Simeon (Luke 2:25–35) can be raised up.

Parents who have similar concerns about their children can share those concerns, pray for each other, and encourage each other. Parents who have overcome feelings of betrayal, stemming from their children's having become missionaries, can comfort other parents and help them to develop a kingdom perspective, rather than only seeking the well-being of their children on this earth.

Local Church Involvement

Korean churches have eagerly been sending missionaries overseas for the last thirty years. Now the Lees desire that local churches see supporting missionaries' parents as also part of their ministry. If congregations catch a vision for PCM, a church located near some of these parents could undertake a ministry of caring for them as a distinctive outreach of the church. The church could ask someone of a similar age to relate to a nonbelieving parent so that maybe through friendship that parent will come to know the Lord. Mission organization PCM workers relate to parents from a distance and have limited opportunities for sharing the Gospel. Ideally, local churches will get involved in sharing the message of salvation with nonbelieving parents.

Parents who are Christians can be recognized as "parents of the church" and treated as are the pastor's parents.[31] Doing so would honor these parents in a way that is culturally relevant. Through the parents, the local church can be connected with a missionary's ministry and so become more missional.[32]

Special attention should be given to parents who are experiencing financial difficulty. If local churches were to provide practical help to missionaries' parents with financial problems, they would provide a good model for honoring parents, and doing so would be a beautiful testimony to the local community. The seventy-three parents whose spouses have passed away compose another group that needs to receive special attention.

Cultural Issues

In the West many people prefer to be financially independent after retirement. In Korean society postretirement support is expected, and coresidence with parents—which both lightens the load of living expenses and enables children to offer practical assistance—is the most common way of helping elderly parents. But living overseas as a missionary makes coresidence impossible. Another way to care for elderly parents is to provide financial help. GBT does not have an official policy, but it allows its members, upon request, to use US$100 per month to help support parents. That amount, however, is a mere token.

The suicide rate among senior citizens in Korea is a critical social issue, and financial difficulty is one of the main reasons for the elderly to commit suicide. Nonbelieving parents of missionaries who are unable to provide for themselves may especially feel that they have been abandoned by their childen for the sake of the children's ministry. Missionary children in turn carry a multiple burden. In addition to the stigma they may feel for seeming to have abandoned their parents, they are unable to help their parents practically through financial support or spiritually by leading them to salvation. They are likely to feel a weight of guilt. Since Korean society expects the first son to play a major role in caring for elderly parents, a missionary who is a first son will be even more burdened. If his parent were to commit suicide because of financial difficulty or loneliness, it would be a major setback for missions. Great social pressure would come from nonbelievers to condemn missionaries for "deserting" their parents. Since in Korean culture the social norm of caring for parents is highly important, this may be an opportune time for GBT to review its financial policy in light of societal expectations. As it does so it will become the "light" (Matt. 5:14) in terms of practicing hyo.

Even though PCM cannot meet all the needs of parents or fulfull their desire to have their children live with them or nearby, it still fills some of the gap by honoring parents in culturally relevant ways. It can help sons and daughters to fulfill their filial role to their parents. At the same time it is good Christian witness to the missionaries' nonbelieving relatives and their neighbors.

Holistic Approach to a Missionary Family Unit

The Lees realize that PCM is a total-care ministry with the purpose of supporting the ministry of missionaries by helping them fulfill their filial duty towards their parents. When missionary children do not have a good relationship with their parents, the Lees also have difficulty building a good relationship with those parents.

The Kahngs discovered that missionaries on furlough were not able to spend much time with their parents because of the demands placed on them by fund-raising and other work GBT asked them to do. Missionaries find it challenging when their parents say things to the grandchildren without understanding how they have grown up on the mission field. The Lees see a need to assist grandchildren in developing good relationships with their grandparents. Ideally, PCM will follow a holistic approach in ministry to each family unit (missionary, missionaries' parents, and missionary kids) by partnering with an MK ministry. This holistic approach is culturally appropriate in the Majority World.

CONCLUSION

Obeying and honoring parents is the first commandment with a promise and is pleasing to the Lord (Ex. 20:12; Lev. 19:3; Deut. 5:16; Eph. 6:1–3; Col. 3:20). God denounces and pronounces a curse upon people who disobey or ignore their parents (Lev. 20:9; Deut. 21:18–21; Deut. 27:16; Ezek. 22:7; Rom. 1:30; 2 Tim. 3:2). In any particular society, however, culture defines what it means to obey and to honor parents. Practices that are acceptable in Western societies, such as allowing parents to enter a nursing home, may be culturally unacceptable in others. For instance, in Korea for children to put their parents in a nursing home without providing any additional financial support is considered to be deserting them. The Bible warns that people who do not provide for their immediate family are worse than unbelievers (1 Tim. 5:8). Being a missionary and serving people around the world is a high calling, but if missionaries cannot fulfill their filial duty because of their ministry, they may court the condemnation of hypocrisy that Jesus pronounced (Matt. 15:5–8; Mark 7:11–13).

This issue is not restricted just to Korea, for, on the one hand, most other Asian countries also rely heavily on children for support of elderly parents, and, on the other hand, most of the countries in East and Southeast Asia are similarly undergoing decreasing filial piety, a rapidly aging population, and rapid economic development.[33] Missionaries from East and Southeast Asian countries will, therefore, experience similar dilemmas with regard to care of aging parents.

Most African countries have a traditional worldview that believes ancestors are intermediaries between god and people and that they influence the living.[34] Africans therefore honor their parents when they are alive and venerate the dead, an outlook that has similarities to Confucian teaching. At present African countries have higher fertility rates than Korea, but as more Africans become missionaries, they may encounter similar issues related to honoring parents.

In Western countries the issues of honoring and caring for parents may lead to very different practices or practical applications from those found in the Majority World. Leaders of international mission agencies do need to be aware of the cultural expectations in the Majority World concerning PCM and to make accommodations in their organizational policies. Not only does ministry to the parents of missionaries fit well in the cultures of the Majority World, which expect children to honor their parents, but it can also become a stepping stone toward stronger mission organizations and outreach. Therefore to operate appropriately within Majority World cultures, mission agencies should consider embracing parental care as part of their ministry.

NOTES

1. Robert Kohls, *Learning to Think Korean* (Boston: Intercultural Press, 2001), 101. In this chapter "Korea" refers to the Republic of Korea or South Korea.

2. I wish to thank those who supplied the information on which this chapter is based. In 2013 Philip and Okja Kahng and John and Esther Lee, PCM workers for GBT, responded to my requests for a number of interviews. Through e-mail Luke Yoon, who initiated GBT's PCM program, supplied answers to my queries regarding the program's history. The current and previous directors of GBT as well as the personnel directors for GBT and Wycliffe USA provided further background on their PCM programs. Information about PCM activities being done by other mission agencies in Korea came from the director of Korea Research Institute for Mission. The directors of Wycliffe Hong Kong, Taiwan, Singapore, and Japan provided information about those organizations' experience doing PCM.

3. Kohls, *Learning to Think Korean*, 101.

4. Sungmoon Kim, "Trouble with Korean Confucianism: Scholar-Official between Ideal and Reality," *Journal of Comparative Philosophy* 8 (2009): 43, doi: 10.1007/s11712-009-9105-1.

5. Hanki Woo, "Hankukeui Kyuyangeul Ikneunda" (Discussion of Korean culture), *Humanist* 5 (2007): 63.

6. Keong-Suk Park, Voonchin Phua, James McNally, and Rongjun Sun, "Diversity and Structure of Intergenerational Relationships: Elderly Parent–Adult Child Relations in Korea," *Journal of Cross Cultural Gerontology* 20 (2005): 289, doi: 10.1007/s10823-006-9007-1.

7. Korean National Statistical Office, "2011 Life Tables for the Nation and Provinces," December 4, 2012, http://kostat.go.kr/portal/english/news/1/17/1/index.board?bmode=read&aSeq=273092&pageNo=&rowNum=10&amSeq=&sTarget=&sTxt=.

8. Korean National Statistical Office, "2012 Statistics on the Aged," September 27, 2012, http://kostat.go.kr/portal/english/news/1/8/index.board?bmode=read&aSeq=268470.

9. In 2011 the fertility rate was 1.24. See Korean National Statistical Office, "Final Results of Birth Statistics in 2011," August 23, 2012, http://kostat.go.kr/portal/english/news/1/8/index.board?bmode=read&aSeq=260076.

10. Population Reference Bureau, "World Population Data Sheet 2012," www.prb.org.

11. Yeon Kyung Chee, "Elder Care in Korea: The Future is Now," *Ageing International* 26 (2000): 27; and Korean National Statistical Office, "Population Statistics," 2011, http://census.go.kr/hcensus/ui/html/data/data_020_010_Detail.jsp?p_bitmId=60482&q_menu=4&q_sub=2&q_pageNo=1&q_div=ALL.

12. Chee, "Elder Care in Korea," 31.

13. Young-Jun Choi, "Transformations in Economic Security during Old Age in Korea: The Implications for Public-Pension Reform," *Aging and Society* 26 (2006): 549, doi: 10.1017/S0144686X06004879; and Ji-Whan Yun, "The Myth of Confucian Capitalism in South Korea: Overworked Elderly and Underworked Youth," *Pacific Affairs*, 83 (2010): 241.

14. Korean National Statistical Office, "2012 Statistics on the Aged," September 27, 2012, http://kostat.go.kr/portal/english/news/1/8/index.board?bmode=read&aSeq=268470.

15. Korean National Statistical Office, "Household Income and Expenditure Trends in the Third Quarter 2012," November 16, 2012, http://kostat.go.kr/portal/english/news/1/7/index.board?bmode=read&aSeq=269155.

16. "In South Korea, total spending (public and private) on education was 13.3% of the GDP in 1984, compared to 5.7% in Japan in 1982 and 6.78% in the United States in 1981 education expenses." See Luis Felipe Ramirez and Julio E. Rubio, "Culture, Government, and Development in South Korea," *Asian Culture and History* 2, no. 1 (2010): 77.

17. Park et al., "Diversity and Structure," 292.

18. Erin Hye-Won Kim and Philip J. Cook, "The Continuing Importance of Children in Relieving Elder Poverty: Evidence from Korea," *Ageing and Society* 31 (2011): 969, doi: 10.1017/S0144686X10001030.

19. Ibid., 965.

20. Kohls, *Learning to Think Korean*, 105.

21. "Korea Must End the Suicide Epidemic," *Chosumilbo*, September 11, 2012, http://english.chosun.com/site/data/html_dir/2012/09/11/2012091101353.html.

22. Sang-Hun Choe, "As Familes Change, Korea's Elderly Are Turning to Suicide," *New York Times*, Feburary 17, 2013, www.nytimes.com/2013/02/17/world/asia/in-korea-changes-in-society -and-family-dynamics-drive-rise-in-elderly-suicides.html?pagewanted=1&_r=2&hp&.

23. Korean Statistical Information Services (KOSIS), "Impulse to Commit Suicide and Reasons (13 Years Old and Over)," http://kosis.kr/eng/; enter "Suicide" in search box.

24. "Korean Parents Spent Too Much on Their Children," *Chosumilbo*, August 29, 2013, http:// english.chosun.com/site/data/html_dir/2012/07/05/2012070501469.html.

25. See www.gbt.or.kr.

26. GBT did not necessarily look for Korean Americans to fill this role. The Kahngs and the Lees were qualified and available. Most GBT members who could have taken this role were translators working in the field and therefore not available.

27. In the remainder of this chapter, the word "child" or "children" usually refers to adult missionaries rather than to MKs.

28. Ramirez and Rubio, "Culture, Government, and Development in South Korea," 78.

29. Dong-Hwa Kim, "Ministry to the Elderly Parents of Missionaries," in *Worth Keeping: Global Perspectives on Best Practice in Missionary Retention*, ed. Rob Hay, Valerie Lim, Detlef Blocher, Jaap Ketelaar, and Sarah Hay (Pasadena, Calif.: William Carey Library, 2007), 366–67.

30. "Majority World" here is a synonym for the non-Western countries belonging to the Global South that traditionally were not missionary sending countries.

31. For missionary parents to be treated as parents of the church or treated in the way the pastor's parents are would mean for them to be honored as persons worthy of respect and recognition from the church members.

32. Alan Roxburgh and Scott M. Boren, *Introducing the Missional Church: What It Is, Why It Matters, How to Become One* (Grand Rapids: Baker Books, 2009).

33. Mui Teng Yap, Leng Leng Thang, and John W. Traphagan, "Introduction: Aging in Asia— Perennial Concerns on Support and Caring for the Old," *Journal of Cross Cultural Gerontology* 20 (2005): 259, doi 10.1007/s10823-006-9005-3; and Kim and Cook, "Continuing Importance of Children," 972.

34. Edwin Zulu, "Reverence for Ancestors in Africa: Interpretation of the Fifth Commandment from an African Perspective," *Scriptura: International Journal of Bible, Religion, and Theology in Southern Africa* 81 (2002): 479.

5

THE "FAMILY PROBLEM": Challenges in Balancing Maternity and Mission in Nineteenth-Century Equatorial Africa

MARY CAROL CLOUTIER

As they answer the call to share the Gospel in diverse places, missionary families frequently face risks and privations. In the twenty-first century, risks and danger may arise from political or religious hostility of which missionaries are direct or indirect targets. For nineteenth-century missionaries, life-threatening risks were more often related to health and the environment. One missionary wrote, "I went as a celibate, being told by the public, and even by missionaries, that white maternity in Africa was fatal to both mother and child. There were those who called African missionary marriage 'murder.' Men and women gave up their work in Africa, unable to face this terrible problem."[1]

Robert Hamill Nassau wrote these words in his defense of having missionary families serve in Africa, even though he had buried one son and two wives in African soil. A medical doctor and pioneer missionary, Nassau argued both that raising a family in Africa was normal and natural and that doing so allowed missionaries to model Christian home life amid their Christian converts and host communities. While many missionary families faced debilitating illnesses and death, Nassau felt that moderation in activity, proper diet and rest, and the availability of medical professionals and supplies did much to increase the life expectancy of missionary families. Nassau's own experience in sending his children to the United States to be cared for by family members led him to argue against this "mistaken sense of duty." It was, he wrote, "heroic in its mistake" and completely uncalled for.[2]

Private and published missionary correspondence of the Presbyterians' Gaboon and Corisco Mission (formed in 1870 by the merger of the Gaboon Mission and the Corisco Mission), in Equatorial Africa, reveal intimate family decisions regarding the health and safety of missionary mothers and children on the field, and their sense of accountability to their family, supporters, and mission board. These archives support Nassau's conviction that missionaries often felt pressured about missionary maternity and that they were torn between their calling and duty as missionaries and their commitment to the health and safety of their families.

This chapter traces the stories of several pioneer missionary families that served during the mid-nineteenth century in what is now northern Gabon and southern Equatorial Guinea. High mortality rates (particularly for women and children) dissuaded some from answering the call to serve on the mission field. Those who obeyed the call found that they would continually need to negotiate the risks, count the cost, and trust God in all circumstances. Missionary parents had essentially three choices regarding their families: to have children and keep them on the field; to send their children away while they, the parents, remained on the field; or to leave the mission field in order to raise their family. The following stories illustrate that no choice was foolproof, clearly right or wrong. Any decision had potential risks and consequences. Missionary communities sometimes preached the Gospel without words by the way they responded to both life and death, fully trusting in God's providence. They also illustrated that God's broader family includes the unmarried, the widowed, and the childless, as well as families with children—each having a place, role, and purpose in his kingdom. Lastly, the stories indicate that with time, experience, improved conditions, and applied wisdom, missionary parents could reasonably expect to raise their children on the mission field and also carry out a fruitful ministry.

MISSION CEMETERIES: MISSION FAMILIES AND THEIR LOSSES

A tour of the Baraka Mission cemetery in Libreville, Gabon, gives little evidence of missionary maternity. In 2005 there were two identifiable gravestones of missionary children, those of Louise Menkel (age five) and infant Arthur Reading. Nearby, the Porter family tombstone marks the common grave of Rollin and Nancy Porter and their infant. The details of their brief lives were recorded in private letters and diaries.

Missionary deaths were often described in heroic terms, such as in the case of Zeviah Walker in 1848: "Having done what she could, she ceased from her labors, and her works do follow her. . . . Several persons who have recently been converted to God, state that her faithful labors, especially her dying entreaties, were made the means of bringing them to repentance."[3] The report cited makes scant mention that for nearly two years William and Zeviah Walker had been running the Gaboon mission on their own, while their missionary colleagues were in the United States seeking to regain their health.[4] Except for the dedicated care of an unmarried African American woman, Jane Cowper, the Walkers were alone during a difficult pregnancy followed by the immediate loss of their newborn son. Zeviah Walker suffered for two more months before death released her.[5]

Missionaries at this time were acutely aware of their mortality, often expressing a willingness to suffer and die for the sake of the Gospel in Africa.[6] The story of Rollin and Nancy Porter is indicative of this zeal, which preempted caution and prudence. When the Porters arrived in June, 1851, the Baraka (Gaboon) Mission cemetery was but seven years old, yet already it contained numerous graves, including those of four young missionary women and two babies, all buried within the previous three years.

In a journal Nancy Porter recorded their adjustment to life in Africa, their assignment to a remote new mission site, and their frequent bouts with "African fever." The journal ends abruptly on June 24, 1852, with reference to her being confined to bed. The mission doctor also being sick, her sick husband was attending to both of them. The rest of the story is told by their tombstone inscription, which states that Rollin Porter died on July 6 and Nancy Porter died days later; no date was given for the birth or death of the infant buried with them. A published account of their deaths paints a vivid image: the Porters were sick with fever in adjacent rooms. When told that her husband would not live until morning, Nancy asked to be taken to him. Her caregivers lifted her into a rocking chair and carried her to his room so that she could bid him farewell. Soon after this, Nancy gave birth to a daughter. Hearing her husband's labored breathing in the next room, she knew he would soon die.

The baby, however, "led the way to heaven. In one hour her father was with her. Mrs. Porter lingered a day or two, and then joined her loved ones in bliss."[7]

What is evident in the Porter journal is that the couple was living in an area unreached by the Gospel, whose inhabitants were frequently engaged in overnight drumming and dancing, intertribal wars, and local disputes. In their one full year of missionary service, the Porters were simultaneously studying the local language, preaching the Gospel, and operating a small school. The resulting loss of sleep and rest, combined with a malarial climate, their frequent journeys in open boats under the tropical sun, and Nancy Porter's (unmentioned) pregnancy, all contributed to their failing health. Seasoned missionary colleagues urged them to remain at the Baraka mission and to rest, but Rollins Porter committed himself to extensive travel and preaching, further compromising his health. He had to be convinced to remain near his bedridden wife.[8] One of Nancy Porter's last journal entries, two weeks prior to their deaths, reflected their extreme weariness and zeal: "We feel that it is not by might or by power but by God's Spirit that the work is to be accomplished, and we can do nothing but lay ourselves with all our rare talents and high attainments upon the altar of sacrifice and beg God to use us as instruments in carrying forward this glorious work. I ask no greater privilege."[9]

The graves in Baraka cemetery show eleven adult missionary deaths in the mission's first fifteen years (some with unborn and newborn babies), but many more missionaries left the field due to broken health and "other considerations."[10] Graves now lost include those of the Walker baby (1848), the Preston baby (date unknown), and the Clemens baby (1857). The only record of their existence consists of brief remarks in the personal journals of missionaries.[11] Similarly, otherwise unknown missionary children are revealed in an 1862 description of the Corisco cemetery, indicating the prevalence of multiple losses among mission families. The article mentions the graves of "Mr. Ogden and his babe" and "Mrs. Loomis and her child," as well as "the first Mrs. DeHeer."[12] Recently, missionaries in Equatorial Guinea cut back the jungle growth to clear the Benita Mission cemetery, the final resting place of little Paull Nassau (1867), Solomon Reutlinger and his infant son (1869), Mrs. (John) Menaul (1870), Mary (Mrs. Robert) Nassau (1870), baby William Gault (1884), and Mary (Mrs. Peter) Menkel and her unborn baby (1893).

While these gravestones are silent reminders of the harsh losses of missionary families, missionary letters and journals give insight into the joy and hopeful anticipation of parenthood. Many missionary children's lives were spared when their parents gave them over to the care of friends and relatives "back home" or left the field for the sake of keeping their family intact.

PREGNANCY AND CHILDBIRTH

Pregnancy and childbirth were "delicate" subjects in the nineteenth century, and mission records rarely mentioned them. Early on, missionaries serving at both the Gaboon and Corisco Missions remained on the field for the birth of their children. In the absence of trained medical doctors, missionaries cared for one another in sickness and in childbirth. This created much stress as the care of one sick person required the time and strength of several others, drawing them away from their regular mission duties. One of the earliest cases recorded was that of Anna DeHeer, who died in childbirth. A fellow missionary took charge of the newborn until her own health and strength failed. The widowed father's health was severely compromised as he cared for his two small daughters (one a newborn), until they were sent to the United States and adopted by kind friends. Cornelius DeHeer remained in missionary service, and lamented his absent daughters.

Phebe Ogden's complicated pregnancy and birth, in early 1861, had a cumulative and catastrophic effect on the mission. According to Walter Clark, this one pregnancy required months of attention by his wife, Maria, and Miss Mary Latta, as well as "a strong and faithful colored nurse from Liberia."[13] Clark's wife was "completely broken down from labor and responsibility," and Mary Latta's health was so compromised that she had to be evacuated for a time to preserve her life. In their absence, the girls' school was virtually suspended. Chauncey Loomis, a medical doctor, was also "much involved in the case," which Clark deemed "an extra and heavy burden upon his mind and hands."[14] Clark attributed Thomas Ogden's death, shortly after the birth of his son, to exhaustion from his wife's illness. Ogden had already been weak in health, and this had been "the last straw." In contrast to Clark's opinion, Loomis, in his year-end report, noted that Ogden had ignored his colleagues' recommendation that he take a furlough to recuperate his health. Just prior to his final illness he had been traveling for ministry. Upon his return, Ogden was presented with his newborn son, to which he replied, "Well, if the Lord will, we shall give Africa another Missionary."[15]

Perhaps a more tragic case was that of the Loomis couple, Chauncey and Harriet, who arrived on the field in January 1860.[16] Chauncey Loomis came to the field expecting to serve as mission physician, but was instead given responsibility for the mission store and accounts, the oversight of several boarding schoolgirls, and provision of meals for schoolteachers and their assistants. Overwhelmed by the burdens of multiple mission assignments and a perceived lack of empathy and friendship from fellow missionaries, Loomis faltered in his own health and emotional well-being.[17] His wife was also pregnant during this stressful time. In mid-July 1861, just three months after the birth of the Ogden baby, and two months after Thomas Ogden's death, Harriet Loomis went into labor. In his brief description of her confinement, Chauncey Loomis noted, "The labor being tedious, and being fearful of harm to the mother, if too long delayed, the child was taken away by instruments."[18] He then expressed his own anguish: "It is hard for a father to be compelled to lift hand against his own child, yet it was a professional duty. It seemed hard to make the coffin and dig the grave with my own hand. But it is done."[19] A month later, Harriet Loomis died of fever. Loomis attributed his family losses to the overwhelming and unrelenting demands of ministry assignments and unsympathetic missionary colleagues.[20]

Having lost Thomas Ogden, the Loomis baby, and Harriet Loomis in the space of three months, the mission determined that Phebe Ogden and her baby should not remain on the field; a missionary widow and her baby would add undue burden, rather than strength, to the community.[21] The missionaries were convinced of the "expediency for pregnant ladies to return home to avoid untimely graves."[22]

RISKS AND CONSEQUENCES

In spite of what may have seemed like a moratorium on missionary maternity on the field, some families carefully weighed the risks and consequences and made decisions that seemed right for themselves. The Clarks returned to the United States for the early years of their family life. Widowed Georgianna (Mrs. George) McQueen left her son with relatives and returned to the field. Mary Latta's first year on the field was largely devoted to caring for sick colleagues and their infants, and attending the burial of three in as many months. In her second year she met and married her colleague, Robert Nassau, a physician as well as an ordained missionary. Nassau offers rare insight into the nineteenth century missionary family in several autobiographical works. His book *Crowned in Palm-Land* is a compilation of his first wife's personal journal and letters home, which chronicle their early married life, her hopes of having a family, and her mixed joy and sorrow in watching her babies reach milestones and then weaken, despite her best efforts in caring for them.[23] These accounts open a deeper understanding of the difficult decisions parents had to make as they sought balance between their commitment to the missionary work and their devotion to the well-being and future of their children.

Difficult Choices

Mary Latta Nassau traveled to the United States to give birth to her first son, Willie, returning to the mission field when her baby was just seven months old. While in Liberia she hired a young Americo-Liberian woman, Mrs. Thompson, to be her baby's nurse at Corisco.[24] Anxious for other young families to join them, she wrote to the Clarks, who were contemplating a return to the mission field with their two young children. Mary's letter assured them that her child was doing well and that there were many such missionary babies along the coast of Africa.[25]

The mission soon faced dangerous conditions, however, including a smallpox epidemic and regional food shortages. The Nassaus were greatly concerned with the declining health of their little boy, Willie. When the ship bringing the Clark family and a supply of nourishing food arrived, the Nassaus determined that the food had come too late to help their son. They made the difficult decision to send him back to the United States to be cared for by relatives.[26] In a later letter, Mary Nassau remarked that they got along without him—he was just fourteen months old when they separated—though they missed him every day. Their work at the new Benita station, on the mainland, was enough to "keep hands and often thoughts engaged; and then we know we acted as God's providence seemed to direct."[27]

Mary noted her son's second birthday and imagined him playing in the snow. In a letter to his caregiver, she reflected on his childhood, which she was missing: "I cannot help longing for a sight of the baby face, and wish that I might hear once more the sound of his baby voice. Do not teach him, as he grows older, to long too much for his papa and mamma so far away. If we come to him, he will learn to love us: and if not—. It is sad for a child from his earliest years to feel the shadow of a great loss. I ask that for my baby's sake. I want his childhood to be a happy one."[28]

Seeking God's Direction and Peace

The Nassaus believed that a missionary family helped to "show the brutal heathen hearts the beauty and dignity of a perfect Christian family."[29] Yet in their desire to have children on the mission field, they were keenly aware of the uncertainty of life. Pregnant with her second child, Mary Nassau wrote, "Buying for the baby always saddens me, especially anything that it will not need for a few months. It seems as though I felt too sure of the little life. Oh, I hope it will live! My little one! My Blessed child! Even if it should not, it is pleasant thinking, talking of, and preparing for it beforehand."[30] Mary described having sought the Lord on this issue and sensed from him the promise of "another little life that might shed some happiness on ours."[31] She wrote, "I know there is a great deal said about its being wrong to have children in Africa. I do not know,—I tried to find something in the Bible,—I prayed for teaching, but perhaps my wishes misled; but I could find only in God's Word that children were a blessing."[32]

The Nassaus' second son, Paull, was born in July 1866, when his older brother in the United States was twenty-eight months old. The African community in their locality had not previously seen a white newborn, and they expressed great disappointment. Their ancient beliefs held that the white man's land was below the sea and that death would bring them to a happy land, full of wealth, where their skin would be changed to white.[33] Yet here was a white child born in the ordinary way: "Now our hopes are dead. Dying, we had hoped to become like you. But, verily, ye are born as we."[34] Local women marveled that the white baby took nourishment from his mother's breast, just as their babies did.[35]

Beginning in his sixth month, little Paull's health was compromised when Mary Nassau became ill with dysentery and was unable to nurse him. After a period of separation, the baby would no longer accept the breast. Robert Nassau was concerned because the child would only take "artificial food," which lacked necessary nutrients. Canned and dry milk supplies were available fifty miles away in the mission store, but intertribal wars had become intense in the area and people were afraid to make long-distance trips across enemy lines. Meanwhile, his child cried for hunger and sickened on unhealthy food.[36] Eventually able to procure fresh goat milk and a supply of nourishing food from America, he expressed hope that little Paull would soon "regain his rosy cheeks and plump legs."[37] He observed, however, that the baby was "fading away, and growing more beautiful as he faded."[38] Paull Nassau died soon after at the age of sixteen months. They concluded that the cause of death was chronic diarrhea, caused by a poor water supply. Mary Nassau reflected, "What need to speak of my sorrow? The loneliness must cling to my heart, and yet I try to be glad for my precious child that was so soon taken to the Saviour's arms. He has found now there is something better even for him than mother's heart on which he loved to lie, or mother's face and voice for which he used to watch and listen when I left him for a little while."[39] In a note to her missionary friend Maria Clark, she wrote, "I have always felt that mothers should not mourn too deeply the little ones gone to glory, and I still feel the same. 'It is well.' May a kind Father spare your little flock."[40] The Clarks (now a family of five) would leave definitively for the United States just three months later.

Compounded Grief

To add to the Nassaus' sorrow, two local Christians came to them in secret, warning them to watch the child's grave, intimating that someone might come and "spoil" it (fetishers believed there was power in the body parts of white persons, and this was a viable concern). The couple made the difficult decision to remove their son from the original grave and on a moonless night quietly reburied him in another, secret location.[41] Telling no one of this change, they "mourned" openly at the original grave and privately at the second. Later, when the gravestones arrived from America, Nassau secretly transferred the child's remains back to the original grave, prior to transferring them to the new mission cemetery. When the child was finally buried under the marble gravestones, Mary Nassau was satisfied that her little son was "rested."[42]

In less than two years after Paull's death, three missionary babies were born. Little Anna Menaul was hastily sent to America after her baptismal ceremony.[43] The Nassaus welcomed a third son, Charley, and the Reutlingers lost a son at birth. Solomon Reutlinger himself died in July 1869, on his wife's twenty-second birthday.

Charley Nassau remained healthy for eight months and then began to lose weight, as his brothers had. The Nassaus were hoping for a furlough in America, after nine years of service with the Corisco Mission, but were unable to leave. The death of Solomon Reutlinger and his widow's transfer to the Gaboon Mission had left them virtually alone.[44] The Menauls needed a health furlough, due to Mrs. Menaul's second pregnancy. The imminent furloughs of the Menauls and DeHeers required the Nassaus to defer their own plans for furlough for at least another two years.[45] Meanwhile, their oldest son turned six, far away in the United States. Mrs. Menaul died after giving birth to a daughter. Mary Nassau cared for the baby girl until the child and her widowed father were strong enough to leave for America.

A few months later, Mary Nassau became dangerously ill with fever. All mission and church work stopped as the small community kept vigil. Robert Nassau, contemplating the few options left to them, decided to transport her to Corisco Island. Through the fog of pain and delirium, Mary Nassau sensed that her death was imminent. She managed to communicate to her husband her wishes that she wanted him to provide future care for their faithful Liberian nurse, Lavinia Sneed,[46] and vetoed their intention to leave behind little Charley as they evacuated her to the Corisco Mission.[47] She died during the voyage, sometime after midnight. Though almost to Corisco Island, they turned the boat back towards the mainland, to their own mission station, Benita. As he gazed upon his lifeless wife, Nassau reflected, "And this form, outlined through the white cover, is [Charley's] mother,—and she had helped me bury baby Paull,—we two, alone, in secret, at night,—and we had sent away her first-born across the sea. All, with a thousand other truths come back."[48] Mary Nassau was buried at the Benita cemetery near her son Paull.[49]

LIBERIAN CHILDCARE ASSISTANTS

The decisions that the Nassaus faced—to have children on the field and whether or not to keep them on the field—were common to missionaries. While many missionaries hired and trained local persons to help care for their households, the Gaboon and Corisco missionaries also employed American-born women of color, many of them Americo-Liberian colonists, whose faithful presence and trusted experience gave missionary mothers relief from the overwhelming demands of home and childcare.

One particular Americo-Liberian woman became a familiar and trusted friend and a comfort to missionary women in their motherhood. Mrs. Lavinia

Sneed, already mentioned in relation to the Nassau family, arrived at Corisco Mission in 1867. She remained with the Nassaus for several years, occasionally relocating to associate with other families and to fill needs for a midwife and nurse. Lavinia Sneed appears to have been indispensible to the missionaries in that vital role. In early 1872, two new missionary couples (Samuel and Sophia Murphy and Jacob and Mary De Bruyn-Kops) were expecting babies and had made the decision to remain in Africa for the births. Though a French doctor was available, the expectant couples were counting on Sneed's presence and care. An unexpected delay in her return from a visit to Liberia, however, caused the two families to reconsider their decision, and both wives returned to America for their confinement.[50] The mission did not have a firm policy on the subject of missionary maternity, and it appears that such decisions (and their repercussions) were left to the couples. In a letter to the secretary of the Presbyterian board, Samuel Murphy expressed regret at their departure, mindful of the expense, the loss of their services, and the "influence upon friends of the Mission at home."[51] Both husbands left the mission less than a year later.[52] Lavinia Sneed remained in Gaboon, assisting a succession of families, for nearly twenty-five years.

MISSIONARY WIDOWERS—AN INTERIM WHOLLY DEVOTED TO THE WORK

Two missionary widowers, William Walker and Robert Hamill Nassau, experienced the grief and loss of their spouses and family homes. Yet in the interim period of their secondary "bachelorhood," both men found freedom and flexibility to do vital, pioneer missionary work. They found both challenge and satisfaction in doing extensive travel into the interior, preaching among unreached people groups, and devoting long hours to language acquisition and translation. Both learned a great deal about their host cultures and became able to live more simply and to adapt to local foods and conditions. For Walker, who buried two wives and one newborn son in his first six years on the field, the period of widowerhood lasted only about two years, yet he accomplished a great deal. With his third marriage, Walker's life returned to the nucleus of home and family, and his ministry was once again based at the main mission of Baraka. He and his third wife, Catherine, did not have children of their own, but adopted into their family several African orphans whom they raised to adulthood.

After the death of his wife, Mary, in 1870, Robert Nassau remained a widower through his next ten-year term in Africa. During those years he opened up several interior missions along the Ogowe River and did the tireless work of missionary pioneer, pastor, and medical doctor. Nassau's two surviving sons, Willie and Charley, remained in America during his absence in Africa.

MISSION FAMILIES ON THE FIELD

After 1870, when the Gaboon Mission and Corisco Mission merged, missionaries seemed more willing to accept the risks of remaining on the field for the birth of their children and raising their children in Africa. Evidence indicates that they also gave full-time care to their own children, perhaps with the help of local African employees.

In 1875 Joseph and Mary Reading arrived with their eighteen-month-old son, Arthur, who was gravely ill, having contracted dysentery from contaminated water onboard ship; he died a few weeks later.[53] Little Arthur's death, unrelated to living conditions in Africa, was the first in the Gaboon Mission in seventeen years. While the Corisco Mission had sustained numerous losses in the 1860s, Gaboon missionaries (especially young couples) left the field when their health was at risk. Only three older, childless couples remained at Gaboon during its last decade before the 1870 merger of the two missions. In the next few years, three children were born to Peter and Charity (Sneed) Menkel, and the Readings returned from furlough with their second child. These were the first missionary families who remained on the field with their growing children. Added to these in the next decade were the Arthur Marling, Adolphus Good, William Gault, and Graham Campbell families. Remarkably, these mission families eventually left due to the illness or death of the missionary husband/father.

A SECOND FAMILY

In 1880, after a decade of living without family, Robert Nassau returned to the United States for a much-needed furlough, during which time he reacquainted himself with his two sons, spoke passionately about the mission work in Africa, and pursued (with the help of trusted friends) the goal of finding a suitable wife.[54] His prayers and efforts were answered in the person of Mary Foster, whom he married just prior to his return to Africa in late 1881. The second Mary Nassau proved to be a strong and capable missionary, unafraid of the deprivations and dangers of the interior. Like the first Mrs. Nassau, she had also been orphaned as a child, and longed for a family of her own. She, too, weighed the desire against the risk of having a baby in Africa, confiding in her colleague, Mary Reading, who had already lost a baby son to dysentery and was raising her little daughter in the interior. Mary Nassau became pregnant in early 1884. Knowing the pain her husband had experienced in living apart from his sons, she asked him to promise that they would keep and raise this child. In *The Path She Trod*, Robert Nassau recounts the details of their life and marriage, her complicated pregnancy and childbirth, and his grief and sense of helplessness as he delivered his tiny and frail infant daughter, and then watched his wife fade away.[55] Honoring his promise to her, Nassau kept his daughter with him in the African interior. For the next seven years his child's life took priority over the relentless demands of the mission work as he focused on her survival and day-to-day care. Nassau lamented the lack of qualified caregivers in his remote location. A photo of the two of them, when little Mary was a toddler, clearly shows a rapidly aging and exhausted father. When the child was three or four, Nassau found a trustworthy caregiver, a young Gabonese woman who had been raised at the Baraka Mission. Their close working and living arrangements led missionaries and members of the church and community to suspect them of impropriety. This period in Nassau's life and ministry was filled with bitterness, sorrow, suspicion, and dissension. When Mary was seven, Nassau took his next furlough. Mary would remain in the United States for the rest of her life, while her father returned to Africa for one more term of service.

HE PUTS THE LONELY IN FAMILIES (PS. 68:6)

Missionaries often felt deprived of extended family relationships they might have enjoyed at home, and they developed close family ties with one another. Miss Susanna Dewsnap was very close to the Reading family, having arrived in Gaboon with them on the same ship in 1875.[56] On the voyage and during baby Arthur's fatal illness, Susanna became a second mother to him. When he died, she helped to wash the body and prepare the casket.[57] Several years later, when the Readings returned from furlough with little Lizzie, they resumed the extended family relationship with Miss Dewsnap. In 1881, when both Lizzie and Susanna fell ill of African fever, Mrs. Sneed and the Readings nursed them. Susanna's case proved to be fatal, however, and her colleagues prepared her for her imminent death.[58] In accord with her final wishes, she was buried near baby Arthur at the Gaboon Mission.[59]

Missionary widows such as Phebe Ogden and Louise Reutlinger remained in missionary service for decades after the loss of their husbands and babies, and likewise found a welcome place in missionary families. Louise Reutlinger, who had lost both her only infant and her husband in her early twenties, became a close friend of the DeHeers, whose daughters (from his first marriage) had been adopted and raised in the United States. The DeHeer grandchildren and great-grandchildren remembered "Aunt Lou" fondly and noted her influence in their young lives.[60] When Louise died, in 1938, sixty-eight years after burying her husband and child in Africa, she was laid to rest at the foot of the DeHeers' grave in Nyack, New York.

ASSESSING MISSIONARY HEALTH

Robert Hamill Nassau, in his 1893 assessment of improvements in missionary health in Equatorial Africa, described some of the mistakes the early missionaries had made that compromised their health and well-being: they allowed their zeal for spreading the Gospel to consume them even though they were aware that the climate required moderation physically, mentally, and spiritually; appropriate dress; and diet adjusted to the environment.[61] Overwork in the equatorial heat and humidity often sapped their strength and compromised all other aspects of their well-being. Missionary home and family life improved after they made certain changes, such as building their homes off the ground and with more durable materials. Well-trained domestic assistants relieved them from being overwhelmed by relentless and arduous household tasks, and freed them to concentrate on ministry tasks. Improved knowledge and understanding of African illnesses helped them to better treat and prevent them. They also received better care from medical professionals. Nassau attributed some early missionary deaths to "mental depression" and "intense homesickness" resulting from their sense of isolation on the mission field. Frequent mail, communications, and support from mission societies and supporters helped to bridge this sense of distance and to give a feeling of "home-love," making "less painful and depressing the isolation which is distinctive of an African missionary's life."[62] The last improvement Nassau noted was the "solution of the family problem—If ever it was right or necessary for [an] African missionary parent to part with his young infant, it is not now necessary. And I go so far as to believe positively that it is wrong."[63] Nassau's 1893 article on missionary health argued that the missionaries of the later nineteenth century were mistaken in their view that missionary maternity was fatal for both mother and child and that children could not survive in the African climate. He remarked on the cruel separation of missionary parents from their small children and their subsequent meetings as "strangers" in later years. Nassau felt that missionaries had an exaggerated sense of their duty and unnecessarily sent their children away for the sake of Christ.[64]

CONCLUSION

Missionary families faced difficult decisions on whether to keep their family on the field, to send their children to live with relatives at "home," or to leave the mission work altogether and return home with their family. The first option—to remain with their children on the field—fulfilled their longing for family and helped to provide a model of the Christian home and family for the new converts and host community. The second option offered a greater likelihood that the child would be well nourished, well reared, and well educated. This did not always guarantee a happy childhood, however, and often caused parents and children to feel alienated from one another. The third option was to leave the mission field and to keep the family intact while serving in home ministry. Though missionaries seemed to regret leaving foreign mission work for the sake of their families, many found satisfying and fruitful "mission" work in the United States.

While nineteenth century missionaries faced great suffering and privation, John Darch cautions us not to exaggerate their hardships, as their contemporaries at home, of every class, likewise experienced sickness, death, and suffering.[65] Anthropologist T. O. Beidelman's research shows that these issues were also common among Church Missionary Society missionary families serving in East Africa during the same time period.[66]

Striking similarities between today's missionary families and their nineteenth-century predecessors exist as well. Darch notes that loneliness and isolation continue to be common problems among missionaries.[67] A recent study of missionary families and risk, by Donald Grigorenko and Margaret Grigorenko, shows that contemporary missionary parents also face criticism as to the wisdom of taking their children to potentially dangerous places and underscores the need for missionaries to develop a theology that recognizes that God sometimes allows pain, suffering, and death as part of the unfolding of his plan of redemption.[68] Jerry Rankin's reflection arising from his family's experience in mission service parallels the sentiment expressed by Nassau that the family helps to embody the message of the Gospel as husbands and wives demonstrate love and respect toward one another and as they work together in the ministry.[69] Their loving relationship with their children and the example they provide of godly parenting likewise set an example. Anneke Stasson's research on Ingrid and Walter Trobisch shows that 1950s-era missionary parents were as prone as their 1850s-era counterparts, such as the Porters, to let zeal for their ministry take precedence over family concerns.[70]

Though nineteenth-century missionaries did not express themselves in terms we use today, their writings indicate that they had worked out a theology of risk and that as Gospel-bearers they recognized that pain, suffering, loneliness, loss, and death would be part of their life and witness for Christ.

NOTES

1. Robert Hamill Nassau, "Some Causes of the Present Improved Health of Missionaries to Africa," *Missionary Review of the World* 6, no. 12 (1893): 926–29.

2. Ibid., 928.

3. American Board of Commissioners for Foreign Missions, *Annual Report of the Board for 1849* (Boston: T. R. Marvin, 1849), 99.

4. American Board of Commissioners for Foreign Missions, *Annual Report of the Board for 1848* (Boston: T. R. Marvin, 1848), 133.

5. Harvey Newcomb, *Cyclopedia of Missions: Containing a Comprehensive View of Missionary Operations Throughout the World; With Geographical Descriptions, and Accounts of the Social, Moral, and Religious Condition of the People* (New York: Charles Scribner, 1854), 94.

6. Nancy Sikes Porter, Diary, June 7, 1851, Nancy Sikes Porter Papers, Ellington Historical Society, Ellington, Connecticut.

7. Erasmus Darwin Moore, *Life Scenes from Mission Fields: A Book of Facts, Incidents, and Results, the Most Material and Remarkable in Missionary Experience, Condensed and Arranged for Popular Use* (New York: Charles Scribner, 1857), 318.

8. Porter, Diary, June 15, 1852.

9. Ibid., June 22, 1852.

10. American Board of Commissioners for Foreign Missions, *Annual Report of the Board for 1861* (Boston: T. R. Marvin & Son, 1861), 27.

11. William Walker, Diary, February 26, 1848, and April 12, 1854, Box 2, William Walker Papers, Wisconsin Historical Society, Library-Archives Division, Madison, Wisconsin (hereafter WHSLAD). Peter Menkel, Diary, August 29, 1884, Box 1 Folder 2, Series I: Diaries, 1875–1897, Peter Menkel Papers, Presbyterian Historical Society, Philadelphia, Pennsylvania (hereafter PHS).

12. Georgianna McQueen, "Corisco Graveyard" (excerpts from letter dated November 12, 1862), *The African Repository* 39, no. 6 (June 1863): 183–84.

13. Walter Clark, letter to Walter Lowrie, corresponding secretary of the Presbyterian Mission, October 15, 1862, Africa Letters, vol. 7, reel 68, letter 124, PHS.

14. Ibid. In mission records, Chauncey Loomis is also often referred to as Charles Loomis.

15. Chauncey L. Loomis, end of year report, 1861, vol. 7, reel 68, letter 91, PHS.

16. William Rankin, "Mrs. H. E. Loomis," *Memorials of Foreign Missionaries of the Presbyterian Church U.S.A.* (Philadelphia: Presbyterian Board of Publication, 1895), 200–202.

17. Loomis, letter to John Lowrie, October 1861, vol. 7, reel 68, letter 89, PHS.

18. Loomis, letter to [Walter or John] Lowrie, August 1861, vol. 7, reel 68, letter 90, PHS.

19. Ibid.

20. Loomis eventually repatriated the remains of his wife and child to the United States, where her elaborately carved tombstone depicts the story of her life in Africa. For the gravestone, see Laurel K. Gabel, "'I Never Regretted Coming to Africa': The Story of Harriet Ruggles Loomis," *Markers: Annual Journal of the Association for Gravestone Studies* 16 (1999): 140–73.

21. Clark, in his letter dated October 15, 1862, argues that missionary women should leave the field during pregnancy, childbirth, and motherhood.

22. Clark, letter, 1862.

23. Robert Hamill Nassau, *Crowned in Palm-Land: A Story of African Mission Life* (Philadelphia: J. B. Lippincott, 1874).

24. Nassau, *Crowned in Palm-Land*, 156.

25. Ibid., 170.

26. Ibid., 174.

27. Ibid., 175.

28. Ibid., 223.

29. Ibid., 232.

30. Ibid.

31. Ibid., 232–33.

32. Ibid., 233.

33. Ibid., 234.

34. Ibid., 233.

35. Ibid., 237.

36. Ibid., 241.

37. Ibid., 243.

38. Ibid., 245.

39. Ibid., 250.

40. Ibid., 251.

41. Ibid., 252.

42. Ibid., 253.

43. Walker, Diary, March 31, 1869, Box 2, William Walker Papers, WHSLAD.

44. Nassau, *Crowned in Palm-Land*, 317.

45. Ibid., 320.

46. Ibid., 338.

47. Ibid., 339.

48. Ibid., 350.

49. Ibid., 360.

50. Samuel Howell Murphy, letter to John Lowrie, July 5, 1872, vol. 9, reel 71, letter 365, Africa Letters—Gaboon and Corisco Mission, PHS.

51. Ibid.

52. Robert Hamill Nassau, *Corisco Days: The First Thirty Years of the West African Mission* (Philadelphia: Allen, Lane, and Scott, 1910), 128. Samuel Murphy would later return for a two-year commitment, though his wife and children remained in the United States during that period.

53. Joseph Hankinson Reading, *The Ogowe Band: A Narrative of African Travel* (Philadelphia: Reading & Company, 1890), 188.

54. Robert Hamill Nassau, *My Ogowe: Being a Narrative of Daily Incidents during Sixteen Years in Equatorial West Africa* (New York: Neale Publishing Company, 1914), 346.

55. Ibid., 457.

56. Reading, *Ogowe Band*, 187.

57. Ibid., 188.

58. Ibid., 189.

59. William Walker, letter to Henry Bacheler, August 21, 1881, as copied into a letter from Bacheler to the family of Susanna Dewsnap; Ruth Benson and John Dewsnap provided materials from records and correspondence privately held by the Dewsnap family via e-mail attachments and CD to Mary Cloutier, January 2006.

60. Holly Lemons, a descendant of Cornelius DeHeer and his first wife, Anna, e-mail to Mary Cloutier, June 30, 2005.

61. Nassau, "Some Causes of the Present Improved Health of Missionaries to Africa," 927.

62. Robert Hamill Nassau, "Africa," in *Historical Sketches of the Missions under the Care of the Board of Foreign Missions of the Presbyterian Church*, 3rd ed. (Philadelphia: Women's Foreign Missionary Society of the Presbyterian Church, 1891), 26.

63. Nassau, "Some Causes of the Present Improved Health of Missionaries to Africa," 927.

64. Ibid., 928.

65. John Darch, "Love and Death in the Mission Compound: The Hardships of Life in the Tropics for Victorian Missionaries and Their Families," *Anvil* 17, no. 1 (2000): 39.

66. T. O. Beidelman, "Altruism and Domesticity: Images of Missionizing Women among the Church Missionary Society in Nineteenth-Century East Africa," in *Gendered Missions: Women and Men in Missionary Discourse and Practice*, ed. Mary Taylor Huber and Nancy C. Lutkehaus (Ann Arbor: Univ. of Michigan Press, 1999), 113–43.

67. Darch, "Love and Death in the Mission Compound," 39.

68. See Donald Grigorenko and Margaret Grigorenko, "Experiencing Risk: Missionary Families in Dangerous Places," pp. 27–46, in this volume.

69. Jerry Rankin, "The Family and Missions: Reflections from the Life of a U.S. Missionary," pp. 47–61, in this volume.

70. Anneke Stasson, "Walter and Ingrid Trobisch and a Missiology of 'Couple Power,'" pp. 5–25, in this volume.

6

WILLIAM CAREY'S VISION FOR MISSIONARY FAMILIES

ANDREW D. MCFARLAND

What shall we make of the story of William Carey and the ragged beginnings of his mission in India? Did he use manipulation or deceit in trying to convince his wife Dorothy to go to India? Were his wife and children prepared for the physical and mental stress of life in India? Today these concerns are certain to be shared by missionary parents and sending organizations alike. But in Carey's case, no missionary interview included questions about the physical or mental health of the wife and children of missionaries.[1] This study seeks to show that in spite of failure, disappointment, and numerous domestic catastrophes, Carey's dogged commitment to the creation of a "mission family" not only preserved the mission, but rescued his own family as well. This strategy for the formation of a small community of missionaries living and working communally proved to be vital for his mission's success. At the same time, the challenges he faced made this plan essential for his family's survival.

On January 9, 1793, Carey, the English Baptist father of three boys and one on the way, pledged his missionary service to God and the newly formed Baptist Missionary Society (BMS) for the propagation of the Gospel in India.[2] In May of that year he published *An Enquiry into the Obligations of Christians to Use Means for the Conversion of the Heathens*, an eighty-seven-page pamphlet that argued for the biblical mandate and practical viability of engaging in foreign mission.[3] His primary concern was the means of mission family support and structure. Therefore, it is not surprising that he volunteered to go with John Thomas, veteran of Indian travel, who had assured the small gathering at Kettering that missionaries could support themselves in North Bengal.[4] And indeed, some missionaries in India already had. The missionary work of the

"Christians of St. Thomas," the Roman Catholics, and the Moravians long preceded Carey's work in India.[5]

Carey's missionary zeal was not shared, however, by his wife, Dorothy, who firmly rejected the idea. Still, some biographers argue that this rejection need not indicate an antimissionary spirit.[6] In reality, a number of possible explanations for Dorothy's resistance can be given. First, she was five months pregnant. This meant that their fourth child was expected to arrive while Carey proposed to be en route to India.[7] Second, she had traveled very little. She and all her family had remained in or near the town of Piddington her whole life.[8] Third, to be a missionary in late eighteenth-century British India was illegal. In spite of the efforts that year of Evangelical statesman William Wilberforce, Parliament refused to allow any amendment to the East India Company's charter that would permit Christian missions in India.[9] Any or all of these reasons, or others, may have contributed to Dorothy's refusal to go.[10]

Thus, Carey faced a significant dilemma: to go to India without his family or to postpone his mission until his circumstances were more agreeable. He chose the former. On March 26, 1793, he left Dorothy and two sons in Piddington, taking with him their oldest son, Felix, hoping to return soon for the rest of his family.[11] Nevertheless, none of them could have anticipated the events that followed. Due to an anonymous note concerning the legality of their residence in India, Carey and Thomas were forced off the *Oxford* before they could depart from the Isle of Wight.[12] Of course, the ordeal was a great disappointment, but Thomas wasted no time securing another ship, in this case, a Danish vessel expected any day.

In spite of Carey's decision to separate his family in pursuit of a mission in India, he did not fail to show his concern for his family. This concern is evident in one of his letters to Dorothy after his delay in leaving England. Carey had received a letter from Dorothy reporting the safe delivery of their child, and he replied to her concluding that the whole ordeal must have been orchestrated by God to reassure him of his wife and child's well-being.[13] In the same letter he mentioned his pleasure in having his oldest son, Felix, with him and how Felix was helping him write this letter to her.[14] He closed the letter by reassuring his wife of his "most affectionate" love for her.[15] Clearly Carey was not as insensitive as some have supposed.[16]

Regardless, Carey and Thomas saw this delay as providential, and towards the end of May they decided to approach Dorothy once more in Piddington, traveling through the night and reaching her by breakfast.[17] By the end of their short visit, Dorothy resolved to go on the condition that her sister, Kitty, join them.[18] As early as May 27, the whole family was on its way to board the *Kron Princessa Maria*, which left England on June 13 bound for India.

Some biographers take this opportunity to charge Carey with coercion. But there is no evidence that he embraced the European attitude of his day, which thought of women and children as property. Rather, he had always assumed that a missionary family would embody the desire to "work together" and "model Christian community."[19] This does not mean he was exempt from making mistakes. After more than a decade in India he admitted, "After I had preached, or rather thought I had, for two years, a man one day came to me and declared that he could not understand me."[20] His struggle to grasp the Bengali language fueled considerable depression and a profound insecurity.[21]

If there was ever a time Carey needed missionary community, it was during this period. And yet his attempts to create a mission family before 1800 were only marginally successful. Not until after that date did he realize his vision. But what did Carey mean by a mission family? The answer has implications for missionary families today.

CAREY'S MISSION FAMILY STRATEGY

As early as 1790, both the *Instructions for the Members of the Unitas Fratrum* and the *Periodical Accounts Relating to the Missions of the Church of the United Brethren* were available in English. Therefore, either of these Moravian publications could have served as Carey's inspiration for his mission family strategy.[22] Already by 1792 he was well aware of the progress of Moravian missions, as he mentions their labors in the *Enquiry*.[23] Regardless, he did not use the word "family" or "mission family" to describe his strategy in this treatise. Instead, he simply suggests, "It might be necessary, however, for two at least to go together, and in general I should think it best that they should be married men. . . . Two or more other persons, with their wives and families, might also accompany them who should be wholly employed in providing for them."[24] At this point, his assumptions were largely pragmatic.

Nevertheless, by 1796 the Moravian influence on his strategy was evident; as Carey acknowledged to Andrew Fuller, secretary of the BMS, "You will find it similar to what the Moravians do."[25] By this time Carey had had three years in India to test the strategy of the *Enquiry*. In the process he had discovered the inadequacy of an approach that lacked Christian fellowship.[26] With this in mind, he now proposed organizing missionaries and converts into one common family. In a letter to John Ryland he called for "the ordering of such a Family."[27] Still, to understand what Carey was suggesting, three letters from the fall of 1796 are necessary, as he laid out different aspects of his strategy in each.[28] For the sake of clarity we will compile his most salient convictions from these letters.

First, well before societies were inquiring about the mental and physical health of missionary families, Carey argued for some form of missionary screening, insisting that the "strictest attention" in selection was "absolutely necessary."[29] After all, one ill-selected missionary or missionary wife could put the whole mission in jeopardy. This was even more important since he envisioned these families laboring together on a "small farm," "living together" in "separate houses" with "fixed rules," but having "one common table," "one common stock," an aim to become "nurseries of the mission," and a willingness to submit to the management of "elected stewards."[30]

Second, Carey assumed that this arrangement would be self-supporting. He concluded that if all members of the mission family had all things in common and were co-laborers, every addition to their missionary community would provide more stability.[31] He was convinced that if they were to rely on support from England, the cost would be far too great. He calculated that the "methods of agriculture" in India could easily support seven or eight families, and he pleaded with the Society to send them out immediately.[32]

Third, Carey perceived that the advantages of this strategy would far exceed an "example of industry." He understood it to include "Christian society, daily worship, a common school, proper rules for appropriation of time, regular preaching excursions, all learning of languages being in one place, a public library, and the accumulation of everyone's knowledge set into one aggregate."[33] He wanted to reassure his brethren in England that this plan was not devised for financial gain. Rather, it was to foster the sharing of missionary life and labor in the propagation of the Gospel.

Fourth, Carey anticipated that the day would come when Indians would join them and be "considered equal" members of the mission family.[34] This arrangement was necessary, he explained, because "should any natives join us, they would become outcasts immediately."[35] Worthy of note is that he fully expected Indian culture, and more precisely Indian Christianity, to be preserved by this emphasis on equality. As a result, he foresaw their itinerant Indian evangelists, pastors, and teachers not as trophies of success, but as co-laborers in evangelization.[36] This vision was Carey's mission family strategy.

So why did he wait so long to formally suggest this strategy? Christopher Smith argues that it was due to his aspirations to become a "solitary mission-ary hero."[37] He goes on to say that once the prospects for a mission family finally arrived in 1799, the development "upset all his mission plans."[38] And yet, for reasons already stated, these conclusions are inconsistent with Carey's intentions during the pre-1800 period. A careful study of the events of 1794, 1795, and 1796 offers some insight.

CHALLENGES OF THE PRE-1800 MISSION FAMILY STRATEGY

During his first years in India Carey was faced by a series of challenges as he sought to refine and implement his mission family strategy. The challenges began almost immediately upon the arrival of the Carey family and John Thomas in India in November of 1793, and they occurred at the most basic level of what a missionary is.

Missionary expectations. The first challenge facing Carey's pre-1800 mission family strategy was the lack of consensus on the character of a missionary. After only two months in Calcutta, it became apparent that Thomas did not entirely match the missionary example Carey had proposed in his *Enquiry*—namely, his expectation that they "be willing to leave all the comforts of life behind them."[39] To make matters worse, he had appointed Thomas as controller of the funds.[40] Carey was mortified and ridden with anxiety over the ease with which Thomas was spending the mission funds on "affluent" living.[41] The situation became intolerable.

In mid-January Carey began to search for an alternative location for the mission, moving his family to Bandel, a Portuguese community near Calcutta, and then to Manicktullo, a then marshy suburb of Calcutta. But when he visited Thomas two days later, he found all their funds depleted and Thomas in debt once again.[42] Now Thomas had no real choice except to abandon the mission for a surgical practice in Calcutta in order to repay his creditors.[43] His departure presented another problem for Carey since he had recommended that no fewer than two missionaries be sent out.[44]

Missionary support. These disappointments led to Carey's second challenge, a lack of monetary and communal support for his family. With no money, no fellow missionary, no real knowledge of the culture, and no mastery of the language, Carey and his family were truly destitute. He described his predicament in his journal, where he confessed, "I am in a strange land, alone, no Christian friend, a large family, and nothing to supply their wants."[45] For Carey, the issue of support became the most urgent matter, but this required their moving twice more before June of 1794. And by this time the ages of their children—Jabez, Peter, William, and Felix—were one, five, six, and nine.[46] Even so, Carey was successful that year, with Thomas's help, in securing employment as the supervisor of an indigo factory.[47] Moreover, the income must have been adequate since he recorded in his journal in mid-June that he intended to request the Society to send no more support.[48]

Physical illness and death. In the fall of 1794 a third challenge presented itself: illness engulfed nearly all of the group. At least since January, Dorothy and Felix had suffered from dysentery, and now Carey and Peter were sick as well. Carey developed a malaria-like fever that wound up incapacitating him for two months.[49] Then sadly, in this environment of illness, their five-year-old, Peter, developed a fever and died. By the end of October the indigo season had ended. The Careys were grieving the loss of Peter while trying to recover from their various illnesses. Moved by their struggle, George Udney, the owner of the indigo factory Carey was managing, recommended a vacation for the family in Bhutan, though Carey explained it as being more of a business venture for Udney.[50] Udney also arranged for John Thomas to go with them, as Thomas was now the supervisor of another of Udney's indigo factories not far away. In spite of the change of pace, however, both he and Dorothy continued to suffer from recurring bouts of illness and fever until December.

Mental illness. Unfortunately, the events of 1795 were no better with Carey's fourth challenge arriving in the spring: Dorothy's gradual loss of sanity. Clinical psychologist and Carey biographer James Beck places the onset of Dorothy's mental illness before March of that year.[51] During this time she had written a secret letter to Thomas charging Carey with adultery, something Thomas perceived to be evidence of her illness.[52] And one of Carey's female biographers, Mary Drewery, makes a useful observation in regard to Carey's treatment of these events, noting that after this date a "conspiracy of silence" about Dorothy appears in the letters and journals of Carey and his colleagues.[53] She implies that this silence resulted from the stigma associated in the eighteenth century with mental illness.[54]

While these conclusions are certainly possible and are supported by Carey's journal and letters, such a conspiracy of silence must have been short-lived, since Carey shattered it in a letter to his sisters on October 5, 1795. He confessed, "I have greater afflictions than any of these in my family, known to my friends here, but I have never mentioned it to any one in England before—in my poor wife—who is looked upon as insane to a great degree by both natives and Europeans."[55] Carey's hesitancy to place himself among those who looked upon her as insane is significant. Thomas even sent Carey an undated letter in 1795, pleading, "Her false surmises bring on true troubles, that are rising to such a height that I know not what will be the issue of it. . . . You must endeavor to consider it as a disease."[56] These clues point to the possibility that Drewery's so-called "conspiracy of silence" about Dorothy may just as easily have arisen from Carey's rejection of the diagnosis and his friends' respecting his convictions.

One of the earliest admissions from Carey that his wife was insane came in April of 1796 in a letter to his sisters. As if it was just discovered, he announced some distressing news, writing, "My poor wife must be considered as insane; and is the occasion of great sorrow. I have [been] obliged to confine her some time back to prevent murder which was attempted."[57] All his hopes for a misdiagnosis evaporated and he was forced to concede that his wife was not likely to recover. At this point some might be tempted to argue that through confinement, he simply cast Dorothy aside in the pursuit of his own ambition, but nothing could be further from the truth. He took seriously his vow to care for her "in sickness and in health." How else could we explain his eleven-year refusal to have her committed to an asylum? Instead of treating Dorothy like an obstacle, we find him choosing to tolerate her outbursts, deflect her accusations, and shield the children from her harm. So we cannot charge Carey with marital abandonment.

Core retention. In the summer and fall of 1796, Carey's fifth challenge became evident, the seemingly impossible task of assembling the right people, at the right time, in the right place. He had already mentioned this problem to his sisters, writing, "The inestimable blessing of Christian Society is enjoyed but scantily here, to what it is in England, for though we have very valuable Christian friends, yet they live 20 or 30 miles distant from us."[58] And the disappointment became even greater when Ram Ram Basu, Carey's Indian *munshi* (or teacher), who he had hoped would soon join them in baptism, was proven guilty of adultery and had to be dismissed.[59]

The arrivals of missionary recruits, John Fountain and Ignatius Fernandez, later that year may have encouraged him to develop and implement the mission family strategy.[60] Fountain's unruliness, however, was to prove as much trouble as Thomas's debt, specifically in regard to his "outspoken political radicalism."[61] And although Fernandez, an Augustinian monk turned Portuguese businessman, joined with them in the work, he stayed only long enough to become Carey's first convert in India.[62] By June 1797 Carey was engaged in building the first Protestant church in Bengal, located at Dinajpur.[63]

SUCCESS OF THE POST-1800 MISSION FAMILY STRATEGY

After the indigo factory in Mudnabati was abandoned in September, 1799, Carey decided on Kidderpore as an ideal location for another indigo factory.[64] By at least July of that year, he had learned of new missionary recruits in route to India and had begun to build "houses and other buildings" in preparation for them.[65] The realization of Carey's mission family, however, would not be found in Kidderpore. Instead, unforeseen events were unfolding that would firmly plant the mission in the obscure location of Serampore. Therefore, in mid-December, 1799, Carey and his family gathered all their belongings and prepared to move for the last time.

At the outset it is important to reiterate that although Carey spoke about his mission family strategy in the pre-1800 period and even tried to implement it on occasion, his vision never quite materialized. Indeed, he admitted to his sisters, "Before our other brethren arrived there was no opportunity of forming a family which should have a common stock."[66] Now with the arrival of so many at once, joining forces with those already there, it was achievable.

The new arrivals included the Marshmans and their three children, the Grants and their two children, the Brunsdons, Ward the printer, and Miss Tidd, who planned to marry Fountain.

Tragically, William Grant died three weeks after arriving. Regardless, his widow and children persisted with the plans of the mission. Then they were all joined by the Careys and their four children, Fountain, and in October even the Thomases.[67] A large house with property was found and purchased from Governor Bie's nephew, and they all went to work hammering out the arrangements.[68] Three reasons for Carey's post-1800 mission family success rise above all others: missionary unity, missionary community, and missionary support.

Missionary unity. Perhaps the first and most fundamental reason for success was the group's consensus in regard to the task—engaging in the formation of a family, not the implementation of a strategy. At what point in the pre-1800 period Carey became convinced of this priority is unclear. As we have stated, in 1796 he argued for the "ordering of such a family."[69] Moreover, he harbored many expectations for his mission family strategy, ranging from the creation of "Christian Society" to the invitation of Indian membership. Somehow he failed, however, to emphasize the significance of the bond that might hold them together.

Now at the conclusion of their first week in possession of the property at Serampore, the group unanimously embraced Carey's mission family strategy, which was recorded in Ward's journal.[70] Ward reported that they formulated plans for "the government of the family" and the superintendence of "the affairs of the family."[71] Two amendments appear that were not previously included in Carey's strategy, the provision of space for "adjusting differences" and the action of "pledging ourselves to love one another."[72] These convictions, more than anything else, contributed to the preservation of the mission and the rescue of Carey's family. Later that year he described their "common family" to a colleague when he wrote, "We love one another and are as the heart of one man in our work."[73] This is the reason Ralph Winter suggests, "It is wise that we try to keep quite separate in our minds the Serampore Brotherhood's inner structure and its field strategy."[74]

With respect to this "inner structure," Ward reported they also embraced Carey's 1796 ideas of laboring together, "living together," "fixed rules," "one common table," "one common stock," and "elected stewards."[75] This arrangement was timely since Carey had recently confessed to his sisters his burdens of "labour, disappointment, and perplexity" coupled with absorption in "temporal concerns" and no encouragement in the task.[76] The Serampore Covenant, as it was called, eventually prepared the ground for the later Form of Agreement, which every mission station was required to read publicly three times annually.[77] Not only did this action nurture mission consensus, but it also eliminated any misunderstanding about missionary expectations.

Missionary community. A second reason for success was the group's shared dedication to Carey's earlier suggestion that their families become "nurseries of the mission."[78] Even before they had arrived in Serampore, Hannah Marshman was caring for the Grants' children.[79] In March the Marshmans opened a boarding school on the premises for European, Anglo-Indian, and missionary children.[80] As J. C. Marshman later explained, they all "repudiated the custom of sending children to England, lest European associations should alienate their minds from India and from the cause of missions."[81] The ages of Carey's children that June were Jonathan, 5, Jabez, 7, William Jr., 12, and Felix, 15.[82] By then Dorothy had been considered insane for approximately five years, and the ordeal had taken its toll on the children.[83]

As the "true mother of the settlement," Hannah Marshman took a special interest in nurturing Carey's children.[84] This was important since Carey's younger children, Jonathan and Jabez, had been more or less deprived of maternal care altogether. All the same, within two years she noted some behavioral problems surfacing in Carey's two older sons, Felix (now 17) and William Jr. (14). For reasons that are unclear, the trouble was not resolved by their weekly meetings for addressing grievances. Feeling that "to refrain longer would be criminal," she complained to John Ryland in England, arguing that Carey was in some ways responsible due to his "domestic affliction" (Dorothy), "perpetual avocations," or what she calls his "easiness of temperament."[85] Regardless, the boys responded to her correction and the trouble was resolved.

As a spiritual mentor, Ward invested himself in the discipling of Carey's two older children through his work with the boys in the printing office. At least Felix directly experienced a "love of Christ" through his efforts.[86] There is some indication that William Jr. did as well.[87] Even Joshua and Hannah Marshman's son John developed a deep relationship with Ward, spending a great deal of time in the printing office.[88] Years later, at the news of Ward's death, William Jr. wrote, "Mr. Ward was very dear to me. How often has he upheld me, when my feet well-nigh slipped."[89]

In spite of struggles, each of Carey's sons continued to demonstrate a strong connection to the mission family into their adult lives. Felix married in 1804 and was serving the mission until 1814. But the following year he experienced a kind of psychotic break and withdrew from the mission family to wander in the region of Assam.[90] Eventually he returned to Serampore due to Ward's urging.[91] William Jr. married in 1808 and was still serving the mission in 1833. Jabez married in 1814, albeit to a woman whom Carey said had a "love of finery," and in 1833 was also serving the mission.[92] For a time, Jonathan's conversion was uncertain and he was living in adultery, yet by 1833 he was married, an attorney of the Calcutta Supreme Court, and the treasurer of the Serampore Mission.[93] In each case, the mission family had played an important role through its willingness to become "nurseries for the mission."

Missionary support. By November of 1801, a third reason for success could be observed: their provision of Christian care. Dorothy's insanity had spiraled out of control. Once again Carey confided in his sisters, writing, "Mrs. Carey is obliged to be constantly confined. She has long got worse and worse, but fear both of my own life and hers, and the desire of the police of the place, obliged me to agree to her confinement."[94] However, putting Dorothy away in the impersonal (and often deplorable) environment of an asylum for what would likely be the rest of her life was unthinkable for him. After all, he had refused such suggestions from friends for at least five years.

Several insights invite a better understanding of Carey's decision about Dorothy's care. First, he did not need to fear traveling back to England for her treatment as he was well aware there was an asylum in Calcutta. Carey and Marshman had had to take Thomas there when he became insane the year before.[95] Second, Carey did not need to fear an increase in bad publicity because of Dorothy's insanity any more than for Thomas's since the condition of both and their connection with the mission were already publicly known. Third, no evidence exists that Carey and Marshman were appalled by the conditions of the asylum. We will remember, Carey left his dear friend of ten years there. Whatever his reasons were for confining Dorothy in the mission house, they could not have been these. Indeed, his determination to make the daily sacrifice of longsuffering with his wife is the most likely explanation. Now members of the mission family could help as well. In fact, James Beck suggests that Carey's arrangement of this "community of Christian care" for her was his "long-term strategy."[96] In spite of all their efforts, she died of a fever in 1807.

CONCLUSION

At the outset of this study it was suggested that Carey's commitment to the creation of a mission family preserved the mission and rescued his family. As has been shown, he did indeed draft the means in 1796 for the future preservation of the mission and the rescue of his family. Using the Moravian approach to missions as his inspiration, he submitted a rough sketch of his idea and set out to implement it. His overarching conception was that in approach missions must be, at the core, interdependent not independent or dependent. In this way his mission family strategy was like a map that charted the course for interdependence.

If this understanding of Carey's strategy is correct, what might we learn from his pre-1800 mission challenges? He had long complained that wherever European expatriates banded together, present also were the origins of prejudice and what he called "inaction." Throughout his writings he pleaded with the BMS to send missionaries anywhere except Calcutta. Sadly, his advice was not heeded, and this very issue would later become the seed of great problems for the mission. Instead, he expected missionaries to practice mission *among* the Indian people and, after their conversion, *with* the Indian people. These two assumptions were the basis for all of Carey's thought.

Even so, Carey was not naïve about what foreign mission would require of Europeans. He had learned by experience the importance of missionary selection, accountability, health, and partnership. Perhaps his biggest regret was having been blind to the significance of some of these issues before leaving England. This is evident in the large volume of letters he wrote to his sons on how they ought to proceed with their missions. Carey's fatherly advice and missionary experience pour from these pages, especially in letters to Jabez.

We might also ask what we can learn from Carey's post-1800 mission success. As we might guess, he wanted to underscore, as much as possible, the importance of the mission family. In letters to his friends and family back in

England, Carey repeatedly found himself without the words to describe the unity they were experiencing at Serampore and resolved to call it "utmost harmony" or "enjoyment." Indeed, on occasion he thought it "impossible" that it should exist at all.

But Carey had never anticipated just how much he would need the mission family's support. He had foreseen the strategy and yet not his own utter reliance on it. Furthermore, he was quite surprised by the bond of love that almost immediately was experienced by all of them. As time passed, he came to understand the significance of that bond. Through his struggle to raise his children as more or less a single parent, and his dodging the rogue accusations of his wife, he had discovered his own need for the mission family. And with the support of some twenty mission stations throughout the region, he became absolutely convinced of Serampore's need for the mission family.

Clearly, the charge that Carey exhibited a "less than perfect family life" is problematic.[97] Certainly he made mistakes, but abandoning his wife and children for the work of the mission was not one of them. After all, they were a large part of his vision for the mission family. Nor can we portray him as authoritarian before or after leaving England. He was wholly committed to the egalitarian ideal throughout his pastorates in England and his mission in India. Carey loved his wife and children. Even when he disagreed with them, he never failed to listen and respond to his family's needs with understanding and respect.

Nevertheless, after the death of Andrew Fuller in 1815, Carey's mission family strategy was marginalized by the BMS. They sought, rather, a new missionary strategy supported and governed by an extensive board in London. This strategy strongly endorsed the practice of European superintendence, thereby discouraging Indian leadership. Furthermore, the new junior missionary recruits from England during this period were in favor of the new strategy. Then, right about the time Carey could have been passing on the mission family leadership to the next generation, the juniors rebelled and founded a rival mission in Calcutta. Although two of his children served the BMS as missionaries after his death, once the last of the Serampore Trio died in 1837, the mission family slowly faded from memory.

Today Carey's mission family strategy is rarely studied, and even fewer have ventured to attempt it. One reason may be that his commitment to interdependent living has been perceived as too risky. Indeed, trust could be abused and tensions could rage out of control in such a close-knit community. When one considers, however, the financial and emotional costs involved in the failure of more solitary missionary efforts, it seems worth the risk. Several missionary families assigned to one location could share in the work of the mission. They could share the burden of the hardships they encounter. They could provide member care for one another in times of discouragement and despair. Above all, their sacrificial love for one another could poignantly illustrate the present reality of God's kingdom for pre-Christian people.

So what shall we make of the ragged beginnings of Carey's mission in India? Has his pleading convinced us of the need for the mission family? These are important questions that deserve thoughtful answers. While the topics of contemporary missiology represent a wide range of missiological concerns, few could be more important than the intersection of mission and family.

NOTES

1. James Beck, *Dorothy Carey: The Tragic and Untold Story of Mrs. William Carey* (Eugene, Ore.: Wipf & Stock, 1992), 190.

2. S. Pearce Carey, *William Carey D.D., Fellow of Linnaean Society* (London: Hodder and Stoughton, 1924), 104. See also Mary Drewery, *William Carey: A Biography* (Grand Rapids: Zondervan, 1979), 44.

3. William Carey, *An Enquiry into the Obligations of Christians to Use Means for the Conversion of the Heathens* (Leicester: Ann Ireland, 1792).

4. *Periodical Accounts Relative to the Baptist Missionary Society*, vol. 1 (Clipstone [Eng.]: J.W. Morris, 1800), 29. See also S. Pearce Carey, *William Carey*, 104.

5. Kenneth Scott Latourette, *A History of the Expansion of Christianity*, vol. 6 (Grand Rapids: Zondervan, 1970), 66, and Stephen Neill, *A History of Christian Missions* (London: Penguin Books, 1990), 122.

6. Beck, *Dorothy Carey*, 15. See also Drewery, *William Carey*, 21.

7. Drewery, *William Carey*, 45. See also S. Pearce Carey, *William Carey*, 107.

8. S. Pearce Carey, *William Carey*, 107. See also Timothy George, *Faithful Witness: The Life and Mission of William Carey* (Birmingham, Ala.: New Hope, 1991), 70.

9. Tom Hiney, *On the Missionary Trail* (New York: Grove Press, 2000), 9. See also S. Pearce Carey, *William Carey*, 141.

10. Beck, *Dorothy Carey*, 71–76, reviews a number of reasons why Dorothy Carey refused to join William in going to India.

11. Drewery, *William Carey*, 46. See also George, *Faithful Witness*, 157, and S. Pearce Carey, *William Carey*, 113. Eustace Carey states that Andrew Fuller expected Carey to return for the family; see his *Memoir of William Carey, D.D.: Late Missionary to Bengal; Professor of Oriental Languages in the College of Fort William, Calcutta* (London: Jackson and Walford, 1836), 76. Beck (*Dorothy Carey*, 77) mentions a letter from Fuller to Stevens expecting Carey to return.

12. S. Pearce Carey, *William Carey*, 122. George (*Faithful Witness*, 84) writes that Thomas's creditors were hunting him down. See also Drewery, *William Carey*, 49.

13. S. Pearce Carey, *William Carey*, 120. See also Drewery, *William Carey*, 51, and George, *Faithful Witness*, 83.

14. S. Pearce Carey, *William Carey*, 120. See also George, *Faithful Witness*, 83.

15. S. Pearce Carey, *William Carey*, 120. See also George, *Faithful Witness*, 83.

16. On the basis of this letter, however, Ruth Tucker charges Carey with insensitivity; see Ruth A. Tucker, "William Carey's Less than Perfect Family Life," *Christian History* 11, no. 4 (1992): 27.

17. S. Pearce Carey, *William Carey*, 126. See also Drewery, *William Carey*, 51, and Beck, *Dorothy Carey*, 81.

18. George, *Faithful Witness*, 85.

19. William Carey, *Enquiry*, 74. See also George, *Faithful Witness*, 157.

20. William Carey, letter to Sisters, August 9, 1808, in *The Journal and Selected Letters of William Carey*, ed. Terry G. Carter (Macon, Ga.: Smyth & Helwys, 2000), 66. All citations of Carey's journal and letters are from this volume; hereafter JSLWC.

21. William Carey, Journal, April 4, 1794, in Carter, JSLWC, 22.

22. David Schattschneider, "William Carey, Modern Missions, and the Moravian Influence," *International Bulletin of Missionary Research* 22, no 1 (January 1998), 11. See also S. Pearce Carey, *William Carey*, 186.

23. William Carey, *Enquiry*, 11.

24. Ibid., 73.

25. William Carey, letter to Andrew Fuller, November 16, 1796, in Carter, JSLWC, 136.

26. William Carey, Journal, June 17, 1794, in Carter, JSLWC, 34.

27. William Carey, letter to John Ryland, November 26, 1796, in Carter, JSLWC, 136.

28. William Carey, letter to Fuller, November 16, 1796; letter to Ryland, November 26, 1796; letter to Society, December 28, 1796, in Carter, JSLWC, 136–37.

29. William Carey, letter to Fuller, November 16, 1796; letter to Ryland, November 26, 1796, in Carter, JSLWC, 136–37.

30. William Carey, letter to Fuller, November 16, 1796; letter to Ryland, November 26, 1796; letter to Society, December 28, 1796, in Carter, JSLWC, 136–37.

31. William Carey, letter to Ryland, November 26, 1796, in Carter, JSLWC, 137.

32. William Carey, letter to Fuller, November 16, 1796, in Carter, JSLWC, 136.

33. William Carey, letter to Society, December 28, 1796, in Carter, JSLWC, 138.

34. William Carey, letter to Fuller, November 16, 1796, in Carter, JSLWC, 137.

35. William Carey, letter to Ryland, November 26, 1796, in Carter, JSLWC, 137.

36. William Carey, letter to Fuller, November 18, 1806, in Carter, JSLWC, 174.

37. A. Christopher Smith, "William Carey: Protestant Pioneer of the Modern Mission Era," in *Mission Legacies: Biographical Studies of Leaders of the Modern Missionary Movement*, ed. Gerald H. Anderson, Robert T. Coote, Norman A. Horner, and James M. Phillips (Maryknoll, N.Y.: Orbis Books, 1994), 248.

38. Ibid., 248.

39. William Carey, *Enquiry*, 75.

40. William Carey, Journal, January 15, 1794, in Carter, JSLWC, 8.

41. William Carey, Journal, January 13, 1794, in Carter, JSLWC, 7.

42. William Carey, Journal, January 15, 1794, in Carter, JSLWC, 8.

43. William Carey, Journal, January 23, 1794, in Carter, JSLWC, 11. See also Drewery, *William Carey*, 69. and George, *Faithful Witness*, 97.

44. William Carey, *Enquiry*, 73.

45. William Carey, Journal, January 15–16, 1794, in Carter, JSLWC, 8.

46. Drewery, *William Carey*, 78.

47. William Carey, Journal, March 31, 1794, in Carter, JSLWC, 21. See also S. Pearce Carey, *William Carey*, 152, and George Smith, *The Life of William Carey, D.D.: Shoemaker and Missionary* (Lexington: Feather Trail Press, 2010), 57.

48. William Carey, Journal, June 19, 1794, in Carter, JSLWC, 34.

49. William Carey, Journal, September 1–October 11, 1794, in Carter, JSLWC, 39. See also Drewery, *William Carey*, 81.

50. Drewery, *William Carey*, 84. See also William Carey, Journal, October 14–20, 1794, in Carter, JSLWC, 41.

51. Beck, *Dorothy Carey*, 108.

52. Drewery, *William Carey*, 83. See also Beck, *Dorothy Carey*, 110.

53. Drewery, *William Carey*, 82.

54. Ibid., 82.

55. William Carey, letter to Sisters, October 5, 1795, in Carter, JSLWC, 281.

56. Beck, *Dorothy Carey*, 110.

57. William Carey, letter to Sisters, April 10, 1796, in Carter, JSLWC, 281.

58. William Carey, letter to Sisters, March 11, 1795, in Carter, JSLWC, 73.

59. S. Pearce Carey, *William Carey*, 167. See also Drewery, *William Carey*, 92.

60. William Carey, letter to Society, December 28, 1796, in Carter, JSLWC, 137.

61. George Smith, *Life of William Carey*, 70. See also Drewery, *William Carey*, 100.

62. S. Pearce Carey, *William Carey*, 170. See also George Smith, *Life of William Carey*, 63.

63. William Carey, letter to Fuller, June 22, 1797, in Carter, JSLWC, 166. See also George Smith, *Life of William Carey*, 63.

64. William Carey, letter to Fuller, July 17, 1799, in Carter, JSLWC, 204.

65. William Carey, letter to Fuller, July 17, 1799, in Carter, JSLWC, 75.

66. William Carey, letter to Sisters, February 25, 1807, in Carter, JSLWC, 275.

67. Drewery, *William Carey*, 118.

68. Leighton Williams and Mornay Williams, *Serampore Letters: Being the Unpublished Correspondence of William Carey and Others with John Williams, 1800–1816* (Memphis: General Books, 2010), 26. See also George Smith, *Life of William Carey*, 78.

69. William Carey, letter to Ryland, November 26, 1796, in Carter, JSLWC, 136.

70. *Periodical Accounts Relative to the Baptist Missionary Society*, vol. 2 (Clipstone [Eng.]: J.W. Morris, 1801), 44. See also S. D. L. Alagodi, "Carey's Experiment in Communal Living at Serampore," in *Carey's Obligation and India's Renaissance*, ed. J. T. K. Daniel and R. E. Hedlund (Serampore: Council of Serampore College, 1993), 21, and George Smith, *Life of William Carey*, 80.

71. *Periodical Accounts Relative to the Baptist Missionary Society*, vol. 2, 44.

72. Ibid., 44.

73. Williams and Williams, *Serampore Letters*, 25.

74. Ralph D. Winter, "William Carey's Major Novelty," in Daniel and Hedlund, *Carey's Obligation*, 128.

75. *Periodical Accounts*, 2:44.

76. William Carey, letter to Sisters, November 30, 1799, in Carter, JSLWC, 108.

77. S. Pearce Carey, *William Carey*, 248. See also George, *Faithful Witness*, 123. George highlights the eleven points of the 1804 Form of Agreement.

78. William Carey, letter to Fuller, November 16, 1796, in Carter, JSLWC, 136.

79. Drewery, *William Carey*, 115.

80. Ibid., 113. See also S. Pearce Carey, *William Carey*, 187, and William Carey, letter to Father, December 1802, in Carter, JSLWC, 273.

81. J. C. Marshman, *The Life and Labours of Carey, Marshman, and Ward* (London: Alexander Strahan & Company, 1864), 77.

82. Drewery, *William Carey*, 78.

83. Beck, *Dorothy Carey*, 115.

84. S. D. L. Alagodi, "Carey's Experiment," in Daniel and Hedlund, *Carey's Obligation*, 27. See also Drewery, *William Carey*, 115; George, *Faithful Witness*, 124; and George Smith, *Life of William Carey*, 116.

85. Drewery, *William Carey*, 115. See also George, *Faithful Witness*, 124.

86. Drewery, *William Carey*, 112.

87. S. Pearce Carey, *William Carey*, 193.

88. Sunil K. Chatterjee, *John Clark Marshman: A Trustworthy Friend of India* (Sheoraphuli: Sunil Kumar Chatterjee, 2001), 45.

89. Drewery, *William Carey*, 184.

90. William Carey, letters to Jabez Carey, November 25, 1814, and October 6, 1815 [should read 1814], in Carter, JSLWC, 288. See also Beck, *Dorothy Carey*, 122, and S. Pearce Carey, *William Carey*, 273.

91. Drewery, *William Carey*, 175.

92. William Carey, letter to Jabez Carey, March 9, 1819, in Carter, JSLWC, 285.

93. William Carey, letter to Jabez Carey, April 12, 1817, in Carter, JSLWC, 283. See also Drewery, *William Carey*, 200.

94. William Carey, letter to Sisters, November 23, 1801, in Carter, JSLWC, 282.

95. Beck, *Dorothy Carey*, 156. See also Drewery, *William Carey*, 122.

96. Beck, *Dorothy Carey*, 142.

97. Tucker, "William Carey's Less than Perfect Family Life."

PART TWO

RESPONDING TO MK SEXUAL ABUSE AND TO REPORTS OF ABUSE BASED ON RECOVERED MEMORIES

INTRODUCTION

RESPONDING TO MK SEXUAL ABUSE AND TO REPORTS OF ABUSE BASED ON RECOVERED MEMORIES

ROBERT J. PRIEST

In one survey of 101 adult children of missionaries, 15 percent recalled having sexual contact with someone four or more years older than themselves before they were eighteen, and 9 percent recalled sexual contact against their will with someone less than four years older than themselves. Altogether 19 percent answered affirmatively to one or both of the sexual abuse questions, with fully 24 percent of females checking one or both.[1] In another survey of 608 adult children of missionaries, 6.8 percent reported having experienced sexual abuse within their "school context" between grades one and six.[2]

Over the last two decades numerous investigations have revealed that Protestant missionaries themselves have sometimes been the perpetrators of sexual abuse.[3] Notable public reports documenting sexual abuse of MKs by missionaries have been published for a variety of mission agencies and boards, such as the Christian and Missionary Alliance,[4] the Presbyterian Church USA,[5] the General Board of Ministries of the United Methodist Church,[6] and New Tribes Mission.[7] Numerous other investigations documenting abuse have been carried out in a wide variety of mission settings, although usually with results less publicized.

MKs who have experienced sexual abuse have often organized themselves (such as with the MK Safety Net[8]) and networked with other MKs who have experienced abuse to push for mission agencies and boards to acknowledge the abuse, care for the abused, and develop new policies and practices that protect children. Lawsuits and criminal trials are increasingly prevalent. New organizations dedicated to fostering best practices in mission agencies and to carrying out or coordinating such investigations have been formed, such as Godly Response to Abuse in the Christian Environment (GRACE)[9] and the Child Safety and Protection Network (CSPN).[10]

Complicating the situation is the fact that some of the accusations by adult children of missionaries against specific named missionaries are based on memories that are not continuous, but that have "surfaced" through the influence of recovered memory therapies. That is, many of the Christian publications that address sexual abuse and many of the individuals who provide leadership in addressing the problem of MK abuse endorse recovered memory ideologies, an endorsement with significant impact on the prevalence of accusations against missionaries based on recovered memories.[11] Since many experts on memory contend that "recovered memories" are likely to be "confabulations" rather than genuine memories, the possibility that a significant number of missionaries are falsely being charged with abuse must also be considered.[12]

In the first chapter below, Theresa Sidebotham provides legal advice on best practices for mission agencies in protecting children from abuse and in responding to historical reports of abuse. Historian Philip Jenkins provides an overview of what happened with the Roman Catholic Church's sexual abuse crisis, and also introduces the reader to the issues raised by recovered memory therapies. Finally, two psychologists, David Dunaetz and Ray Phinney, provide critical overviews on what research psychologists now understand about memory in relation to the difficult area of "recovered memory" of sexual abuse, showing the implications for mission agencies.

NOTES

1. Robert J. Priest, "Etiology of Adult Missionary Kid (AMK) Life-Struggles," *Missiology: An International Review* 31 (2003), 180.

2. David Wickstrom, e-mail to Robert J. Priest, January 1, 2010; comments based on his survey of adult children of missionaries.

3. For a dramatic recent example in the news, see Lee Moran, "Florida Missionary Sentenced to 58 Years in Prison for Sexually Abusing Indigenous Girls in Amazon," *New York Daily News*, January 30, 2014, www.nydailynews.com/news/crime/missionary-sentenced-sexually-abusing-girls-amazon-article-1.1596392.

4. Geoffrey B. Stearns et al., *Final Report of the Independent Commission of Inquiry to the Board of Managers of the Christian and Missionary Alliance*, 1997, www.mksafetynet.net/usa/reports/invcmareport.html.

5. Howard Beardsley et al., *Final Report of the Independent Commission of Inquiry, Presbyterian Church (U.S.A.)*, 2002, www.pcusa.org/resource/icireport/; James Evinger, Carolyn Whitfield, and Judith Wiley, *Final Report of the Independent Abuse Review Panel Presbyterian Church (U.S.A.)*, 2010, www.pcusa.org/resource/final-report-independent-abuse-review-panel -presby). See also B. Hunter Farrell, "Broken Trust: Sexual Abuse in the Mission Community; A Case Study in Mission Accountability," in *Accountability in Missions: Korean and Western Case Studies*, ed. Jonathan J. Bonk (Eugene, Ore.: Wipf & Stock, 2011), 206–15.

6. Marshall L. Meadors et al., *Final Report of the Independent Panel for the Review of Child Abuse in Mission Settings, General Board of Ministries of the United Methodist Church*, 2009, http://new.gbgm-umc.org/about/globalministries/childprotection/finalpanelreport/.

7. GRACE (Basyle Tchividjian, Victor Vieth, Diane Langberg, Janet Brown, Duncan Rankin), *Amended Final Report for the Investigatory Review of Child Abuse at New Tribes Fanda Missionary School*, 2010, www.bishop-accountability.org/reports/2010_08_28_GRACE _Fanda_Report.pdf. See also the video series by Scott Ross, *Abuse: The Hidden Secret* (Sanford, Fla.: New Tribes Mission, 2003).

8. MK Safety Net, www.mksafetynet.net/.

9. GRACE: Godly Response to Abuse in the Christian Environment, http://netgrace.org/.

10. Child Safety and Protection Network, http://childsafetyprotectionnetwork.org.

11. For documentation, see Robert J. Priest and Esther E. Cordill, "Christian Communities and 'Recovered Memories' of Abuse," *Christian Scholar's Review* 41, 4 (2012): 381–400, and their "Response to Evinger and Darr's 'Determining the Truth of Abuse in Mission Communities,'" *Christian Scholar's Review* (forthcoming).

12. Priest and Cordill, "Christian Communities and 'Recovered Memories' of Abuse."

7

GETTING IT RIGHT, HEALING THE WRONG:
Legal Issues in Protecting Children and Organizations from Child Sexual Abuse

THERESA LYNN SIDEBOTHAM

Child sexual abuse is endemic in human society. This chapter examines the current landscape of child sexual abuse, addresses prevention of abuse, offers wise approaches to investigation of alleged sexual abuse, identifies steps toward healing and justice, and discusses sex abuse litigation.[1]

CURRENT LANDSCAPE OF CHILD SEXUAL ABUSE

Child sexual abuse reports fall into two categories, present and historic. Many reports of abuse in religious organizations, including missions, are from the distant past. Present and historic claims must be addressed in slightly different ways. While no sharp dividing line between the two can be established, it is helpful and necessary to distinguish between them. Roughly, present cases involve current or recent abuse claims by minors or young adults that fall within the statute of limitations; historic claims are ones made by much older adults and are often outside the statute of limitations. On this point, data for abuse in the Roman Catholic Church in the United States is instructive (see chart 7.1). The incidence of abuse rose in the sixties, peaked in the seventies, fell sharply in the eighties, and has continued to fall.[2]

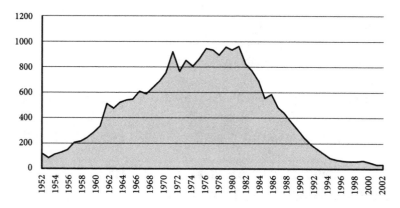

Chart 7.1
Number of incidents of abuse by U.S. Roman Catholic priests by
year of occurrence, 1950–2002

Note that the counts include all years of multiyear incidents of abuse. For example, if an abusive relationship between a priest and a youth persisted for four years, that incident is included in the count for each year of the duration of the abuse. (Copyright © U.S. Conference of Catholic Bishops; used by permission.)

Although previously unknown cases are reported each year, the cases follow a pattern of being mostly historic, so the "peak of the curve is not moving forward or broadening as time goes on."[3] For instance, only 7–10 credible reports of abuse were lodged by current minors in 2011 and 6 credible reports in 2012 across the entire Roman Catholic Church.[4] The church's many steps to prevent child abuse and to reach out to victims are also instructive.[5]

Though other organizations have not conducted in-depth audits similar to those carried out by the Catholic Church, patterns of past and present abuse elsewhere appear to be similar. Mission organizations have also faced abuse allegations from the distant past.[6] Organizations that track sexual abuse allegations against missions, such as the Child Safety and Protection Network, see both current and historic sexual misconduct claims.[7]

In a new development, law enforcement has pursued religious leaders with criminal charges because of failure to protect children. In Philadelphia, Monsignor William Lynn was convicted of endangering children and sentenced to prison. In Missouri, Bishop Robert Finn was convicted of a misdemeanor for failing to report suspected abuse. Victims' advocacy groups wanted him sent to jail.[8] In the Protestant world, five employees of Victory Christian Church in Oklahoma were arrested and charged because they delayed two weeks in reporting sexual abuse in August 2012.[9] The court refused to dismiss the charges and scheduled the cases for a jury trial.[10] By March 2013, all five had pleaded to charges, and three faced some jail time.[11]

In sum, any organization that has worked with children over time should assume that historic cases exist, even though unknown. Any organization currently working with children should assume that abuse is an ongoing risk.

PREVENTION OF ABUSE: POLICIES, SCREENING, AND TRAINING

Adequate child safety policies are gradually being established as a standard of care. Strong evidence shows that good policies protect children and protect an organization. Prevention should be based on situational factors or "routine activities theory," which teaches that abuse requires three factors: first, a motivated abuser; second, a potential victim; and third, lack of a "capable guardian" or, put another way, an environment that gives access.[12] Studies show that addressing these three factors reduces child sexual abuse by limiting opportunities to commit it.[13] Methods of prevention can include policies, screening, training of adults and children, and audits.

Policies. Establishing codes of conduct for all staff and volunteers sets clear standards of behavior. Beyond sexual abuse these standards should cover behaviors that are boundary violations, lack integrity, or lack Christian purity, such as dirty jokes, inappropriate touching that is not sexual abuse, sexual harassment, and adult pornography. Religious organizations have the advantage of legal protection in enforcing religious moral standards.

Policies regarding conduct should be widely available to all staff and be incorporated into training.

Screening. Criminal background checks are considered a key step. The Catholic Church has run well over two million checks on employees and volunteers, but has uncovered few, if any, sexual offenders.[14] Possibly, background checks scare offenders away from applying. At a minimum, background checks show that the organization takes child protection seriously.

Mission leaders need to be aware of government regulations on background checks. In the United States the Fair Credit Reporting Act (FCRA) applies to both credit reports and criminal records.[15] Adverse employment actions based on these reports must comply with FCRA standards. Note that because of worry that screening for criminal backgrounds disproportionately affects minorities, the U.S. Equal Employment Opportunity Commission (EEOC) has issued guidance on when and how arrest and conviction records may be used.[16]

Checking references is a useful screening tool. When former employers are reluctant to discuss reasons why an employee left,[17] a written permission and waiver of liability allows them to be candid without fear of retribution.[18]

Background questionnaires are useful. They can ask about applicants' history of working with children. Religious organizations can ask about religious morals. Sample screening documents are available through organizations such as Child Safety and Protection Network, MinistrySafe, or an organization's insurer. Organizations should have their attorneys review application and screening documents.

The usefulness of screening documents is not invalidated by the possibility that prospective employees with a history of inappropriate behavior would simply lie on a questionnaire. Indicators such as questions not answered, or dubious answers, often appear.

Training. Training is critical to a good child protection program. If children know what behavior is not acceptable and what steps to take if they are threatened, they are less likely to be victims.

Training also addresses the "capable guardian" and environmental access. If all other adults understand red flags and danger signals and see the first signs of boundary violations, they are more likely to take action to protect children. Clear understanding of what constitutes a safe environment empowers adults to take appropriate action rather than being afraid to cause trouble.

All personnel and volunteers should be trained initially and at stated intervals. Organizations can share resources through groups such as Child Safety and Protection Network.

Audits. Some large organizations conduct audits to evaluate compliance with hiring, training, and conduct policies. The Catholic Church conducts a massive annual audit, which is one reason it may now be the safest organization for children. An audit can also demonstrate to observers that the organization has not been negligent.[19]

WISE APPROACHES TO INVESTIGATION OF ALLEGED SEXUAL ABUSE

Since allegations of child sexual abuse are almost inevitable, leaders must be ready to face them. They must resist any impulse toward denial, but not jump to conclusions. Allegations of child abuse present a crisis, and missteps can compound the damage. They can further hurt victims, disrupt ministry, mistreat alleged offenders, lower morale, destroy public image, and result in legal action. Good policies equip administrators to handle crisis situations well. Important steps to be taken in response to allegations of sexual abuse include reporting, investigating, making findings, healing victims, disciplining offenders, and managing public relations. Under the present heading I deal with various facets of the reporting and investigating process.

Reporting: internal and external. Organizations should have procedures in place for reporting reasonable suspicions of sexual misconduct. "Reasonable suspicion" is a legal term, and its definition may vary according to regional statutes. Generally it means "sufficient knowledge to believe that criminal activity is at hand," based on specific facts. The standard is lower than for probable cause or "probably true."[20] Reports of misconduct made within an organization should trigger an investigation. Depending on the nature of the allegations, reports must also be made to civil authorities. For immoral adult activity that does not involve child abuse but that violates the Christian principles of the organization (such as adultery or other illicit sexual behavior), restriction to an internal report alone may be appropriate.

All states of the United States and many other countries now make reporting of child abuse mandatory, and reasonable suspicion of child abuse usually must be reported promptly to law enforcement. A prompt but brief preliminary investigation may or may not be appropriate to determine if specific facts support reasonable suspicion. External reports to law enforcement should be made in accordance with relevant local law, and all alleged abuse involving minors, including historic claims, should be reported.[21] Filing such a report indicates reasonable suspicion but does not mean that a finding of abuse has been made. Failure to report may have serious consequences.

Alleged sexual abuse that takes place overseas should be reported to local authorities there in accordance with local law and culture. For a U.S. citizen, allegations of abuse at home or overseas should also be reported in the home states of the victim and the perpetrator. Reporting is similar for citizens of many other countries. Finally, for U.S. citizens, alleged child sexual abuse that occurs overseas can be reported to federal authorities for possible prosecution under the Federal PROTECT Act of 2003, which criminalizes "illicit sexual conduct" abroad by United States citizens and permanent residents.[22] Reporting to local embassies or consulates may also be wise. When specific reports are not stipulated by law, organizations can take into account the alleged victim's wishes for reporting. But in any case, required reports must be made.

If a law enforcement agency plans to investigate, usually the organization will defer its own investigation until after completion of the criminal investigation so that evidence is handled correctly.

Organizational culture. The culture of an organization—and the experience members, staff, and employees have of it—have an impact on reporting and investigations. Organizational culture may also have an impact on the likelihood of abuse occurring at all. Inappropriate culture can lead to failure to deal with abuse. In addition to having reporting policies and procedures in place, organizations should evaluate their interior culture to see if members will be likely to carry out policies in a meaningful, helpful way. The 2012 report on Penn State, for instance, disclosed a culture that was not favorable to reporting of abuse because of problems with power and control in the hierarchy.[23] The culture of the Catholic Church that fostered "isolation, separation, and obedience" and a "code of silence" helped to make child abuse possible in that church.[24] Changes to organizational culture are possible but take great intentionality.

Characteristics of good investigations. If a single lesson has been learned from past mistakes, it is that allegations must be investigated quickly and thoroughly. Anyone posing a current risk should be suspended from ministry or placed on leave while an investigation is conducted. Whether to make an investigation public calls for discretion. A baseless allegation could ruin a person's career and ministry.

An investigation of current abuse allegations must first protect the alleged victim and other children. Obtain the services of an investigator with in-depth training in interviewing children. A historic investigation may encounter problems in locating witnesses, and the investigation may be more documentary. Historic allegations also may involve more difficult decisions on how broadly to frame an investigation. Investigating too widely may reinjure people who have moved on, or even trigger false claims, but investigating too narrowly may foreclose healing for victims.

When abuse is reported, investigation should begin promptly, especially in a current case in which victims may be at risk. An immediate investigation honors the claimant's report, prevents further harm, and protects the organization from claims of negligence. It also provides a fair process and quick resolution for the alleged offender, who may be innocent. The first step is for the organization's leadership to put together a fact-finding team.

Responsibilities and competencies of a fact-finding team. A fact-finding team must address competing goals. First, it must discern the truth—the accurate, unvarnished truth without any presuppositions either way. It must probe deeply, ask follow-up questions, and view all statements and evidence with an open mind. Second, the team must avoid further wounding the alleged victim and close family or friends. Third, the team must be aware of and collect information about others who could be harmed. Fourth, the team must objectively administer justice concerning the alleged offender. Fifth, the team must avoid creating unnecessary liability for the organization. This should include reporting confidentially to the organization's attorney and ultimately to organizational leadership.

The fact-finding team should be assembled carefully. Two or three is a good number, depending on how extensive the investigation will be. The gender of the team should be mixed unless everyone interviewed will be of a single gender.

The team must have experience. Competencies should include psychological training in sexual abuse, legal knowledge of the unique sexual abuse issues, and knowledge of the organization and its ministry. A trained team will know how to get evidence and how to evaluate it. Specialized knowledge required may include how to interview children without contaminating evidence, how to interview alleged offenders, and cross-cultural understanding. If criminal charges may be filed, evidence must be handled properly, with attention to such issues as chain of custody, so that evidence can be proven to be valid and uncontaminated.

Advantages and disadvantages of an outside investigative team. Whether an investigative team should be an independent team from outside the organization is subject to debate. The Child Safety and Protection Network recommends that, to preserve objectivity, at least one person on the team be from outside the mission. Some victim advocacy groups insist that the entire team should be independent of the organization. Teams drawn solely from within an organization create higher risk that investigations will stop too soon. Anecdotal reports from the Catholic Church scandals to Penn State demonstrate the tendency for internal investigators to take a minimal approach. Additionally, an organization may lack adequately skilled personnel. Also, media and victims' groups may accuse the organization of bias.

Outside teams may have a higher level of professional expertise, but they will have less knowledge of an organization's history and structure. An outside team is not automatically free from bias. If a group positions itself, or historically acts, as advocating either for victims or for organizations, it should not be used. In addition, as discussed below, use of an outside team could undermine privacy and confidentiality of information for both the organization and the individuals involved.

A mixed team has at least one member from within the organization and at least one from outside. Mixed teams facilitate understanding an organization's culture but also bring objectivity. For this reason they may be the best option.

Probably the main reason organizations resist using outside investigative team members is the much higher cost. In the world of child sexual abuse, placing the consideration of cost first misses the bigger picture. First, the damage to children's lives must be properly addressed, even if it is costly. Second, defending even one lawsuit resulting from an inadequate investigation is likely to dwarf the costs of an external investigation.

Role of attorneys. An attorney may bring useful training and legal knowledge and will help to preserve privacy and confidentiality rights. Attorney time is costly, however, and few attorneys focus on this area of law.

Attorneys can take various roles. On the investigative team an attorney seeks impartial truth. An attorney advising the organization has a different role, an obligation of loyalty to the client. Keeping these two roles separate prevents possible conflicts of interest.

In some cases the investigation itself should be kept confidential or privileged, with only limited information disseminated for general consumption. If there is a possibility that litigation could occur, the investigation should be carefully structured with the assistance of an attorney, especially with respect to outside investigators.

Even if an attorney is not to be a member of the investigative team, the organization needs to be advised by an attorney with deep experience in child protection and sexual abuse litigation. An attorney should monitor each step of the investigation, receive the reports, help determine whether the investigation is being done effectively and adequately, help determine whether justice is being done to the accused, recommend healing responses to care for victims, and help the organization position itself for any legal defense that may be needed.

Considering issues of privacy and privilege. Investigations are about information. Once information is set free, it cannot be recaptured. This affects both personal reputations and an organization's legal defenses.

In an investigation, privacy is a key value. Victims will not likely wish to have their personal information broadcast. They may not even want the organizational leadership to have it. The fact-finding team can report to leadership using numbers rather than names and keep a separate key. Also, those accused should generally not be publicly identified until after some kind of due process has occurred, such as a law enforcement proceeding or a disciplinary action by the organization. Publishing unsupported accusations violates U.S. canons of justice and opens the organization to a defamation claim.

In a lawsuit some evidence must be turned over to the other side, but some is legally protected. Society labels some information confidential or, in a legal term, "privileged." Communications between clergy and people under their pastoral care are privileged. Other confidential or privileged communications are those between attorneys and clients, doctors and patients, and husbands and wives.

Communications that are privileged in these various ways may be kept private and usually need not be revealed in a lawsuit. But these privileges can be waived or lost by giving documents or information to anyone outside the tight circle of privilege. Once privileges are waived, they cannot be restored. Mismanagement, that is, undiscriminating management, of information may waive privilege and make the organization more vulnerable to a lawsuit.

Therefore, before an investigation begins, organizations need to consider carefully how they will manage the resulting information. How will information be discussed and by whom will it be reviewed so that it is kept within the circle of privilege? How publicly will the information be revealed? Attorney advice is helpful here.

After an investigation ends, leadership will need to consider carefully what aspects of the report should be released to claimants, to constituents of the organization, and to the public.

STEPS TOWARD HEALING AND JUSTICE

Steps toward healing and justice involve outreach to victims, acknowledgement of harm and hurt inflicted, and provision of therapy and other assistance toward healing. But justice also involves discrimination; not all claims are equally valid or credible, and not all misconduct is equally culpable. Often parties have conflicting interests and claims on justice. Protecting children must take priority, which requires instituting a policy of zero tolerance for child sexual abuse.

Outreach to victims and healing responses. If someone reports abuse, the report should be received promptly and sensitively and be taken seriously. Unfortunately, many victims feel they have had to fight to get recognition of what has happened to them. Rather than being embraced, they have been rebuffed and wounded further. Organizations must give attention to healing and reconciliation for victims of child sexual abuse. Responding to abuse in only a strictly legal fashion is inadequate and does even more damage to victims.

Many victims express a primary need for someone to hear their story and to affirm that what happened to them was evil. When abuse has been substantiated, an apology from the organization, given by someone high in leadership, can be healing. Other approaches to healing include offering therapy, sponsoring support groups, holding retreats, and giving victims input on improving child safety going forward. When possible, victims need compassionate care and a pastoral response.[25]

The complex truth about claimants. Many claimants are telling the tragic truth about their lives. In many cases they have suffered horrific abuse that is sickening to consider. The full scope of these findings should be presented to the organization's board or leadership. Other claimants are exaggerating, perhaps unconsciously. Over time, incidents can come to be perceived as having been more grave, frequent, or brutal, and injuries can grow from a mildly disturbing episode to a life-threatening trauma.[26] When stories are shared, others may unintentionally appropriate true accounts and make them part of their own experience. Occasionally claims are completely fraudulent.

At times, claimants' memories of abuse are "recovered," meaning that the alleged abuse was not continuously remembered but was retrieved (or created) later. For some time psychologists have doubted the reliability and accuracy of recovered memories.[27] Best practice calls for independent corroboration of the accuracy of recovered memories.

Even for genuinely injured claimants, the level of wounding varies. Astonishingly, some studies show that at the time it happens, child sexual abuse may not be particularly traumatic if it is nonviolent touching perpetrated by a "friend." The child does not understand sexuality and may be confused or uncomfortable, but not initially traumatized. Later, trauma sets in after the child realizes the depth of the betrayal and the evil that occurred.[28] For other children, abuse produces more immediate symptoms.

Trauma levels may vary in time and may depend on other factors, such as the emotional health of the person at the time of cognitive processing of the abuse and the level of support available.[29] Treating abused children shortly after the injury occurs helps prevent later complications.[30] (Sometimes both organizational leadership and family members need help in understanding this, as the child's initial symptoms may be very subtle.) The benefit of timely intervention underscores the importance of prompt investigations.

Balancing conflicting interests of parties. The mission seeks to serve justice in several ways. First, and most important, it must protect children. Preventing harm to present-day children by moving to correct unsafe situations is critical. Next, it does justice to the alleged victim (who may or may not presently be a child) by hearing the story promptly and attentively and thoroughly investigating the claims. If the mission finds that child abuse has occurred, it seeks to provide healing to the victim by offering counseling and other action steps. It provides justice to the alleged offender by an impartial investigation that protects privacy interests until allegations have been established and by having an investigative structure that provides due process. It is desirable to have some kind of appeal process in place. If the organization finds abuse, it disciplines the offender, and it may need to provide some carefully thought-out notification to others who need to know. If the accused is exonerated, it moves to restore the person's reputation and discredit false charges. (Inconclusive findings require careful consideration of what is just to all parties.) Finally, it carries out the investigation in a way that protects the legal interests of the mission.

Zero tolerance. Historically, religious organizations have been inept in their handling of offenders. Early efforts, consistent with the idea of forgiveness and reconciliation, sought to rehabilitate offenders. Ministries today still struggle, with varying answers, with the question of whether a repentant sexual sinner should be allowed to return to ministry. The decision is tough when removing a gifted person will destroy a successful ministry.

The lesson of history, however, is clear, at least with respect to sexual abuse of children. Others have repeatedly tried the experiment, and the dangers of keeping an offender in ministry are too great. If an allegation of child sexual abuse is determined to be true, the person should be removed immediately and permanently from ministry—no matter how charismatic, vibrant, and successful that person may be otherwise.

FACING LITIGATION AGAINST THE ORGANIZATION

At times, healing responses to allegations of abuse are inadequate or not accepted. Factors outside an organization's control usually drive lawsuits.

Victims have a moral right to healing responses. But litigation is combative and destructive, and the organization may need a strong defense.

What drives sex abuse litigation? Plaintiffs' attorneys drove the Catholic Church's sexual abuse scandal. Seldom has a righteous cause been so profitable. Filing claims of child sexual abuse is enormously lucrative for attorneys, because they receive 35 to 50 percent of the result, over and above their expenses.[31] Given that the total payout on the claims was around $1.5 billion in just five years, attorneys' earnings have been substantial.[32] Total Catholic defense expenditures since the claims began (including the $1.5 billion just mentioned) exceed $2.5 billion and are still growing.[33]

Claims may be filed against both alleged offenders and institutions. Fiscal reality dictates that claims be filed against institutions, whether or not the evidence shows the institution ever had knowledge of the abuse problem. True offenders deserve to be punished, but they rarely have money, and they may be dead, in which case the claims are filed against the institution alone.

Claims include negligent supervision, vicarious liability (employers being liable for acts or omissions of employees), breach of fiduciary duty (a type of breach of trust), fraudulent concealment, and others. Courts have found some of the claims legally viable and others not. Plaintiffs file them anyway. Whether or not they are legally sound, they put pressure on the defending organization. Cases rarely go to trial; the vast majority of the cases settle.

Because even ancient Catholic sexual abuse claims are gradually drying up, plaintiffs' attorneys seem to be seeking new markets. Missionary boarding schools have become a good target because they provide a large pool of former children. So do other religious organizations that have worked with children in the last fifty years. Cases are much more profitable when developed in groups and waves. Further litigation can be anticipated. A proactive approach to investigations and healing, both for current and historic abuse, is the best preparation for the gathering storm.

Why keep statutes of limitations? Victims' groups applaud removing statutes of limitations. These statutes, they argue, hinder justice by permitting old crimes to go unpunished. They claim victims may not yet remember what happened or that they have lacked the psychological strength to come forward, sometimes for decades. In some regions, plaintiffs' attorneys have helped to change laws to revive old, time-barred claims. In Connecticut, for instance, the statute of limitations is now thirty years. In California the statute of limitations was suspended for a one-year window to file old claims, triggering around a thousand new lawsuits.[34] A current "window" bill that would revive old claims is being debated in Pennsylvania.[35]

But statutes of limitations serve a valid purpose and have always been a vital component of our legal system. Mission leaders need to understand how they work. First, the clock starts when a child reaches majority, commonly at age eighteen. Then the clock runs for the length of time provided by state statutes, often three to six years, though much longer in some states. So someone abused at age twelve might have until age eighteen plus the length of the statute of limitations to file a claim.

For cases to be allowed to be filed against institutions for abuse that allegedly occurred decades earlier becomes problematic. Early notice to an institution helps it to correct dangerous conditions so that others are not injured. This principle is one way that governments justify granting only short time frames for complaints against themselves. (In Colorado, for instance, in order for people to sue the government, they must give notice within 180 days of the wrongful act.)

Statutes of limitations help in achieving good adjudication of claims. Old claims, often made after the offenders are dead, are subject to the hazards of fading memories, lost documents, and missing witnesses. Recent studies show that even current eyewitness testimony may be unreliable because of memory inaccuracies. Of 297 convictions that have been overturned by DNA evidence, more than 70 percent were based on (presumably well-meant) eyewitness testimony.[36] Thus, old claims create a greater possibility of doing injustice to the accused. And testimony is not always well-meant. Fraud is much more difficult to detect and prove for old claims, especially if the only other person supposedly involved in the incident has dementia or is dead. Many old claims may be exaggerated or completely fabricated.

Justice issues are different in current and historic abuse cases. In a lawsuit about current abuse (a lawsuit that is brought at the latest within a few years after the accuser becomes an adult), recollections and evidence are relatively fresh, and it is easier to evaluate the actual degree of injury. In historic abuse, the injury, while it may be very real, is also somewhat or quite old, and evaluating it becomes difficult because of its being tangled up with all the other griefs and difficulties of life. In addition, in historic cases the financial burden for wrongdoing gets shifted by decades. After forty or fifty years, not only is litigation difficult, but it also resembles reparations. The current organization is being asked to pay for something done long ago by someone else. To the present members of the organization, that does not feel like justice.

Insurance purchased forty or fifty years ago, with a certain set of assumptions about risk, is seldom adequate. Often the insured institution cannot even locate such old policies. If insurance is not available, today's members and donors must pay for mistakes made generations earlier. Current church or missions programs suffer. It is not those responsible for any wrongdoing who pay, but their institutional descendants.

Reasonable statutes of limitations ensure that defendants are judged by contemporaneous standards of care.[37] Medical standards, for example, have changed enormously since 1970; no medical decision made then should be held accountable to the standards of 2014. Yet litigation in historic abuse cases routinely evaluates decisions made in 1970 by the standards of today's research and knowledge. In those days, instead of prison, offenders were sentenced to treatment until they were "cured."[38] At the time, leaders did not realize this was ineffective. Another difference in the standard of care for historic cases is that most U.S. child protective services and child abuse reporting laws were not yet in place, let alone laws covering international offenses. Organizations are within their rights to insist on applying the statutes of limitations.

Should not repressed memory or recently recovered memory delay the onset of statutory limitations? Arguments for extending or ignoring statutes of limitations are often made on the basis that sexual abuse is so traumatic that either victims repress their memories or they do remember them but require time to gain strength enough to confront the institution. Some experts, such as Elizabeth Loftus, consider repressed-memory theory to be largely junk science.[39] Memories retrieved after a long period of time are suspect, even when the claimant remembers them in good faith. Research has established both that memory is plastic and that false memories can be created.

In therapy, dealing with a "recovered memory" is an important goal, because a negative memory carries trauma and emotion whether it is entirely true, partially true, or not at all true. For therapy, it may not matter much whether or not the memory is true, because it truly affects the person. But legal settings are different. If allegations of abuse mean that someone is to lose a career or be convicted of a crime, or if an organization is to pay out large sums of money, then corroborating evidence is needed that the abuse really happened. The same recovered memory that is taken seriously as the basis for therapy may not have sufficient evidentiary support to warrant legal consequences or to destroy an alleged offender's personal and professional life.

While normal statutory limitation periods do not start running until a child victim becomes an adult, allowing repressed memory or "psychological strength" claims to change the statutory period makes the claims period effectively lifelong. While mission organizations should reach out compassionately to former MKs with recovered memories, they can require recovered memory to pass certain tests before being accepted as evidence.

Litigation will attempt to circumvent the statute of limitations. Because historic cases cannot otherwise be litigated, plaintiffs' attorneys plead theories such as repressed memory, psychological inability to come forward, or lack of knowledge of the organization's culpability, to circumvent the statute of limitations. Some courts have recently accepted these arguments and some have not.[40]

Given that these arguments are common, mission organizations should prepare to face them from the beginning of any investigation and should not lightly waive them or permit others to do so on their behalf.[41]

Litigation strategy. Counsel and insurers are key players in litigation strategy. A very early step is to put the insurer on notice and to get the insurer involved in the defense. Child sexual abuse cases in religious organizations are highly specialized, and usually plaintiffs' attorneys have the immense advantage of being repeat players. The legal defense team must understand the specific patterns of this type of litigation. Consider whether your organization's or insurer's attorneys are litigators with this kind of experience, and if not, work with them to hire a defense attorney who practices in this area. Litigation defense counsel will help address issues about document privileges (confidentiality) as well as litigation holds (making sure that relevant documents are preserved).

Defense counsel will also work with the organization's general counsel to assess the costs and goals of the case and to devise a strategic approach. The defense team has available certain constitutional and religious law principles as well as more ordinary defenses. Organizations should be aware that litigation is expensive, and they need to plan and prepare financially. Early stages of the litigation may involve motions to dismiss or for summary judgment because of the statute of limitations. Litigation around discovery may include disputes over privileged documents, or resisting extraordinarily broad requests for documents that plaintiffs' attorneys use to uncover more claims.

Most civil litigation ends in settlement; therefore, throughout the case, litigation counsel will strategize toward the possibility of settling the case. But achieving settlement often means being well prepared for going to trial if necessary.

Lawsuits by alleged offenders. If an accusation is false and is acted on, essentially a person's life will be destroyed. Other types of lawsuit arising from sexual abuse investigations are those filed by the alleged offenders for defamation, negligent supervision of the investigation team, or wrongful termination. These lawsuits are a very real risk. Both considerations of justice and litigation risk are reasons to conduct investigations carefully and in accordance with best practices, including due process for the accused. Legal counsel can help balance competing risks and can also help formulate findings and statements that reduce legal liability.

CONCLUSION

Child sexual abuse may be the most noxious plant that can take root and grow in a religious organization. Preventing child sexual abuse or rooting it out is a difficult and expensive challenge, but critical for both children and the organization. As the chief financial officer of one major mission has posed the issue, "The continued work of the mission is just one bad child abuse case away from being ended." Organizations must get it right to protect children and the organization, and when abuse has happened, to do what they can to heal the wrong.

NOTES

1. Theresa Lynn Sidebotham, "Protecting Children and Organizations from Child Sexual Abuse: An Overview of Legal and Practical Issues," a white paper, is a more extended version of this chapter. Copies are available from the author at www.telioslaw.com.

2. John Jay College of Criminal Justice of the City University of New York, *Nature and Scope of Sexual Abuse of Minors by Catholic Priests and Deacons in the United States, 1950–2002* (Washington, D.C.: United States Conference of Catholic Bishops, 2004), 24–35, www.usccb.org/issues-and-action/child-and-youth-protection/upload/The-Nature -and-Scope-of-Sexual-Abuse-of-Minors-by-Catholic-Priests-and-Deacons-in-the-United -States-1950-2002.pdf.

3. National Review Board, *A Ten Year Progress Report* (Washington, D.C.: United States Conference of Catholic Bishops, 2012), 1, www.usccb.org/issues-and-action/child-and -youth-protection/upload/10-year-report-2012.pdf.

4. Secretariat of Child and Youth Protection for the National Review Board, *2011 Annual Report on the Implementation of the "Charter for the Protection of Children and Young People"* (Washington, D.C.: United States Conference of Catholic Bishops, 2012), 3–4, www .usccb.org/issues-and-action/child-and-youth-protection/upload/2011-annual-report.pdf; Secretariat of Child and Youth Protection for the National Review Board, *2012 Annual Report on the Implementation of the "Charter for the Protection of Children and Young People"* (Washington, D.C.: United States Conference of Catholic Bishops, 2013), 3, www.usccb .org/issues-and-action/child-and-youth-protection/reports-and-research.cfm.

5. Keeping Our Promise to Protect, www.usccb.org/search.cfm?site=newusccb&proxystyleshe et=newusccb_frontend&q=%22Keeping+our+promise+to+protect%22&btnG.x=22&btnG .y=18&lang=eng; or go to www.usccb.org/ and place "Keeping Our Promise to Protect" (including the quotation marks) in the search box.

6. For examples, see Melissa Steffan, "Missionary Group Fires Sex Abuse Investigator," *Christianity Today*, February 12, 2013, www.christianitytoday.com/gleanings/2013/february /missionary-group-fires-sex-abuse-investigator.html; Leslie Scanlon, "Six Persons Named by Abuse Review Panel in Physical, Sexual Abuse Investigation," *The Presbyterian Outlook*, August 11, 2010, www.pres-outlook.org/component/content/article/44-breaking -news/10520-six-persons-named-by-abuse-review-panel-in-physical-sexual-abuse -investigation-.html; *GRACE Amended Final Report for the Investigatory Review of Child Abuse at New Tribes Fanda Missionary School*, August 28, 2010, www.bishop-accountability .org/reports/2010_08_28_GRACE_Fanda_Report.pdf; "Final Report of Independent Panel," *Global Ministries in the United Methodist Church*, http://new.gbgm-umc.org/about /globalministries/childprotection/finalpanelreport/; and John W. Kennedy, "Missions: From Trauma to Truth," *Christianity Today*, April 27, 1998, www.christianitytoday.com /ct/1998/april27/8t5016.html.

7. See http://childsafetyprotectionnetwork.org.

8. John Eligon and Laurie Goodstein, "Kansas City Bishop Convicted of Shielding Pedophile Priest," *New York Times*, September 6, 2012, www.nytimes.com/2012/09/07/us/kansas-city -bishop-convicted-of-shielding-pedophile-priest.html?_r=0.

9. Gregory S. Love and Kimberlee D. Norris, "Church Employees Arrested/Charged for Failure to Report Sexual Abuse," *Ministry Safe Blog*, September 25, 2012, http://blog.ministrysafe.com/blog/post/church-employees-arrestedcharged-for-failure-to-report-sexual-abuse.aspx.

10. Jarrel Wade, "Judge Rules against Victory Christian Ministers," *Tulsa World*, November 20, 2012, www.tulsaworld.com/news/crimewatch/judge-rules-against-victory-christian-ministers/article_88497413-9a6a-59d7-9521-22d975701e8c.html.

11. Lori Fullbright, "Victory Christian Staff Members Plead No Contest to Failing to Report Teen Rape," *WNOW News on 6*, March 22, 2013, http://wnow.worldnow.com/global/story.asp?s=21767011.

12. Research Team of John Jay College, *Causes and Context*, 5, 16.

13. Research Team of John Jay College, *Causes and Context*, 99.

14. National Review Board, *Ten Year Progress Report*, 8.

15. 15 U.S.C. § 1681 *et seq.*, www.law.cornell.edu/uscode/text/15/1681.

16. U.S. Equal Opportunity Commission, *EEOC Enforcement Guidance*, no. 915.002, April 25, 2012, www.eeoc.gov/laws/guidance/arrest_conviction.cfm.

17. Jeffrey L. Seglin, "Too Much Ado about Giving References," *New York Times*, February 21, 1999, www.nytimes.com/1999/02/21/business/the-right-thing-too-much-ado-about-giving-references.html.

18. Whether to use this approach will depend on the law in different jurisdictions. Also, note that some states grant protection by statute to former employers acting in good faith.

19. Diane Heldt, "Regents: All University of Iowa Employees Should Have Sexual Harassment Training," *Gazette*, February 6, 2013, http://thegazette.com/2013/02/06/regents-all-university-of-iowa-employees-should-have-sexual-harassment-training/.

20. See Farlex, *Free Dictionary*, http://legal-dictionary.thefreedictionary.com/Probable+Cause+and+Reasonable+Suspicion.

21. Most privileges, such as the counselor-client privilege, do not shelter persons from reporting child abuse, though clergy confidentiality is absolute in many jurisdictions.

22. Federal PROTECT Act of 2003, 18 U.S.C. § 2423(c), www.law.cornell.edu/uscode/text/18/2423.

23. Freeh Sporkin & Sullivan, LLP, "Report of the Special Investigative Counsel Regarding the Actions of the Pennsylvania State University Related to the Child Sexual Abuse Committed by Gerald A. Sandusky," July 12, 2012.

24. Tom Barth, "Crisis Management in the Catholic Church: Lessons for Public Administrators," *Public Administration Review*, September/October 2010, p. 785.

25. National Review Board, *Ten Year Progress Report*, 2.

26. Intense focus such as that created by involvement with a victims' group or a lawsuit may lead to unconscious exaggeration, as the person becomes obsessed with the injuries.

27. Robert J. Priest and Esther E. Cordill, "Christian Communities and 'Recovered Memories' of Abuse," *Christian Scholar's Review* 41, no. 4 (Summer 2012): 381–400.

28. Susan A. Clancy, *The Trauma Myth* (New York: Basic Books, 2009).

29. Sometimes it may be not so much that memory is repressed or lost, as that the abuse had relatively little significance or effect until the person came to realize—rather than to remember—what actually happened.

30. For a more detailed overview, see B. E. Saunders, L. Berliner, and R. D. Hanson, eds., *Child Physical and Sexual Abuse: Guidelines for Treatment (Revised Report: April 26, 2004)* (Charleston, S.C.: National Crime Victims Research and Treatment Center, 2004), 25–26.

31. One sample fee agreement for this type of case gave the attorneys 40 percent of gross recovery if the case settled or went to trial, and 50 percent if there was an appeal. In addition, attorneys received all their costs. Fees would be divided between local counsel and one of the national plaintiffs' firms. Costs are high. For instance, one national plaintiffs' consultant and expert witness charges $700 per hour. In the end, the amount of money available for the actual plaintiff may be rather small.

32. From 2004 to 2009, settlement payments alone totaled $1,499,088,412, apart from other payments and costs. See Center for Applied Research in the Apostolate, "2009 Survey of Allegations and Costs: A Summary Report for the Secretariat of Child and Youth Protection, United States Conference of Catholic Bishops, February 2010," in *2009 Annual Report on the Implementation of the "Charter for the Protection of Children and Young People"* (Washington D.C.: United States Conference of Catholic Bishops, 2010), 41, www.usccb.org/issues-and -action/child-and-youth-protection/upload/annual-report-on-the-implementation-of-the -charter-for-the-protection-of-children-and-young-people-2009.pdf.

33. Laurie Goodstein and Erik Eckholm, "Church Battles Efforts to Ease Sex Abuse Suit," *New York Times*, June 14, 2012, www.nytimes.com/2012/06/14/us/sex-abuse-statutes-of -limitation-stir-battle.html.

34. Ibid. Estimates vary on the California window, but there seem to have been around 800 persons who alleged abuse by priests and around 1,000 total allegations of abuse.

35. Jan Murphy, "Pa. Lawmakers Push for Extending Statute of Limitations for Child Sex Abuse Victims," *Penn Live*, Sept. 25, 2013, at www.pennlive.com/midstate/index.ssf/2013/09 /pa_lawmakers_push_for_extendin.html.

36. Douglas Starr, "False Eyewitness," *Discover Magazine*, September 2012, 40, http:// discovermagazine.com/2012/nov/04-eyewitness#.UTztRRlifNA.

37. Changing standards of care for children may be illustrated simply. When I lived in Indonesia, everyone commented on what nice, round heads my children had. I explained that it was because American doctors had determined it was safer for children to sleep on their stomachs (and much easier for them to roll over and crawl). Indonesian babies had flat heads from lying on their backs. About the time my last round-headed baby had graduated to a regular bed, the Americans doctors changed their minds and the standard of care and decided that, after all, it was much safer for babies to sleep on their backs. It turned out the mothers of the flat-headed babies were right after all.

38. In an address presented to the Irish bishops on March 10, 2009, Monica Applewhite gave an excellent summary of historic standards of care and the Catholic sexual abuse scandal. See www.safeguarding.ie/dr-monica-applewhite-irish-bishops/.

39. Elizabeth Loftus and Katherine Ketcham, *The Myth of Repressed Memory: False Memories and Allegations of Sexual Abuse* (New York: St. Martin's Press, 1994).

40. See Colomb v. Roman Catholic Diocese of Burlington, No. 2:10-cv-254 (D. Vt. Sept. 28, 2012) (denying summary judgment for abuse in 1974; www.leagle.com/decision/In%20FDCO%2020121031810); but see Quarry v. Doe 1, 272 P.3d 977 (Cal. 2012) (dismissing case as barred by statute of limitations; http://scocal.stanford.edu/opinion/quarry-v-doe-i-34062.).

41. For example, the outside investigator GRACE recommended that New Tribes Mission submit to binding arbitration for all claims brought by missionary children and that it agree to waive all statutes of limitations defenses. See *GRACE Final Report*, August 23, 2010, p. 51.

8

OUT OF THE PAST:
Assessing Historical Reports of Sexual Abuse

PHILIP JENKINS

Since the 1970s, Western attitudes toward the scale and seriousness of child abuse have been revolutionized, with claims that abuse has been very widespread and systematic in church and institutional settings. Increasingly such claims are also made about evangelical mission agencies. My goal is to describe the common patterns of such accusations, particularly in religious settings, and means of assessing the credibility of these charges. I will focus especially on debates concerning memories of early abuse or molestation.

ASSESSING HISTORICAL REPORTS OF SEXUAL ABUSE

When historians write the history of religion in modern America, they will pay special attention to one issue of one newspaper. In 1985 the *National Catholic Reporter* published what was at the time an explosive revelation of charges concerning so-called pedophile priests. At the time, it was the first comprehensive statement of the view that sexual abuse might be pervasive in a religious community or denomination, and that aspects of that religious culture actively facilitated abusive behavior. The fact that its statements now seem so utterly standard and unsurprising is an acknowledgment of the social and cultural revolution that has overcome the American religious world since that date—and which, indeed, has now traveled far around the globe.[1]

Recently abuse charges have rent the world of evangelical missionary schools as well, but I do not propose to address that situation directly, nor do I comment on any specific case or investigation. Rather, I will offer a historical perspective on abuse crises in a religious setting, addressing two separate themes. Each in its way concerns the theme of interpreting and explaining past events, whichever denomination or faith tradition might be involved. My emphasis throughout will be on the Catholic aspects of the crisis, not because these are necessarily the most heinous or prevalent, but because they have been most intensely studied, and they have many lessons for other traditions, religious and secular.[2]

I will first address the changing climate of opinion concerning child sexual abuse. My point in doing this is assuredly not to justify misconduct—or outright evil—but rather to suggest why churches or agencies sometimes responded in a way that today seems bafflingly callous. This change in the climate of opinion is important in understanding the roots of abuse. If we find, for instance, that a particular church acted in this way in, say, the 1970s, it is tempting to try to explain its attitudes in terms of its ideology or administrative structure. That is misleading because, at the time, religious organizations acted no differently from secular counterparts in such matters. Very generally, the behavior of one was neither more nor less shocking than that of the other. If we are looking for the roots of a "culture of abuse," we will not find them in religious ideologies, of any shade.

History also helps us understand means of exploring and investigating charges from earlier eras. Of its nature, sexual abuse is often not recognized at the time of occurrence, and only comes to light much later, sometimes decades later. Ever since the 1980s, naturally enough, the study of child abuse has been intimately bound up with concerns over memory: How are memories of abuse recalled? Are they dependable? Can they be suppressed or distorted? By training, I am not a psychiatrist. Over some thirty years, though, I have closely studied these issues as a historian and social scientist and can trace the memory debate against its social and cultural context. The story offers potent warnings for anyone hoping to rely on so-called recovered memories as a reliable means for investigating past events.[3]

Finally, I will discuss some possible lessons from the Catholic abuse crisis for present debates in the missiological world.

"THE PAST IS A FOREIGN COUNTRY"

English novelist L. E. Hartley famously declared that "the past is a foreign country: they do things differently there."[4]

That is nowhere more true, perhaps, than in attitudes toward sexuality. If we look back at just the past seventy years or so, the United States has gone through several successive waves of concern about sexual threats to children, and these shifting attitudes have to be understood if we are to look at the responses of particular agencies to reports of abuse. Most important, we see that lenient or neglectful responses to abuse charges were not the preserve of any religious institution: rather, they were supported by the weight of expert secular opinion. While today all competent authorities agree that child sexual abuse is a monstrous and horrible crime, and abusers are uniquely dangerous offenders, those perceptions are historically very new, dating back only some thirty years. Radically different attitudes prevailed before that time.[5]

As is widely acknowledged, social attitudes change over time, and different kinds of crime and deviancy are treated differently in different eras. At this point, though, it might be objected that this comment is surely not relevant to discussions of child sexual abuse, which is utterly condemned in all civilized communities. Actually—and shockingly—such changes have occurred in these matters, too. In fact, viewed over the course of the past century or so, attitudes toward the definition, seriousness, and prevalence of child sexual abuse have shifted perhaps as substantially as have opinions about almost any other type of illicit conduct. Only by understanding this sea change can we appreciate the responses of institutions and agencies in earlier times—and only thus can we avoid the dangers of 20/20 hindsight. The chronology is critical in understanding the responses of agencies facing reports of child molestation, whether that agency was religious or secular in nature—and whether we are looking at a Catholic diocese, a public school, or a mission school.

In some eras the conventional view of the behavior treats it as extremely serious and threatening, and deserving of urgent intervention. In other time periods, little attention is paid to child abuse issues, and the issue is regarded as trivial in its effects. Particularly malleable over time is the definition of what constitutes abuse. Up to the 1880s, the age of sexual consent in the United States was ten. Attitudes towards abusers or molesters have also changed dramatically over time. In some eras they are regarded as highly pernicious, persistent, and dangerous, while at other times molesters are seen as almost pitiable figures requiring only light treatment rather than harsh punishment. In different eras, therefore, abuse-related matters have been viewed with varying degrees of gravity.

So enormous have changing attitudes towards child sexual abuse been within the past few decades that we can almost speak in terms of a cultural revolution. Today the views of child abuse and molestation held by medical and psychiatric experts, in addition to mainstream media sources, treat the behavior as extremely damaging and threatening and urge that severe remedies be taken against abusers. These perceptions, however, have grown up only in quite recent times, since the late 1970s and early 1980s. In the previous era—between the mid-1950s and mid-1970s—radically different views prevailed, both of the offense itself and of the character of its perpetrator.

Remarkably, the term "child abuse" only acquired its present meaning of sexual misconduct as recently as 1977.

A CALLOUS AGE

The history of American attitudes toward child abuse over the past half century may be sketched briefly. During the 1940s and early 1950s the United States experienced what historians describe as a sex offender panic, when extreme and unsubstantiated charges were made about the scale of child endangerment. Sensational cases led the mass media to suggest that thousands of homicidal sex criminals were at large. In response to these fears, many legislatures passed sweeping laws targeting not just child molesters but also other sexual deviants whose actions were believed, wrongly, to be connected with crimes against children, including adult homosexuals. In the 1950s a reaction set in against this earlier wave of panic. Psychiatrists, therapists, criminologists, and sociologists argued that earlier fears had been overblown, and new ideas and interpretations became commonplace. These newer and far more relaxed interpretations prevailed until the late 1970s, and they conditioned responses to child abuse allegations arising in these years.

One significant contrast to modern attitudes was that from the mid-1950s through the late 1970s, child sexual abuse was not regarded as a grave or pressing problem, and accordingly, it attracted little attention in terms of publications, whether scholarly or popular. The scarcity of expert or professional literature itself conveyed a message about the proper degree of concern about issues of sexual abuse, molestation, and pedophilia. Surely—one might have thought—if nobody was writing about a topic, it could not really be that serious, could it? No book specifically on pedophilia was available in English before 1964.

The writing that was available from prestigious psychiatrists and criminologists suggested interpretations almost diametrically opposite from what today would represent conventional wisdom. I stress that the opinions to which I refer here derived from the best-known and most-respected experts, not from eccentric or fringe writers. Reacting against the panic atmosphere of earlier years, the consensus of expert opinion in the 1956–76 era held that

- While molestation and sexual abuse occurred, these acts were not necessarily serious or devastating in their effects.
- The degree of harm depended largely on the official response to a complaint. Heavy-handed actions by police and/or courts were likely to traumatize a molested child at least as seriously as the original act of abuse. Parents were cautioned to consider these effects carefully before deciding whether to bring an official complaint.
- Molesters were not considered to be persistent or compulsive offenders. Most of the literature portrayed them as confused inadequates, and their actions as isolated. The threatening image of the serial molester or pedophile was discussed only in order to be dismissed as hysterical media hyperbole dating back to the "sex fiend" era.
- The appropriate response to molesters was felt to be therapy rather than punishment, and leading psychiatrists suggested that such treatment, even for relatively short periods, could be highly effective in curing molesters.

In case those comments sound incredible or far-fetched, let me offer a few illustrations. One of the leading criminologists of the 1950s, Paul Tappan, rejected the view "that the victims of sex attack are 'ruined for life'" as one of the pernicious myths diverting social policy. He argued that little lasting harm *need* be caused by the experience of "rape, carnal abuse, defloration, incest, homosexuality or indecent exposure":

In some instances the individual does carry psychic scars after such an experience. Characteristically the damage is done far more, however, by the well-intentioned associates of the victim or by public authorities than by the aggressor. This is not to condone the offense, but merely to emphasize that its implicit danger has been grossly exaggerated, and that the possible traumatizing of the individual is almost always a product of cultural and individual responses to the experience rather than because of the intrinsic value of that experience itself. . . . The young individual in our own society who has not been exposed to an excess of parental and community hysteria about sex can absorb the experience of a socially disapproved sexual assault without untoward consequences.[6]

The Kinsey researchers agreed: "The emotional reactions of parents, police officers and other adults who discover that the child has had such a contact may disturb the child more seriously than the sexual contacts themselves," and the danger was all the worse given "the current hysteria over sex offenders."[7]

Among the greatest psychiatric scholars of the 1950s were figures such as David Abrahamsen, Benjamin Karpman, and Manfred Guttmacher. What did they think about sex offenders? Strikingly, they paid so little attention to child abusers that the reader would obviously draw the conclusion that this type of individual was not a common or dangerous phenomenon. But the remarks they did make are jaw-dropping. Reported studies claimed excellent results with a variety of therapies, including group therapy and brief psychoanalysis, which in one experiment was believed to have cured seven out of eight pedophiles. Remission and cure are both reported confidently in the literature, so that "recidivism in sexual offenses is low in general," with the lowest rates being found among heterosexual pedophiles. These experts were still being read as respected authorities into the 1970s and beyond.[8]

THE 1970s

Forgiving or easygoing attitudes toward sexual offenses of all kinds, including acts involving children, reached a new height in the post-1967 decade, when many criminologists and psychiatrists advocated the decriminalization of many offenses, the reduction or elimination of criminal penalties, and a fundamental shift towards treatment solutions, preferably in a noninstitutional setting. Numerous court decisions enhanced the rights of accused or convicted sexual offenders. In addition, some legislatures showed themselves sympathetic to calls for legal reform, lowering the age of sexual consent to the early teens. The relaxed attitude is also suggested by official inaction towards child pornography of the most blatant and harrowing kind, which became freely available in adult bookstores between 1972 and 1977.[9]

According to the mores prevailing in the society at large before the mid-1970s—and according to much professional writing at the time—the offense of child molestation was no more serious than an act of adult homosexuality, probably less so, and neither should be penalized with particular severity. Any resort to the criminal justice system in a case of this sort would have been viewed as unnecessary, and in fact likely to cause mental trauma to the children involved. The appropriate treatment for the offender was therapy, probably of brief duration. Although this is a deeply painful matter to report, much of the abuse literature in these years suggested that the child victim him- or herself was often to blame for the misconduct, and that the danger of false charges was acute.

From a modern perspective, many of the attitudes and theories described here may seem abhorrent in their spirit and simply incorrect in their interpretation; for instance, in the common view of pedophilia as casual and non-compulsive. The experts were not just wrong; they were dreadfully, dangerously wrong. These ideas, however, were not simply widespread; they represented the commonplace assumptions of the best expert opinions of the time. They were the principles guiding individuals and institutions who had to decide how to respond to complaints of abuse.

Of course, matters changed. In 1977, child sexual abuse suddenly entered the national agenda with an explosion of research and publication. Over the next seven or eight years, concern about abuse and its effects surged, as new theories emerged concerning the persistent nature of molesters' behavior. Charges of both child pornography and child sex rings gained national attention. Experts stressed the extreme harm that abuse might cause, and offered startlingly high estimates for the scale and prevalence of misconduct. From the mid-1980s, knowledge and concern about abuse and molestation became intense, and the alarm over religious-centered abuse must be seen in that context. We can identify a series of key scandals and revelations in the mid-decade, not least the sensational McMartin School affair, which came to national attention in 1984, and the beginnings of the clergy abuse scandal in 1985.

Since that date, child abuse has remained a matter of deep concern that has even intensified, for instance with the new focus in the 1990s on sexual predators and compulsive sex criminals. By this point, we can see something like the familiar cultural world we know today.

In many ways this cultural transformation benefited society and benefited children. It dispelled many of the pernicious myths of the previous thirty years or so, and placed a vital new premium on children's welfare. Everything I will say here must be founded on that basic principle. To acknowledge that this was substantially a change for the good, however, does not mean that we should treat all its manifestations sympathetically or uncritically. Alongside the praiseworthy new sensibility, there were also excesses, some of which were quite as alarming in their way as the callousness of the 1960s and 1970s.

REMEMBERING ABUSE

The chronology I offer here is essential to understanding the debate over memory in matters of child abuse.

Briefly, the concern over child sexual abuse in the 1980s spawned a highly uncritical attitude towards investigative techniques, resulting in wild and wholly bogus speculations about so-called cult ritual abuse, or Satanic Ritual Abuse (SRA). Such a topic may seem wildly bizarre, outré, but it is in fact highly relevant to contemporary concerns. As I will explain, the SRA panic led directly to modern debates over Recovered/False Memories, which have to be understood in that context. The best argument against therapeutic techniques intended to reclaim so-called recovered memories is that these were deeply, unforgivably, implicated in the ritual abuse panic, which is now recognized as a disastrous farrago.[10]

Although this era has faded from contemporary discourse and slipped into the historical record, its horrors must not be forgotten. From the late 1970s, investigators became willing to accept children's testimony as objectively accurate, even when elicited by questionable investigative techniques. Reluctance to doubt victim testimony induced investigators to accept as authentic outlandish stories of bizarre abuse and torture, and to make sense of them in the only way possible, by presuming that atrocities were the work of a ritualistic cult. Other evidence for sinister practices arose from memories recovered—during therapy—from adult "survivors" of abuse, and here too, fantastic accounts could only be explained within the larger narrative of cult rituals.

To interpret these bizarre charges, investigators and therapists turned to a sensationalistic 1980 book that would have a vast impact on attitudes toward child abuse during the coming decade: *Michelle Remembers*, in which a psychiatrist describes therapy sessions with a woman who recalled ritualistic sexual abuse inflicted on her as a child in Vancouver during the mid-1950s. Culprits belonged to a clandestine cult that caged, molested, and tortured children, and sacrificed animals. Such stories provided a blueprint for understanding the tales now coming to light.

Between 1985 and 1994, America suffered a far-reaching panic alleging the widespread existence of satanic cults that victimized children en masse and practiced widespread human sacrifice. It was difficult to look at any media source, including the most respectable and sober, without finding credulous references to these ridiculous charges.

Therapeutic professions were deeply implicated. During these years, therapists persuaded at least several thousand vulnerable patients to recover supposed memories showing that they were the victims of atrocities inflicted by people within satanic cults. These warped beliefs persuaded many patients to sever relations with the families who had, presumably, participated in such atrocities. The scale of this crisis can be suggested by a simple statistic: The number of alleged victims of ritual abuse who surfaced in the 1984–94 era was roughly comparable to the total number of victims of sex abuse by Catholic clergy for the whole 1950–2002 period, as identified by the John Jay report.[11] But in the Jay report, the vast majority of victims were reporting genuine offenses, whereas in the ritual abuse affair, the number of authentic victims was precisely zero.

I reiterate that critical point. Despite thousands of allegations and alleged "recovered memories," there was never a single documented or confirmed episode of such cult sexual abuse, satanic ritual abuse, or human sacrifice: not a single one. There was in fact a vast amount of smoke, and precisely no fire.

BELIEVE THE CHILDREN

The refusal to disbelieve children's supposedly spontaneous testimony was in large measure a reaction against the callous therapeutic attitudes of the 1950s and 1960s. It also owed much to the precedent of the feminist anti-rape campaign of the 1970s, which had so criticized the insensitivity of police and courts to adult victims. By extension, the new child abuse professions asserted that children never lied about matters of sexual abuse, and that once children admitted to being abused, this fact must be accepted and affirmed with tenacity. Therapists were haunted by the example of Sigmund Freud, who had withdrawn early claims about the widespread and damaging nature of childhood sexual abuse, and resorted to claims that allegations were fantasized.

The truth of abuse must be believed. Falsehoods might be harmless frills, irrelevant to the substance of the accusation, but the nonsensical quality of the tales could indicate that ingenious molesters were deliberately committing their crimes in fantastic settings in order to discredit children's accounts. The ideology of "Believe the Children" contributed to a readiness to accept apparently outrageous stories of ritualistic abuse. To express skepticism was to deny the reality of victimization, and tacitly to acquiesce in it.

These cultural attitudes now shaped the rise of the recovered memory movement. Belief in recovered memory originally had nothing to do with satanic claims. The idea had its roots in core Freudian beliefs about the power of infantile experiences connected with sexuality, and the repression of memories in later life. These assumptions became a powerful therapeutic trend during the early 1980s, when failings and anxieties encountered by adult patients were traced to forgotten instances of early abuse, which the therapist recovered through hypnosis or suggestion. In 1987 Judith Herman and Emily Schatzow published what would become a classic study of the recovery of abuse memories by a group of women in therapy.[12]

Once identified as incest survivors, patients could confront their problems and begin a process of healing their "inner child," usually through self-help groups of comparable survivors, following the familiar model of Alcoholics Anonymous. This vision was publicized in self-help books such as *The Courage to Heal*, by Ellen Bass and Laura Davis. Already copious "Recovery" sections in bookstores expanded to meet the needs of *Secret Survivors* of incest, the victims of *Toxic Parents*.[13]

Therapists accepted a strong likelihood that abuse had occurred despite a lack of corroborating evidence, except for ill-defined symptoms that others might identify as accidental personality traits. *The Courage to Heal* assured readers that

> If you are unable to remember any specific instances . . . but still have a feeling that something abusive happened to you, it probably did. . . . If you think you were abused and your life shows the symptoms, then you were. . . . Survivors go to great lengths to deny their memories. One woman convinced herself it was all a dream.[14]

Skepticism was discouraged: E. Sue Blume wrote that "if you doubt you were abused, minimize the abuse, or think 'Maybe it's my imagination,' these are symptoms of post-incest syndrome." That patients believed that horrible acts had been done to them was in itself a fact of enormous significance, while skepticism on the part of the therapist would violate the trusting relationship believed essential for successful treatment. Counselors were instructed in the cardinal doctrines of recovery: "Be willing to believe the unbelievable. . . . No one fantasizes abuse. . . . Believe the survivor."[15]

As SRA was so integral a part of therapeutic culture in the mid-1980s, elements from that mythology influenced the tales that therapists now drew forth from their cooperative subjects, so that the imagined reality of this era was back-projected into earlier decades to form a surreal nightmare pseudo-history. *The Courage to Heal* included an influential section on ritual abuse and murder, with confirmatory citation of *Michelle Remembers.*

The number of therapists active in memory recovery treatment grew dramatically from the late 1980s. Acceptance of these ideas was encouraged when celebrities like Roseanne Barr and Oprah Winfrey declared themselves incest survivors, providing a newsworthy tag that resulted in articles in popular magazines such as *Cosmopolitan.* Several well-publicized criminal cases used recovered memories to convict individuals of serious crimes, including murder, while memories of victimization provided the basis for civil actions, offering a fertile field for attorneys.

Legislatures were sympathetic. In 1990, California was the first state to extend the statute of limitations in abuse cases from the age of 19 to age 26, and also to permit actions to be brought within three years after the time that a person of any age *recalled* an offense, a lead followed by over twenty states in the next two years. This reform massively expanded the potential for civil litigation, and several hundred suits followed in the next three years, generally involving adult women suing members of their family.

CHRISTIAN THERAPY

Recovered memory theories also strongly influenced evangelical writers and therapists, such as Fred and Florence Littauer, and Dan Allender. James Friesen's 1991 book *Unlocking the Mystery of MPD* was a comprehensive statement of the claims then being made about Multiple Personality and recovered memory. Friesen argued for instance that "pulling unconscious, dissociated memories into the client's awareness lies at the heart of therapy for dissociators. . . . The wounds must be thoroughly exposed, so that the client can receive healing."[16]

Adding to the impact of such work was that these books usually came from distinctively evangelical publishers and were then distributed through the Christian bookstores which at that time were such a common feature of American retailing. Friesen's book, for instance, was produced by the California press Here's Life, which also published Josh McDowell.

These evangelical authors took charges of satanic cults and SRA very seriously, and some continue to do so. Friesen's current website offers a document dated 2011 in which he lists "indicators" of SRA that might surface during recovered memories.

If a person cites even a few of these twelve indicators in a recalled memory, it is very likely about SRA. There may be other items, but these cover what have been reported to me, virtually all of the time. There is also violent sexual abuse, the killing a sacrifice, and there is dismemberment, destruction and consumption of the sacrificial offering. These perpetrating acts are present virtually all of the time, and they also point to SRA. These indicators and violent acts are present when people worship Satan. . . . There have been at least 75 persons who have reported being victimized by SRA to me in my work as a psychologist, over a period of 25 years.[17]

MEMORY WARS

Some academics and psychologists had long been dubious about the potential for recovering supposedly lost memories, suspicious both of the techniques employed in therapy and of the chance that recollections would accurately reflect events that had genuinely occurred. These criticisms were reinforced by pressure groups composed of people who complained that they had suffered as a result of wrongful abuse prosecutions. VOCAL (Victims of Child Abuse Laws) grew out of a ritual abuse case in Jordan, Minnesota, in 1984–85, and the False Memory Syndrome Foundation claimed several thousand members by the mid-1990s. From 1992, the mass media became increasingly active in their attacks on recovered memory. The charge was that concern over sex abuse had led to the creation of a therapeutic industry with a vested interest in the identification of sexual trauma, while dubious therapies were giving rise to false accusations.

This was particularly scandalous in the case of multiple personality disorder (MPD) cases that supposedly resulted from abuse. This diagnosis was extremely rare and tentative prior to the sensational 1973 book *Sybil* (filmed 1976), but by the late 1980s, thousands of instances were being claimed each year, often with a degree of fragmentation that beggared belief. Patients were said to have dozens or hundreds of separate personalities, some claiming knowledge and linguistic skills that the conscious personality could never have acquired, some ostensibly drawing on experiences from previous incarnations. MPD was beginning to look more like demonic possession than an authentic personality disorder, with "alters" appearing and vanishing just as demons were said to behave in ancient stories of exorcism. But while allegations seemed fantastic, the same credibility extended to children was felt to be appropriate for adult survivors. Even more egregiously than recovered memory, MPD remains an utterly tainted area of modern therapeutic history.[18]

The dual attack on ritual abuse and recovered memory reached impressive dimensions between 1993 and 1995. There was soon an impressive scholarly literature on the debate over memory and false memory syndrome. Hostile critiques were publicized in books with titles like *The Myth of Repressed Memory*, while the title *Victims of Memory* epitomized the theme that therapeutic zeal to protect children had damaged innocent lives. An attack on false memories became almost an obligatory feature for all major media outlets.

These often took as their text the academic findings of psychologist Stephen Ceci, who showed how repeated questioning of children over lengthy periods would generate false but plausible-sounding memories, which subjects would report with conviction as objective reality: in the right circumstances, the question became the answer. Elizabeth Loftus also showed how easily "memories" could be created.

Against the abuse "survivor," the false memory movement counterposed the "retractor," the person (again, usually a woman) who came to realize that allegations that she had made did not reflect objective reality. A new hostility to therapy was exhibited in legal cases in which wrongly accused parents successfully sued therapists who had produced such charges, on the grounds of malpractice or slander. Doubts about abuse accusations were enhanced by well-reported instances in which abuse charges were cynically employed as weapons in child custody cases, an issue which had aroused concern since the late 1980s.

Recovered memory claims faced multiple problems, including definition of such basic terms as "loss" and "recovery." Contrary to the assumption of fiction writers, it is exceedingly difficult to find a single case in which an individual has suddenly recollected memories that were wholly suppressed, and where that recovered event can be verified or validated to any degree. Abuse cases that reputedly involved recovered memories rarely fit this pattern. Rather, as in some notorious Catholic clergy cases, individuals did indeed retain memories of the abuse, but at a low level of awareness. They were continuous, rather than repressed. These became acute and agonizing following some stimulus or association that drove the victim to investigate further. It is fiercely controversial whether abuse memories are ever lost altogether.

Tellingly, nobody has ever reported finding wartime survivors of German concentration camps or extermination camps who suppressed those memories, only to recall them in later life. In other words, sufferers of the most profound traumas recorded in modern history never took refuge in memory suppression or repression. Why, then, would alleged victims of childhood sexual abuse be so different?

Perhaps the final blow to the recovered memory industry was the growing number of patients who under therapy produced accounts of abuse and abduction by alien beings and UFOs. Such experiences simply could not have happened as objective events, yet these reports were buttressed by exactly the same arguments as accounts of childhood abuse. For abductees, as for SRA survivors, the same stories were reported across the nation, and indeed around the world, and both types of subject reported remarkably similar types of experience, even to the same alleged scars or physical traces of abuse. If UFO events had not literally occurred, why should any credence be placed in reported memories of ritual abuse, or abuse of any kind? Belief in SRA already demanded an acceptance of real-life sorcerers and witches; must one also believe in space travelers from other worlds?

The main professional associations of the therapeutic world came under intense pressure to resolve the recovered memory/false memory debate. In the mid-1990s, critical reports by the American Psychological Association and American Medical Association cast grave doubts on the validity of such memories, especially in providing reliable evidence of actual abuse that might be used in court. The American Psychological Association's Working Group on Investigation of Memories of Childhood Abuse agreed that recovered memories conceivably might resurface in some instances, although overwhelmingly, people who had suffered abuse retained memories and did not wholly suppress them. The report further warned that "it is also possible to construct convincing pseudo-memories for events that never occurred." The APA asserts that "at this point it is impossible, without other corroborative evidence, to distinguish a true memory from a false one."[19] Meanwhile, "the AMA considers recovered memories of childhood sexual abuse to be of uncertain authenticity, which should be subject to external verification." In the 1980s, feminist activist Diana Russell was a primary advocate of recovered memory claims. By 1999 she wrote that "the majority of retrieved memories are false."[20]

That remains the state of psychological knowledge on these matters. My own position is that recovered memory therapy remains so utterly suspect that it should never be used as a basis for abuse investigations, still less litigation.

LESSONS FROM THE CATHOLIC ABUSE CRISIS

How can we avoid the evils of the callous years of the mid-twentieth century, without falling into the credulity of the ritual abuse panic of the 1980s? With the historical overview just reported as my background, let me conclude with some observations based on the experience of the Catholic Church since the 1980s, an era of extraordinary crisis and conflict. I will focus on three fundamental issues.

- We have no worthwhile idea of how different organizations or professions compare in their record of child sexual abuse.
- Any discussion of child sexual abuse must begin with a discussion of the term "abuse," as well as "child."
- Child abuse must always be understood in its cultural context.

My conclusion expands upon each of these statements briefly.

We have no worthwhile idea of how different organizations or professions compare in their record of child sexual abuse. "Everybody knows" that Catholic clergy have a very high rate of sexual misconduct. To my knowledge, though, there is no comparative basis for such claims. Further, what we know about any topic depends on how we know it. In the case of the Catholic Church, we are dealing with an extremely bureaucratic organization that keeps excellent records over time. Once a lawyer or investigator gains access to those records, it is easy to establish a trail to multiple previously unknown cases. No other denomination or profession has such revealing materials or has ever been subject to a searching investigation like the John Jay inquiry of 2004 and its successors.

For anyone with any interest in abuse issues in a religious context, or in any institutional context, the John Jay inquiry and its successors are absolutely required reading.

We know that Catholic clergy in the second half of the twentieth century had an abuse rate of 4.2 percent. We have zero idea whether that is higher or lower than the rate for other denominations, or for secular professions dealing with children, such as school-teaching. Based on what we know historically, the rate of abuse among Catholic clergy could have been ten times greater than in the general population, or ten times less. We know nothing that would allow us to narrow these parameters.

Nor, critically, do we know how abuse rates have increased or decreased over time. Recorded figures for abuse are just that, incidents that are recorded. The process of recording depends on many factors beyond the actual rate of incidence. It would involve, for instance, perceived sensitivity to threats of child abuse in a community; education of children in such matters; police willingness to investigate allegations; and the variety of means available to children to report offenses, as well as their comfort level with those opportunities. Arguably, a heightened sensitivity to abuse might even result in a decline in the real incidence of offenses even while reported offenses were actually rising.

Any discussion of child sexual abuse must begin with a discussion of the term "abuse," as well as "child." However unsavory the topic, it is impossible to discuss this problem without knowing what kinds of behavior are under discussion. The "abuse" label is so vast as to be unhelpful without further information. The sexual molestation of prepubescent children is a singularly ghastly crime, and it should not be conflated with lesser forms of sexual offense.

This is especially problematic when dealing with older teenagers, who might be children in the view of the law but who can still give a degree of consent. Such at least is the view of the many jurisdictions around the world that have established ages of consent at 14 or 16. The forcible rape of a ten-year-old child should not, in other words, be confused with a consensual sexual contact between a thirty-year-old man and a seventeen-year-old youth. Both acts might be sinful and illegal, but the degree of culpability differs enormously.

On a related matter, we must be very careful with seemingly technical labels such as pedophile. A pedophile is a man (usually) who is sexually interested in prepubescent children. The word is uniquely damaging in its implications, and it should not be applied rhetorically to cases involving older minors.

Issues of definition and age are critical.

Child abuse must always be understood in its cultural context. Sexual misconduct with minors occurs in all societies. A man can become a serial molester, though, only if he is constantly allowed to escape detection and punishment.

Whether behavior becomes pervasive and persistent, then, depends on the cultural and institutional environment. If an offender is detected, is he (usually he) likely to be stopped and sanctioned? But what will ensure that result? Partly, it is a matter of the institution itself, but also of the broader social climate that shapes that culture.

I offer one telling Catholic example. When we read about Catholic clergy cases, it is tempting to see this as a problem of celibacy. As I have said, there is no evidence that Catholic clergy were more abusive than any other group or profession. But we can say that in particular eras, that church was much more open to abuse than at other times.

Let us look at the original 2004 John Jay Report on abuse among U.S. Catholic clergy between 1950 and 2002. If celibacy were the prime issue, then we would expect the problem to be fairly constant. In fact, it is anything but that, based on what we can say about the dates at which the recorded misbehaviors occurred. One astonishing table in the report shows a Himalayan peak in reported abuse between 1975 and 1980, an awful six-year period that produced over 40 percent of all recorded incidents for the whole fifty-two-year span under study. Reported incidents have plummeted since the late 1980s, and this change probably reflects a real decline in abusive behavior. Certainly the vast majority of dioceses toughened their response to abuse in these years, and most introduced quite draconian codes of conduct in response to the crises of 1992–94. In that sense, the nightmare is past.

We might ask: what on earth went so badly wrong in the late 1970s? Largely, it was a matter of control and supervision. Moral and disciplinary controls over priests did undergo a grave decline, in consequence of the hemorrhage of men leaving the priesthood. Higher authorities simply felt they had to tolerate levels of misbehavior that they would once have stamped on in the knowledge that the offenders could easily be replaced—but that older assumption was no longer valid in 1975 or 1980. Also, clergy in the 1960s and 1970s were not immune from social pressures towards sexual experimentation, the sense that old injunctions against adultery or pederasty were destined to perish in the new age of ethical relativism. As I have stressed, these were exactly the years when social and expert attitudes toward adult-youth sexuality were at their most perilously tolerant.

For whatever reason, the Catholic "abuse crisis" was at least in part a generational phenomenon associated especially with a cohort of priests who began their careers in the chaos following the Second Vatican Council. The "typical" priestly offender grew up within the certainties of the church of the 1950s, and saw them progressively demolished in the late 1960s. Perhaps naturally, he saw no reason why the process would not continue indefinitely. Why should he not indulge his desires? A shocking 10 percent of priests ordained in 1970 would ultimately be the subject of plausible abuse allegations.

I cannot tell you how to create a society free of child sexual abuse. But I can certainly point to social structures and values that permit such misbehavior, if they do not actually promote it. And it is very hard for any one institution to remain immune from these social trends.

NOTES

1. Philip Jenkins, *Pedophiles and Priests* (New York: Oxford University Press, 1996); and *The New Anti-Catholicism* (New York: Oxford University Press, 2003).

2. By way of declaring an interest, I should explain that I have on numerous occasions in the past decade served as an expert witness in abuse cases involving churches, usually the Roman Catholic Church.

3. Robert J. Priest and Esther E. Cordill, "Christian Communities and Recovered Memories of Abuse," *Christian Scholars Review* 41 (2012): 381–400.

4. L. P. Hartley, *The Go-Between* (London: Hamish Hamilton, 1953), 9.

5. My discussion here is drawn from Philip Jenkins, *Moral Panic* (New Haven: Yale Univ. Press, 1998).

6. Paul Tappan is quoted from Fred Cohen, ed., *Law of Deprivation of Liberty* (St. Paul, Minn.: West, 1980), 669–70.

7. Alfred C. Kinsey, Wardell B. Pomeroy, Clyde E. Martin, and P. H. Gebhard, *Sexual Behavior in the Human Female* (Philadelphia: W. B. Saunders, 1953), 121.

8. Jacob H. Conn, "Brief Psychotherapy of the Sex Offender," *Journal of Clinical Psychopathology* 10, no. 4 (1949): 347–72; compare Benjamin Karpman, "A Case of Pedophilia Cured by Psychoanalysis," *Psychoanalytic Review* 37, no. 3 (1950): 235–76; Johann W. Mohr, Robert E. Turner, and Marian B. Jerry, *Pedophilia and Exhibitionism: A Handbook* (Toronto: Univ. of Toronto Press, 1964), 85, 170.

9. Philip Jenkins, *Moral Panic* (New Haven: Yale Univ. Press, 1998); Philip Jenkins, *Beyond Tolerance* (New York: New York Univ. Press, 2001).

10. From a vast literature on ritual abuse, see for instance Robert D. Hicks, *In Pursuit of Satan* (New York: Prometheus, 1991); Debbie Nathan and Michael Snedeker, *Satan's Silence: Ritual Abuse and the Making of a Modern American Witch Hunt* (New York: Basic Books, 1995); Philip Jenkins, *Mystics and Messiahs* (New York: Oxford Univ. Press, 2000).

11. John Jay College of Criminal Justice of the City University of New York, *Nature and Scope of Sexual Abuse of Minors by Catholic Priests and Deacons in the United States, 1950–2002* (Washington, D.C.: United States Conference of Catholic Bishops, 2004), www.usccb.org /issues-and-action/child-and-youth-protection/upload/The-Nature-and-Scope-of-Sexual -Abuse-of-Minors-by-Catholic-Priests-and-Deacons-in-the-United-States-1950-2002.pdf.

12. Judith L. Herman and Emily Schatzow, "Recovery and Verification of Memories of Childhood Sexual Trauma," *Psychoanalytic Psychology* 4, no. 1 (1987): 1–14.

13. The literature on recovered memory/false memory is immense. See for instance Jennifer J. Freyd, *Betrayal Trauma* (Cambridge: Harvard Univ. Press, 1997); Paul S. Appelbaum, Lisa A. Uyehara, and Mark R. Elin, eds., *Trauma and Memory* (New York: Oxford Univ. Press, 1997); Elizabeth A. Waites, *Memory Quest* (New York: Norton, 1997); Nicholas P. Spanos, *Multiple Identities and False Memories* (Washington, D.C.: American Psychological Association, 1996); Kenneth S. Pope and Laura S. Brown, *Recovered Memories of Abuse* (Washington, D.C.: American Psychological Association, 1996).

14. Ellen Bass and Laura Davis, *The Courage to Heal* (New York: Harper and Row, 1988), 86, 345–47, 417–21.

15. E. Sue Blume, *Secret Survivors* (New York: Ballantine, 1991).

16. Fred and Florence Littauer, *Freeing Your Mind from Memories That Bind* (San Bernardino, Calif.: Here's Life, 1992; orig. 1988); Dan B. Allender, *The Wounded Heart* (Colorado Springs, Colo.: NavPress, 1990); James G. Friesen, *Uncovering the Mystery of MPD* (San Bernardino, Calif.: Here's Life, 1991), 167.

17. James G. Friesen, "Satanic Ritual Abuse Indicators," www.jamesgfriesen.com/PDF-Files /Satanic-Ritual-Abuse-Indicators.pdf. For a critical view of evangelical SRA theories, see Bob and Gretchen Passantino, "The Hard Facts about Satanic Ritual Abuse," www.equip .org/articles/the-hard-facts-about-satanic-ritual-abuse/#christian-books-1.

18. Ian Hacking, *Rewriting the Soul* (Princeton, N.J.: Princeton Univ. Press, 1995); Debbie Nathan, *Sybil Exposed* (New York: Free Press, 2012).

19. Final Report of the Working Group on Investigation of Memories of Childhood Abuse, 1998, at www.apa.org/pubs/journals/special/2190404.aspx; "Can a Memory Be Forgotten and Then Remembered?," www.apa.org/topics/trauma/memories.aspx.

20. Diana Russell, *The Secret Trauma*, rev. ed. (New York: Basic Books, 1999), xxvi.

9

RECOVERED MEMORIES AND ACCUSATIONS OF SEXUAL ABUSE:
A Review of Scientific Research Relevant to Missionary Contexts

DAVID R. DUNAETZ

The consequences of childhood sexual abuse are devastating. Victims experience higher levels of depression, posttraumatic stress disorder (PTSD), anxiety disorders, alcoholism, antisocial behavior, social phobia, and attempted suicide.[1] Although the vast majority of cases of childhood sexual abuse occur within the context of the child's family, cases of abuse by clergy and other full-time Christian workers is a tragic problem.[2] Between 1950 and 2000, approximately 4 percent of Catholic priests were accused of sexual abuse of a minor.[3] One estimate of pedophilia among Protestant workers is 2–3 percent, but the prevalence of sexual abuse in Protestant ministries is difficult to determine because of the lack of a central organization.[4] Nevertheless, insurance companies (which have access to the most reliable records) charge Protestant and Catholic organizations approximately equal rates for sexual misconduct coverage, although they do charge organizations with large children's ministries higher rates.[5]

Strong evidence indicates that the prevalence of childhood sexual abuse in religious contexts has declined sharply since the early 1990s, when the dangers of such abuse became more widely known and policies were instituted to limit the likelihood of its occurring.[6] In the Roman Catholic Church, reports of childhood sexual abuse by clergy are especially prevalent for the period 1955 to 1995, peaking during the late 1970s and early 1980s with rates approximately fifty times higher than at present.[7] A similar trend of rise and decline in incidence may have occurred in Protestant ministries as well, as sexual mores in Western cultures evolved, becoming more sexually permissive from the 1950s to the 1970s, and as awareness of the importance of protecting minors from sexual abuse increased in the 1980s and 1990s. A search of the Internet for "missionary abuse" quickly provides documented cases of abuse in evangelical missions that also occurred during this period.[8]

Victims of childhood sexual abuse suffer catastrophic aftereffects, but others, also innocent, may be caught up in allegations of sexual abuse and suffer unfair and devastatingly negative consequences. The point is controversial, but simply stated, it may be that not all accusations of sexual abuse are true. If false accusations are made, the consequences may be quite real, resulting in criminal prosecution, shattered relationships, and terminated careers, even among evangelical missionaries.[9] At the heart of the controversy surrounding false accusations lies the concept of *recovered memories*, memories of traumatic abuse that have supposedly been repressed (subconsciously blocked) but that have once again become conscious. At the end of the nineteenth century Freud was the first to propose that traumatized individuals may repress memories in order to protect themselves.[10] During the 1980s and early 1990s, the concept was popularized by the press, spurred on by fascination with the McMartin Preschool case.[11] The moral panic that ensued, interacting with the popularity of the New Age movement, led many psychotherapists to develop therapies that involved suggesting to clients that they had previously been abused by those closest to them.[12] During the same period various Christian groups focused on recovering repressed memories. A book from that period that advocates recovering memories of supposedly repressed abuse (and filing of civil suits against the alleged perpetrators), *Courage to Heal*, by Ellen Bass and Laura Davis, is still popular in Christian circles and is available through Christian book distributors such as christianbooks.com and cokesbury.com.[13] Robert Priest and Esther Cordill offer an overview of the extent to which such ideas are present in Christian literature.[14]

Since the mid-1990s, however, academic researchers have moved away from belief in repressed and recovered memories.[15] Many recovered memories are now considered to be *false memories*. Although a general consensus exists in the scientific community concerning the dangers of false memories, many counselors and therapists, including many who are evangelical Christians, are not aware of the advances made by the cognitive sciences and the dangers associated with false memories.[16] This issue is important for mission organizations because accusations of child abuse by their members must be dealt with appropriately. Most, if not all, mission organizations want to act quickly and decisively to stop any abuse that has occurred, to remove child abusers from their organizations, and to provide all the support possible to victims of abuse. To act upon false accusations, however, may have extremely negative consequences for those accused of abuse, potentially destroying both their careers and their families.

In order to help mission organizations to respond properly to accusations of abuse, I will address three questions:

- Does scientific evidence show that recovered memories truly exist? If so, under what conditions?
- Does scientific evidence show that false memories occur? If so, under what conditions?
- In missionary contexts, are there indicators that show a memory is more likely to be false?

Answers to these questions should enable leaders of mission organizations to act more wisely and justly in order to protect the innocent, help the abused, and discipline the guilty. Developing the ability to respond justly not only benefits those directly involved, but also creates an atmosphere of trust in the organization that enables all its members to function more effectively for the glory of God.[17]

SCIENTIFIC EVIDENCE CONCERNING RECOVERED MEMORIES

Although the repression of traumatic memories has long been hypothesized and the concept has taken firm root in Western culture, only in the past thirty years, as accusations of childhood sexual abuse have multiplied, has the question of whether recovered repressed memories actually exist (and if so, under what conditions) been the subject of serious research by cognitive psychologists. To demonstrate that recovered memories of repressed trauma exist, three criteria must be met:[18]

- It must be demonstrated that abuse took place.
- It must be demonstrated that the memory of the abuse was forgotten and inaccessible for a period of time.
- It must be demonstrated that the abuse was later remembered accurately.

To conduct experiments to test whether memories of trauma could be repressed and recovered would be unethical. Therefore, researchers must depend on cases studies. Such research works with three types of case studies: retrospective studies (involving participants who already claim to have recovered memories), prospective studies (involving victims of confirmed abuse who are interviewed to discover whether they can remember the abuse), and corroborative studies (examining supporting evidence offered by people who claim to recall forgotten abuse).

Evidence from Case Studies

Much of the popular literature on repressed memories is based on case studies as reported by individual therapists. Issues of confidentiality make it difficult or impossible to verify whether the individuals reported on were actually victims of abuse.[19] The subjects of these studies certainly believe now that they were abused, but evidence that they actually were usually does not exist, limiting the usefulness of case studies. In a well-known Jane Doe case, Elizabeth Loftus and Melvin Guyer demonstrated, using public records to track down the individuals involved, that the supposed abuse by the mother is highly unlikely ever to have occurred.[20] The "memories" of abuse were most likely implanted by the father and step-mother during a custody battle. In most such cases, the only verification available is the supposed victim's word that abuse has occurred.

Therapists who report recovered memories may, in fact, be highly motivated to believe that these memories are of authentic events. During the 1980s and 1990s recovering repressed memories was a major generator of income for certain therapists. The financial incentives that come from being able to produce memories with such emotional impact may prevent therapists from being unbiased in their interpretation of common symptoms, such as depression and anxiety, that occur among both the abused and the non-abused. Practices involving direct suggestion, guided imagery, hypnosis, age regression, and dream analysis have been common techniques (in spite of the controversies that have surrounded each of these techniques) used by therapists to recover supposedly repressed memories. Mental health professionals today have perhaps less motivation to recover repressed memories in clients, for both the American Medical Association and the American Psychiatric Association have issued statements warning about the dangers of these techniques.[21] In addition, therapists have been sued for implanting false memories and have had their licenses revoked.[22] Nevertheless, both licensed and unlicensed therapists and counselors, especially those who were trained before the turn of the century or who were trained at professional schools (such as many Christian schools, in contrast to research universities), may still use memory recovery techniques.

Evidence from Retrospective Studies

As with case studies, most retrospective studies (that is, studies of individuals who report having already recalled the supposed abuse) have not provided evidence that the abuse actually did occur. If evidence is provided, its verification is typically ambiguous, such as an out-of-court settlement without an admission of guilt or joining an online incest survivors group without having memories of having been abused.[23] In some cases, however, the abuse has been verified.[24]

In most cases of childhood sexual abuse, the trauma is not forgotten. Events that are traumatic are strongly imprinted on the mind and are difficult to forget, often leading to posttraumatic stress disorder.[25] Forgetting traumatic events is especially difficult when physical reminders of the abuse are present, such as interactions with the abuser, discussions that mention the abuser, or remaining in (or returning to) the place of abuse. These reminders prevent victims from forgetting their experience. Nevertheless, some situations exist in which the abuse is forgotten. The most frequent situations in which this occurs are when the abuse is not considered traumatic at the time, when the abuse is not interpreted as sexual, or when the abuse occurs while the child is very young.[26]

However difficult it may seem to believe that sexual abuse would not be viewed by the victim as traumatic or sexual at the time the abuse occurred, sexual abusers often try to mask their actions. A three-year-old, for example, may not be able to distinguish between groping and roughhousing. Such abusers would most likely be caught only if a third party adult observed the act. That the three-year-old will have little or no memory of the event is quite possible. The fact that child abuse is not always viewed by the victim as being traumatic can help to explain why approximately 50 percent of adults who are raped (both male and female) suffer from PTSD, but only about 20 percent of children who have been sexually abused develop PTSD.[27]

Similarly, even teens may not view abuse as sexual. A teenage boy, for example, might be touched inappropriately by a youth worker but shrug it off as an accident. Only later, perhaps years later, when he shares his experience with others and hears that they, too, were touched inappropriately by the same youth worker, will he understand that this was most likely a form of sexual abuse.

In such cases, the abuse is generally not forgotten or repressed. The victim, however, might not have reason to recall the events or to think of them for a period of several years or more. Such memories remain accessible and, if required, can be recalled. The retrieval may occur spontaneously when some reminder of the events occurs, such as a discussion concerning the abuser or revisiting the place where the abuse occurred. Such cases cannot be considered instances of repression since the memories have always been accessible, although the victim might interpret the recalled memory as having been repressed.[28]

Evidence from Prospective Studies

Studies of victims of confirmed abuse who are interviewed to discover if they can remember the abuse are called prospective studies. In one well-known study, Linda Meyer Williams examined interviews about unwanted sexual experiences gathered from 129 women whose hospital records indicated childhood sexual abuse.[29] Over a third of them did not mention the events recorded in the hospital records, a fact that Williams interpreted as evidence of repressed memory. Although this study has often been cited (even in Christian circles, e.g., see Stephen Tracy, *Mending the Soul*[30]) to demonstrate that a large percentage of abused women repress memories, the study has been criticized strongly because phenomena other than repression could account for the women's not having told the interviewers about the events.[31]

Many of the acts of abuse occurred when the child was less than two years old; normal childhood amnesia, not repression, is a better explanation of why some of these events were not recalled.[32] Also, the study was designed so that the interviewer would specifically not mention to the victim the verified act of abuse; if that act had been mentioned, perhaps the victim would have been able or willing to recall it. Also quite possibly some of the women, who did not previously know the interviewers, chose not to reveal to a stranger all of their memories of unwanted sexual experience. Incidents they passed over might have included memories of the verified abuse.

In an attempt to reproduce the Williams study, Gail Goodman and colleagues found a much smaller percentage of victims who were unable to recall verified abuse.[33] Those who were younger when the abuse occurred, who received little emotional support from their mothers, and who were less severely abused were less likely to recall the abuse. In such situations, the events were apparently not experienced as highly traumatic at the time they occurred. In addition, people who tended to have frequent dissociative experiences (instances of being unable to integrate real events into their thoughts, for example, finding themselves somewhere without knowing how they got there, or not being able to remember important events in their lives such as their wedding) were also less likely to recall childhood sexual abuse. Often dissociation may be a defense mechanism to protect oneself from painful memories of traumatic events, and among these interviewees repression may have actually occurred.[34]

Evidence from Corroborative Studies

Another line of evidence, corroborative studies, examines the rate at which childhood sexual abuse memories that were perceived as being previously forgotten and are now considered remembered are verified. Corroboration may come from the testimony of other people abused by the same person (who did not forget the abuse), the testimony of people who either witnessed the abuse or discovered it near the time it occurred, or the confession of the perpetrator. Various studies have found that the rate of corroboration for spontaneously recovered memories (that is, memories recovered outside of therapy but due to some "trigger," such as a discussion or visiting the place of abuse, serving as a reminder of the incident) is about 40 percent, approximately the same as for never forgotten memories of abuse.[35] Memories recovered during therapy, in contrast, have corroboration rates of only 3 percent or even less. These low corroboration rates are not consistent with the hypothesis that accurate memories are often repressed and later restored during psychotherapy. They are consistent, however, with the hypothesis that interactions with therapists (who may actively seek to recover repressed memories) may generate false memories of abuse.[36]

In summary, it does not appear that traumatic sexual abuse is often repressed, later to be recalled in therapy.[37] It is possible that some victims, especially those suffering from dissociation, might experience loss of memory of traumatic events, but normal forgetting (due to childhood amnesia or because the events were not perceived as traumatic) is a more likely mechanism by which memories of childhood sexual abuse are lost.[38] Therefore, recovery of allegedly repressed memories of childhood sexual abuse could, in fact, be *false memories*, a hypothesis which will now be considered.

SCIENTIFIC EVIDENCE CONCERNING FALSE MEMORIES

Is it possible for people to develop false memories, memories of events that never really happened? We will first consider the experience of people who claim to have recovered memories of abuse in therapy or in support groups. Second, we will consider laboratory evidence that false memories can be implanted in unsuspecting individuals.

Impossible False Memories of Trauma

In most cases involving recovered memories of childhood sexual abuse, it is impossible to determine whether the abuse occurred or not. A number of reported cases of recovered memories of abuse and trauma, however, have proven to be false. These false allegations include memories of having been gang-raped in a satanist organization although the person's hymen remained unaltered, memories of having had one's clitoris removed although a medical doctor verified its presence, and memories of witnessing the murder of a person later found to be still alive.[39] Other memories that cannot be true, but which are sometimes claimed to be recovered, include personal experiences that occurred before the age of six months.[40] Given what we know about the human brain, such memories are impossible due to juvenile amnesia.[41]

Other traumatic memories which are relatively common, but are most likely false, concern satanic ritual abuse and space alien abductions. Unlike abuse which may or may not occur, these two phenomena can be dismissed with less uncertainty. Although many people claim to be victims of satanic ritual abuse or alien abduction, little verifiable evidence of their existence is available. No large networks of violent satanists have ever been discovered,[42] and 95–100 percent of memories of satanic ritual abuse are "recovered" during some type of therapy.[43] Similarly, no strong evidence for space alien abductions exists, but experimental research on people who believe that they remember having been abducted by aliens indicates that they (as well as people who claim to recall past lives) are more prone to false memories than are people who do not claim to have such memories.[44]

Additional evidence for false memories comes from retractors, people who at one time claimed to have recovered memories but later realized that these memories were false. Some retractors have taken the step of suing their therapists, a trend that has put a strong damper on the recovered memories movement. Studies made of retractors have shown a common pattern: Individuals seek therapy for depression with therapists who use memory recovery techniques (such as suggestive visualization or hypnosis); this process leads to "recovered" memories of abuse and a false accusation of abuse; the individuals later realize that their supposed recovered memories were false memories implanted by the therapist and retract their accusations.[45]

The experiences of people who have memories of impossible events and the retractions from people who once claimed to have recovered repressed memories of abuse all point to the existence of false memories. Strong evidence for false memories is also found in experimental studies.

Laboratory Studies of False Memories

The abundance of anecdotal evidence and case studies concerning false memories has motivated a broad range of laboratory studies that have experimentally examined the possibility of false memories and the conditions under which they are most likely to be produced. Before looking at who is most vulnerable to false memories, an overview will be helpful of three of the most common experimental designs used to understand false memory: the mousetrap experiment,[46] the spilled wedding punch experiment,[47] and the Bugs Bunny at Disneyland experiment.[48]

In light of the McMartin Preschool panic in which young children recalled being sexually abused by many preschool teachers and workers in satanic rituals involving underground tunnels and local churches, Stephen Ceci and colleagues conducted a study to find out if preschoolers could develop false memories.[49] Over a period of weeks, preschoolers were repeatedly asked to think about if they had ever had their hand stuck in a mousetrap which had to be removed at the emergency room. Approximately 40 percent of the three and four year olds reported that the event truly happened, and more than 30 percent of the five and six year olds reported that it happened. These proportions were relatively stable throughout the experiment. This experiment demonstrated that false memories could easily be created by suggesting that an event might have happened and showed that the false memories are relatively stable. Asking preschoolers to think about whether they had experienced something was enough for many of them to believe that they had actually experienced it when, in fact, they had not.

Although it might be easy to create false memories in preschoolers, the question remained as to whether false memories could be created in adults. The *spilled punch at a wedding* series of studies attempts to implant memories in adults through a false narrative that is supposedly from a trustworthy informant.[50] Typically, a young adult has been told by the researchers that they have contacted his or her parents to get information about an embarrassing event that occurred when he or she was young. The participant is presented with an embarrassing or memorable story (such as accidently spilling punch on the bride's parents at a wedding) and asked to recall it. The average false memory rate in this type of experiment is 31 percent.[51]

The spilled punch at the wedding experiment demonstrates that is easy to create false memories in adults by using deceptive information, but the question remains of whether false memories can be created in adults by simple suggestion. Also, the spilled punch at a wedding experiment was criticized because many adults may actually have spilled punch on someone at some event when they were small and their memories of such an event therefore were not completely false. To address these issues, the *Bugs Bunny at Disneyland* experiment was designed.[52] Participants were exposed to an ad which asked them to remember the feelings they had as a child when they shook Bugs Bunny's hand at Disneyland. As Bugs Bunny is a Warner Brother's character, this was an impossible event. Only participants who had never visited a Six

Flags park were included in the study because of the possibility that they might have met Bugs Bunny there. When later asked if they had ever met Bugs Bunny at Disneyland, between 16 percent and 36 percent of the participants in these types of studies indicated that they could remember meeting him, some indicating that they remembered hugging him, touching his ears, or hearing him say, "What's up, Doc?"[53] Thus merely suggesting to adults that they try to remember something can create a false memory of the event.

More recently, quite sophisticated false memory generating techniques have been developed that have led to false memories in up to 78 percent of adults and 88 percent of children.[54] In light of these studies and in light of what we know about memories of traumatic events, we can conclude that not only is recovery of repressed memories, at best, a rare phenomenon, but also that it is relatively easy to implant false memories in normal humans. These conclusions have significant missiological applications in light of the dangers of false accusations.

FALSE MEMORIES IN A MISSIONARY CONTEXT

In this final section we will first discuss the reasons why false accusations of child abuse are especially dangerous in a missionary context. We will also examine which individuals are most vulnerable to false memories, and, finally, we will look at the signs that a recovered memory is more likely to be false.

Dangers of False Accusations in Missionary Contexts

"Acquitting the guilty and condemning the innocent—the LORD detests them both" (Prov. 17:15 NIV). One of God's primary attributes is righteousness or justice. He is never pleased when the guilty are acquitted or the innocent are condemned. When the innocent are falsely accused, even if no formal judgment is made against them, relationships may be broken and trust damaged. False accusations against full-time Christian workers, especially those involved in cross-cultural ministry, are particularly damaging.[55]

False accusations against missionaries may have more negative consequences for the accused than for members of other professions. Missionaries tend already to suffer from high levels of stress due to multiple demands involving unrealistic expectations. In their home culture, not only are most missionaries expected to change the world (or at least one culture) for Christ, but they are also expected to raise their own funds to do so. In the culture in which they are serving, missionaries are subject to the intrusive demands that are often placed on clergy: personal criticism from multiple sources, unrealistic expectations that might not be expressed, ambiguity of boundaries involving personal and professional life, and criticism of family life.[56] These stressors by themselves are enough to lead to burnout; when false accusations are added to the mixture, the increased stress can be traumatic.[57]

When false accusations are made, a missionary's social, financial, and spiritual support systems crumble. He or she may be abandoned by churches both at home and abroad. False accusations which lead to forced termination may be financially devastating. Missionaries have no unemployment insurance, and because of their low salaries they may have little in savings. The stigma associated with being accused of child sexual abuse will most likely make it impossible to continue in their career. Marcus Tanner of Texas Tech University leads a research program on forced termination of clergy. In one study, Tanner found that 46 percent of the participants had symptoms that would allow for a PTSD diagnosis if forced termination were considered a traumatic event.[58] If borne out, Tanner's figures indicate that the rate of PTSD may be greater than that of victims of childhood sexual abuse (12.2 percent for males and 26.5 percent for females, according to one study).[59]

This means that mission organizations must do all they can not only to prevent childhood sexual abuse, but also do to protect missionaries from false accusations of child sexual abuse. Both sexual abuse and false accusation are devastating to the victims. Most mission organizations have taken steps to lower the risk of childhood sexual abuse; they must also be prepared to deal justly with accusations of abuse that might be false.

Individuals More Likely to Experience False Memories

Although it is possible to create false memories in many people, no known technique is capable of creating false memories in everyone. The question arises: Under what conditions are people more likely to develop false memories?

People undergoing therapy with therapists who seek to recover repressed memories are the most likely candidates for false memories.[60] In the past twenty years many therapists have been sued for implanting false memories;

in consequence, the practices associated with memory recovery (such as hypnosis, suggestion, guided imagery, dream interpretation) are perhaps less common than they used to be. Therapists and unlicensed counselors who were trained before the late 1990s, however, and those trained outside of a research university (something that is common in Christian circles) may still use techniques that frequently generate false memories.

In addition, research has found that people who think it is likely that they will one day begin psychotherapy tend to believe that the therapist will be able to uncover repressed childhood trauma, thereby predisposing themselves to even inadvertent suggestions of abuse.[61] Similarly, people who participate in online support groups for *survivors of childhood abuse* will be exposed to suggestions that they were abused and are thus more susceptible to false memories.[62] Susceptibility to false memories also increases after exposure to media coverage of people claiming to have recovered repressed memories.[63]

Children of missionaries (MKs) may also be more susceptible to the implantation of false memories. Due to being raised in two or more cultures, MKs may have more psychosocial challenges as they move into adulthood than do monocultural individuals.[64] Some MKs may see having been raised multiculturally as the source of the challenges they face; others may seek other reasons for these challenges. People who desire an external cause for their internal struggles may be especially prone to developing false memories. Research has shown that one especially effective way to account for one's problems without having to accept personal responsibility for them is to accuse others of wrongdoing. Innuendo and accusations concerning others potentially lead to higher evaluations of the accuser, both in the eyes of the accuser and of third parties.[65] By increasing the apparent guilt of a target, the culpability of the accuser is decreased. This technique is especially effective when the reputation of the accuser is in question; such accusations reduce reservations that a third party might have concerning an accuser's character.[66]

When Are "Recovered" Memories of Abuse More Likely to Be False?

Because both child abuse and false accusations may have devastating effects, mission organizations need to deal with accusations and to discern the underlying truth. The therapeutic techniques that are most likely to implant false memories are still used by some counselors. In addition, some attorneys may seek to develop new markets by encouraging lawsuits against Protestant organizations now that settlements against Catholic organizations are beginning to decline.[67]

The following list, adapted from Richard McNally and Elke Geraerts, describes situations in which recovered memories of childhood sexual abuse are more likely to be false.[68] The presence of any of these indicators does not prove that a recovered memory is false, but they are statistically validated signs whose presence indicates a higher likelihood that the memories are false. In addition, it should be noted that false accusations may be made which are not based on false recovered memories; false accusations can be made for any number of possible reasons. The following signs simply reflect, based on empirical research, how false recovered memories tend to differ from true memories.

Claims for recovery of memories are more likely to be false when

- *The claimed abuse is perceived as having been traumatic when it occurred.* Traumatic sexual abuse tends not to be forgotten. If the abuse was not perceived at the time as traumatic, however, it may be forgotten until reminders occur in the victim's environment.
- *The claimed abuse occurred multiple times.* Multiple instances of abuse are more likely to be traumatic and not likely to be forgotten. Abuse that occurred once or just a few times is more likely to be forgotten.
- *The claimed abuse was understood to be sexual when it occurred.* Abuse that is perceived to be sexual is more likely to be remembered than abuse that was not perceived to be sexual.
- *The offenders or places where the claimed abuse occurred continued to be present in the life of the abused.* Places and people present at the place of abuse serve as reminders of the abuse. If the victim continues to have these in his or her life after the abuse, they serve as reminders and forgetting the abuse is less likely.
- *The recollections of abuse occur gradually as an adult.* Verified recovered memories of abuse tend to occur suddenly when the victim encounters a reminder of the abuse. In contrast, false memories tend to develop slowly as individuals try to develop a narrative that explains their present condition.

- *The recollections as an adult occur in therapy, survivors groups, or media exposure to recovering of repressed memories.* Such exposure increases the likelihood of suggestions of childhood sexual abuse which can become false memories.
- *There is no corroborating evidence.* The presence of corroborating evidence may be the best indicator that the claims of abuse are real.

Childhood sexual abuse is always tragic. False accusations of childhood sexual abuse are also tragic. Mission organizations must do what they can to prevent abuse from occurring as well as to prevent false accusations from destroying lives. Empirical studies of false memories and real memories have given tools that can help us to distinguish between the two and to fulfill the biblical injunctions to "hate what is evil; cling to what is good" (Rom. 12:9 NIV).[69]

NOTES

1. Stephen Dinwiddie et al., "Early Sexual Abuse and Lifetime Psychopathology: A Co-twin-control Study," *Psychological Medicine* 30, no. 1 (2000): 41–52; Robert D. Levitan et al., "Childhood Adversities Associated with Major Depression and/or Anxiety Disorders in a Community Sample of Ontario: Issues of Co-morbidity and Specificity," *Depression and Anxiety* 17, no. 1 (2003): 34–42; Cathy Spatz Widom, "Posttraumatic Stress Disorder in Abused and Neglected Children Grown Up," *American Journal of Psychiatry* 156 no. 8 (1999): 1223–29.

2. Health and Human Services, ed., *Child Maltreatment 2009* (Washington, D.C.: U.S. Department of Health and Human Services, 2009); L. M. Nussbaum and Theresa Lynn Sidebotham, "Are Protestant Ministries a New Market? Lessons Learned from the Catholic Sexual Abuse Scandal," 2011, www.rothgerber.com/files/10436_AreProtestantMinistriesaNewMarketv3 .pdf; Karen J. Terry et al., *The Causes and Context of Sexual Abuse of Minors by Catholic Priests in the United States, 1950–2010: A Report Presented to the United States Conference of Catholic Bishops by the John Jay College Research Team* (Washington, D.C.: United States Conference of Catholic Bishops, 2011).

3. Terry et al., *Causes and Context.*

4. G. Lloyd Rediger, *Ministry and Sexuality: Cases, Counseling, Care* (Minneapolis: Fortress Press, 1990).

5. Nussbaum and Sidebotham, *Are Protestant Ministries a New Market?*

6. Terry et al., *Causes and Context.*

7. Ibid. Some reports of abuse were not voiced until long after the alleged incidents. See the considerations raised by Theresa Sidebotham in chapter 7 of this volume.

8. See, for example, the confession posted at www.youtube.com/watch?v=kT9j8WNAw1M.

9. Elizabeth F. Loftus and Kathrine Ketcham, *The Myth of Repressed Memory: False Memories and Allegations of Sexual Abuse* (New York: St. Martin's Press, 1994); Mark Pendergrast, *Victims of Memory: Sex Abuse Accusations and Shattered Lives* (Hinesberg, Vt.: Upper Access Books, 1996); Robert J. Priest and Esther E. Cordill, "Christian Communities and 'Recovered Memories' of Abuse," *Christian Scholar's Review* no. 41 (4) (2012): 381–400.

10. Sigmund Freud, "The Aetiology of Hysteria," in *The Standard Edition of the Complete Psychological Works of Sigmund Freud*, ed. Anna Freud and James Strachy (London: Hogarth Press, 1962), 187–221.

11. Mary Young, "The Devil Goes to Day Care: McMartin and the Making of a Moral Panic," *Journal of American Culture* 20, no. 1 (1997): 19–25.

12. Margaret Thaler Singer and Abraham Nievod, "New Age Therapies," in *Science and Pseudoscience in Clinical Psychology*, ed. Scott O. Lilienfeld, Steven J. Lynn, and Jeffrey M. Lohr (New York: Guilford Press, 2003), 176–204; Elizabeth F. Loftus and Laura A. Rosenwald, "Buried Memories, Shattered Lives," *American Bar Association Journal* 79, no. 11 (1993): 70–73.

13. Ellen Bass and Laura Davis, *Courage to Heal: A Guide for Women Survivors of Child Sexual Abuse* (New York: Perenniel Library, 1988).

14. Priest and Cordill, "Christian Communities and 'Recovered Memories' of Abuse."

15. Loftus and Ketcham, *Myth of Repressed Memory*; Meredith Maran, *My Lie: A True Story of False Memory* (San Francisco: Jossey-Bass, 2010); Pendergrast, *Victims of Memory*.

16. Joyce W. Lacy and Craig E. L. Stark, "The Neuroscience of Memory: Implications for the Courtroom," *Nature Reviews Neuroscience* 14, no. 9 (2013): 649–58; Lawrence Patihis et al., "Are the 'Memory Wars' Over? A Scientist-Practitioner Gap in Beliefs about Repressed Memory," *Psychological Science* 25, no. 2 (2014): 519–30.

17. David R. Dunaetz, "Organizational Justice: Perceptions of Being Treated Fairly," in *Serving Jesus with Integrity: Ethics and Accountability in Mission*, ed. Dwight P. Baker and Douglas Hayward (Pasadena, Calif.: William Carey Library, 2010), 197–221.

18. H. G. Pope and J. I. Hudson, "Can Individuals 'Repress' Memories of Childhood Sexual Abuse? An Examination of the Evidence," *Psychiatric Annals* no. 25 (1995): 715–19.

19. Elizabeth F. Loftus and Deborah Davis, "Recovered Memories," *Annual Review of Clinical Psychology* 2 (2006): 469–98.

20. David L. Corwin and Erna Olafson, "Videotaped Discovery of a Reportedly Unrecallable Memory of Child Sexual Abuse: Comparison with a Childhood Interview Videotaped 11 Years Before," *Child Maltreatment* 2, no. 2 (1997): 91–112; Elizabeth F. Loftus and Melvin J. Guyer, "Who Abused Jane Doe? The Hazards of the Single Case History, Part I," *Skeptical Inquirer* 26, no. 3 (2002): 24–32.

21. American Medical Association, *Memories of Childhood Abuse. Report #5-A-94 of the Council of Scientific Affairs* (Washington, D.C.: American Medical Association, 1994); American Psychiatric Association, *Statement on Memories of Sexual Abuse* (Washington, D.C.: American Psychiatric Association, 1994).

22. Susan P. Robbins, "Social and Cultural Forces Were Partially Responsible for Satanic Panic," in *Satanism*, ed. Tamara L. Roleff (San Diego: Greenhaven Press, 2002), 91–102.

23. Loftus and Davis, "Recovered Memories."

24. Richard J. McNally and Elke Geraerts, "A New Solution to the Recovered Memory Debate," *Perspectives on Psychological Science* 4, no. 2 (2009): 126–34.

25. Rachel Yehuda, "Post-Traumatic Stress Disorder," *New England Journal of Medicine* 346, no. 2 (2002): 108–14.

26. McNally and Geraerts, "New Solution to the Recovered Memory Debate."

27. Yehuda, "Post-Traumatic Stress Disorder"; Ronald C. Kessler et al., "Posttraumatic Stress Disorder in the National Comorbidity Survey," *Archives of General Psychiatry* no. 52 (12) (1995): 1048–60.

28. Loftus and Davis, "Recovered Memories"; McNally and Geraerts, "New Solution to the Recovered Memory Debate."

29. Linda Meyer Williams, "Recall of Childhood Trauma: A Prospective Study of Women's Memories of Child Sexual Abuse," *Journal of Consulting and Clinical Psychology* 62 no. 6 (1994): 1167–76.

30. Steven R. Tracy, *Mending the Soul: Understanding and Healing Abuse* (Grand Rapids: Zondervan, 2005).

31. Loftus and Davis, "Recovered Memories."

32. Josef Perner and Ted Ruffman, "Episodic Memory and Autonoetic Conciousness: Developmental Evidence and a Theory of Childhood Amnesia," *Journal of Experimental Child Psychology* 59, no. 3 (1995): 516–48.

33. Gail S. Goodman et al., "A Prospective Study of Memory for Child Sexual Abuse: New Findings Relevant to the Repressed-Memory Controversy," *Psychological Science* 14, no. 2 (2003): 113–18.

34. Ibid. For an alternative view, see Emily A. Holmes et al., "Are There Two Qualitatively Distinct Forms of Dissociation? A Review and Some Clinical Implications," *Clinical Psychology Review* 25, no. 1 (2005): 1–23.

35. McNally and Geraerts, "New Solution to the Recovered Memory Debate"; Richard J. McNally et al., "Clinical Characteristics of Adults Reporting Repressed, Recovered, or Continuous Memories of Childhood Sexual Abuse," *Journal of Consulting and Clinical Psychology* 74, no. 2 (2006): 237–42; Elke Geraerts et al., "The Reality of Recovered Memories: Corroborating Continuous and Discontinuous Memories of Childhood Sexual Abuse," *Psychological Science* 18, no. 7 (2007): 564–68.

36. Geraerts et al., "Reality of Recovered Memories."

37. Gail S. Goodman, Jodi A. Quas, and Christin M. Ogle, "Child Maltreatment and Memory," *Annual Review of Psychology* 61 (2010): 325–51; Loftus and Davis, "Recovered Memories."

38. Goodman et al., "Prospective Study of Memory for Child Sexual Abuse."

39. Daniel L. Schacter, *Searching for Memory: The Brain, the Mind, and the Past* (New York: Basic Books, 1996); Daniel L. Schacter, *The Seven Sins of Memory* (New York: Houghton Mifflin, 2001); Richard J. McNally, *Remembering Trauma* (Cambridge, Mass.: Harvard Univ. Press, 2003); Loftus and Davis, "Recovered Memories."

40. R. Arnold Barr, *My Lives* (New York: Ballantine, 1994).

41. Perner and Ruffman, "Episodic Memory and Autonoetic Consciousness."

42. Loftus and Ketcham, *Myth of Repressed Memory*; Loftus and Davis, "Recovered Memories."

43. McNally, *Remembering Trauma*.

44. Richard J. McNally, "Explaining 'Memories' of Space Alien Abduction and Past Lives: An Experimental Psychopathology Approach," *Journal of Experimental Psychopathology* 3, no. 1 (2012): 2–16.

45. Joseph de Rivera, "The Construction of False Memory Syndrome: The Experience of Retractors," *Psychological Inquiry* 8, no. 4 (1997): 271–92; Harold I. Lief and Janet Fetkewicz, "Retractors of False Memories: The Evolution of Pseudo-memories," *Journal of Psychiatry and Law* 23 (1995): 411–35; James Ost, Alan Costall, and Ray Bull, "False Confessions and False Memories: A Model for Understanding Retractors' Experiences," *Journal of Forensic Psychiatry* 12, no. 3 (2001): 549–79.

46. Stephen J. Ceci et al., "Repeatedly Thinking about a Non-event: Source Misattributions among Preschoolers," *Consciousness and Cognition* 3, no. 3 (1994): 388–407.

47. Ira E. Hyman, Troy H. Husband, and F. James Billings, "False Memories of Childhood Experiences," *Applied Cognitive Psychology* 9, no. 3 (1995): 181–97.

48. Kathryn A. Braun, Rhiannon Ellis, and Elozabeth F. Loftus, "Make My Memory: How Advertising Can Change Our Memories of the Past," *Psychology & Marketing* 19, no. 1 (2002): 1–23.

49. Young, "Devil Goes to Day Care"; Ceci et al., "Repeatedly Thinking about a Non-event."

50. Hyman, Husband, and Billings, "False Memories of Childhood Experiences"; Elizabeth F. Loftus, "Make-Believe Memories," *American Psychologist* 58, no. 11 (2003): 867–73.

51. D. Stephen Lindsay et al., "True Photographs and False Memories," *Psychological Science* 15, no. 3 (2004): 149–54.

52. Braun, Ellis, and Loftus, "Make My Memory."

53. Loftus, "Make-Believe Memories."

54. Maryanne Garry and Kimberley A. Wade, "Actually, a Picture Is Worth Less than 45 Words: Narratives Produce More False Memories than Photographs Do," *Psychonomic Bulletin & Review* 12, no. 2 (2005): 359–66; Lindsay et al., "True Photographs and False Memories"; Henry Otgaar, Ingrid Candel, and Harald Merckelbach, "Children's False Memories: Easier to Elicit for a Negative than for a Neutral Event," *Acta Psychologica* 128, no. 2 (2008): 350–54.

55. Marcus N. Tanner, Jeffrey N. Wherry, and Anisa M. Zvonkovic, "Clergy Who Experience Trauma as a Result of Forced Termination," *Journal of Religion and Health* 52, no. 4 (December 2013): 1281–95, doi:10.1007/s10943-012-9571-3; Marcus N. Tanner, Anisa M. Zvonkovic, and Charlie Adams, "Forced Termination of American Clergy: Its Effects and Connection to Negative Well-Being," *Review of Religious Research* 54, no. 1 (2012): 1–17, doi:10.1007/s13644-011-0041-2.

56. Cameron Lee, "Specifying Intrusive Demands and Their Outcomes in Congregational Ministry: A Report on the Ministry Demands Inventory," *Journal for the Scientific Study of Religion* 38, no. 4 (1999): 477–89.

57. Tanner, Wherry, and Zvonkovic, "Clergy Who Experience Trauma as a Result of Forced Termination."

58. Ibid.

59. Kessler et al., "Posttraumatic Stress Disorder in the National Comorbidity Survey."

60. Loftus and Davis, "Recovered Memories."

61. David C. Rubin and Adriel Boals, "People Who Expect to Enter Psychotherapy Are Prone to Believing That They Have Forgotten Memories of Childhood Trauma and Abuse," *Memory* 18, no. 5 (2010): 556–62.

62. Loftus and Davis, "Recovered Memories."

63. McNally and Geraerts, "New Solution to the Recovered Memory Debate."

64. Karen A. Wrobbel and James E. Plueddemann, "Psychosocial Development in Adult Missionary Kids," *Journal of Psychology and Theology* 18 (1990): 363–74; Michael J. Klemens and Lynette H. Bikos, "Psychological Well-Being and Sociocultural Adaptation in College-Aged, Repatriated, Missionary Kids," *Mental Health, Religion, and Culture* 12, no. 7 (2009): 721–33.

65. Derek D. Rucker and Anthony R. Pratkanis, "Projection as an Interpersonal Influence Tactic: The Effects of the Pot Calling the Kettle Black," *Personality and Social Psychology Bulletin* 27, no. 11 (2001): 1494–1507.

66. Derek D. Rucker and Richard E. Petty, "Effects of Accusations on the Accuser: The Moderating Role of Accuser Culpability," *Personality and Social Psychology Bulletin* no. 29 (10) (2003): 1259–71.

67. Nussbaum and Sidebotham, *Are Protestant Ministries a New Market?*

68. McNally and Geraerts, "New Solution to the Recovered Memory Debate."

69. I thank Robert J. Priest and several anonymous reviewers for helpful comments that have served to improve this chapter in multiple ways.

10

MALLEABILITY OF MEMORY:
Evaluating Testimony and Accusations within the Mission Community

RAYMOND PHINNEY

Memory—what it is; its strengths and what it can offer; its limitations, even defects; and its reliability—at first glance seem to be an arcane topic at some distance from the concerns of missionaries and mission administrators. Evangelical mission organizations, however, increasingly face accusations of sexual misconduct allegedly perpetrated by missionaries on the field decades earlier. In some cases the only evidence is the accuser's memory. In extreme cases accusers allege their memory was repressed or forgotten and then recovered more recently, either spontaneously or through memory recovery therapy. Although rare, these extreme cases are not as rare as might be thought. One survey suggests a figure as high as one case per year per mental health professional. Considering the number of therapists in North America, such accusations are not infrequent.[1]

By the mid-1990s the American Psychological Association determined therapeutically recovered memories to be of dubious utility or accuracy and cautioned therapists not to suggest or instigate memory recovery therapies.[2] The idea, however, that detailed but inaccessible memories can be retrieved through clinical intervention (or self-help workbooks) has persisted. Though more likely to be the case among social workers (M.S.W.) than psychologists, it reportedly persists among Christian therapists and a few other demographics.[3]

Most people believe that accusations based on recovered memory are either true or a lie. But a third possibility exists. The accuser may believe the accusations, in which case they are not a lie, but may still be entirely false. The temptation to think categorically is strong, that is, to think that either (1) all memory is unreliable for establishing guilt (due to documented memory errors), or (2) if a horrible event such as sexual abuse is remembered, it must have occurred largely as reported. But things are not so simple. Research tells us that memory is not entirely suspect, but that it is vulnerable to certain types of errors under certain conditions.

An accurate, detailed understanding of memory function and vulnerability is critical for ranking memories as more or less dependable. We do know that continuous memories, or those recovered in a brief time without therapy, are much more likely to be accurate than those recovered in therapy over a period of time.4 To lay the groundwork for missions leaders to make informed judgments, this chapter first gives an overview of what memory provides and how it functions. Second, it examines claims made for "recovered memories" and memories said to have been recovered during therapy. Third, it concludes with considerations mission leaders should bear in mind when confronted with memory-based accusations, particularly those based on recovered memories of abuse said to have occurred long before.

MEMORY: AN OVERVIEW

Most laypersons believe memory primarily functions to provide conscious knowledge of the past. Memory researchers, however, believe that memory guides current behavior based on past experience. Conscious knowledge may be a side effect or one means to achieve guidance, but it is not the system's real objective. An implication of the scientific theory is that recovery of accurate memory, once lost, is unlikely. Efforts at memory enhancement are more likely to amplify motives for one's current behavioral predispositions and run a strong risk of reducing memory accuracy for the events in question.

Most people believe that memory works like videotape; to relive recorded events one simply replays the video. Memory based on weak evidence is expected to manifest some problem with the "videotape" analogous to scratches, blurs, and blotches on a tape. Using this folk theory, when people experience detailed, vivid memories with no telltale "video" deficiencies, they are likely to be confident—mistakenly—of their memories' accuracy. "Computer models" of memory can also be misleading, suggesting that (a) memory encoding is encyclopedic and very detailed, (b) "storage" is static retention of information, unchanged until recalled, and (c) recall is mainly determined by the past events. None of these is true.

In life, attention limitations allow only a portion of our perceptual experience to be *encoded*. Memory *storage* is not static, as on a hard drive. Information in our memories is updated after the fact with context and real world knowledge. Finally, *recall* depends not only on past events but also on one's current context. Memory *retrieval* involves a *reconstruction* of the event based on fragments of encoded, updated, and inferred information, subject to constraints arising from the recall situation.

ENCODING

Most information stored in memory is limited to what we directly attend to with our limited-capacity attention system. An experiment known as the Illinois Door Study demonstrates how little we actually encode, often only basic information about people, such as "direction asker," not noticing clothing, height, and hairline changes.[5] Ultimately, only information that is attended and rehearsed is translated into semantic information (meaning) for later recall.

Repetition powerfully strengthens memories but has diminishing returns; each repetition adds less strength than the last.[6] While more processing is better, the type of processing is also critical. In "levels of processing" theory, "deeper" cognitive processes support better memory.[7] Memory is optimized to retain meaning (semantics), not sensory (visual or acoustic) information.[8] Encoding transforms a small subset of sensory information from an event into a semantic code. The limited nature of encoding necessitates updating in storage and reconstruction at recall in order to yield a complete narrative of past events.

STORAGE

Between encoding and retrieval, information in memory is not simply warehoused; it is updated, that is, supplemented with information from later similar events, others' verbal accounts, and one's current contextual knowledge concerning such events. All possible sources of information are used to make a memory as detailed and accessible as possible for later use. Information with similar *meaning* is stored together, regardless of *when* the information was obtained. Therefore we often recall ourselves as having experienced something during an event that we only learned about or felt after the event.

Memory elements are distributed throughout the cerebral cortex, visual elements in visual cortex, auditory information in auditory cortex, and the hippocampus consolidates or binds those separate brain representations together. Studies of amnesiacs have shown that hippocampal function is essential both for memory encoding and for later recall.[9] The hippocampus not only consolidates brain representations but also reconsolidates information each time it is recalled. During reconsolidation the memory can incorporate new information and is therefore vulnerable to change or even deletion.[10] This vulnerability, a seeming weakness, is also a strength. It is adaptive because one may gain further information regarding an event after it occurs. If the memory were not labile, it could not be improved with ongoing learning. Since memory is semantically organized, later information is stored with the original memory, enhancing future adaptive responses to similar situations.

Unused memories decay, becoming less accessible over time. Rehearsing or using information builds memory strength, combating decay. Levels of processing, discussed under encoding, also affect retention. Deeper, semantic information is retained longer than shallower, sensory information.[11]

Thus, retained information is updated, not static. Furthermore, updating can lead to enhancement or deletion of memories. It can be adaptive, but it can also be a source of errors. Misinformation experiments, discussed below, elucidate how this occurs.

RETRIEVAL

To be used, information in memory must be retrieved, often automatically. An example is priming, in which primed targets are more quickly retrieved than unprimed targets.[12] For instance, the word *puppy* primes faster subsequent recognition of the word *dog*, but not *lramn* (a non-word) or *blanket*, because *dog* is semantically related to *puppy*. Priming is not restricted, however, to semantically related information. As paired-list experiments show, priming can be arbitrary.[13] Pairing words caused subjects to associate them, and the first words could then prime access to the second words, even though they were semantically unrelated. Priming can even occur with no explicit pairing.[14] Forgotten items not accessible at a particular time or under certain conditions can be recalled later if more effective retrieval cues are available. For instance, looking at our old yearbook pictures primes recall of names and events we could not otherwise retrieve that day.

Context effects are related to priming. The context—that is, the environmental, mental, and physical conditions—in which an item is learned is automatically associated with it and can prime recall of it. Being in a similar context later can improve recall of the item. For instance, people who learned word lists on land or underwater remembered more words if later tested in the same environment.[15] Internal environment can exert this same effect. State dependent memory yields enhanced recall when internal state (e.g., inebriation versus sobriety) is similar at encoding and recall.[16] Mood dependent memory yields enhanced recall when mood is similar at encoding and recall.[17] Another mood effect, mood-congruent memory, entails enhanced recall when the remembered items' meanings are congruent with one's current mood.[18] Depressed persons often exhibit both effects. They better recall information encoded while depressed (mood dependence) and information with a depressing meaning (mood congruence).[19]

Recall relies crucially on current environment, not just past events. What one recalls tends to be congruent with one's current context. For instance, when in an angry state, one is more likely to remember a given event as containing angry words.

RECONSTRUCTION

The concept of memory retrieval usually evokes a search analogy, such as for an artifact—a detailed, accurate, unchanged representation of a past experience. No such representation exists. Recall is not retrieval of a faithful reproduction of the event. Recall involves reconstructing aspects of the event from limited, stored, updated information, plus current knowledge and context.

Reconstruction is typically accurate due to real world knowledge, for instance, invariants. For example, the earth is invariably below, the sky above; light comes from above, and so on. By abstracting and using such invariants, humans economize information processing and storage.[20] We need not store every aspect of an experience, because certain attributes covary with others. Reconstruction capitalizes on context and invariants to supply missing information, usually correctly. Sometimes, however, economizing leads to inaccuracy. The effect of misinformation supplies an example. One study had participants answer questions after watching a video of low-speed car crashes with no vehicle damage.[21] One group was asked to estimate the cars' speed as they "hit" each other. The verb for the other group was "smashed." One week later, the "smashed" group falsely reported seeing broken glass at the scene at twice the rate of the "hit" group. The minor change of wording distorted later memory of crash severity.

People may even recall entirely false events, such as getting lost as a child at a Disney park and being found by Bugs Bunny[22] or seeing a nonexistent video of an event they know happened, such as the No. 30 bus explosion in the 2005 London Tavistock Square bombing.[23] False memories become even more detailed and vivid when subjects are encouraged to simply talk about whether the supposed event *might* have happened, as one may do in psychotherapy or recovery groups.[24] Over successive sessions, subjects "recall" more detail and develop more emotion about the false event. Those memories, as judged by the subject and by third parties, then become indistinguishable from true memories. Merely imagining an event increases false recall, yet at the same time increases one's confidence in that recall.[25]

Some proponents of recovered memory therapies contend these experiments do not involve the intensity and personal nature of sexual abuse. They argue that such trauma changes memory mechanisms, sparing them from misinformation or suggestion. Recent experiments using personal threatening events in an army mock POW camp at Survival Training School, however, indicate otherwise. Well-trained individuals misidentified their interrogator 93 percent of the time when given incidental misinformation about him versus 50 percent of the time when not misinformed.[26] Participants were physically, emotionally, and verbally abused by their interrogators and were punished if they looked away from the interrogators' faces. Yet when misinformed, they could not accurately identify them. Clearly stress did not spare those memories from distortion.

The final stage of reconstruction is plausibility checking.[27] At the conscious level, plausibility checking determines our confidence in the accuracy of a particular memory.

MEMORY "FAILURES"

False and distorted recall due to misinformation is only one kind of memory error. Daniel Schacter has classified memory failures into seven "sins."[28] He argues these "sins" are not errors, but rather the infrequent downsides of adaptive trade-offs that yield efficient, useable memory systems. The bare fact that memories are sometimes inaccurate does not justify regarding all memory as equally erroneous or unreliable. Our memory systems have specific vulnerabilities that are likely to yield distortions.

Failure to recall information, such as the inability to put a name to a familiar face, is an instance of *blocking*. It often occurs for someone we have not met or thought of recently. Given limited resources, only activated memories are prioritized for strengthening. *Transience*, loss of information over time, is another downside of decay. But decay is adaptive; it roughly mirrors the environmental likelihood of exposure to similar information in the future.[29] *Absent-mindedness* is forgetting information that was not properly attended to at encoding. Settling an argument between my children immediately upon arriving home interrupts my normal routine as I lay my keys down. My diverted attention is not on key placement, which is quickly forgotten. Later I cannot find them. This seems a failure, but given limited processing capabilities, priority was given to processing things that were important enough to attend to. The downside? If I am distracted, something may be unattended and not be properly encoded. These three "sins" are different costs of decay and loss, but that loss is not arbitrary. Attended and used information is conserved.

Suggestibility is distortion based on post-event misinformation. It is the downside of updating. Post-event information usually improves one's understanding of and future response to an event. Sometimes, however, post-event information can be misleading, as in the car crash study mentioned earlier. An inference from a single word in post-event questions was stored with the representation of the actual collision, since both concerned the same event, and later led to distorted recall. Pseudomemories from memory recovery therapy are partially generated by suggestion, as discussed below.

Attributing information to the wrong source is *misattribution*. When we remember something but forget when and where we learned it, we experience source amnesia. Our system, trying to make meaning, is always trying to reattach this memory to a source. Reattachment usually is accurate, but sometimes can be erroneous. The concept "smashed" in the car crash study came from the post-event question, but was attributed to observation of the accident. Similarly, leading questions, poor interviewing technique, and repeated interviewing can distort eyewitness testimony. Even careful questioning may cause distortions. Misattribution is one reason imagination inflation occurs and some false memories form.

Bias is memory distortion due to one's expectations. Since memory is semantically organized, the similar meaning of one's expectations and one's actual observations at an event are difficult to separate in later recall. Sometimes one's understanding of what occurred at an event is misattributed as due to observations at that event, when it is really due to pre-event expectations. Expectations also guide attention. Proper expectations direct focus to the most important issues, facilitating memory for them. Likewise, misplaced expectations can bias one's memory for the meaning or details of an event.

Persistence is intrusive and unwelcome recall, such as occurs in post-traumatic stress disorder (PTSD). It can also occur after less extreme stresses such as an office argument. Afterwards, it is quite adaptive to relive it, analyzing and modeling how things might have gone differently, to improve future responses. The possible downside is that some people under some conditions are over-aroused by reliving the event, causing sensitization to the trauma rather than habituation. The prevalence of persistence in PTSD and other cases indicates that trauma most commonly triggers persistence, not repression or forgetting. Contrary to claims made by proponents of repression, sexual trauma is better remembered and less often forgotten than other events, especially if it is violent, significant, or repeated over time.[30]

These "sins" of memory are not inefficiencies, dooming all memory to error. They are the costs of an adaptive and efficient system.[31] Rather than declaring all memories equally fallible, one must wisely assess a memory to determine if it is more or less likely to have triggered one of these downsides. These "sins" also demonstrate that the system's main purpose is not conscious knowledge of one's past, but behavioral guidance.

MEMORY OF LONG PAST EVENTS

The two main types of long-term memory—semantic and episodic—can vary in their accuracy. Semantic memory concerns facts we know, such as my memory that Columbus sailed the Atlantic on the *Niña*, the *Pinta*, and the *Santa Maria*. Episodic memory concerns the occasions and timeline of our life, such as my memory of my kindergarten teacher telling the story of Columbus as we colored three ships on the sea. Although I can recall and rehearse either, it is much easier to verify the ships' names than the details of that day in class. Semantic memory is thus less susceptible to distortion through misinformation, suggestion, and context effects. Episodic memory is typically rehearsed less often and less reliably than semantic memory.

I have, for instance, a vivid memory of what I did on the morning of September 11, 2001, because I have repeatedly thought about and told others about those events. I have, however, no memory of September 10, 2001. I do not recall ever recounting those events to anyone. Likely, no one ever asked. My memory of 9/11 is an example of a flashbulb memory of an important and emotional event. These memories were once thought to be accurate because of their vividness.[32] People's recall of such events, however, changes over time, as has been shown for the announcement of the O. J. Simpson murder verdict,[33] the Challenger space shuttle explosion,[34] and 9/11.[35]

Why do these stories change if they are so important to us and we retell them all the time? Elizabeth Marsh observes that retelling is not the same as recalling.[36] A retelling is intended to affect the listener, not practice complete recall. One omits details that are "boring," complicate the story, or detract from the desired effect. Untold details are rehearsed less and may become irretrievable. If asked about the unrehearsed information, we are able to reconstruct the answers. Though often accurate, the reconstruction may involve misattribution of items for which the teller had source amnesia. Some details may be overemphasized, leading to later exaggeration of details or of the importance of one event versus another. Or the speaker may misattribute and remember some aspect of a retelling as having actually occurred in the event. One is thus much more likely to be inaccurate about episodic than semantic information. Lacking ability to verify the facts, an often retold or remembered story can change, even on its main points.

"THERAPEUTICALLY RECOVERED MEMORIES"

With this background we are now prepared to assess the validity of therapeutically recovered memories. The folk "videotape" theory of memory supports belief in the idea that amplifying or strengthening the memory system improves accuracy of recall. It discounts the likelihood of pseudomemories being generated because it suggests that inaccuracies would be obvious "edits" to the "videotape." Sadly, although almost all researchers repudiate this view, many therapists still indulge this folk theory.[37] Thus it can happen that both therapist and client believe there is a detailed and accurate event memory that is eminently recoverable in all its details and that any false memories will feel qualitatively different to the client, who will then know to reject them. Details "recalled" after therapy starts are thus assumed to be accurate.

Unfortunately for such conceptions, behavioral guidance theory strongly indicates that the only thing therapeutic "amplification" is likely to strengthen is motives associated with current behavioral predispositions. If a memory has not been retrievable for some time, it is unlikely to be accurately recovered. As reviewed above, most sensory details never were encoded. Those that were encoded decayed more quickly than semantic information. Storage was not static, and the retrieval context exerts a powerful effect on reconstruction. Extra details "recalled" during therapy are mostly inferred from presently known information, shaped by current context and goals, and involve suggestion and misinformation effects introduced by the therapist and the client's own motivations. Furthermore, there is no known way to examine the memory itself to determine which details were recalled through accurate encoding, storage, and retrieval, and which were additively reconstructed. Memory itself does not differentiate between accurate and inaccurate reconstructions.

The likelihood of therapeutic recovery of an *accurate* memory is dubious at the very best. All the memory enhancement techniques we know of are prospective or require detailed contextual knowledge.[38] Memory enhancement carried out after the fact is quite difficult and always leads to some degree of distortion. What little evidence is cited in support of the accuracy of therapeutically recovered memory is overblown and often is interpretable other than as supporting the recovered memory. Studies of supposed recovered memories often use subjects who also have freestanding memories, so some of the recovery rate is really just normal memory.[39] Mounting evidence documents that reports of memories recovered in therapy are often memories that people recalled and forgot several times in the course of their lives. Any accuracy in these memories is likely due to intermittent rehearsal, as is the case for freestanding memory and spontaneously recovered memory.[40]

The less the client remembers as therapy begins, the more influence the current context has. Therapists' questions and even open-ended prompts influence retrieval, since the details of the encoding context cannot be known independently of the client's own incomplete memory. The mismatch between the original and the therapeutic context biases recall to fit the therapeutic context. The filling-in of information via reconstruction is automatic, similar to the way the blind spot in one's retina is filled. Neither the client nor the therapist has the means to determine which details, if any, are accurate.

Suggestion is rampant in such therapies. Even a therapist with no agenda can influence clients' reconstruction processes as they piece together a recovered memory. A mild therapist agenda, such as a tentative belief that a male relative or family friend abused the client who is currently repressing the memory, can powerfully bias the client's reconstruction process. Stronger therapist agendas, such as a firm belief that the client must have been sexually abused and repressed it, are even more corrupting. An open-ended and inclusive question can cause suggestion and misinformation depending on the client's interpretation of the question, the wording, and the intent of the therapist. These negative effects are stronger when the retention interval is long, as is common in most memory recovery cases. Imagination inflation, misattribution, and misinformation effects also become more powerful over repeated sessions of discussing possible past events.[41] In combination, the effects of the therapeutic context all exploit memory vulnerabilities to maximize "recall" and thus make therapeutically recovered memories categorically less reliable than freestanding memories.

Many therapists who use memory recovery therapy follow the flawed logic displayed by this syllogism.

a. IF one was sexually abused as a child,
b. THEN one will have certain symptoms.
c. The client has those symptoms.
d. THEREFORE, the client was probably sexually abused in the past, even if the client does not remember it.

In such conditional logic, the syllogism can properly yield the conclusion "D" only if "C" affirms the antecedent "A." However, "C" actually affirms the consequent "B," a logical fallacy known as "affirming the consequent."

There are other circumstances that could produce the same symptoms (such as suffering any trauma, not just sexual abuse). If a therapist suggests this line of reasoning, clients believe it is plausible, relying on the expert and not noticing the fallacy. They are then more likely to "recall" new details consistent with childhood sexual abuse. Assumptions that client symptoms point to repressed sexual abuse, even if not stated baldly to the client, will nevertheless be inferred from the phrasing of questions and will bias memory reconstruction.

INFLUENCE OF EXPERTISE

The last stage in memory reconstruction, plausibility checking, is informed by one's beliefs both about the world and about the way memory works.[42] Expert opinion strongly influences especially this latter belief. Once a therapist tells clients that people can suffer sexual abuse, forget it, and then later recover it, the scenario gains plausibility. If asked to think about and discuss any evidence that such a thing ever happened, the more clients discuss such a possibility the more likely they are to produce details that seem to substantiate the suspicion.[43]

PATTERN PERCEPTION

Once clients accept the flawed logic and begin guided imagery, hypnosis, journaling, dream interpretation, and such, they will begin remembering snippets of experience that might be interpretable as sexual abuse. Any scary events that they remember but for which they have source amnesia may be grafted into a growing abuse narrative. Both misattribution and suggestibility help to form the narrative. In trying to reconstruct this event, all their pattern perception and plausibility mechanisms will automatically be at work. Most likely they will eventually "recover" a memory of abuse at the hands of a plausible person. It will often be a close male with whom the client feels emotional distance or conflict and who was alone with them one or more times.

PROPER CLINICAL GUIDELINES

The American Psychological Association Working Group on Investigation of Memories of Childhood Abuse, writing in 1998, rejects the idea that any symptomology is an indicator of child sexual abuse. But they go further, noting,

When clients report what they phenomenologically experience as memories of previously unrecollected trauma, therapists should ... avoid imposing a particular version of reality on these experiences and ... reduce risks of the creation of pseudomemories.... [T]he goal of therapy is not archeology; recollection of trauma is only helpful insofar as it is integrated into a therapy emphasizing improvement of functioning.

Therapists should carefully consider all alternative hypotheses, including that the retrieved material is (a) a reasonably accurate memory of real events; (b) a distorted memory of real events ... due to developmental factors or source contaminations; (c) a confabulation emerging from underlying psychopathology or difficulties with reality testing; (d) a pseudomemory emerging from exposure to suggestions; or (e) a form of self-suggestion emerging from the client's internal suggestive mechanisms.[44]

Thus even if clients already believe they are remembering real sexual abuse, therapists are encouraged to keep an open mind. Such an approach will lessen the danger of falling into the logical fallacy and (mis)influence of expertise warned of above.

RECOVERED MEMORY THERAPY AND MEMORY DISTORTION

Any recovered memory therapy that relies primarily on the client's memory or that of his or her allies—and that does not make early use of memories from persons with contrary viewpoints, public records, common sense, and fact checking—will tend toward memory distortion. A therapist-initiated approach based on observed symptomology without freestanding memories of abuse is an egregious logical and clinical error that encourages confabulation and often leads to pseudomemories. Memories that are freestanding or that were unexpectedly recovered outside of therapy can be corroborated by other evidence at a much higher rate than those recovered in therapy.[45]

HANDLING OF ACCUSATIONS BASED ON THERAPEUTICALLY RECOVERED MEMORY

How should accusations of sexual misconduct based on recovered memories be handled? We can begin by remembering that memory is not a videotape of the past. Normal memory processes can include many types of distortion. Therefore, the best practice is to use physical evidence, other witnesses' accounts, and similar means to corroborate any person's recall and correct for distortion. Therapeutic memory recovery, by contrast, maximizes distortion-generating influences. It can and has generated pseudomemories and distortion, including distortion of the perpetrator's identity, the time and place of the event, and even whether the event actually occurred. As stated, therapeutically recovered memories are less reliable than freestanding memories or spontaneously recovered memories. Also, if the victim understood the abuse as sexual and traumatic when it occurred, and the place it occurred and the offender were continuously present in the victim's life, any recovered memory is less likely to be accurate, since those factors all make forgetting the abuse in the first place highly unlikely. Further, discontinuous memories that were recovered all at once are more reliable than those recovered one detail at a time over an extended period.

Therefore, if accusations warrant further investigation and the accused is notified and asks for an accounting, the accused should be specifically apprised that therapeutically recovered memory is the impetus for the charges. Since such memories tend toward distortion, they should not be transcribed in any public documentation of the investigation (regardless of outcome) unless they are corroborated in detail.

USE OF REMOTE MEMORY IN ASSESSING ACCUSATIONS

Faced with an accusation, what steps should mission agencies take? First, a primary consideration is to distinguish discreetly but clearly between accusations based on freestanding memory and those based on recovered memory. While memory recovery therapy and allied memory self-help workbooks are known to distort memory strongly and even to generate false memory, everyday memory is usually accurate about the most important elements of a memory. Signs of a dependable memory include that the rememberer was paying attention at the initial event, could rehearse and verify information over time, and could always retrieve the memory. But since the recall context can powerfully influence reconstruction, verification of these conditions must occur as unobtrusively as possible. If a mission organization learns of an accusation, it should get as detailed a statement as possible while influencing that detail as little as possible.

It is important to avoid the common mistake of assuming that vivid, detailed, sincere memories of traumatic events are more accurate than other memories. There is no property of a memory *qua* memory that can indicate if it is false. Pseudomemories have been shown to persist, contain great detail, evoke emotional response, and affect behaviors such as food preferences just as real memories do.

The first step is to solicit a statement with careful, non-directive language. Prompt complainants to report what they saw, heard, felt, and so on. Have them specify what they thought those perceptions meant and how they thought about them at the time and over time since then. Have them take their time and rewrite the statement to form a coherent, linear description of the events and the recall process.

After the narrative is as complete and linear as the complainant thinks possible, ask well-planned questions to clarify inconsistency or ambiguity in the complaint or differences between the complaint and other known information. Construct questions carefully, based on a thorough reading of the complaint and other information known to the organization, to limit the possibility of suggestion and misinformation effects. Avoid giving information not supplied or suggesting things not alleged.

Since complainants may not always volunteer that their memory is a result of therapy, the initial report should include answers to general prompts concerning the status of their allegations between the time of the alleged occurrence and the complaint. The questions should be broad enough to include not only discussions with psychotherapists but also pastors, survivor groups, and self-help workbooks about psychology or trauma. Ascertain as clearly as possible whether complainants' memories were freestanding or discontinuous. If discontinuous, how did recovery occur? Was it in therapy or spontaneously? If the complainant did undergo memory recovery therapy, it is useful (if possible) to ascertain whether the therapist ever committed the logical errors concerning symptomology or exerted other undue influence on reconstruction. Thus, contacting the therapist and carefully interviewing them is another reasonable step. The entire process of recording the complainant's allegations and directed interviews based on those allegations should be recorded (at least in writing if not videotaped) for later review, to assess whether any suggestions were planted in the process.

As previous discussion has indicated, no guarantee exists that a memory is accurate. Thus, determining the relative reliability of a memory should only be a small part of an investigation. Both corroboration *and* disconfirmation should be sought. A further psychological issue that may affect an inquiry is confirmation bias. Investigators often have a "hunch" early on and then try to confirm it with their investigation. Appointing different persons or subcommittees to seek corroborative versus disconfirming evidence may help to limit the effects of confirmation bias.

In considering long past events for which not much is discoverable, it is tempting to look at the complaint itself to determine its accuracy. Unfortunately, no known property of the memory itself can differentiate a genuine memory from a pseudomemory.[46] No differences in detail, emotion,[47] durability,[48] or effect on behavior[49] have been observed. If the memory was discontinuous, however, there are properties of the recovery and circumstances recalled that may help determine whether the memory is more likely to be accurate.[50] Memories unexpectedly recovered without therapy have a better corroboration record than therapeutically recovered memories. Memories recalled slowly though a self-help workbook should be considered analogous to therapeutically recovered memory. If the accuser perceived the abuse as traumatic or sexual at the time it occurred, and if the offender and the location of the abuse were still present in the accuser's life after the abuse, it is unlikely that it would have been forgotten. Therefore, if recovered, it is more likely to be a false memory.

Finally, a licensed clinical mental health professional should be a member of or consultant to any investigating committee. Since the judgments this person might make relative to the accusations often involve assessing another's clinical acumen and involve high degrees of scientific literacy in the relevant areas, it would be appropriate for this person to hold doctoral-level supervision and research qualifications.[51]

NOTES

1. Ellen Legault and Jean-Roch Laurence, "Recovered Memories of Childhood Sexual Abuse: Social Worker, Psychologist, and Psychiatrist Reports of Beliefs, Practices, and Cases," *Australian Journal of Clinical and Experimental Hypnosis* 35, no. 2 (2007): 111–33; Jean-Roch Laurence and Shelagh Freedman, "Research Brief: Number of Clients at Risk for Developing False Memories of Abuse: Addendum to Legualt and Laurence (2007)," *Crime Scene* 16, no. 1 (2009): 15–16.

2. By then use of suggestive memory recovery techniques by doctoral-level therapists had already declined to below 25 percent. See Scott O. Lilienfeld et al., "Why Many Clinical Psychologists Are Resistant to Evidence-Based Practice: Root Causes and Constructive Remedies," *Clinical Psychology Review* 33, no. 7 (November 2013): 883–900, doi:10.1016/j.cpr.2012.09.008.

3. Paul Simpson, *Second Thoughts* (Nashville, Tenn.: Thomas Nelson, 1996). For details of a recovered memory case involving an evangelical mission and a selective summary of major inquiries in missions organizations that supported the use of recovered memory in the 1990s and 2000s, see Robert J. Priest and Esther E. Cordill, "Christian Communities and 'Recovered Memories' of Abuse," *Christian Scholar's Review* 41, no. 4 (2012): 381–400.

4. Elke Geraerts et al., "The Reality of Recovered Memories," *Psychological Science* 18, no. 7 (2007): 564–69.

5. Daniel J. Simons and Daniel T. Levin, "Failure to Detect Changes to People during a Real-World Interaction," *Psychonomic Bulletin and Review* 5, no. 4 (December 1998): 644–49, doi:10.3758/BF03208840; Daniel J Simons et al., "Evidence for Preserved Representations in Change Blindness," *Consciousness and Cognition* 11, no. 1 (March 2002): 78–97, doi:10.1006/ccog.2001.0533.

6. Peter L. Pirolli and John R. Anderson, "The Role of Practice in Fact Retrieval," *Journal of Experimental Psychology: Learning, Memory, and Cognition* 11, no. 1 (1985): 136–53.

7. Fergus I. M. Craik and Robert S. Lockhart, "Levels of Processing: A Framework for Memory Research," *Journal of Verbal Learning and Verbal Behavior* 11, no. 6 (1972): 671–84.

8. Fergus I. M. Craik and Endel Tulving, "Depth of Processing and the Retention of Words in Episodic Memory," *Journal of Experimental Psychology: General* 104, no. 3 (1975): 268–94, doi:10.1037/0096-3445.104.3.268.

9. Larry R. Squire and Stuart M. Zola, "Structure and Function of Declarative and Nondeclarative Memory Systems," *Proceedings of the National Academy of Sciences of the United States of America* 93, no. 24 (1996): 13515–22; Larry R. Squire, Craig E. L. Stark, and Robert E. Clark, "The Medial Temporal Lobe," *Annual Review of Neuroscience* 27 (January 2004): 279–306, doi:10.1146/annurev.neuro.27.070203.144130.

10. Natalie C. Tronson and Jane R. Taylor, "Molecular Mechanisms of Memory Reconsolidation," *Nature Reviews: Neuroscience* 8, no. 4 (April 2007): 262–75, doi:10.1038/nrn2090.

11. John R. Anderson, "Verbal and Propositional Representation of Sentences in Immediate and Long-Term Memory," *Journal of Verbal Learning and Verbal Behavior* 13 (1974): 149–62.

12. David E. Meyer and Roger W. Schvaneveldt, "Facilitation in Recognizing Pairs of Words: Evidence of a Dependence between Retrieval Operations," *Journal of Experimental Psychology* 90, no. 2 (1971): 227.

13. Michael J. Watkins and Endel Tulving, "Episodic Memory: When Recognition Fails," *Journal of Experimental Psychology: General* 104, no. 1 (1975): 5.

14. Endel Tulving and Zena Pearlstone, "Availability Versus Accessibility of Information in Memory for Words," *Journal of Verbal Learning and Verbal Behavior* 5, no. 4 (1966): 381–91.

15. D. R. Godden and A. D. Baddeley, "Context-Dependent Memory in Two Natural Environments: On Land and Underwater," *British Journal of Psychology* 66, no. 3 (1975): 325–31.

16. Donald W. Goodwin et al., "Alcohol and Recall: State-Dependent Effects in Man," *Science* 163, no. 3873 (1969): 1358–60.

17. Eric Eich, "Searching for Mood Dependent Memory," *Psychological Science* 6, no. 2 (1995): 67–75.

18. P. H. Blaney, "Affect and Memory: A Review," *Psychological Bulletin* 99, no. 2 (March 1986): 229–46.

19. Mood-incongruent memory yields enhanced recall of items with *opposite* meaning from one's current mood, aiding mood regulation. Mood regulation further highlights that memory's primary function is behavioral guidance, not furnishing conscious knowledge of the past. See Gerrod Parrott and Matthew P. Spackman, "Emotion and Memory," in *Handbook of Emotions*, ed. Michael Lewis and Jeanette M. Haviland-Jones, 2nd ed. (New York: Guilford Press, 2000), 476–90.

20. James J. Gibson, *Perception of the Visual World* (Boston: Houghton Mifflin, 1950).

21. Elizabeth F. Loftus and John C. Palmer, "Reconstruction of Automobile Destruction: An Example of the Interaction between Language and Memory," *Journal of Verbal Learning and Verbal Behavior* 13 (October 1974): 585–89, doi:10.1016/S0022-5371(74)80011-3.

22. Kathryn A. Braun, Rhiannon Ellis, and Elizabeth F. Loftus, "Make My Memory: How Advertising Can Change Our Memories of the Past," *Psychology and Marketing* 19, no. 1 (2002): 1–23. Bugs Bunny is a Warner Brothers character, not a Disney character.

23. James Ost et al., "Familiarity Breeds Distortion: The Effects of Media Exposure on False Reports Concerning Media Coverage of the Terrorist Attacks in London on 7 July 2005," *Memory* 16, no. 1 (January 2008): 76–85, doi:10.1080/09658210701723323.

24. Lauren French, Rachel Sutherland, and Maryanne Garry, "Discussion Affects Memory for True and False Childhood Events," *Applied Cognitive Psychology* 20, no. 5 (July 2006): 671–80, doi:10.1002/acp.1219; Stefanie J. Sharman, Charles G. Manning, and Maryanne Garry, "Explain This: Explaining Childhood Events Inflates Confidence for Those Events," *Applied Cognitive Psychology* 19, no. 1 (January 2005): 67–74, doi:10.1002/acp.1041; Christopher

M. Heaps and Michael Nash, "Comparing Recollective Experience in True and False Autobiographical Memories," *Journal of Experimental Psychology: Learning, Memory, and Cognition* 27, no. 4 (2001): 920–30, doi:10.1037//0278-7393.27.4.920.

25. Maryanne Garry et al., "Imagination Inflation: Imagining a Childhood Event Inflates Confidence that It Occurred," *Psychonomic Bulletin & Review* 3, no. 2 (1996): 208–14.

26. C. A. Morgan et al., "Misinformation Can Influence Memory for Recently Experienced, Highly Stressful Events," *International Journal of Law and Psychiatry* 36, no. 1 (2013): 11–17, doi:10.1016/j.ijlp.2012.11.002.

27. Daniel L. Schacter, "Illusory Memories: A Cognitive Neuroscience Analysis," *Proceedings of the National Academy of Sciences of the United States of America* 93, no. 24 (November 26, 1996): 13527–33.

28. Daniel L. Schacter, *The Seven Sins of Memory: How the Mind Forgets and Remembers* (Boston: Houghton Mifflin, 2001).

29. John R. Anderson and Lael J. Schooler, "Reflections of the Environment in Memory," *Psychological Science* 2, no. 6 (November 1991): 396–408, doi:10.1111/j.1467-9280.1991 .tb00174.x; John R. Anderson and Lael J. Schooler, "The Adaptive Nature of Memory," in *Handbook of Memory,* ed. Endel Tulving and Fergus I. M. Craik (New York: Oxford Univ. Press, 2000), 557–70.

30. Deborah Davis and Elizabeth L. Loftus, "The Scientific Status of 'Repressed' and 'Recovered' Memories of Sexual Abuse," in *Psychological Science in the Courtroom: Consensus and Controversy,* ed. Jennifer L. Skeem, Kevin S. Douglas, and Scott O. Lilienfeld (New York: Guilford Press, 2009), 55–79.

31. Daniel L. Schacter, Scott A. Guerin, and Peggy L. St. Jacques, "Memory Distortion: An Adaptive Perspective," *Trends in Cognitive Sciences* 15, no. 10 (October 2011): 467–74, doi:10.1016/j.tics.2011.08.004; Daniel L. Schacter, Joan Y. Chiao, and Jason P. Mitchell, "The Seven Sins of Memory," *Annals of the New York Academy of Sciences* 1001 (October 2003): 226–39, doi:10.1196/annals.1279.012; Schacter, *Seven Sins of Memory: How the Mind Forgets and Remembers.*

32. Roger Brown and James Kulik, "Flashbulb Memories," *Cognition* 5, no. 1 (January 1977): 73–99, doi:10.1016/0010-0277(77)90018-X.

33. H. Schmolck, E. A. Buffalo, and Larry R. Squire, "Memory Distortions Develop over Time: Recollections of the O. J. Simpson Trial Verdict after 15 and 32 Months," *Psychological Science* 11, no. 1 (2000): 39–45.

34. Ulric Neisser and Nicole Harsch, "Phantom Flashbulbs: False Recollections of Hearing the News about Challenger," in *Affect and Accuracy in Recall,* ed. Eugene Winograd and Ulric Neisser (New York: Cambridge Univ. Press, 1992), 9–31.

35. Jennifer M. Talarico and David C. Rubin, "Confidence, Not Consistency, Characterizes Flashbulb Memories," *Psychological Science* 14, no. 5 (2003): 455–61.

36. Elizabeth J. Marsh, "Retelling Is Not the Same as Recalling: Implications for Memory," *Current Directions in Psychological Science* 16, no. 1 (2007): 16–20.

37. Lawrence Patihis et al., "Are the 'Memory Wars' Over? A Scientist-Practitioner Gap in Beliefs about Repressed Memory," *Psychological Science* 20, no. 10 (2013): 1–12.

38. For the differences between retrospective, prospective, and corroborative studies of memory, see David R. Dunaetz, "Recovered Memories and Accusations of Sexual Abuse: A Review of Scientific Research Relevant to Missionary Contexts," pp. 169–88, in this volume.

39. For a study that includes people with freestanding memories and very low standards for corroboration, see Judith L. Herman and Emily Schatzow, "Recovery and Verification of Memories of Childhood Sexual Trauma," *Psychoanalytic Psychology* 4, no. 1 (1987): 1–14, doi:10.1037/h0079126.

40. Elke Geraerts et al., "Forgetting of Prior Remembering in Persons Reporting Recovered Memories of Childhood Sexual Abuse," *Psychological Science* 17, no. 11 (November 2006): 1002–8, doi:10.1111/j.1467-9280.2006.01819.x.

41. French, Sutherland, and Garry, "Discussion Affects Memory"; Heaps and Nash, "Comparing Recollective Experience"; Sharman, Manning, and Garry, "Explain This."

42. Julia T. O'Sullivan and Mark L. Howe, "Metamemory and Memory Construction," *Consciousness and Cognition* 4, no. 1 (March 1995): 104–10, doi:10.1006/ccog.1995.1011.

43. French, Sutherland, and Garry, "Discussion Affects Memory"; Heaps and Nash, "Comparing Recollective Experience"; Sharman, Manning, and Garry, "Explain This."

44. Judith L. Alpert et al., "Final Conclusions of the American Psychological Association Working Group on Investigation of Memories of Child Abuse," *Psychology, Public Policy, and Law* 4, no. 4 (1998): 933–40, doi:10.1037//1076-8971.4.4.933.

45. Elke Geraerts et al., "The Reality of Recovered Memories: Corroborating Continuous and Discontinuous Memories of Childhood Sexual Abuse," *Psychological Science* 18, no. 7 (July 1, 2007): 564–68, doi:10.1111/j.1467-9280.2007.01940.x.

46. Daniel M. Bernstein and Elizabeth F. Loftus, "How to Tell If a Particular Memory Is True or False," *Perspectives on Psychological Science* 4, no. 4 (July 2009): 370–74, doi:10.1111/j.1745-6924.2009.01140.x.

47. Cara Laney and Elizabeth F. Loftus, "Emotional Content of True and False Memories," *Memory* 16, no. 5 (January 2008): 500–516, doi:10.1080/09658210802065939.

48. Cara Laney et al., "The Persistence of False Beliefs," *Acta Psychologica* 129, no. 1 (September 2008): 190–97, doi:10.1016/j.actpsy.2008.05.010; Bi Zhu et al., "Brief Exposure to Misinformation Can Lead to Long-Term False Memories," *Applied Cognitive Psychology* 26 (2012): 301–7; Elke Geraerts et al., "Lasting False Beliefs and Their Behavioral Consequences," *Psychological Science* 19, no. 8 (August 2008): 749–53, doi:10.1111/j.1467-9280.2008.02151.x.

49. Cara Laney et al, "Asparagus, a Love Story," *Experimental Psychology* 55, no. 5 (January 1, 2008): 291–300, doi:10.1027/1618-3169.55.5.291; Daniel M Bernstein et al., "False Beliefs

about Fattening Foods Can Have Healthy Consequences," *Proceedings of the National Academy of Sciences of the United States of America* 102, no. 39 (2005): 13724–31.

50. Richard J. McNally and Elke Geraerts, "A New Solution to the Recovered Memory Debate," *Perspectives on Psychological Science* 4, no. 2 (March 2009): 126–34.

51. Patihis et al., "Are the 'Memory Wars' Over?"; Lilienfeld et al., "Why Many Clinical Psychologists Are Resistant."

PART THREE

FORUM ON SEXUAL ORIENTATION AND MISSION:
An Evangelical Discussion

INTRODUCTION

FORUM ON SEXUAL ORIENTATION AND MISSION:
An Evangelical Discussion

DWIGHT P. BAKER

The person who thinks that the issue of same-sex attraction is a simple and straightforward matter may safely be judged not to have thought deeply about it or to have dealt with friends and family members whose lives are embroiled with it. The issue quickly plunges to the depths of who we are as persons and whose we are. What is the attitude of the church toward LGBTQ persons? What should it be? Is there a gap between "is" and "should be"? If there is a discrepancy, in which direction does the current between them flow? How can the gap be bridged? Or can it? Is the distance between more like a gulf, too wide to bridge and with only frail rowboats for braving treacherous seas and crashing breakers? Are the winds so high and the waters so deep that either to go or to come is to court disaster?

What about the LGBTQ community—or, in evangelicals' favored formulation, LGBTQ individuals—and mission? At the most basic level, what about mission *to* persons with same-sex attraction? What shape and configuration does Gospel witness take to be Good News to them? Is it a question of "Change your orientation first, then we can talk"? Must the LGBTQ person first become straight, after which, possibly, the weightier matters of new birth, justification, and sanctification can be considered? Is that the way the grace of God presents itself in Scripture, in church history, in our own lives?

What of same-sex attraction as a matter for missionary member care and for care of missionary families? Various estimates can be found for the number of missionaries—and diverse definitions of the word "missionary," also—but by any accounting, missionaries and missionary families constitute a sizable group of people. Statistically, therefore, we can expect to find a significant presence of persons with same-sex attraction within and related to the members of the missionary community: missionaries themselves experiencing struggles with their own sexual orientation; children of missionaries; brothers and sisters, members of missionaries' immediate families; members of their extended families, nephews, nieces, uncles, aunts, brothers- and sisters-in-law. Answering the call to missionary service is no guarantee of a smooth pathway to glory.

How are evangelical mission agencies ministering to the needs and concerns of the mission community? Is sex on the agenda? Are issues of sexual orientation and attraction being addressed with candor, sensitivity, and insight in ways that are helpful to Gospel servants who are themselves pilgrims on the way, persons whose own journey is not yet complete and whose sight, therefore, is still imperfect?

What role is there for LGBTQ persons in the church and in Christ's mission? Or is that better phrased: Is there any role at all—of even the most minimal sort—for LGBTQ persons? Is that a question that can be answered categorically? Or do categorical answers necessarily misconstrue and mislead? By contrast, are categorical answers the only thing that can rescue a rowboat in danger of sinking beneath raging waves?

These concerns and more are raised in the evangelical forum on sexual orientation and mission that follows. Missiological anthropologist Sherwood Lingenfelter frames questions that are intended to clarify the current debate. His presentation is personal and familial; it is also ecclesial and Gospel centered. Quoting Mark Yarhouse, he asks, "To whom do these young people belong?" Calling upon the resources of biblical studies, theology, ethics, anthropology, and what we have learned about hermeneutics, he presses the questions of whether there is a place in the church and in mission for persons with same-sex attraction.

Thirteen evangelical scholars—with expertise and experience in anthropology, sociology, psychology, biblical studies, systematic theology, ethics, practical theology, university administration, missiology, and mission agency administration—were invited to serve as discussants. Their observations are of high caliber, offering pointed questions and suggesting even more fields to bring into the discussion. As one would hope, the tone throughout is irenic and respectful. Our thanks to them.

And our thanks to Sherwood Lingenfelter, who opened the discussion at major personal investment of himself and his family. He concludes the discussion with a response to his interlocutors.

Take, read, reflect, and carry the discussion forward. But also be informed, act in the light of the Gospel, and in doing so, serve the living Christ.

11

GAY AND LESBIAN CHRISTIANS:
Framing Questions and Clarifying the Debate about a Place in Church and Mission for Evangelical LGBTQ Youth

SHERWOOD G. LINGENFELTER

The issues at the heart of this chapter are best told in the story of Nicodemus, son of a conservative Baptist pastor, who accepted Christ as a twelve-year-old boy and was baptized by his father. Active in Young Life while in high school, he enrolled in a state university, and while earning his B.A. degree, he was deeply involved in a parachurch ministry on that campus. After graduating, Nicodemus joined the staff of that ministry and has been serving effectively up to the time of the writing of this chapter in 2013.

During the last five years Nicodemus has struggled deeply with his sexual identity; while he occasionally dated girls, he had no romantic interest in any, and he found himself strongly attracted to young men in his ministry group. Knowing that any public expression of these attractions would destroy his ministry, Nicodemus secretly began looking at male pornography on the Internet. Yet he had no peace about this activity. Each time he yielded to the temptation, he felt dirty, guilty, and deceitful, and crippled in his daily devotional life and ministry.

Finally, Nicodemus shared his struggle with one of the other staff members and asked for help to overcome his growing addiction to male pornography.

They invited one other man to join them, and together they covenanted to pray for deliverance and to hold Nicodemus accountable. They together agreed that Nicodemus would not use his iPad or computer without one of them being present. While this has helped Nicodemus deal with the pornography, he finds that even walking on campus brings him into contact with men to whom he is attracted. In despair, he has cried out to Jesus, and to his pastor father, for love and help. He has not yielded to temptation to have a sexual affair with another man, yet he has them all the time in his mind. His father and mother were totally surprised and shocked by what Nicodemus revealed to them, and they are prayerfully seeking counsel and the wisdom of God as to how to respond out of love for their son.

The challenge facing evangelical Christians today is how do we love, mentor, and guide committed Christian youth, students, and graduates of our colleges and universities who have same-sex attraction and are passionate about following Jesus and serving God? Mark Yarhouse, a clinical psychologist at Regent University, notes that homosexual orientation is reported for at least 2–3 percent of the U.S. population, but in cities it is closer to 10 percent.[1] If we consider only the Protestant and Catholic college and university campuses in the United States, more than 28,000 students (2 percent of the more than 1,425,000 students) in any given year experience struggles similar to that of Nicodemus.[2] Given the large number of evangelical and Catholic students in private and public universities, the population is much larger.

I have experienced this challenge in a very personal way. In 2001, at the age of thirty-six, my only daughter, Jennifer, who graduated with a Bible major from Moody Bible Institute and from Biola University with a doctorate in psychology, announced to my wife and me that she is lesbian. She and her Latina partner have since adopted two infant boys, who are now our grandsons. My daughter Jennifer's story is in part, and perhaps in whole, my story on this question. Without our journey together, I would not have written this chapter.[3]

Before my daughter "came out" to us in 2001, I was much more sure of my traditional position on gay issues. Jennifer's testimony, her journey through Moody and Biola, and her continuing commitment to know and follow Christ as a lesbian has had a profound effect on my thinking and emotions as a father. At the same time, while serving as provost at Fuller Theological Seminary, I was challenged by students to create a more compassionate and caring community for the men and women enrolled at Fuller who have same-sex attraction and who experience critical and hostile language and feelings of fear and oppression because of their sexual orientation.

WHAT ARE THE ESSENTIAL QUESTIONS?

Four topics and related questions have framed my research and writing on this subject. The most common queries by Christians are, What are the causes of same sex attraction? and Is it possible to change from a gay to a straight orientation? Second, and the core question for evangelicals, is, What does Scripture say about homosexual behavior? Third, many evangelicals are asking, Is it possible to be Christian and gay? Some, like Jennifer and Nicodemus, profess openly that they love Jesus, they accept the Gospel message that salvation is by faith alone, and their hope is in the death and resurrection of Jesus Christ. Others in evangelical churches reject them and say that a gay or lesbian who is not celibate cannot be a Christian.

The question perhaps most important to people with same-sex attraction is, What implication does my sexual orientation have for my identity? Growing up in a context where people like them are called names (fag, queer, homo, and other terms of disparagement), many ask, "Who and what am I?" The word "homosexual" has become offensive language both to those who find themselves attracted to persons of the same sex, and to their straight friends in the colleges and universities of America. Much of the literature on this topic uses the term homosexual, but, with the exception of quoting these sources, I will not use it in this chapter out of respect for the people who find it offensive. I will use same- and opposite-sex attraction to refer to sexual feelings and emotions, and for the identities of persons with same-sex attraction, I will use gay or LGBTQ (lesbian, gay, bisexual, trans-sexual, and queer)—words that people with same-sex attraction use for themselves.[4]

In the pages that follow I explore all four of these topics in greater depth. My assumption is that the factors driving current evangelical conversations are multiplex. The etiology of same-sex attraction is so complex that the best current research is inconclusive; the cultural and political pressures upon the church are so intense that they cloud our thinking, research, and interpretation of data; the alternatives presented to us by the secular society are without moral compass, inadequate biblically and theologically, and yet we are hard pressed to engage meaningfully with them.

It is not my intention, nor do I have the expertise, to answer these questions. Rather, the objective of this chapter is to argue that no single person, or small group of people, is able to answer for the church, and that what is needed is a commitment on the part of evangelical scholars and church leaders to gather the best minds and diverse viewpoints for extended conversations together to seek appropriate responses for our time, for our LGBTQ children, and for the generations of evangelicals who will follow us. I do not know what those responses will be, but I trust in the power of God and the work of the Holy Spirit to teach us through his body, the church.

THE MOST FREQUENT QUESTIONS—CAUSE AND CHANGE

In the nineteenth century the common explanations for same-sex attraction and behavior were of two kinds, either criminal behavior or a medical problem.[5] The criminal view assumed moral choices based upon a sinful lifestyle. Medical explanations included psychological immaturity or various pathologies including genetic, hormonal, or emotional disorders, the latter deriving from faulty parenting. In the 1960s my evangelical community took a common sense view of such behavior. We assumed same-sex behaviors were conscious choices, that is, spiritual rebellion by people we presumed were driven by a "playboy" or "playgirl" mentality, leading to all kinds of sexual promiscuity. Such views were validated by lurid stories of gay sexuality in the pre-HIV/AIDS era in cities such as San Francisco, Hollywood, New York, and Amsterdam, and further enhanced by the open sensuality of Gay Pride parades and other public displays of same-sex affection shown on television and in other news media.

In 1974 the American Psychiatric Association and the American Psychological Association adopted resolutions rejecting the notion that homosexual orientations were a form of mental illness.[6] In spite of these resolutions, Stanton Jones notes that social conservatives persist in viewing homosexuality as a mental illness of psychological or spiritual origin, and that "persons could change their orientation if they simply tried hard enough." Jones concedes that these views are rightly rejected by scholars of human sexuality, yet he also notes that after three decades of medical, genetic, and social science research, no single explanation for same-sex orientation has been found.[7]

The question of the etiology of same-sex attraction has not been, and perhaps cannot be, separated from the political debates for and against LGBTQ people and behaviors. In his critical review of research about causes of same-sex and bisexual orientation, Jones suggests that many of these studies are compromised by relying upon voluntary rather than random population samples, and in some cases by the political bias of the researchers. Yet, he concludes, "Contrary to the assumptions of many social conservatives, biology does appear to play a modest part in determining sexual orientation. Contrary to the assumptions of many social progressives, [however,] psychological and environmental variables also appear to play at least a modest part in determining sexual orientation."[8]

Yarhouse concurs with Jones that the causes of same-sex orientation are complex, and that we cannot state with any degree of certainty which of these many variables are the critical ones for any single person. Both Jones and Yarhouse conclude that there are multiple influencing factors, "multiple homosexualities," and significant differences in their expression between men and women.[9] Further, same-sex attraction or orientation is not something people choose. But they do, Yarhouse states, have choices to make about behavior and identity.[10]

Can someone change sexual orientation? After reviewing both psychoanalytic and Christian recovery ministry interventions, Yarhouse concludes that "most people will not change their orientation, if by that we mean moving from 'completely gay' to 'completely straight.' But change can occur along a continuum." Change, for those who experience it, is usually a decrease in same-sex attraction, that is, lessening of temptation to seek a same-sex partner and, sometimes, an increase in contentment with a life of chastity. A smaller number of persons may actually experience an increase in opposite-sex attraction, whether to a spouse or to another person.[11]

Yarhouse and Jones also conclude that the risk that a person may be harmed by seeking to change is minimal, provided that she or he is adequately informed in advance of the limitations of such ministries or therapy. This conclusion is challenged, however, by the study of the American Psychological Association task force cited above and by the testimony of numerous individuals who have undergone reparative therapy. On June 19, 2013, the leaders of Exodus International, the oldest and largest Christian ministry doing reparative therapy, apologized publicly to their constituency for "ignorance that perpetuated hurt"; the stigmatization of parents; and the pain, shame, and guilt felt by individuals in therapy when their sexual attractions did not change.[12]

WHAT DOES SCRIPTURE SAY ABOUT LGBTQ BEHAVIOR?

I will not presume to try to provide an answer to the question, What does Scripture say about LGBTQ behavior? My purpose here is to highlight issues that are debated by biblical scholars and theologians on the subject. I will not argue in support of any of their positions, but rather try to discern the nature of the debate and frame the issues in a way that I hope will be productive for future conversations.

1 Corinthians 6:9–10 and 1 Timothy 1:8–10

For me the big surprise during my research was that Bible scholars have only minor disagreements about what the words of Scripture say, regardless of their position on the topic; what they do disagree about is the interpretation of those words in context and the theological implications of what is said. For example, in considering 1 Corinthians 6:9–10 and 1 Timothy 1:8–10, my sources all agree that *arsenokoitai* is a combination of Greek words *arseno*, "male," and *koites*, "beds." They note that this word appears nowhere in Classical Greek literature, but appears to be drawn from the Septuagint translation of Leviticus 18:22 and 20:13, which refer to a man who beds another man, as a man beds a woman.

Interpreting on the basis of cultural context, Robin Scroggs and Dale Martin argue that Paul is referring specifically to the widespread Greek practice of men of high class and rank having intercourse with slave boys in their households. David Garland reports this same material in his notes on the text, but rejects it as not relevant to his interpretation. Scroggs further notes that 1 Timothy 1:8–10 connects the two categories just mentioned with a third, the slave dealer who sells boys for prostitution.[13]

Robert Gagnon, David Malick, and David Peterson, along with Garland, reject the argument that Paul is referring only to the common Greek practice of sex between master and slave boys. Gagnon also rejects Scroggs's interpretation of 1 Timothy, arguing that the list in Timothy merely corresponds to the order of commandments 5–9 of the Ten Commandments. Of these, Gagnon's presentation is the most persuasive, gathering all possible textual evidence to show by reasonable inference that Paul is condemning all same-sex male relations, and particularly what has been labeled homosexual behavior in the twentieth century.[14]

The difference of opinion can be summed up this way: The Scriptures speak clearly against males bedding males; the debate is whether these texts are limited in scope, referencing Greek high class married or unmarried men bedding subordinate males (an abuse of power over vulnerable persons), or are universal in application, applying to males with same-sex attraction bedding each other.

Leviticus and Romans

The debates about the Leviticus texts and Romans 1 are more complex and open to wider interpretation. Dan Via argues that the Levitical prohibition against homosexual practice must be understood in the cultural context of the whole of Levitical law. He concludes that the law against a man bedding another man focuses on four critical issues: out-of-bounds uncleanness (18:22; 20:13), compromising the purity of male heirs to ancestral land, separating Israel from pagan nations (18:3, 24), and assaulting male honor. Via also notes, along with many others, that the only references to such behavior in the Old Testament are Genesis 19 and Judges 19. In both of these cases, gangs of men, presumably married and unmarried, seek to gang rape vulnerable men.[15]

Gagnon counters that the Levitical code views all male/male intercourse as a "first-tier" sexual offense. Further, he argues from Ezekiel, Jude, and 2 Peter that sexual licentiousness and abomination characterize all male/male sex, and that Sodom (Gen. 19) and the case in Judges are examples of such behavior. Peterson and Donald Wold agree that Leviticus is about holiness, and any act of a man lying with a man is unholy.[16]

Gagnon, Garland, and Malick argue that Romans 1 is about perversion of nature, and Malick concludes that the text "describes homosexuality as an evil in itself."[17] Via argues that the sin in Romans 1 is rebellion, the "foolish human choice" of rejecting God's truth, and that "same sex relations are not so much sin itself—or at least *the* sin—as the consequence of sin, what God gave people up to."[18] Scroggs proposes that Romans 1:24–27 refers to married men who, in their lust, "exchanged" or "gave up" their natural sexual relations with women and were consumed with passion for one another.[19]

CLARIFYING THE ISSUES

The sources I found most helpful for clarifying the debate were *Homosexuality and the Bible: Two Views*, by Dan Via and Robert Gagnon, and *Bible, Gender, Sexuality: Reframing the Church's Debate on Same-Sex Relationships*, by James Brownson. Via argues on interpretive grounds of context that Scripture, reason, and experience suggest grounds for the justifiability of monogamous homosexual practice. Gagnon counters that there is no biblical alternative to heterosexual marriage or celibacy.[20] Brownson critiques the moral logic of both traditionalist and revisionist readings of Scripture, and then through a broader exploration of biblical texts on sexuality proposes alternative frames of moral logic.[21]

Finally, John Goldingay and colleagues in the Anglican Communion, taking a traditionalist position, have presented a persuasive argument against same-sex marriage by examining gender, sexuality, and marriage from the whole of Scripture. Citing New Testament texts that reference God's creation of male and female, and God's ordaining of marriage between them for the purpose of procreation and godly offspring (Gospels and Paul), they conclude that the blessing of same-sex unions is untenable in light of Scripture.[22] Citing critical reviews of the literature on causes of same-sex attraction, and the ambiguity of current evidence about causation and possible change, they conclude that same-sex attraction is not "natural" and should not be attributed to God's creation.[23] This last point is widely debated by those who are sympathetic to LGBTQ persons, some of whom see God's creation through a critical realist lens in which the Garden of Eden does not explain paleontology, cycles of life and death, the extinction of species, genetic variability, chemical mechanisms in genes that produce the human fetus, and the diversity resulting from these processes.

What does Scripture say about same-sex behavior? Are we willing to bring the biblical scholars and church leaders who disagree on these matters to meet together with committed Christian scholars in anthropology, sociology, biology, psychology, medical science, philosophy, and ethics, and to ask that they together grapple with these questions?

IS SEXUAL ORIENTATION AT THE CORE OF HUMAN IDENTITY?

For more than two decades, anthropologists have given particular attention to the cultural formation of "identity." From that research, they have discovered significant diversity in cultural conceptions of identity and the values associated with them.[24] Anthropologist Jenell Paris summarizes the way gender and sexual orientation are expressed differently around the globe and states that American sexual identity categories—heterosexual/homosexual, gay/straight—are not universal, but rather a creation of our medical professionals in the twentieth century.[25] For some Christians, this social construction elevates those who are straight as being somehow morally superior in nature and substance. Paris argues that most cultures do not have this distinction. Rather, people are male and female, with gender roles in social life and sexual behavior for procreation.

Paris further argues that the affirmation of heterosexuality among American evangelicals creates a privileged identity for some and a subordinate, unprivileged, and stigmatized identity for gays; the markers "gay," "queer," and "bisexual" illustrate the subordination of people with these feelings.[26] For men such as Nicodemus and Justin Lee, same-sex attraction is a biochemical, brain-based reality. When they see an attractive, even seductive woman, their brains and body chemistry produce no chemical response; but when they see an attractive man, they experience the same chemical reaction most men have to seductive female bodies. This becomes a grave cultural liability in cultures like that of the United States that place high value on the "straight" male identity. To paraphrase Lee, "I didn't want it, and I can't get rid of it, and everybody condemns me for it."[27] The biochemical experience of lesbians is different. Lisa Diamond speaks of fluidity, nonexclusivity, and attraction to person, not gender, as part of their experience, yet they share in common the social stigma of rejection and alienation because of their same-sex attractions.[28]

Yarhouse's research suggests that Paris is correct in her assessment of this "chasm" and its distortion of human identity as created in the image of God. Yarhouse concludes that young people with same-sex attraction in the United States are in a process of identity formation that is socially constructed. He distinguishes three phases or tiers in that process:

- *same-sex attraction*: having sexual feelings about others of the same sex, possibly along with bisexual or opposite-sex attraction
- *homosexual orientation*: being attracted to the same sex alone, with no feelings toward the opposite sex
- *centering on a gay identity*: making the sociocultural category of "gay-ness" central to one's self-identity and affiliation[29]

Acknowledging that many gays find this to be "splitting hairs," Yarhouse sees value in keeping these variables distinct and suggests that young people experience a process of identity formation that begins with same-sex attraction combined with ambivalence about why they are different and who they really are. Paris would argue that this ambivalence is in fact a product of the wider social context in which individuals face intense pressure to appear heterosexual. As they struggle to understand their feelings and how they differ from their gender peers, young people often go through a period of time in which they try on different roles. Dating with opposite-sex persons is a common strategy, but it often occurs at the same time young people are seeking friendships with sympathetic persons of the same sex. Yarhouse suggests that young people begin with an identity dilemma, move on to identity development, and end in an identity synthesis as gay, lesbian, bisexual, or transgendered persons.

Perhaps the most important insight for mission and the church is what Yarhouse terms the "Gay Script."[30] Summarizing sources by gay and lesbian authors, he characterizes the script as follows:

- Same-sex attraction is "natural."
- Same-sex attraction is the real you (discovery).
- Your sexual attraction is the core of who you are.
- The natural extension of that core is to engage in sexual behaviors that are natural.
- Self-actualization consists of homosexual behavior, thereby fulfilling your identity.

This script is the solution provided by LGBTQ activists to the identity crisis of young people with same-sex attraction, and they proactively encourage youth in this period of crisis to "self-actualize," that is, to enjoy sexual intimacy and to join with others in celebrating their newfound sexual identity.

Yarhouse suggests that for Christians there is a possible alternative script:[31]

- Same-sex attraction is one of many human experiences.
- Sex does not (or should not) define your identity (agreeing with Paris).
- You may choose to integrate your experience into a gay identity, or you may choose to center your identity on other experiences.
- The most compelling aspect of personhood is identity in Christ.

The strength of Yarhouse's alternative is that he validates the emotional and physiological feelings of LGBTQ persons—their biochemistry is real, their attractions are powerful—and at the same time he recognizes that our sexual drive is not the most compelling aspect of human life. The most compelling aspect of personhood is the "image of" and "longing for" God, which is fulfilled in our relationship to and identity in Christ. Yet this is not the script presented by most evangelical churches.

CAN A PERSON BE CHRISTIAN AND GAY?

To the question, Can a person be Christian and gay? many evangelicals would answer with a resounding, No! Yarhouse and Jones surveyed students in three schools affiliated with the Council for Christian Colleges and Universities (CCCU). They found that students who identified as sexual minorities had several identity scripts—scripts around Christ or some other facet of who they were. They noted, however, that the colleges' negative atmosphere related to sexual minorities pushed such students toward the gay script. For example, only three of the twelve CCCU schools they contacted would allow students to participate in the survey. Yarhouse concludes that Christian colleges and churches do not want to talk about this and seek to deny the existence of these youth in their communities. He then poses what I believe is the most important question: "To whom do these young people belong?"[32]

Yarhouse notes that the gay community claims all who have same-sex attraction, and they get very angry when they lose some to the "hostile" evangelical community. We in the church, on the other hand, expel these folks and hand them over to gay unbelievers. As a case in point, Justin Lee narrates how many evangelicals refused to accept him with his same-sex attraction, insisting that he become heterosexual and even isolating him, although he was celibate.[33] On this issue, Yarhouse and Lee independently arrive at the same conclusion: we need to embrace Christian young people with same-sex attraction as our own and to work out ways to make clear their calling and place in Christian community.

Cultures marked by the Protestant tradition have embraced romantic love, sexual fulfillment, and marriage as the norm for Christian living, and they have relegated singles to the pejoratively labeled statuses of "old maid" and "uncommitted bachelor."[34] In these Protestant traditions, persons unable to commit to marriage are marginalized in family and society, and often find themselves living in isolation and loneliness.

Within the Roman Catholic tradition, monastic communities have provided havens for men and women with same-sex attraction, in which a religious rule of life, including occupation, relationship, and worship, supported both the sacramental tradition of chastity and a community of confession and penance for those who failed to uphold the rule. Nevertheless, in America the personal journey of people with same-sex attraction has been difficult in Catholic religious communities as well. Catholic scholars note that integrating gay applicants into an American Catholic seminary or communal life has strong parallels to integrating ethnic and racial minorities—offensive language, a climate of superiority/inferiority, and policies that discriminate. The approach to celibacy taught by the Catholic Church has been one of "human love competing for divine love." Lesbian nuns are rejecting this interpretation for one that emphasizes instead "developing close, intimate friendships," rather than sexual love.[35]

The late Henri Nouwen was a Catholic priest who suffered from same-sex attraction over his full adult life. He kept his commitment to celibacy, yet Yancey notes the "unspoken agony that underlay what he wrote about rejection, about the wound of loneliness that never heals, about friendships that never satisfy."[36]

As I reflect on Yarhouse's question, "Whose people are they?" I see that he and I, as well as others cited in this chapter (Paris, Paul Jewett and Marguerite Shuster, Andrew Marin, Lee), share a common concern.[37] It is that evangelical churches have just one script for gays:

- Same-sex attraction is a danger that we exclude from our churches.
- Change of orientation and opposite-sex marriage is the only choice for lifelong relationship.
- Chastity that leads to celibacy is the only option for singles.
- Celibacy does not remove the danger of same-sex attraction, so one's ministry options are limited, and one must live in isolation, loneliness, and self-denial in order to be accepted.

ALTERNATIVE SCRIPTS FOR "QUEER" EVANGELICAL YOUTH?

The most pressing question on sexuality for evangelical churches in 2014 is, What alternative scripts are we willing to consider for young and old in our churches and colleges who struggle with same-sex attraction? Do Nicodemus's friends have any precedents to guide them as they seek to support him? As possible answers to those questions, I have found three alternative scripts framed by Western evangelicals. I present a brief review of each.

Open Celibate Leaders: Martin Hallett

Martin Hallett tells the story of his conversion as a practicing gay man in England. After his conversion, he became convinced that the hungers driving him were for intimate love, which he sought but did not find in sex. His promiscuity stopped when he developed deep friendships with two "special persons," the Lord Jesus and the person who led him to Christ. Canon Roy Barker, the vicar of a large evangelical church, saw Hallett's potential and encouraged him to share his story and to invite interested people to join a "consultation" on homosexuality. Thus began his journey as a uniquely valued member of the body of Christ.[38]

For three years he had virtually no struggle with his sexuality, and then "God sent me a 'sexual thorn in the flesh' and I became aware of my homosexual struggles."[39] Because of the strength of his relationships in the church and his relationship with Christ, he writes, "There was, for me, no turning back." Hallett observes, however, that singleness is not valued among evangelicals, and that among evangelicals, if someone is single, "something is wrong with us." This attitude poses a problem that bars the establishment of healthy relationships for both singles and married people who have addictions that marriage does not resolve.

Hallett proposes that the church needs more "open" leaders, gays and lesbians like himself, who are willing to live in submission to Christ and to minister to all. He concludes that his sexuality is a gift that God has used to bless others. Yet for Hallett and others like him, such ministry is possible only for those who see same-sex behavior as wrong and reject it to follow Christ.

Open Dialog, Diverse Pathways to Discipleship: Justin Lee

Justin Lee, a deeply committed Southern Baptist Christian, suffered much from evangelical friends because he was attracted to men and not women. Drawing the parallel between his friends, who were sure that he was a sinner, and Job's friends, he writes: "Christians weren't such great people to be around if you were gay. They might lecture you, talk down to you, or quote the Bible at you, but they weren't likely to make you feel loved. Quite the opposite."[40]

In 2001 Justin Lee established the Gay Christian Network (www.gaychristian .net) for mission to young people who had been rejected by family and church because of their experience of same-sex attraction. Using his own resources, he created opportunities for dialog and insisted from the beginning that the dialog be open to Side A (those who support same-sex marriage) and Side B (those who promote celibacy for Christians with same-sex attractions). The network enables young people caught in the cross fire between these opposing sides to discover for themselves how to live a life in submission to Christ and committed to spiritual growth.

Recognizing that this work cannot be done in isolation, the network focuses on creating safe communities for fellowship among LGBTQ Christians and on strengthening relationships among family and friends by helping them process questions and misunderstandings. From the very beginning, Lee has sought to represent Christ and his Christian commitments to the wider LGBTQ community and to invite individuals to reconsider the invitation to new life in Christ.

Affirming "Queer" Evangelicals: Soulforce

More radical voices framing new alternatives for young people like Nicodemus also appear among those evangelical Christians who have come out about their same-sex attraction. Evangelical Christian author Mel White and his partner

Gary Nixon founded Soulforce, an organization that sponsors symposiums on topics pertinent to LGBTQ interests and, in cooperation with Christian college campuses, promotes justice for gay students. It also develops programs for education about "nonviolent direct actions" for social change.[41] Soulforce embraces same-sex marriage and the ordination of gay men and lesbian women for ministry. Working from the nonviolent traditions of Gandhi and Martin Luther King, Jr., they actively oppose Christian organizations that promote "homophobia and religious bigotry."

Creating Dialog on College, University, and Seminary Campuses

OneTable, OneWheaton, and Queer Underground are examples of nonformal movements, often stimulated and encouraged by Soulforce, present on various college and seminary campuses to gather students and faculty for dialog about LGBTQ issues. Through monthly fellowship meals, film screenings, and presentations by invited speakers, these student groups seek to create dialog about LGBTQ issues and to foster collaboration among evangelicals so as to forge new directions. At Fuller Theological Seminary, "OneTable exists as a safe space for all who desire to be a part of the conversation surrounding faith, sexual orientation, and gender identity."[42] OneWheaton and Biola University's Queer Underground are groups of gay and lesbian students and alumni who have joined together to engage the faculty and administration around issues of faith and sexuality.[43] Their websites are representative of scores of underground LGBTQ websites in member schools belonging to the Council of Christian Colleges and Universities.[44]

Several themes recur on these websites. The students affirm they are committed evangelical Christians even when some faculty state openly that they cannot be evangelical and gay. They yearn for open dialog about their issues in their respective communities. They hope for a safe and welcoming community in which they can grow in their faith and can create a theologically meaningful framework for their future lives and ministries. They insist that people take their experience seriously, and they reject "tradition" that has dismissed their pain and isolation. If a poll of these groups were taken in January 2014, it would be found that most were still waiting for faculty and leaders to invite them into serious dialog.

CONCLUDING REFLECTIONS

In the year 2014 there is much uncertainty and distress among evangelicals about the LGBTQ movement in the United States. Many would like to dismiss these people and their political and religious agenda, but their numbers are too large and the issues are too complex—a fact that I hope this chapter has made clear—for a simple "biblical" or "political" solution. *Christianity Today* reports that 42 percent of "LGBT adults identify as Christians" and 29 percent say they have felt "unwelcome at a place of worship."[45] As we have seen, many LGBTQ followers of Jesus take issue with traditional readings of Scripture and particularly with the cultural history that has produced them. Further, those with a political agenda have gained wider public support and momentum.

But Christians and the church must not allow the culture or politics to set our agenda, nor can we rely upon the cultural solutions of the last century to meet these challenges. As with the great theological questions throughout history, this issue requires adaptive leadership. It calls for men and women of God to come together to examine the issues afresh and to seek the whole counsel of God for his church and for his children who suffer persecution for their same-sex attraction.

Toward that end I suggest a few guiding principles that may help us in this process.

- We must get on the "balcony" and look and listen, seeking not just a local, but a global perspective on these issues for the church.
- We must listen to the wounded in our midst and to the competing voices that offer new readings of Scripture, bringing their different and perhaps complementary perspectives to these questions.
- We must begin locally, convening conversations that bring together church leaders, biblical and theological scholars, scholars researching human sexuality, and LGBTQ students and graduates of our seminaries and universities. (Though a few small local conversations have begun, it is to be regretted that LGBTQ persons and research scholars on sexuality are usually excluded.)

- Finally, we must covenant with God to be faithful servants, obedient to his Word, and committed to God's mission of reconciling the world to himself.

I conclude with my personal reflections, mentioning some of the cultural issues that I believe should be a part of our reflections on Scripture and part of our future conversations about the whole counsel of God and God's mission to and for LGBTQ people in the United States and around the globe.

Cultural Context and Scripture?

As a cultural anthropologist, I offer two propositions for consideration in the interpretation of Scripture and then apply them briefly to texts on sexuality.

- All revelation from God must be interpreted within the *limiting effects* of the cultural context in which it is given.
- *Redundancy* (story told from several perspectives, multiple contexts) corrects the cultural distortions and makes truth more accessible to diverse cultural audiences.

Some cultural material may interfere with the message, but when the message is stated in various ways in multiple biblical contexts, such as the four Gospels, the overall truth and theological meanings become clear.

Biblical texts on sexuality illustrate the *limiting effects* of culture in Scripture in several ways. Abraham, for example, is married to his half-sister Sarai (father's daughter by a second wife), which is clearly incest in our culture and in Leviticus, but Scripture makes no comment. Isaac and Jacob marry first cousins, where other societies prohibit such close marriages as incestuous. David has seven wives, ten concubines, and a young virgin to lie with him in his old age, all of which would be unacceptable and illegal in our contemporary society. The Scriptures are silent on these issues while quite explicit on others. We clearly ignore these texts and we at the same time affirm these people as heroes of the faith because other redundant texts give them honor and praise.

As my Fuller colleague John Goldingay states, "The attempt to discover what the Bible has to say about same-sex relationships involves looking to it for answers to questions it does not pose, at least in the precise form we need to ask them."[46] This insight is important for any conversation on this issue, regardless of one's bias toward either tradition or revision. In the cultures of the patriarchs, heads of families arranged marriages for their children; men and women had little, if any, choice, regardless of their sexual attractions or lack of them. In the cultures of Greece and Rome, one finds very different cultural rules for the regulation of sexual behavior than those of the patriarchs, and also from those of our Western cultures in the twenty-first century. Could it be that for the inspired writers of Scripture the possibility of "same-sex couples" just did not and could not exist in those cultures? And if so, what might that mean for our theological reflections on the Gospel and biblical teaching about human sexuality and discipleship for today?

A Hierarchy of Sins?

In *Who We Are: Our Dignity as Human,* Paul Jewett and Marguerite Shuster grieve that religious people—the church in all of its various expressions—have practiced abusive and destructive discrimination against LGBTQ people, applying a hierarchy of sins of which homosexuality is the most grievous and intolerable.[47]

This issue has puzzled me as well. Scroggs observes that in the three lists of vices in 1 Corinthians (5:10, 5:11, 6:9–10), the immoral, greedy, robbers, and idolaters appear in all three, and the reference to "men who bed with men" in only one.[48] I wonder why sexual immorality, and particularly LGBTQ sexuality, has risen to the top of evangelical conversations, and we rarely ever consider the pervasive sins of greed and the "idolatry of work" as detrimental to our spiritual and collective health as professing disciples of Jesus. Very few evangelicals would find themselves excluded from ministry for idolatry of work, and many are disciplined but then received back into ministry after committing adultery. What are the social, economic, and political pressures that drive us to accept such a hierarchy?

Part of the issue that I see here is a possible distortion of our self-image, based upon our "normal" sexuality. As Paris has suggested and Malick has affirmed, in the hetero/homosexual dichotomy of our culture, being "straight" is good and being "homosexual" is evil. But Elizabeth Stuart, a lesbian Roman Catholic theologian in Britain, well reminds us, "In the end gay is not good, straight is not good, no one is good but God alone and redemption does not come through gender or sexuality, rather these are taken up in the process of redemption."[49]

The Wideness of God's Grace and Mercy?

How wide is God's grace? Jewett and Shuster pose the question:

> When we defined marriage as a unique relationship between a man
> and a woman, should we have added, "or occasionally between a
> man and a man, or between a woman and a woman"? Is there a
> real possibility here that we have somehow missed? . . . Or must we
> wait for the ultimate resurrection of the body when there will be no
> marrying or giving in marriage, and our focus and identity will be
> wholly on Christ?[50]

Sexual promiscuity of any kind is clearly rejected for the people of God in
Scripture, a truth that we accept unconditionally; but as Jewett and Shuster
ask, could there be a place for monogamous same-sex relationships? As
polygamy was permitted to provide sexual and economic support for young
widows in Israel, is it possible that same-sex partnerships (civil marriages, if
Goldingay and others are correct) might be permitted by God as the solution
for LGBTQ individuals who have confessed Jesus as Christ and Lord and who
have cast themselves upon the mercy of God? If so, the standard of holiness
for such couples is the same as Paul's instruction for holiness in male/female
marriages (1 Cor. 7:2–3, 8–9). As we see recorded in Scripture the story of
God's discipline and grace given to David, king of Israel—a man of great sexual
hunger, adultery, and murder—can we hope for both God's discipline and
grace in our time? To what extent does God accept our weaknesses, condone
the hardness of human hearts, and work in grace within our cultural limitations? This is perhaps the most difficult question to answer, because God,
and God alone, decides!

Andrew Marin's focus in his ministry in gay communities of Chicago is
on faithfulness to Scripture, the wideness of God's mercy, and leading gay
men to become obedient followers of Jesus. He does not try to define how
wide or narrow that grace and mercy might be, yet he never wavers in leading
any willing gay man into deep study of the Bible toward a relationship with
Christ.[51] Paraphrasing his ministry, I believe Marin has hope that his gracious
God might "look upon the misery" of our youth with same-sex attraction, who
are fleeing our churches, and might "restore to [them] his covenant blessing
instead of his curse" (2 Sam. 16:11–12).

Missional Questions

As I reflect on our past performance, I see that I along with most of my colleagues at Biola and Fuller, as well as most evangelicals, have avoided this conversation and the questions raised in this chapter. Until my daughter came out, same-sex attraction was a nonissue for me, and the traditional response of the church was my own. At this point I invite readers to consider with me the following questions and commit together to engage in conversations about alternative ways to love and minister to LGBTQ persons.

- How might the experience of rejection by the church shape gay and lesbian reflections on the meaning of the Gospel? How does it affect their understanding of how God views them?
- Is it possible to see the seven crucial biblical passages in a light that moves from condemnation to redemption (see Marin's effort in this regard)?
- Would we consider conversations with radical nonformal LGBTQ student groups about their potential roles in God's mission to a lost world?
- Are we willing to do serious work with Christians of same-sex attraction on framing new scripts and new ideals for community life and mission that include or are exclusively for unmarried men and women?

Many, of different persuasions, including Martin Hallett, Andrew Marin, Justin Lee, and Mel White, have sought to define new ways to invite people with same-sex attraction and LGBTQ identities and sexual behaviors to reconsider the Gospel and a life of discipleship and mission in Jesus Christ. Are we willing to join them in this quest and to frame new scripts for evangelical youth that will enable them to rediscover what it means to be a new creation in Christ Jesus, called to his service and for his mission through the church to a lost world?

NOTES

1. Mark A. Yarhouse, *Homosexuality and the Christian* (Minneapolis: Bethany House, 2010), 76–77.

2. My figures are based on data from College Stats; see http://collegestats.org/colleges/Christian.

3. See Jennifer Lingenfelter, "Reflections of a Gay Christian," *The SEMI* (June 29, 2012), and Sherwood Lingenfelter, "Reflections of a Father," *The SEMI* (June 29, 2012). Both articles are available at http://infoguides.fuller.edu/lingenfelter/otherpapers.

4. For discussion of the significance of terminology, see Andrew Marin, *Love is an Orientation: Elevating the Conversation with the Gay Community* (Downers Grove, Ill.: IVP, 2009), 60–61, and Justin Lee, *Torn: Rescuing the Gospel from the Gays-vs.-Christians Debate* (New York: Jericho Books, 2012), 52–53. For a brief but helpful reflection on the LGBTQIA coalition, see Andy Crouch, "Sex without Bodies," *Christianity Today*, July/August 2013, 74–75.

5. See APA Task Force on Appropriate Therapeutic Responses to Sexual Orientation, *Report of the Task Force on Appropriate Therapeutic Responses to Sexual Orientation* (Washington, D.C.: American Psychological Association, 2009), 21.

6. Ibid., 23–24.

7. Stanton L. Jones. "Same-Sex Science: The Social Sciences Cannot Settle the Moral Status of Homosexuality," *First Things* 1 (2012), www.firstthings.com/article/2012/01/same-sex-science.

8. Ibid., 5.

9. Yarhouse, *Homosexuality and the Christian*, 103.

10. Ibid., 77–78.

11. Ibid., 94–95.

12. See Exodus International, http://exodusinternational.org.

13. Robin Scroggs, *The New Testament and Homosexuality: Contextual Background for Contemporary Debate* (Philadelphia: Fortress, 1983), 110–20; Dale B. Martin, "*Arsenokoites* and *Malakos*: Meanings and Consequences," in *Biblical Ethics and Homosexuality: Listening to Scripture*, ed. Robert Brawley (Louisville: Westminster John Knox, 1996), 117–36; and David E. Garland, *1 Corinthians* (Grand Rapids: Baker Academic, 2003), 194–218.

14. Robert A. J. Gagnon, "The Bible and Homosexual Practice: Key Issues," in Dan O. Via and Robert A. J. Gagnon, *Homosexuality and the Bible: Two Views* (Minneapolis: Fortress, 2003), 41–92; David E. Malick, "The Condemnation of Homosexuality in 1 Corinthians 6:9," *Bibliotheca Sacra* 150 (October–December 1993): 479–92; David Peterson, ed., *Holiness and Sexuality: Homosexuality in a Biblical Context* (Milton Keynes: Paternoster Press, 2004); and Garland, *I Corinthians*.

15. Dan O. Via, "The Bible, the Church, and Homosexuality," in Via and Gagnon, *Homosexuality and the Bible*, 7–8.

16. Gagnon, "Bible and Homosexual Practice," 62–65; David Peterson, "Holiness and God's Creation Purpose," in Peterson, *Holiness and Sexuality*, 15–16; and Donald J. Wold, *Out of Order: Homosexuality in the Bible and the Ancient Near East* (Grand Rapids: Baker Books, 1998), 133–36, 212–13.

17. Malick, "Condemnation of Homosexuality in I Corinthians 6:9," 481.

18. Via, "Bible, the Church, and Homosexuality," 13–14.

19. Scroggs, *New Testament and Homosexuality*, 110–14.

20. Via and Gagnon, *Homosexuality and the Bible*, 29–39, 93, 101.

21. James V. Brownson, *Bible, Gender, Sexuality: Reframing the Church's Debate on Same-Sex Relationships* (Grand Rapids: Eerdmans, 2013), 53.

22. John E. Goldingay, Grant R. LeMarquand, George R. Sumner, and Daniel A. Westberg, "Same-Sex Marriage and Anglican Theology: A View from the Traditionalists," *Anglican Theological Review* 93, no. 1 (2011): 41.

23. Ibid., 35.

24. In surveys of cultural values among middle class employees of major corporations in seventy-six nations, Geert Hofstede ranks differences between cultures in terms of their value preferences for masculine or feminine qualities in leadership. He defines masculine as "emotional gender roles are clearly distinct: men are supposed to be assertive, tough, and focused on material success" and feminine as "emotional gender roles overlap: both men and women are supposed to be modest, tender, and concerned with the quality of life." Comparing Hofstede's data with the recent Pew study "Gay Marriage around the World" affords the intriguing discovery that ten of the fifteen nations that have legalized "gay marriage" rank in the bottom third, the feminine end of Hofstede's scale. Only two of the fifteen, England and South Africa, fall in the top third, with relative scores of 66 and 63 on a scale in which the highest masculine scores are 98 and 110 (Japan, Slovakia). See Geert H. Hofstede, Gert Jan Hofstede, and Michael Minkov, *Cultures and Organizations: Software of the Mind*, 3rd ed. (New York: McGraw-Hill, 2010), 140–45; and Pew Research, "Gay Marriage around the World," www.pewforum.org/2013/07/16/gay-marriage-around -the-world-2013. In a parallel vein, see "Same Sex Relationships Are Still Criminalized in 76 Countries, according to the United Nations. Almost All Are in Africa and the Middle East," *The Week*, December 20, 2013, 14.

25. Jenell Williams Paris, *The End of Sexual Identity: Why Sex Is Too Important to Define Who We Are* (Downers Grove, Ill.: IVP, 2011), 62–71.

26. Ibid., 40–54.

27. Lee, *Torn: Rescuing the Gospel*, 33.

28. Lisa M. Diamond, *Sexual Fluidity: Understanding Women's Love and Desire* (Cambridge, Mass.: Harvard Univ. Press, 2008), 90.

29. Yarhouse, *Homosexuality and the Christian*, 41–43.

30. Ibid., 48–50.

31. Ibid., 51–53.

32. Ibid., 162–64.

33. Lee, *Torn: Rescuing the Gospel*, 108–15.

34. Paris, *The End of Sexual Identity*, 112.

35. Jeannine Gramick and Pat Furey, *The Vatican and Homosexuality: Reactions to the "Letter to the Bishops of the Catholic Church on the Pastoral Care of Homosexual Persons"* (New York: Crossroad, 1988), and Robert Nugent and Jeannine Gramick, *Building Bridges: Gay and Lesbian Reality and the Catholic Church* (Mystic, Conn.: Twenty-Third Publications, 1992), 74, 129–33.

36. Phillip Yancey, *Soul Survivor: How My Faith Survived the Church* (New York: Doubleday, 2001), 302.

37. For Paul K. Jewett and Marguerite Shuster, see their *Who We Are: Our Dignity as Human; A Neo-Evangelical Theology* (Grand Rapids: Eerdmans, 1996).

38. Martin Hallett, "Homosexuality: Handicap and Gift," in Peterson, ed., *Holiness and Sexuality*, 120–45.

39. Ibid., 124.

40. Lee, *Torn: Rescuing the Gospel*, 115.

41. Mel White, *Stranger at the Gate: To Be Gay and Christian in America* (New York: Plume, 1995); see www.soulforce.org.

42. The quotation comes from www.onetablefuller.com, the OneTable website.

43. For Biola, see www.thebiolaqueerunderground.com; for Wheaton and other schools, see "At Evangelical Colleges, a Shifting Attitude toward Gay Students," *Indianapolis Recorder*, Thursday, April 4, 2013, www.indianapolisrecorder.com/religion/article_8771308a-9d5c -11e2-827f-001a4bcf887a.html.

44. Besides Biola, a sample of Christian schools with LGBTQ underground protest organizations and websites includes Bob Jones University (www.bjunity.org), Cedarville University (www.facebook.com/CedarvilleOut?hc_location=timeline), George Fox University (www .onegeorgefox.org), Harding University (www.huqueerpress.com), Seattle Pacific University (www.supportspuhaven.wordpress.com), Westmont College (http://westmontlgbt .wordpress.com), and Wheaton College (www.onewheaton.com).

45. "Go Figure: Homosexuality," *Christianity Today*, September 2013, 14.

46. John Goldingay, "Biblical Interpretation and Same-Sex Relationships," 7, www.fuller.edu /sot/faculty/goldingay; click the tab "Interpretation."

47. Jewett and Shuster, *Who We Are*, 348–50.

48. Scroggs, *New Testament and Homosexuality*, 103.

49. Elizabeth Stuart, *Gay and Lesbian Theologies: Repetitions with Critical Difference* (Burlington, Vt.: Ashgate, 2003), 114.

50. Jewett and Shuster, *Who We Are*, 350.

51. Marin, *Love Is an Orientation*, 114–39.

12

LINGENFELTER RAISES QUESTIONS OTHER THAN THOSE HE HAS STATED

ANDREW J. B. CAMERON

Lingenfelter has clarified the debate well. But he raises questions other than those he has stated. To explain that claim, I will describe the sadness his article triggered for me, some areas where I strongly agree, and a puzzling *aporia* (absence).

TRIGGERS FOR SORROW

"Others in evangelical churches reject them." "We in the church on the other hand expel these folks, and hand them over to gay unbelievers." "The traditional response of the church was my own." These sentences are hard to read, and hard to weigh. Does the "traditional" response *consist* in rejection and expulsion? I suspect this language weights the discussion against churches that seek to uphold a particular relational "ecology," where faithfully married couples fellowship with chaste singles who have good friendships. The emotive force of the language makes me edgy: was it really "expulsion" and "rejection," or was it the kind of disagreement that necessitated a parting of ways?

But I am saddened by the likely kernel of truth, that churches masquerading as "evangelical" have become cozy clubs of familiarity rather than beacons of light and hope to all sorts and conditions of people. The latter was the kind of church Paul rejoiced in: "Such were some of you," he says, after listing nine vices that bedevil humanity, and from which they were sanctified and justified (1 Cor. 6:9–11). Paul knows these vices have not been extinguished in their community; but unbelievers are entering, being amazed and convicted, and changing (1 Cor. 14:24–25). Churches challenge all who enter and assist us to lay our vices to rest (which takes time). But a church cannot habitually *expel* one vice over another. If selective expulsion has become a common feature of evangelical church life, then the first question becomes, When may we stop calling such a church "evangelical"?

I am saddened to hear of straights somehow being regarded as "morally superior in nature." People who identify as GLBTI are right to reject this failed, anti-Christian anthropology. In the biblical account there are no "natural" moral superiors (except One). There is a lost race, all bearing God's image, all diversely broken, all offered rescue in Christ, whose Spirit alone knows how to remake our humanity more like Christ's. So even the much-quoted Romans 1 includes the little-quoted point that the *first* way people become "unnatural," after losing God, is in idolatry (v. 23) and then in *every* form of sexual lust (v. 24). On this account, my incessant envy when I already have enough, or an obsession for someone other than my wife, is absolutely as disordered and unnatural as any other vice. This point is often observed, yet it rarely takes root in Christian consciences. So Nicodemus's parents are "surprised and shocked"—at what? That he is a sinner, like them? Hardly. When GLBTI people say, "Accept us," at one level they are simply demanding the same latitude we give to our casual daily acceptance of whatever drives us. So to frame a second question, How might Christians stop self-justifying our desires, begin interrogating them in comparison to Christ, and start believing that we *all* need the Spirit to reorder what we love?

POINTS OF AGREEMENT

It was helpful to read of how sexual thoughts and feelings become interpreted as "scripts." Great churches show how Christ redeems and reshapes *all* of our oddball identity stories, not only our sexual scripts. I also agree that "cultures marked by the Protestant tradition have embraced romantic love, sexual fulfillment, and marriage as the norm for Christian living," and marginalized singles to lonely isolation. It becomes unintelligible for evangelicals to suggest single celibacy to *anyone*, when *everyone* (both Christian and secular) fetishizes sexualized coupling and regards singleness as a personal failure. But the Bible clearly commends chaste singleness among "brothers" and "sisters," even as it does faithful marriages that are open to welcoming children, as the two honorable forms of life to be upheld at the core of our new communities. Marriages open to children and chaste singleness open to a fellowship of friends are unveiled by Scripture as the ways to receive and inhabit a sexed body.[1]

A PERPLEXITY

This issue leads me to the puzzling *aporia* in Lingenfelter's piece, which I will approach by way of another social scientist, James Davison Hunter:

> The credibility of one's beliefs depends on certain social conditions that reinforce those beliefs . . . the language, the symbols, and the social practices all woven into everyday life that underline and buttress those beliefs. These social conditions comprise what Peter Berger famously calls "plausibility structures." . . . It is true that there are religious virtuosi who maintain strong beliefs on their own with little or no social support but these individuals are rare. . . . Strong and coherent beliefs require strong institutions enveloping those who aspire to believe. These are the conditions that turn belief into settled convictions.[2]

Nicodemus has the thinnest of social or cultural grounds from which to consider his sexuality. Few will honor a life of chaste singleness for him. Indeed, a gay advocate once accused me of "infinite cruelty" to suggest such a thing. Why? Because the culture fetishizes sexualized coupling across the board, from "family values" evangelicalism, which overtly drives young men toward marriage, through to the most egregious, unbelieving licentiousness. Nicodemus has also been robbed of any meaningful discourse about a purposive aspect of his sexuality, for the raising of children. It has become outlandish to attempt that connection, as if sexuality has "graduated" beyond procreation, and is now solely for bonding with someone. Nicodemus's thinking is further affected by the blurring of sexual activity into sexual identity, whereas Scripture mainly addresses sexual acts, viewing them as the primary category for moral consideration. This scriptural emphasis has become genuinely puzzling for modern people; we would do well to help them rediscover why it matters.

Christian communities that make the single life both thinkable and liveable help to sustain people such as Martin Hallet, mentioned by Lingenfelter, and

Wesley Hill.[3] Other same-sex-attracted people such as Rosaria Butterfield and Peter Ould discover in Christian community how marriage can be thinkable for them.[4] I hope for more churches that accept all sorts and conditions of people, searching together for the biblical account of true humanity. Such churches will deeply and truthfully accept GLBTI persons as precious human beings, without simply granting their account of true humanity. They will seek to recover a human ecology that retrains desire, reconnects faithful married sexuality and gender difference to the task of welcoming children, and does not think of sexual expression as necessary for intimate friendships.

Lingenfelter hints, however, that the questions, assumptions, and demands of GLBTI youth should prevail against such communities, which seem destined always to reject them. Surely, though, as a cultural anthropologist he might suggest *how* more churches like ones that I hope for can come into being (and how freedom of religious assembly can be the peacemaking circuit breaker among the competing accounts of true humanity). If I am espousing a mad form of theological idealism, he should say so; but I reckon the cultural anthropologists can help us forward.

HIDDEN QUESTIONS

It is not that I reject the interesting questions Lingenfelter ends with. Rather, I think they mask other, hidden questions that we should ask of ourselves. What does it mean to remain "evangelical" toward those who do not construe their humanity as we do? Why will we not *really* believe that we are ourselves on the same difficult journey, to discern and inhabit the true "nature" God dreams of for his people? How can we challenge our silly terror of singleness, a terror that the Lord Jesus obviously did not share? What is needed to make chaste singleness both plausible and joyful, whether for widows, widowers, divorced persons, same-sex attracted, or those without an opportunity to marry? ("Same-sex marriage" cannot be settled without settling these questions first—and doing so before no one remembers the historic purposes of marriage.) And, how can churches be re-engineered to assist all who walk in the door?

I am thankful for Sherwood Lingenfelter's reflections, and for the opportunity to respond.

NOTES

1. Andrew Cameron, *Joined-Up Life* (Nottingham, U.K.: InterVarsity Press; Eugene, Ore.: Wipf & Stock, 2011), pp. 233–59; Christopher Roberts, *Creation and Covenant* (New York: T&T Clark International, 2007).

2. James Davidson Hunter, *To Change the World* (New York: Oxford Univ. Press, 2010), p. 202.

3. Wesley Hill, *Washed and Waiting* (Grand Rapids: Zondervan, 2010).

4. Rosaria Butterfield, *The Secret Thoughts of an Unlikely Convert* (Pittsburgh: Crown & Covenant, 2012), and An Exercise in the Fundamentals of Orthodoxy: The Website of Peter Ould, www.peter-ould.net.

13

SAME-SEX RELATIONSHIPS: Toward an Old Testament Orientation

M. DANIEL CARROLL R.

The debate regarding same-sex relationships is increasingly complicated. Social mores are changing, and legal challenges are on the rise. Views have been shifting in mainline denominations for some time, and change is appearing within evangelical circles. Testimonies of those struggling with sexual identity and faith are surfacing, and student GLBTQ groups are being organized on college and seminary campuses. These trends trigger questions about the biblical basis for the traditional negative stance towards same-sex relationships. Rethinking can be prompted by personal experiences, such as the coming out of a child. Such is the case with Sherwood Lingenfelter.

The Old Testament debates focus on three areas. First, background research: How did the cultures surrounding ancient Israel perceive and legislate same-sex relationships? The second area is the study of the biblical text. What does the Old Testament teach? The third engages theological, hermeneutical, pastoral, and missiological concerns. Is the Old Testament authoritative today, though it comes from a different time and cultural context? If so, how might it direct today's church on community life, marriage, family, and missional outreach and calling?

Some argue for reformulating the biblical stance toward a more affirming posture.[1] Others contend that the Old Testament does not condone same-sex unions and sexual practices.[2] My response aligns with the latter, while appreciating the sincerity of that more open position and the pain of those, on all sides, who wrestle with these complex issues. In this response I look at three facets of the Old Testament witness on sexuality.

FOUNDATION: THE CREATION NARRATIVE

It is common to hear that only seven passages deal with same-sex relationships (Gen. 19; Judg. 19; Lev. 18:22; 20:13; Rom. 1:24–27; 1 Cor. 6:9; 1 Tim. 1:10). The topic, however, must be placed against a wider biblical understanding of human sexuality, starting with creation.

Sexual differentiation is fundamental to the creation of humanity (Gen. 1:26–28; 5:2). Humans are gendered from the beginning, and sexuality is linked to procreation as one of its purposes. Humanity is to "be fruitful and multiply." This mandate is not limited to humanity; all creatures are to reproduce (1:22). The necessity and urge to reproduce are fundamental to creaturely existence, and a biblical theology of sexuality must include procreation. Procreation is grounded in the natural order; the mandate cannot be dismissed as simply reflecting the ancient patriarchal cultural need to secure heirs. The creation framework suggested here does not marginalize those who cannot bear children; that struggle is a reality in biblical narratives. Tellingly, even same-sex couples desire children, though the natural process of procreation challenges same-sex unions. Their yearning reflects their creatureliness.

Man and woman are to complement each other in the stewardship of God's creation. Becoming one flesh emphasizes the mystery of a unique, joyous, lasting bond (Gen. 2). It suggests, too, that sexuality is not restricted to having children. The Old Testament celebrates erotic love between a man and a woman (Song of Songs; Prov. 5:18–20).

Differentiation of male and female in marriage is made more significant by its employment as a metaphor for the relationship between God and his people in the Old and New Testaments.

HETEROSEXUAL LOVE WITHIN A FALLEN WORLD

These divine ideals stand in stark contrast to human behaviors in several narratives. Examples include the attempts at homosexual gang rape by citizens of Sodom (Gen. 19) and Gibeah (Judg. 19). They are condemned, because same-sex acts and sexual violence against innocent victims contradict the creation pattern (cf. Jude 7). It is inadequate to argue that the problem is a breach of hospitality (the verb "know" makes this view untenable). That Genesis 19 is clouded in sexual aberration is underscored by the sin of Lot's daughters in its closing scene. Sodom's rebellion included more than sexual sin (Ezek. 16:49–50), but its presence cannot be denied. These two passages do not apply to consensual same-sex relationships, but they are pertinent to a discussion of such unions.

Polygamy deserves mention. While not explicitly proscribed in the Old Testament, it contradicts the thrust of Genesis 2:24 and consistently is problematic for all involved. For much of its history, most of Israel lived within an agrarian, subsistence-level economy. Large families could be crucial to survival; children would have been essential for working the land. This might explain why some opted for this arrangement (e.g., 1 Sam. 1). Incest and homosexual unions would negatively impact child bearing.

Finally, it is hermeneutically unsound to project gay relationships onto the friendships between Ruth and Naomi and David and Jonathan. The vocabulary of affection, "love" (1 Sam. 18:3–4, 15–16) and "take delight" (19:1), should be situated within its cultural setting. Both terms appear in 18:22, with no suggestion of a homosexual relationship. Overlords and vassals also used this language. Hiram is called a "lover" (1 Kgs. 5:1 [MT 5:15]; NIV, "friend") of David. David kisses other men (2 Sam. 14:33; 2 Sam. 19:39), as was the custom (1 Sam. 10:1; 2 Sam. 15:5; 20:9). To interpret these expressions of appreciation erotically reflects impoverished Western views of same-sex interaction.

OLD TESTAMENT LEGISLATION

Israel's law codes condemn violations of the divine ideals.[3] There are prohibitions against rape, premarital sex, adultery, and prostitution. Disruption of natural boundaries, such as incest and bestiality, is censured. Same-sex acts also are proscribed (Lev. 18:22; 20:13). The Hebrew Bible uses a default masculine gender for everyone in its laws (e.g., the Ten Commandments), so same-sex proscriptions applied to both men and women.

Critics of the traditional interpretation claim that juxtaposition to a cultic law (18:21) demonstrates that 18:22 concerns ritual, not moral, aberration and thus pertains only to that ancient context. To cite child sacrifice, however, and not other ceremonies makes sense in this chapter, which focuses on unacceptable practices of other peoples (vv. 2–3, 24–29). Incest (vv. 7–18), adultery (v. 20), bestiality (vv. 23), and same-sex acts (v. 22) are improper ways to bear children. Sacrificing children destroys that gift of God.

The evaluation of same-sex acts as "detestable" (NIV) emphasizes the seriousness of this prohibition. The liaisons listed in Leviticus 18 together are labeled "detestable things" (vv. 26–30), but this one is singled out as "detestable" (18:22; cf. 20:13).

CONCLUSION

In sum, a theology of sexuality grounded in the creation order and procreation is the framework for debates on same-sex matters. The disapproval of the Old Testament is consistent, and this trajectory continues into the New.[4] While the Old Testament may not conceive of some of these relationships as they are understood today, the creation ideals remain the touchstone for assessing sexuality.

This biblical teaching must serve as the foundation for evangelical engagement with the LGBTQ community and the broader society. It does not negate the faith of LGBTQ Christians. Nor can it be used to rationalize attitudes and actions that contradict the love of Christ or to deny the civil rights of LGBTQ persons.

NOTES

1. Dan O. Via, "The Bible, the Church, and Homosexuality," in Dan O. Via and Robert A. J. Gagnon, *Homosexuality and the Bible: Two Views* (Minneapolis: Fortress, 2003), 1–39; Jack Rogers, *Jesus, The Bible, and Homosexuality: Explode the Myths, Heal the Church*, rev. ed. (Louisville: Westminster John Knox, 2009); James V. Brownson, *Bible, Gender, Sexuality: Reframing the Church's Debate on Same-Sex Relationships* (Grand Rapids: Eerdmans, 2013); cf. Martti Nissinen, *Homoeroticism in the Biblical World: A Historical Perspective*, trans. K. Stjerna (Minneapolis: Fortress, 1998). Queer studies are more extreme. See Deryn Guest et al., *The Queer Bible Commentary* (London: SCM Press, 2006); Anthony Heacock, *Jonathan Loved David: Manly Love in the Bible and the Hermeneutics of Sex* (Bible in the Modern World; Sheffield, U.K.: Sheffield Phoenix Press, 2011).

2. Donald J. Wold, *Out of Order: Homosexuality in the Bible and the Ancient Near East* (Grand Rapids: Baker, 1998); James B. De Young, *Homosexuality: Contemporary Claims Examined*

in *Light of the Bible and Other Ancient Literature and Law* (Grand Rapids: Kregel, 2000); Robert A. J. Gagnon, *The Bible and Homosexual Practice: Texts and Hermeneutics* (Nashville: Abingdon, 2001); Richard M. Davidson, *Flame of Yahweh: Sexuality in the Old Testament* (Peabody, Mass.: Hendrickson, 2007).

3. For comparisons with other ancient laws, see Wold, *Out of Order*, 29–61; Gagnon, *Bible and Homosexual Practice*, 44–56; Davidson, *Flame of Yahweh*, 134–42; cf. Nissinen, *Homoeroticism in the Biblical World*.

4. William J. Webb, *Slaves, Women, and Homosexuals: Exploring the Hermeneutics of Cultural Analysis* (Downers Grove, Ill.: InterVarsity, 2001); Willard M. Swartley, *Homosexuality: Biblical Interpretation and Moral Discernment* (Scottdale, Pa.: Herald, 2003).

14

URGENT QUESTION, BUT WITH MARKED RESERVATIONS

GRAHAM A. COLE

This brave essay raises a very real and urgent question: "The challenge facing evangelical Christians today is how do we love, mentor, and guide committed Christian youth, students, and graduates of our colleges and universities who have same-sex attraction and are passionate about following Jesus and serving God?" An excellent question. Sherwood Lingenfelter's great strength lies in the questions he asks and his sensitivity to the complexity of the issues. He is clearly animated by a deep pastoral concern. His own experience of evangelical church life is that few churches or their tertiary institutions offer officially endorsed safe places for such questioning.

The story of Lingenfelter's own daughter's coming out has made him revisit the Scriptures, his theology, and his own attitudes. He suggests the need for a deep listening on the part of evangelicals to LGBTQ people and the imperative for locally convened conversations on the subject. He draws attention to how Scripture reflects the limiting effect of culture in ways that "we"—who are the "we" here?—ignore (e.g., David's many wives). He also argues that evangelicals can operate with a notion of a hierarchy of sins that places same-sex sexual relations at the very top and ignores other sins (e.g., the idolatry of work). He appears to believe, although it is couched in the form of a question, that there is such wideness in God's mercy that God may "accept our weaknesses, condone the hardness of human hearts, and work in grace within our cultural limitations." In the end he calls the reader to be committed missionally to conversation on the subject and to the quest for new scripts to enable faithful discipleship for evangelical youth, Christians of same-sex attraction, and unmarried Christians.

A THINK TANK APPROACH

As an evangelical Anglican theologian and ethicist, I have heard the suggestions that Lingenfelter makes and have been in that intramural conversation for over twenty years now. I have not been part of a church that has ignored the conversation, so there are aspects of the essay with which I do not identify. My own experience generally speaking has been that the call to listening and conversation has been the prelude to increasingly loud calls on the part of some for either the modification of or the abandonment of traditional Christian sexual morality; namely, fidelity within a one-flesh heterosexual covenantal union and chastity outside such a bond. Even so (and especially in light of James 1:19–20, "My dear brothers and sisters, take note of this: Everyone should be quick to listen, slow to speak and slow to become angry, because our anger does not produce the righteousness that God desires" [TNIV]), who can be against listening? And who can be against searching the Scriptures afresh? And how can one ignore the Gospel call to love our brothers and sisters in Christ, our neighbors, and our enemies? I know LGBTQ folk in each of these categories.

The wisdom of Lingenfelter's piece lies in his call for a think tank approach to the issues. Theologian John Macquarrie pointed out years ago that there are ethical issues today (e.g., genetic engineering) that are so complex that one person will have trouble mastering the matter. Christians with different areas of expertise need to address the "problematic" together. For evangelicals with a high view of biblical authority, the construal of Scripture and faithfulness to the Gospel will be at the heart of any such conversation.

MY CONCERNS

The chief concerns I have with the essay lie in how Scripture figures in the argument. Lingenfelter asks, "Is it possible to see the seven crucial biblical passages in a light that moves from condemnation to redemption (see Marin's effort in this regard)?" That is only half of the induction needed. The other half has to do with the biblical teaching of a heterosexual one-flesh union as the context for sexual expression. That teaching begins in Genesis and is reaffirmed by both our Lord and the apostle Paul (see Gen. 2:24; Song of Songs *passim*; Matt. 19:1–9; 1 Cor. 6:12–20; Eph. 5:22–33). Ephesians 5 is especially important; how do a male-male union and a female-female union reflect Christ's marriage to the church? Both strands of biblical testimony need to feature in any conversation on the subject.

Yes, David had many wives, but here some distinctions are vital for clarity's sake. There are descriptive passages in Scripture (e.g., like his father, Solomon had his many wives), prescriptive passages (e.g., love your enemies), proscriptive passages (e.g., do not commit adultery), and permissive ones or concessive ones (e.g., one may marry or not marry, according to Paul). Citing descriptive passages does not further Lingenfelter's argument, nor does it encourage my confidence in his approach. There is not enough wrestling with the proscriptive passages to persuade.

Reading Foucault one might think that for modern/postmodern people, sex has replaced the soul. My sexual attraction to the other is the key to my human identity, is my destiny. On that basis it is hard to know how human is an eighty-year-old Alzheimer's patient who is towards the end of that sad journey. I think that the person who says that she or he is a Christian who has same-sex attraction could be in a very different place from the person who says, I am gay, lesbian, bisexual, transsexual, intersex, or queer. Nouns and adjectives matter when it comes to identity questions. I know personally both sorts of folk. Does Lingenfelter do sufficient justice to the identity issue? In my view, working with same-sex attraction as the key descriptor in the way Lingenfelter does, does not enable deep enough analysis and raises the question for me as to how countercultural Christian sexual morality is. I find that the demands of the Gospel cut across my interests at a number of places. Sexual morality is one such place.

15

ASKING THE BIBLE FOR ANSWERS TO QUESTIONS IT DOES NOT ASK

JOHN GOLDINGAY

In "Gay and Lesbian Christians," my colleague and friend Sherwood Lingenfelter twice refers to my views, and it amuses me to note that there is some tension between the two references. The first speaks of a "persuasive argument against same-sex marriage." The second notes that in asking the Bible about same-sex relationships in the form in which we need to discuss them in our culture, we are asking a question that the Bible does not ask.

As an Episcopalian and a Californian, I live in a cultural context in which it is simply assumed that same-sex relationships are just as moral and natural and good as heterosexual relationships, but the argument that goes with that first reference makes me unable and unwilling simply to assimilate to my culture. With regard to the second reference, one could add to this comment the fact that the Bible nevertheless does suggest a framework for thinking about a question such as this one that it does not discuss. It does so when it distinguishes, on the one hand, between the way things were by God's creation design and, on the other hand, the way Scripture's instructions also make allowance for human stubbornness (e.g., Matt. 19:1–9). It is a framework that Jesus relates to a question that people did ask in his day, the question of the propriety of divorce, and one we might consider in relation to questions we need to ask.

THE CREATION IDEAL IN A STUBBORN WORLD

Over the past century or two, the church has faced a number of tricky questions about the relationship between God's creation ideal for marriage and the way things are in a stubborn world. As well as the questions of divorce and same-sex relationships, there are also the questions of polygamy and the deliberate avoidance of procreation. All four fall short of the creation vision in Genesis. In general, Western Christians are horrified by polygamy; Protestant Christians take birth control for granted and do not look askance at the idea of a couple's avoiding having children; and we go through the motions of being horrified about divorce, but generally welcome divorced and remarried Christians into the fellowship of the church without asking too many questions. But evangelical Christians in the West are in turmoil over same-sex relationships.

Genesis points towards a marriage relationship that involves one man and one woman for life in a relationship that will generate children. All four of the issues I have noted involve relationships that fall short of God's creation ideal at some point. Yet we treat them very differently. I am especially struck that the issue the New Testament most explicitly discusses, divorce and remarriage, is the one over which Christian attitudes have most remarkably changed over the past fifty years or so. The change has come about not as a result of more careful attention to Scripture, but because the church regularly adjusts to cultural realities. I am vaguely aware that there has been considerable missiological reflection on attitudes toward polygamy. I do not know if there has been similar reflection on divorce and remarriage. Perhaps such reflection would help us to think about same-sex relationships.

GUIDELINES FOR THINKING ABOUT TRICKY MORAL QUESTIONS

As well as commenting about the difference between God's creation vision and the way Scripture makes allowance for human stubbornness, Jesus has some other guidelines for thinking about tricky moral questions. One of them is his observation that the entirety of the Torah and the Prophets is an exposition of love for God and love for one's neighbor. One can see how the rule about divorce illustrates this principle as well as the stubbornness principle. In a world gone awry, marriages break down, and in particular, men throw their wives out because they are tired of them or because they cannot have children. In a traditional society this action leaves the wife in a vulnerable position, without anywhere to live, without means of survival, and without any documentation of her position. The rule about divorce papers provides her with some evidence of her status, and is thus both a concession to human stubbornness and an expression of love.

A question Lingenfelter's essay raises is whether there could be some equivalent proper expression of love toward those who are attracted to people of the same sex. I understand that some states have two forms of marriage, regular marriage and covenant marriage. The terms are rather odd, as one would have thought that all marriage was covenantal, but the distinctiveness of covenantal marriage is that the couple forgo (much of) their right to divorce. I have heard it suggested that we need to broaden the idea of two forms of marriage. There could be marriage—with the potential to match the creation ideal—between two people of the opposite sex who do not have a former partner still living and who are open to having children, and another form of marriage for people who lack one of these elements. I cannot see, however, any way in which we can simply agree with the culture that same-sex marriage is just as good as heterosexual marriage.

QUESTIONING ASSUMPTIONS

My final comment is as follows. In a panel discussion at Fuller Theological Seminary, I was once asked what I thought was the biggest thing to be wary about at seminary. I said "sex." The questioner responded with a follow-up query that indicated his assumption that I was referring to same-sex relationships. I was not. I was referring to the fact that our culture assumes that there is nothing wrong about consensual sex between a single man and a single woman, and that Christian young people commonly make the same assumption. They do not see any harm in sexual relationships between single people. That assumption seems to me a much more important issue than same-sex relations. "The Bible contains six admonishments to homosexuals and three hundred and sixty-two admonishments to heterosexuals. That doesn't mean that God doesn't love heterosexuals. It's just that they need more supervision" (Lynne Lavner).[1]

NOTE

1. The comment comes from the cover of Jewish lesbian comic Lynne Lavner's album *Butch Fatale*. See John Goldingay, *Key Questions about Christian Faith: Old Testament Answers* (Grand Rapids: Brazos Press, 2010), 326.

16

EXPERIENCE AT THE HEART OF THE MATTER

JOSHUA W. JIPP

I take it as intellectually honest and methodologically appropriate that Sherwood Lingenfelter begins his essay with appeals to contemporary experience. Each of the accounts he presents should be recognized as an appeal voiced because of the difficulties created by the tension between contemporary experience and the church's teaching on sexuality.

Lingenfelter immediately places experience at the heart of the matter: "My daughter Jennifer's story is in part, and perhaps in whole, my story on this question." This statement is helpful for drawing attention to the way contemporary experience is driving the conversation regarding same-sex attraction and providing the stimulus to reread biblical passages and reframe the church's understanding of sexuality. For the conversation to move forward, this pivotal role of contemporary personal experience must be acknowledged even though the issue needs also to be critically reflected upon in light of Scripture. While evangelicals affirm Scripture as the ultimate authority for ethical decisions, the conversation is not taking place *only* at the level of biblical exegesis. Rather, "the factors driving current evangelical conversations are multiplex"—the two most significant probably being those just mentioned: Scripture and the role of experience.

THE ROLE OF EXPERIENCE IN BIBLICAL INTERPRETATION

Given this state of affairs, I want to raise two related questions about the relationship between experience and biblical interpretation.

First, what role(s) does experience play in our understanding of biblical interpretation and human sexuality? There are at least three broad ways of articulating the relationship.

- Experience is authoritative and *stands over and against* the biblical commandments regarding human sexuality.[1]
- Experience is not authoritative, but it *enables* us to see and understand the teachings of Scripture differently and more accurately.[2]
- Experience should not be given hermeneutical priority over the biblical teaching on sexuality, but it ought to inform how we *apply* biblical teaching on sexuality. The biblical texts, however, must always shape our understanding of experience.[3]

Due to space constraints I will not elaborate upon these ways of construing the relationship. I do want to suggest, though, that this line of reasoning constrains us to probe further: Whose experience is authoritative? How do we adjudicate between competing experiences? Do we give priority to the experience of those we love, or do we give the same weight to the experience of others and include those not part of our context?

A second question about the relation between experience and biblical interpretation: assuming, as I do, that the Scriptures are the final authority for the church, what do the Scriptures themselves say about the role of experience and its relationship to biblical interpretation and ethical discernment? The Scriptures contain many resources that can help us in thinking about this relationship. For example, see the way interpretation and discernment are worked out in the Book of Acts, where God's acts are almost always surprising. Whether it is Judas's apostasy, the outpouring of the Spirit, or Paul's decision to go to Macedonia, God acts in surprising ways *within human experience* that demand interpretation and discernment about what God has done.[4]

A PARADIGMATIC EXAMPLE

What I am describing is seen in clearest form in the foundational event whereby the Gentiles are included within God's people. In Acts 10:1–11:18,

Luke is at pains to show how the church *comes to recognize* Gentile inclusion apart from circumcision as God's will.

The story begins with two accounts of human experience of divine activity: Cornelius's vision of God's angel, who commands him to call for Peter (10:3–6), and Peter's vision during prayer (10:9–16). In response to Peter's refusal to eat clean and unclean food, the voice speaks again: "What God has made clean, you must not call profane" (10:15b). *God* has rendered insignificant the social divisions between Jew and Gentile, and his command requires that Peter's understanding undergo transformation. Luke again portrays the non-obvious nature of divine activity by emphasizing Peter's confusion (10:17). Though Peter does not understand, he obeys by going down to meet with Cornelius's men (10:20), who declare that they have been sent "for you to come to his house and to hear what you have to say" (10:22). Peter, not yet understanding the meaning of the event, responds with obedience by inviting them to receive hospitality (10:23).

The rest of the story narrates Peter's progressive growth in his ability to interpret God's activity within these events. Finally, within Cornelius's home, Peter declares, "God has shown me that I should not call anyone profane or unclean" (10:28b). Through the visions and shared hospitality, Peter goes further in his declaration of divine identity: "I truly understand that God shows no partiality" (10:34). Peter's statement is an insight into Israel's Scriptures, where God is described as impartial (e.g., Lev. 19:15; Deut. 10:17–19; 2 Chron. 9:17; Ps. 82:2). But never had texts such as these been used as the basis to provide for full inclusion of the non-Jew *qua* non-Jew within God's people. When the Gentiles experience the outpouring of the Spirit, Peter baptizes them since they have experienced the Spirit "just as we have" (10:47). In his report to the Jerusalem church, Peter has no doubt that God has acted in these events (11:17), and the story ends with the church praising God, saying, "Then God has given even to the Gentiles the repentance that leads to life" (11:18).

Peter's affirmation of God's activity has been the result of a process of *experience and encounter* with divine work: visions, hospitality with strangers, and the work of the Spirit. Though the event surprises Peter, Luke presents the inclusion of the Gentiles as (in the judgment of James) aligning with Israel's Scriptures (Acts 15:14–18), Jesus' own inclusion of outcasts, Jesus' commission to preach "to all nations" (Luke 24:47), and the initiative of the Spirit (Acts 11:15–17).

FOUR CHARACTERISTICS

We have just seen in Acts four characteristics that guide human interpretation of divine activity. God's acts (1) are discerned through human experiences, (2) align with the teachings, actions, and life of Jesus in the Gospels, (3) conform to the testimony of Israel's Scriptures, and (4) are understood and *agreed upon* within the ecclesial community. I do not suggest that every act of God within Acts conforms to this abstraction (though numerous examples are present within Luke's account of the early church), only that these characteristics are the primary elements that govern interpretation of divine activity.

My goal in this response is to draw attention to the powerful role experience plays in Lingenfelter's essay and to reflect with Scripture about how we might think about the role experience does and should play in contemporary discussions. Christians who would continue the legacy of Acts must reflect upon how God acts in the world in accordance with biblical revelation. If one thinks that a contemporary experience is disclosing something new about God and God's world, we should expect it to conform to how we see the early church reflecting upon God's activity. We are thereby drawn back to examining what Israel's Scriptures say about the matter, to checking whether the experience conforms to the teaching, character, and life of Jesus in the Gospels, and to examining the experience of all of us, carried out together in a communal context.

NOTES

1. This is the position of Luke Timothy Johnson, "Scripture and Experience," *Commonweal*, June 11, 2007, 14–17, www.commonwealmagazine.org/homosexuality-church-1.

2. I think here of events that have transformed previous interpretations of Scripture, for example, the Copernican revolution and the Bible's cosmology or the U.S. Civil War in relation to the New Testament's household codes.

3. I wish to thank Rory Tyer for help in articulating option 3.

4. For fuller discussion, see Joshua Jipp, "The Beginnings of a Theology of Luke-Acts: Divine Activity and Human Response," *Journal of Theological Interpretation* (forthcoming).

17

THE CHURCH'S DEFINITIVE TEACHING

STANTON L. JONES

In "Gay and Lesbian Christians," Sherwood Lingenfelter frames his argument in terms of four questions: What causes homosexual orientation and can it be changed? What does Scripture say about homosexual behavior? Is it possible to be Christian and gay? What about sexual orientation and identity? His objective is that the church suspend judgment while reexamining sexual morality, trusting "in the power of God and the work of the Holy Spirit to teach us through his body, the church."

In responding, I seek to be faithful to the teaching of Scripture and to manifest Christ-like love in doing so. I begin by acknowledging, as I long have, the many ways in which the church has sinned against sexual minority persons through ignorance, hatred, intolerance, and abuse, and by challenging us to better love as Christ loves.[1]

MORAL STANDARDS AND COMPASSION

First, the definitive teaching of the church for two millennia—put forth on the basis of the foundational scriptural teaching that God created humankind, male and female, as physical, sexual, and erotic beings in his image and that we best reflect that image in monogamous marriage of a man and a woman *and* in celibate singleness in community—has been the uniform condemnation of homosexual conduct. Sexual immorality fails to manifest the image of God as intended in creation. Christ taught conformity with the Hebraic moral law (Matt. 5:17–20), and sexual purity is affirmed emphatically in the

New Testament, including in the first ecumenical council (Acts 15) as well as in the epistles. Why, if Lingenfelter trusts "in the power of God and the work of the Holy Spirit to teach us through his body, the church," would we suspend moral teaching on these specific variants of what has been viewed as sexual immorality?

What would justify Lingenfelter's call to fashion "alternative [ethical] scripts"? He offers two justifications. First, he attributes the vigorous defense of traditional sexual morality to a putative "hierarchy of sins of which homosexuality is the most grievous and intolerable." This common trope in contemporary moral debate is a claim I reject. The morality of homosexual conduct, rather, is a preoccupation because we live in a cultural moment when unqualified acceptance of sexual minorities is being demanded. I, for one, have been preoccupied because it has—unlike the equally or more heinous sins of pride, callousness towards the poor, greed, the idolatry of work, and unjustified divorce—an organized movement advocating that such attitudes or actions be declared morally righteous, healthy, and normal. "LGBTQ sexuality . . . has risen to the top of evangelical conversations" because of unrelenting pressure to revise the church's moral teaching to affirm that which Scripture does not.

Second, in arguing that "Christians and the church must not allow the culture or politics to set our agenda" and that today we cannot "rely upon the cultural solutions of the last century," Lingenfelter seemingly regards the "traditional readings of Scripture" as a mere byproduct of the church having allowed "the culture or politics to set our agenda." He fails, however, to offer a persuasive argument establishing this. To the contrary, the consistency of the church's teachings across time and cultures is evidence against Lingenfelter's critique of such provincialism. If Lingenfelter trusts "in the power of God and the work of the Holy Spirit to teach us through his body, the church," then why has not the consistent witness of the church over two millennia, and the contemporary witness of the Roman Catholic and Orthodox communities—along with the vast conservative evangelical and Pentecostal Protestant communities in the developing world—settled the matter?

Lingenfelter fails to establish a case justifying suspension of our moral teaching, especially given that it is regarding a matter of eternal significance in the lives of individuals. In light of the apostle Paul's teaching that "wrongdoers will not inherit the kingdom of God" (1 Cor. 6:9), how can we adopt a noncommittal stance? If mere disagreement should trigger suspension of judgment, the church would never have a cohesive teaching about anything theological or moral; there are always those who do not understand, concur, or submit to any particular teaching. An individual can remain indecisive (perhaps with eternal consequences, as in the life of the Rich Young Ruler), but the call of the church is to fearlessly proclaim the Word of God received, and that includes moral exhortation toward holiness for those who seek to be faithful disciples of Christ.[2] In Christ, we are called to daily, lifelong repentance, and cannot expect less or offer less to our brothers and sisters who struggle with sexual immorality (no matter whether straight or LGBTQ).

At this point, some will dismiss my argument as lacking in compassion, but true compassion must mirror the compassion of the loving, triune God. Lingenfelter makes a fundamental virtue of compassion for those who have been wounded by lack of affirmation and acceptance. My heart goes out to a father of a lesbian daughter and to those who grapple with same-sex attraction. But we must not confuse compassion with acceptance of moral choices that contradict the Christian ethic; it is out of his infinite compassion that God diagnoses our sinful brokenness so that the strong remedy of infinite and costly grace might be applied. To revise our theology and ethical standards to accommodate LGBTQ moral choices in contradiction of biblical teaching would be a denial of genuine compassion.

ORIENTATION, IDENTITY, AND ETHICS

But what of the implications of sexual orientation for identity? Lingenfelter's argument subtly moves, as is so common today, to replace the question of the moral governance of *behavior* with the politics of identity. If being gay or lesbian *is* my identity as a person, how can it be something on which moral judgment could be passed? If ethics is to be driven by identity (heterosexual versus other identities) and not by behavioral standards (sex between one man and woman in marriage, and not outside that boundary), we are shifting the foundation of ethics. The guiding moral paradigm becomes faithfulness not to the standards of a holy God as revealed in the Bible, but fidelity to my experienced identity.

How many identities are legitimate, and what is it that establishes their legitimacy? Lingenfelter explicitly includes BTQ individuals—bisexual, transsexual, and queer—along with lesbians and gays in his request for moral reconsideration, seemingly affirming the legitimacy of these alternate identities despite the lack of clarity of the entailments of this affirmation. What is it that makes the identities and subsequent lifestyle choices of bisexual, transsexual, and queer persons virtuous to the point of being Christlike and hence worthy of affirmation as we send them forth as missionaries? Do other identities merit affirmation? Jenell Williams Paris recently updated the list with a fourteen-letter acronym: LGBTQQPA(H)BDSM: lesbian, gay, bisexual, transgender, queer, questioning, pansexual, asexual, heterosexual, bondage, domination/discipline, submission, sadomasochism.[3] If identity drives ethics, then each unique identity has a unique ethical calling to be respected on its own terms. In the process, the Christian understanding of the very purpose of sexuality and its boundaries blurs.

CONCLUSION

At the most basic level, Lingenfelter's overall argument is the call of a father, an academic, and an evangelical arguing from the grounds of individual experiences. He fails to give proper weight to the compelling theological and biblical grounds for the traditional sexual ethic and the consistent teaching of the body of Christ over the course of centuries. Contemporary science, I have argued elsewhere, fails to make a compelling case meriting revision of these standards.[4]

Lingenfelter was right in his call that we *must* trust "in the power of God and the work of the Holy Spirit to teach us through his body, the church." The power of God through the Holy Spirit was indeed mightily revealed in the inspiration of the Scriptures and in the consistent apostolic teaching of the church through the last two millennia. Homosexual erotic intimacy is not a path affirmed by God, and we are called not to indecision or debate, but to faithful obedience and to faithful proclamation of the truth.

NOTES

1.   Stanton L. Jones, "The Loving Opposition," *Christianity Today*, July 9, 1993, 18–25.
2.   Politically and pragmatically, evangelicals must note the empirical record of mainline denominations that have gone down this path. Lingenfelter's proposed procedure guarantees indefinite suspension of judgment (and paralysis of moral continuity with traditional teaching), because such dialogues always deadlock, resulting in retreat from traditional teaching.
3.   Jenell Williams Paris, *The End of Sexual Identity: Why Sex Is Too Important to Define Who We Are* (Downers Grove, Ill.: IVP Books, 2011), 72.
4.   Stanton L. Jones, "Same-Sex Science: The Social Sciences Cannot Settle the Moral Status of Homosexuality," *First Things* (February 2012): 27–33, www.firstthings.com/article/2012/01 /same-sex-science.

18

THE IMPACT OF CONTEMPORARY TRENDS IN SEXUALITY ON MISSION AGENCIES

PHILLIP MARSHALL

A young Western doctor does a short-term medical stint in West Africa and returns home emotionally wounded. He subsequently leaves his church and identifies with the gay community. Few in the mission agency know his story. A young Asian missionary ministering in a Muslim context is challenged when her lesbian relationship is discovered. While undergoing accountability sessions, she covertly continues various same-sex relationships in a destructive spiral of deception. Finally she agrees to leave her agency. Two MKs at boarding school experiment with same-sex activity and are expelled by the school, requiring their families to return home. How do we evaluate these outcomes in terms of screening and member care?

BEING GLOBAL

The issues raised by Sherwood Lingenfelter go far beyond the United States. Where I sit in Asia, as part of a global missionary organization, we see contemporary trends in sexuality having a small but increasing impact on world missions. He writes, "We must get on the 'balcony' and look and listen, seeking not just a local, but a global perspective on these issues for the church." Mission agencies and missionaries dive from the balcony into the global square; they need anthropological eyes as well as God-directed hearts in order to make sense of the worlds around them, worlds of identity that go beyond geography, ethnicity, and culture, and embrace sexuality.

Missionaries as global citizens have the potential to speak, as Sherwood suggests, into our churches; however, as "jars of clay" they are vulnerable in their own identity and sexuality. The stresses of cross-cultural life, of finding themselves in unaccustomed relationships and activities, and of creating new identities to fit new contexts, challenge understandings of being and sexuality. Singles, the majority of whom are women, continue to be undervalued in missions and have at times been required to live together for reasons of security, finances, or support. Culturally diverse teams have to negotiate complex issues of personal space, touch, gender roles, and same-sex and opposite-sex relationships. Loneliness and exposure to new possibilities, along with ready access to the Internet, can lead a missionary to explore different expressions of sexuality. Member care today must be "open-ended" rather than closed in terms of the questions it asks.

LIVING WITH COMPLEXITY

Sherwood reflects on how today's conversations are going beyond heterosexual and homosexual stereotypes, preferring to use the term LGBTQ to signal respect and complexity. Jenell Williams Paris explores this global complexity in her *End of Sexual Identity*.[1] See, for example, chapter 3, "The Trouble with Homosexuality," where she takes issue with popular and Christian Western stereotypes. Trust is the glue that binds mission agencies and teams together; as evangelicals we agree that trust is built by loving God and loving our neighbor. But trust can be quickly eroded in disagreements and miscommunications arising out of our differences over sexuality. Sadly, this reality is very familiar to many women and singles, as well as those with less power (whether through language, education, wealth, or other criteria) who come into our mission agencies.

While, as Lingenfelter states, "the factors driving current [U.S.] evangelical conversations are multiplex," the global conversations on sexuality are currently arising out of a multitude of cultural contexts and being expressed through many voices. The mission director in Colorado Springs or Charlotte needs to be cognizant of the many social, ecclesiastical, and legal issues surrounding sexuality, both in the United States and in each country in which his or her workers serve. Issues surrounding sexuality present a legal minefield—one that is not always apparent—for mission agencies and churches, which are required to be scrupulous and current in their procedures and documentation. Yet another context is the diverse teams on which mission workers operate, held together by trust. Finally, how do partner organizations, donors, and sponsors view these global changes, whether in the United States or overseas (where homosexual activity may even warrant the death penalty)? Writes one mission leader in a private e-mail: "Where we may be vulnerable is that as evangelical organizations and churches adopt divergent positions, we may need to consider how we partner."

A CASE STUDY

SIM, the global mission agency in which I work, declares that it wants "flourishing people" who are "above reproach." Its principles and practice statement on sexual conduct reads: "It is essential that missionaries maintain an unblemished reputation in matters of sexual morality. As part of our commitment to holy living, we uphold the biblical principles of chastity before marriage and faithfulness within marriage. We celebrate God's good gifts of both heterosexual sex within marriage and celibate singleness. We believe these are God's only patterns for human sexuality."

The Bible not only commands abstention from sexual impurity but also calls God's servants to live "above reproach." The primary consideration must be the credibility of the missionary's life and witness to the host community, which may have stricter standards than those of the sending community, the supporting church, or even the missionary family. In many non-Western societies an action is judged by the context and not only by proof of an act.

While such a statement leaves SIM's doors open to those who experience same-sex attraction, we clearly have little room here for Christians who categorize themselves as actively homosexual or as LGBTQ. "Any sexual misconduct including but not limited to premarital and extramarital sexual relationships, homosexual acts, use of pornography, child abuse and sexual harassment is unacceptable in those who serve as part of SIM. . . . Previous moral failure will not necessarily disqualify anyone from service, and each case will be considered on its merits." In Lingenfelter's account, Nicodemus, Jennifer, and Justin would be considered for service only if they practiced celibacy and agreed to SIM's understanding of "moral failure." For those who are members and engage in homosexuality or other behavior contrary to SIM practice, the statement of principles spells the steps to be followed: "In the case of a suspected moral failure, steps will immediately be taken to establish the truth.... The person or people concerned may be suspended from ministry activity, pending a full investigation.... Counselling is provided, informally or formally as is appropriate to the circumstances, with the purpose of restoring the person to fellowship and, where possible, to ministry, whether in SIM or in another situation."

As Sherwood has shown, such a position will not be acceptable to many, and perhaps increasingly so in some quarters. SIM connects with thousands of churches, mission agencies, and other partners in the United States and around the world. In doing so it desires the reputation of being characterized by God's grace as a Christlike community, and not by "homophobia and religious bigotry." It recognizes that it has on occasion failed in the past, yet it stands firm on this position on sexuality. SIM's leadership is aware that many aspects of our Christianity, including our understanding of sexuality, will be scrutinized and challenged in coming years.

NOTE

1.   Jenell Williams Paris, *The End of Sexual Identity: Why Sex Is Too Important to Define Who We Are* (Downers Grove, Ill.: IVP Books, 2011).

19

A COMPLEX
MULTILEVEL ISSUE

CRAIG OTT

Sherwood Lingenfelter draws our attention with personal poignancy to the complexity of same-sex attraction and the urgency for the church to address the issue in a comprehensive and compassionate manner. I will respond to Lingenfelter by examining four levels at which the issue must be engaged.

THE BIBLICAL-ETHICAL LEVEL

What behaviors and values are consistent with biblical teaching, and how broad are the parameters allowing for cultural diversity? For evangelical Christians this is largely an exegetical-theological undertaking. Lingenfelter opens the door to alternative interpretations of relevant biblical texts on homosexuality. While we should be open to the possibility that received interpretations need reconsideration, I nevertheless personally find the revisionist interpretations outlined here exegetically implausible and unconvincing, being too narrowly focused and overly indebted to contemporary cultural ideologies.

As the Gospel enters a culture it inevitably challenges and transforms the culture at many points. Good contextualization is often countercultural. No one more masterfully contextualized the Gospel than the Apostle Paul. Yet he continually exhorted believers, counterculturally, to live sexually pure lives (e.g., 1 Cor. 6:15–18). As contemporary Western culture becomes increasingly post-Christian, we should not be surprised if biblical ethics—particularly sexual ethics—are increasingly rejected and the church increasingly finds itself on the defensive in its attempt to advocate biblical morality. Nevertheless the church must remain faithful to its best understanding of biblical teaching.

THE PHENOMENOLOGICAL LEVEL

What are the causes of same-sex attraction? What psychological, social, and biological factors are at play? Can such attraction be changed? How do people experience their sexuality, and how does that influence their personal identity? Irrespective of how one might answer the biblical-ethical question, how is one to wisely counsel affected individuals if the counselor cannot first answer these questions? Abstract ethical principles can take us only so far. Lingenfelter notes that the phenomenological dimension remains in need of more research. Lack of scientific consensus here makes informed response at the following two levels more difficult. Even on points at which Christians disagree with contemporary discourse and framing of human sexuality, they must seek to understand the issue in terms of the perceived reality of those most directly impacted.

THE PASTORAL LEVEL

How can the church help persons live according to a biblical ethic? What kind of support should churches offer? How should persons with same-sex attraction be counseled? Lingenfelter recounts the personal stories of struggle, hurt, and marginalization that persons with same-sex attraction face in the evangelical church. When addressing this concern one must take into consideration both of the first two levels. Moreover, missionary experience has taught us that for cultural transformation to occur at a deep level, persons most affected must be part of the hermeneutical community that discerns God's standards and the appropriate course of action. In this sense Lingenfelter's call for dialogue is an important one.

Most evangelical churches indeed lack a thoughtful approach to ministry to persons with same-sex attraction. Leaders are perhaps unaware or are in denial of the pervasiveness of the problem. Most seminaries are not preparing pastors and counselors to deal with the issue at a pastoral level. Churches are not serving their constituencies well if they fail to address these questions and meet the needs in ways that are both biblically and phenomenologically informed.

The manner in which nineteenth-century missionaries dealt with the problem of polygamy is instructive. When polygamists became Christians they were often forced to divorce all but their first wives as a condition for baptism and receiving Holy Communion. If a believer became polygamous, he must divorce or be excommunicated from the church. Thus the church became a promoter of divorce.[1] As Sam Owusu writes, "The church's policy, in many instances, also led to deceit, death, and divorce. Some polygamists lied to the church in saying that they would send their extra wives away, but in fact they would merely ask their wives to stay away from home until they had been baptized."[2] Furthermore, this practice often led to extreme economic, social, and psychological hardship for the divorced wives, including leading to prostitution or even death, not to mention the severe negative consequences for their children.[3] Thus in pursuit of a moral ideal, a greater evil was created. This illustrates how ethical dilemmas and compromises are inevitable when the Gospel enters fallen societies. A deep understanding of the social and psychological factors related to the dilemma is essential if solutions are to avoid harmful unintended consequences.

Now fast forward 150 years, move from Africa to North America, and imagine this scenario: A same-sex, legally married couple with children comes to faith in Christ. Then suppose they come to see homosexual marriage as deviating from God's ideal for marriage. What should they do? How should the pastor counsel them? Should they divorce as a condition for baptism? What might be the emotional and social fallout of a divorce? And what would become of the children? Or can they remain married and become church members, but not serve in leadership? How much understanding will the congregation have for the complexity of the situation? I suspect that few pastors or churches have contemplated how they will respond to this situation, which is no longer hypothetical.

Lingenfelter's essay describes the alienation that persons with same-sex attraction can feel in the church, even when those persons are committed to a celibate lifestyle. Churches have offered various forms of support for persons wrestling with other sins and temptations, such as pornography addiction. The existence of these ministries is not a sign of ethical compromise. On the contrary, they provide compassionate and practical assistance in the pursuit of godliness. Unfortunately, too few churches offer similar support or acceptance for those wrestling with same-sex attraction and sexual identity issues.

THE APOLOGETIC LEVEL

How are Christians (and the Christian message) perceived by the general culture in light of this issue? Evangelicals have a credibility problem due to both their real and perceived attitudes related to homosexuality. Nothing more quickly arouses disdain among young people towards evangelicals than this topic. This in turn negatively impacts receptivity to the Christian message as a whole.

The apologetic response must be twofold. First, we must find ways to communicate our ethic compellingly to those both inside and outside the church. This will likely involve a reframing of the public discussion. Second, we must demonstrate a civil and understanding posture in the manner that the issue is addressed. 1 Peter 3:15b–16 (NIV) might be adapted as follows: "Always be prepared to give an answer to everyone who asks you to give the reason for *your convictions about sexuality.* But do this with gentleness and respect, keeping a clear conscience, so that those who speak maliciously against your good behavior in Christ may be ashamed of their slander." We must learn to live and act with grace, truth, and respect so as to remain winsome in a society increasingly hostile towards biblical values and convictions.

NOTES

1. See Timothy Willem Jones, "The Missionaries' Position: Polygamy and Divorce in the Anglican Communion, 1888–1988," *Journal of Religious History* 35, no. 3 (September 1, 2011): 393–408, and Adrian Hastings, "The Church's Response to African Marriage," *AFER* 13, no. 3 (July 1, 1971): 193–203.

2. Sam Owusu, "Towards a Theology of Marriage and Polygamy," *Direction* 36, no. 2 (September 1, 2007): 195.

3. Ibid.

20

EXPLORING CONVERSATIONS ON SAME-SEX ATTRACTION

JENELL PARIS

If all Sherwood Lingenfelter were asking was that evangelicals converse about same-sex matters with civility and well-informed views, that would be challenge enough. He goes further, raising the possibility of expanding the range of "cultural scripts" available for devout Christians of same-sex attraction, beyond the current "celibacy-only" script.

A tall order, but delivered by a credible and persuasive voice. One of evangelicalism's most astute elders, Lingenfelter has provided leadership to missions, anthropology, and seminary education. His current interest in both the biblical witness regarding sexuality and the lived experience of LGBTQ persons is grounded in his personal experience as father to a lesbian daughter, and grandfather to children raised by this daughter and her partner. A father's love is evident here, but also an anthropologist's craft. Valuing and respecting the Other (not necessarily affirming or promoting) is core to anthropological practice. Lingenfelter's approach blends Christianity and anthropology seamlessly in regard for the Other.

He doubts the sufficiency and the humanity of traditional evangelicalism's single cultural script for LGBTQ persons: homosexuality is a sin, therefore homosexuals should either change or live in celibacy. This insistence on an ethical abstraction—*what should be*—seems unresponsive to *what is*. It simply *is* the case that devout Christians find themselves with persistent, lifelong same-sex attraction. The anthropologist gives close attention to *what is*, and in this case, Lingenfelter reports deep dissatisfaction and pain among evangelical same-sex-attracted young adults and their friends, who are living and thinking their way toward faithful, conscionable consideration of alternate scripts. Because of past shaming, punishing, and excluding experiences in churches, they are doing so largely without the guidance and wisdom of their elders.

WIDENING THE CONVERSATION

Lingenfelter is not arguing for mere concession: *if you can't beat 'em, join 'em.* He summarizes leading exegetical work on relevant passages, and describes several leading alternate scripts offered by new religious leaders such as Justin Lee, Martin Hallet, and Andrew Marin, and the group Soulforce. This portion of his chapter is mostly summative, and not comprehensive, reflecting Lingenfelter's recent scholarly interest in these topics. For instance, examples of important evangelical groups and trends include only males. A fuller perspective would include lesbians, of course, and smaller groups such as transgender or intersex. Theological reflection here is extremely limited, but nonetheless rich, offering insight on gender, sexuality, and personhood. Witness from believers in other contexts would also enlighten; for example, how do Thai Christians view and treat *kathoey*? How does Philippine Christian theology make sense of *bakla*? How could Christian engagement with various marriage forms (arranged marriage, polygamy, serial monogamy, and others) inform our understanding of same-sex marriage? Lingenfelter points to the importance of global perspectives; the next step is for anthropologists to bring their expertise to this topic with specific and fine-grained detail.

Christians of good faith already disagree, and will certainly do the same when considering Lingenfelter's questions about biblical interpretation, alternate scripts, and trends in evangelical public leadership. He anticipates this, and offers foundational encouragements for entering into such dialogue. First (merging two of his principles), our local conversations should be supported by global perspectives. Anthropologists and others have documented various ways that humans live out, symbolize, and codify same-sex relationships; ethnology sheds much-needed light on U.S. sexualities that are sometimes dismissed as idiosyncratic or strange, or, on the other hand, glossed as universal and "natural."

A second principle is to listen to the wounded: specifically, same-sex-attracted Christians who report alienation, misunderstanding, and even cruelty from other believers or from their churches.

A third principle is that we each should deepen our own spiritual lives as we pray, worship, and serve the Lord.

It is hard to argue with these principles, which, if actually practiced, would likely bring us to the table better prepared to discuss any issue, including the one at hand.

SEEKING CLARITY

Throughout his chapter, Lingenfelter presses past distraction to find the heart of the matter: "How do we love, mentor, and guide committed Christian youth, students, and graduates of our colleges and universities who have same-sex attraction and are passionate about following Jesus and serving God?" Wise in its main point, the question nonetheless struck me as unnecessarily focused on youth, especially since the central story was about his daughter, who came out in her thirties. A broader literature base, as well, would show that sexual orientation can shift over time, particularly for women. Coming out as LGBTQ, or discovering a new dimension to one's sexual identity, can happen at any time in life. Gay marriage and gay parenting also show this issue to be about more than personal sexual pleasure; traditional Christians have long supported all families in our pluralist society. It remains to be seen whether and how "family values" may be expansive enough to include gay families. These are questions for the church as a body, not a question for (uncomplicated) adults to answer and then share with (complicated) youth.

Too many Christians push their views on same-sex issues, seeming to believe that theological homogeneity will save us. Lingenfelter takes a more patient approach, warning that "cultural and political pressures upon the church are so intense that they cloud our thinking, research, and interpretation of data." Clarity will come not by purifying our churches or groups, or by refusing to engage the issues, or by arrogant or bombastic talk. Clarity will come as we practice the Christian life together, gathering to pray, worship, and reason together even as we disagree about important matters. What may become clear, however, is that theological homogeneity is no longer possible except at very high human and ecclesial cost.

I find Lingenfelter's ideas to be worth engaging not because I always agree, but because he is a man whose ideas, life, and leadership have been shaped by love. He is made vulnerable as a leader, and as a Christian, because he loves his daughter. Standing so firm in one's faith that one becomes malleable is a beautiful sign of a life centered on Jesus' transforming love.

21

BREAKING THE EVANGELICAL SILENCE ON SEX—WITH CLARITY

KERSTEN BAYT PRIEST

First of all, I wish to thank Sherwood Lingenfelter for his brave, personal scholarship in this invited chapter. I was present for public presentations of the paper en route to its final form and can attest to the tremendous interest his work generated.

As a sociologist (with anthropological training) I will focus my comments on sex, gender, arousal, and identity. Lingenfelter's title and essay, it seems to me, assume contemporary mainstream U.S. "folk" (emic) sexual categories—that is, essentialized (static) sexual identities where each individual is categorically either L, G, B, T, Q, or heterosexual. And yet there are reasons to question whether such categories are cross-culturally valid or are adequate tools for the analysis we need. Conflation of categories *and* concepts hinders culturally relevant Christianity.

DISTINGUISHING SEX AND GENDER

Scientifically speaking, the identifier "sex" is an ascribed status, based on primary characteristics required for reproduction, such as testes or ovaries (with a small percentage of people being intersex, having for example both an ovary and a testicle). In contrast, gender is an achieved status, built on secondary characteristics that develop during adolescence (e.g., body hair, voice, breasts, musculature, skeletal structure). These secondary characteristics are the dimension of the self actively "shaped"—shaved, cinched, clothed—with reference to a social community. Gender then involves the way individuals through interaction are coached and "cued" toward culturally contingent ideals of masculinity and femininity. Anthropologist Margaret Mead famously studied the variability of gender expression across three non-Western societies, one of which uniquely positioned *ideal* men as "flamboyant, flighty, and flirtatious" while *ideal* women were "practical, staid, and business-oriented."[1] Gender elaboration and sexual reproductive capacity are distinct and yet overlap somewhat because certain aspects of gender are deemed "important" for authenticating a person's reproductive or sexual categorization.

Historically in the United States we have tended toward a strong bi-polar expectation for gendered expression, with femininity idealized as Barbie doll–like, emotionally expressive, and submissive, and masculinity idealized as tough and confident, as epitomized by superheroes or men in business "powersuits." Only relatively recently have we explored other gender possibilities, such as the female athlete or the metrosexual male. As my students have noted, however, female athletes run the risk of being called lesbian ("not really a woman"), and the stylishly dressed man is asked if he is gay ("not really a man"). The folk assumption is that ideal gender indexes sex and, by extension, sexual behavior and desire. Interestingly, not all societies limit gender roles to only two (e.g., *masculine, feminine,* and *fa' afa' fine,* in Samoa). As my grey-haired, petite, neo-Marxist feminist professor used to say, "We are *all* doing drag all the time." In short, everyone must *work* to achieve gender. Societies sanction those who fail to achieve or align with specified gender ideals (regardless of sexual activity). Saying this does not mean, however, that the labels are, objectively speaking, "natural," "true," or "real."

ATTRACTION AND AROUSAL

It is important not only to analytically differentiate sex and gender, but also to distinguish the dimension of sexual arousal (sexual attraction) from them. Again, folk ideas about sexual drive (or lack thereof) and what that means are present in every society. Alfred Kinsey was the first to investigate arousal scientifically. Despite sampling issues and ethical questions, his research findings were important because they indicated greater variability than had been thought to exist among humans, including greater variability for a given individual (e.g., bisexual desire).[2] Although Lingenfelter's essay is centrally focused on his daughter, the science of female sexuality is not strongly supportive of the fixity of arousal and identities. Recent research on men's and women's sexual arousal shows that a majority of women are easily aroused by both male and female erotica, whereas males are usually aroused by female erotica with only a minority of men aroused by male erotica. Less frequently are men aroused by both.

Why does this matter? If studies of human sexuality are correct, many people at various points in their lives are likely to experience arousal that is outside the norm even for their personally expected sex or gender role (especially is this true for women). As a Christian social scientist, I find this illuminating. Identity is not necessarily determined by what genitalia may feel at any given moment (recall the apostle Paul's dilemma in Romans 7 between what his body urges him to do and what his soul believes he should not). The notion that if you "feel aroused" then it must be "authentic" to act on it (i.e., consistent arousal = orientation = identity) is a folk idea based on supposed cellular-level "truth." But if we know anything at all about the way culture works, we know that any cultural context will put limitations and specified expectations on all human urges. What an individual might wish to eat is not completely open to any and all choices. As anthropologist Mary Douglas elegantly argues, some things/behaviors are considered "clean" and others "unclean."[3] Humans worldwide expend much effort to shape their group members culturally. Sexual urges, like appetite cravings, have cultural rules that apply.

READING NATURE; SHAPING CULTURE

Finally, it is important to recognize that every society (or community) attaches moral sentiment to what is believed to be "right" or "wrong." Few areas of social life are more fraught than sexual behavior. Societies have always prescribed "ideal" sexual relationships. The United States has traditionally idealized man-woman coupling (licit and illicit). That has changed. Margaret Mead's groundbreaking first publication, in 1928, pushed back against the man-woman cultural ideal, extolling the idyllic South Pacific sexual freedom of Samoan youth (girls with boys, girls with girls, girls with both, and boys with boys).[4] *Coming of Age in Samoa: A Psychological Study of Primitive Youth for*

Western Civilization became standard reading in universities and community colleges for decades.

Not until years later, when Derek Freeman carried out follow-up research, was key contradictory evidence discovered.[5] Mead's counter-cultural predisposition certainly slanted her scholarly view and skewed the "objectivity" of her research. Indeed, it is debatable if any discussion on sexuality can ever be completely objective or neutral. But U.S. society was ready to disrupt sexual norms and actively seek to create new cultural options. Mead's ethnography provided a tool for doing so. Today we are living at a time in which not just the United States, but the whole global community, is rethinking what is sexually right and wrong. National surveys show that American evangelicals are especially reticent to talk about sex.[6] For this reason Lingenfelter's article is groundbreaking. Greater clarity and nuancing is needed, however, especially regarding recognition of the *universal* nature of sex, gender, and arousal coupled with full recognition of the cultural malleability of gender and arousal in conjunction with *specific* moral communities (e.g., spiritual feminist lesbian, white evangelical, AfroBaptist, Christian gay celibate, white mainline, Mormon, and Catholic).

CONCLUSION

Notre Dame sociologist Christian Smith writes that evangelicals are a vibrant growing group precisely because we actively incorporate broader cultural tools as means to attract people to the church. According to Smith, while evangelicals hold to the core of our faith, we also recognize the importance of relevance to the broader society, therefore having what I would call a uniquely negotiated boundary.[7] Lingenfelter's essay exemplifies this evangelical value. He is pushing us to engage the deep cultural shifts taking place in America today, especially as they relate to our Christian communities and families. When he insistently asks, "To whom do these [non-heterosexual] young people belong?" he is implicitly asking a question of the church: Are we willing to engage this debate in creative ways so that we can extend the boundaries of our evangelical community? I do not think it will be an easy conversation, but it matters greatly. Thank you, Sherwood, for nudging us.

NOTES

1. Margaret Mead, *Sex and Temperament in Three Primitive Societies* (New York: W. Morrow, 1935).

2. See www.kinseyinstitute.org/research/ak-hhscale.html. For recent research showing even more variability among women than was found in Kinsey's work, see Roy F. Baumeister, "Gender Differences in Erotic Plasticity: The Female Sex Drive as Socially Flexible and Responsive," *Psychological Bulletin* 126, no. 3 (2000): 347–74), and Meredith F. Chivers, "Leading Comment: A Brief Review and Discussion of Sex Differences in the Specificity of Sexual Arousal," *Sexual and Relationship Therapy* 20, no. 4 (2005): 377–90.

3. Mary Douglas, *Purity and Danger: An Analysis of Concepts of Pollution and Taboo* (New York: Praeger, 1966).

4. Margaret Mead, *Coming of Age in Samoa: A Psychological Study of Primitive Youth for Western Civilization* (New York: Morrow, 1928).

5. Derek Freeman, *Margaret Mead and Samoa: The Making and Unmaking of an Anthropological Myth* (Cambridge, Mass.: Harvard Univ. Press, 1983), and *The Fateful Hoaxing of Margaret Mead: A Historical Analysis of Her Samoan Research* (Boulder, Colo.: Westview Press, 1999).

6. Mark Regnerus, *Forbidden Fruit: Sex and Religion in the Lives of American Teenagers* (New York: Oxford Univ. Press, 2007).

7. Christian Smith, *American Evangelicalism: Embattled and Thriving* (Chicago: Univ. of Chicago Press, 1998).

22

ADDITIONAL QUESTIONS

STEVEN C. ROY

I want to begin with an expression of deep appreciation to Sherwood Lingenfelter for his essay. He has performed a valuable service to the Evangelical Missiological Society and the broader evangelical church by identifying key questions that are currently being discussed relating to gay and lesbian Christians and proposing new questions that need to be. The breadth of his brief survey is impressive, touching on issues of scriptural interpretation, social science research, lived experience, cultural realities, and missional responses. Lingenfelter does all this with a spirit of humility, honesty, and courage. So it is with gratitude and appreciation that I enter into this discussion.

Since Lingenfelter's stated goal is primarily to frame key questions rather than to answer them, I will respond with some questions of my own. They fall into three areas.

THE ROLE OF EXPERIENCE

One of the great contributions of this essay is the way it raises the issue of the relationship between lived human experience and Scripture. What is the proper role of story, of biography, in doing theology? Lingenfelter forces us to grapple with this question by introducing his discussion with the stories of Nicodemus and his daughter, Jennifer.

The force of these stories guarantees that the essay will not languish as a mere abstract discussion of biblical exegesis and ethical theories. A great strength of the essay is that the stories force both author and reader to grapple with the issues being discussed in light of real life and real people. Far too often, evangelicals have engaged in discussions of this topic from the detached stance of the scholar rather than with the engaged connection of those called by God to love him and our neighbors. We need to listen carefully and empathetically to the stories of gays and lesbians who love Christ and are seeking to follow him (both those who are persuaded that the way to do so is a disciplined life of celibacy and those who are persuaded that faithfulness to Christ can involve committed, faithful, life-long same-sex relationships). These stories can help us to see Christ and his Word more clearly—and often to do so with fresh eyes.

That said, I believe it is also possible to use biography too much. While too little experience leads to dry, sterile discussions far removed from real life, too much can end up shaping our biblical interpretations and personal and ministry responses to fit the experience. Is that the case with Lingenfelter's essay? Do the stories he cites give us fresh eyes and open up new possibilities as we engage with Scripture, social science research, culture, and mission? Or do they shape his and our views with unwarranted power and in the end cede first place to the authority of experience? These questions are important. They need to be grappled with intentionally and honestly, in broad conversations within the community of faith.

These questions become all the more urgent when the stories are intensely personal, as is the case with Lingenfelter's daughter, Jennifer. The extraordinary power of this God-given relationship forces us to come to terms with the role that these unique stories and relationships should have in our understanding and our responses. These questions are especially challenging and, as Lingenfelter says, we need to grapple with them together.

BIBLICAL INTERPRETATION

Lingenfelter's survey of biblical teaching on LGBTQ behavior focuses exclusively on the specific passages that explicitly address this topic. This narrow focus, however, raises another question: Are only those biblical texts that explicitly mention an issue relevant for assessing it? Or do other biblical texts and theological themes contribute to forming the framework for a biblical understanding? I am troubled, for example, by the lack of attention given in this essay to the creation accounts of Genesis 1–2. I would suggest that they are worthy of a more central place in the discussion. They form the foundation for our understanding of human sexuality, informing our understanding both of the creational purpose of God and of the range of sexual sin (both opposite-sex and same-sex) in a fallen world. This creational framework is endorsed by Jesus in his teaching on marriage and divorce in Matthew 19:4–6. The creation accounts also frame Paul's discussion of homosexual practice in Romans 1 (see 1:19–20). All of these factors make it important that biblical teaching on creation be central to this discussion.

Other theological themes such as the Fall and the way it shapes our experience of God's good creation, the "already and not yet-ness" of our redemption in Christ, and the ultimate eschatological goals of God for his people all need to be explored to gain a holistic biblical and theological understanding of same-sex attraction and relationships.

THE WIDENESS OF GOD'S MERCY AND THE ISSUE OF REDUNDANCY

As we seek to interpret Scripture, Lingenfelter calls for us to pay close attention to the *redundancy* of the biblical message (the same truth "stated in various ways in multiple biblical contexts"), which can help correct cultural distortions arising out of the *limiting effects* of its original culture. He also suggests that the wideness of God's mercy may well lead him to permit faithful, monogamous same-sex partnerships, even as he permitted polygamy and accepted the weaknesses of a man like David. But Lingenfelter does not relate these two issues. This is unfortunate, in my opinion.

Like Lingenfelter, I am convinced that God's mercy is wide and surprising, and that it regularly transcends barriers that humans have sinfully constructed. But as attractive as I might find Lingenfelter's suggestion to be in relation to LGBTQ behavior, I would be more open to the suggestion's appeal if I saw less redundancy within the canon on this issue. As I read Scripture, the negative portrayal of LGBTQ behavior is uniformly consistent. I do not see tension within the biblical witness, with some texts being positive and others negative. No trajectories toward greater acceptance appear over the span of the canon. As Richard Hayes points out, "The NT offers no accounts of homosexual Christians, tells no stories of same-sex lovers, ventures no metaphors that place a positive construal on homosexual relations."[1] These observations, then, leave us with the question: How does the wideness of God's mercy relate to the redundancy of biblical teaching about same-sex relationships? And how do both issues relate to the experience of Christians with same-sex attractions? Once again, these are important and substantive questions, deserving of broad and ongoing discussion.

Space does not permit me to touch on the missional questions Lingenfelter raises, other than to say that I find it very helpful to frame them, as he suggests, in terms of the new "scripts" for the relationship between same-sex attraction, personal identity, community life, and mission that can and must be developed in dialog with Christians of same-sex attraction.

Thanks again to Sherwood Lingenfelter for his essay. May the additional questions that I have raised enrich what I pray will be an ongoing, God-honoring, and very fruitful dialogue.

NOTE

1. Richard Hayes, *The Moral Vision of the New Testament* (San Francisco: HarperSanFrancisco, 1996), 395.

23

WIDENING THE FIELD
OF VISION

MICHAEL A. RYNKIEWICH

How to engage the rise and spread of LGBTQ cultures with the Gospel of Jesus Christ?—that is a missiological question. Yet in the present chapter by Sherwood Lingenfelter, scant attention is paid to the diversity of cultures in the world, particularly to ethnographic accounts of beliefs and behaviors related to same-sex attraction. Current forces of urbanization and globalization that affect the diffusion and adoption of or resistance to emerging gay cultures throughout the world also are slighted. At this juncture the strategies of mission history and mission anthropology—in addition to biblical theology and personal narrative—would be appropriate to help us frame the issues.

CULTURE

How have cultures addressed same-sex attraction, if at all? Melanesian anthropology offers some insights into issues of identity formation and sexual practice. First, the work of Marilyn Strathern and others provides a caution against pretending that Western conceptions of personhood are somehow scientific while others are not.[1] There are many systems for constructing identity, perhaps as many as there are cultures.

Second, the work of Kenneth Read and others in Papua New Guinea reveals in traditional cultures a widespread concern with gender formation.[2] Of particular concern is that boys raised by their mothers need to go through initiation rites in order to be separated from the polluting influence of women, a result accomplished by their being properly fortified with male influences in the form of semen deposited on the head, in the mouth, or in the anus.[3] It was thought that only in this way would boys transition to become men.

Third, Gilbert Herdt, in *Rituals of Manhood*, recounts the ways in which people create their own sexual identities and notes how fluid these rituals are through time. The Sambia imagined that while the exchange of semen was important so as to move boys along to adolescence and adolescents along to manhood, the end result was to become a heterosexual male and not to remain in these earlier developmental stages featuring same-sex behavior.[4]

Fourth, Bruce Knauft provides us with ethnographic accounts of the hunting and gathering Gebusi, including their practice of same-sex behavior among young men on extended hunting trips. Sexual behavior was variable, depending on the social context.[5]

Taken together, these brief references from ethnographic accounts from a small sample of the range of cultures in the world should humble us concerning what we think that we know about sexuality in cross-cultural perspective. This is a lesson that we should have learned long ago through missiology.

CHANGE

Knauft followed up his ethnographic work with another period of fieldwork carried out twenty years later.[6] By this time the people had been touched by global flows of capitalism in the form of a nearby mine, and Christianity brought by missionaries. Knauft recounts an incident in which he heard a word in conversation that he did not understand. He asked if it was related to the aforementioned practice of young men in hunting parties. The men did not know what he was talking about and took offense at the suggestion that that had ever been a part of their culture. He quickly changed the subject.

Global flows of people, products, and perspectives include not only capitalism and Christianity, but also homoerotic cultures; and in each case, there is local resistance, reinvention, rejection, or adaptation. Peter Jackson describes the way that global cities are linked to each other, and thus how Bangkok became a "gay capital."[7] Jackson pays due attention to traditional Thai understandings, identities, and practices, and then shows how Thais negotiate "global queering."[8] These global flows include people (migration and tourism) as well as ideas and are linked mostly to port cities in capitalist trading networks. Thus urbanization and globalization intersect to create sites for the exploration of new understandings of sexuality—a cultural and social phenomenon, not just a personal one as imagined in the United States. Another lesson learned in missiology: people are caught in webs of significance not all of their own making, but they are resourceful in negotiating their way through the maze.

From a missiological standpoint, we have been here before. The construction of male and female identities, and how that affects marriage and family life, is a long-standing missiological interest—though we last discussed it under the guise of "polygamy." Auli Vähäkangas reminds us that this conversation has not gone away, since childlessness is still an issue in many societies, including those of Tanzania.[9] Childlessness raises issues of wholeness (identity), salvation, and immortality—all mission concerns.

Finally, a missiological perspective must include the "new faces of Christianity" of which Philip Jenkins writes.[10] Insofar as the church's center of gravity has shifted south and east, so has the center of the sending mission, leaving the "First World" on the periphery. No conversation about LGBTQ issues can long continue without voices from the Global South being heard. As Jenkins shows, if we did not already know, the kinds of readings of Scripture proposed in the West are not at all what Christians in the Global South churches practice, nor, I might add, what missionaries sent out by Global South churches teach. To Christians in the Global South, current Western readings of Scripture must look like a case of syncretism, or, at best, poorly contextualized Christianity.

The sum is that critical appropriation of history, theology, and anthropology in a mission "trialogue" remains the best way forward in developing mission policies and practices for this urbanized, globalized, and newly gendered world.[11]

NOTES

1. Marilyn Strathern, *The Gender of the Gift: Problems with Women and Problems with Society in Melanesia* (Berkeley: Univ. of California Press, 1988). Others whose work in Melanesia bears on this topic include Kenneth E. Read, "Morality and the Concept of the Person among the Gahuku-Gama," *Oceania* 25, no. 4 (1955): 233–82; Andre Iteanu, "The Concept of the Person and the Ritual System: An Orokaiva View," *Man* 25 (1990): 35–53; Lisette Josephides, "Metaphors, Metathemes, and the Construction of Sociality: A Critique of the New Melanesian Ethnography," *Man* 26 (1991): 145–61.

2. Kenneth E. Read, *The High Valley* (New York: Columbia Univ. Press, 1980).

3. Mervyn J. Meggitt, "Male-Female Relationships in the Highlands of Australian New Guinea," *American Anthropologist* 66 (1964): 393–407.

4. Gilbert H. Herdt, "Ritualized Homosexual Behavior in the Male Cults of Melanesia, 1862–1983: An Introduction," in *Rituals of Manhood: Male Initiation in Papua New Guinea*, ed. Gilbert H. Herdt (Berkeley: Univ. of California Press, 1984), 1–81; "Semen Transactions in Sambia Culture," in ibid., 167–210; *The Sambia: Ritual and Gender in New Guinea* (New York: Holt, Rinehart, and Winston, 1987). Sambia is a pseudonym.

5. Bruce Knauft, "Text and Social Practice: Narrative 'Longing' and Bisexuality among the Gebusi of New Guinea," *Ethos* 14 (1986): 252–58; "Homosexuality in Melanesia," *Journal of Psychoanalytic Anthropology* 10 (1987): 155–91.

6. Bruce Knauft, *The Gebusi: Lives Transformed in a Rainforest World*, 3rd ed. (New York: McGraw-Hill, 2012).

7. Peter A. Jackson, "Gay Capitals in Global Gay History: Cities, Local Markets, and the Origins of Bangkok's Same-Sex Cultures," in *Postcolonial Urbanism: Southeast Asian Cities and Global Processes*, ed. Ryan Bishop, John Phillips, and Wei-Wei Yeo (New York: Routledge, 2003), 151–63.

8. Dennis Altman developed this concept in his "Rupture or Continuity? The Internationalization of Gay Identities," *Social Text* 14, no. 3 (1996): 77–94. See also Jackson, "Gay Capitals," 153.

9. Auli Vähäkangas, *Christian Couples Coping with Childlessness: Narratives from Machame, Kilimanjaro* (Eugene, Ore.: Pickwick Press, 2009).

10. Philip Jenkins, *The New Faces of Christianity: Believing the Bible in the Global South* (Oxford: Oxford Univ. Press, 2006).

11. See Harvie Conn, *Eternal Word and Changing Worlds: Theology, Anthropology, and Mission in Trialogue* (Phillipsburg, N.J.: P & R Publishing, 1992).

24

THE VIEW
FROM A UNIVERSITY
PRESIDENT'S OFFICE

DAVID WRIGHT

Universities exist to discover and teach truths about life's important questions. Christ-centered universities undertake this work within the integrating framework of Christian faith and scholarship. It is through the rigorous examination of the day's most pressing issues that Christian universities put the riches of our faith into service for the common good. Clearly one of the most pressing issues of our day involves the remarkable contemporary shift in the way Western societies treat homosexuality. Every day we are plied with the hopeful message that homosexuality is a normal and acceptable variation of human identity and experience.

Within a decade a majority of Americans have come to believe that to deny gay and lesbian persons their identity and lifestyle is to wrongfully discriminate against them. To question this view publicly is to be accused of living on the wrong side of history. In the words of one observer, what was once an infirmity has become an identity. This identity is increasingly afforded the protections of the law within even the most conservative states in this country. In taking this step, our society is embracing a point of view that is at odds with beliefs that have guided our religious communities for generations.

Further, this shift is less and less a theoretical issue and more a personal experience. Most of us have family members, friends, or colleagues who are openly gay and lesbian. Our students have gay and lesbian friends. When they graduate they will live and work alongside openly gay persons. Christian universities cannot avoid or evade this tide of social change. Nor can we simply repeat our convictions about the moral dimension of homosexual sexual relations. How do we live out our belief about the morality of such a lifestyle in a society that attaches no moral significance to that lifestyle and that sees any resistance to that lifestyle as itself an act of immorality?

TWO MESSAGES

Our students face two polarized messages.

On the one hand, our religious communities believe that homosexual lifestyles, while they may be experienced as an unchosen orientation, are a fundamentally disordered form of sexual intimacy. Taken in isolation this conviction has come to be viewed by many of our contemporaries as a horrifying belief, but our religious communities simply do not approach questions of morality in isolation. They are part of a larger understanding that all of us fall short of God's glory. All of us, in our moments of honesty and humility, admit that we know what it is to desire something that feels natural and good, but that is in fact sinful and disordered. This truth is the great inconvenient fact that the Bible makes clear about human nature.

But we do not experience this truth as bad news. We believe that the recognition of this truth is the first step toward forgiveness and redemption. In our more lucid moments we know that our happiness and well-being lie not in the affirmation of our disordered loves, but in the narrow and difficult path of submitting our loves to the lordship of Christ. The one is a pleasing enticement to heartbreak. The other is a faithful promise of well-being. We know all too well the easy path that leads to destruction. We are called to the narrow and unfamiliar way that leads to life. This is one narrative offered to our students.

On the other hand, progressive Christians and social liberals offer their own passionately held belief that homosexuality is simply one of many possible distinguishing characteristics that persons may bear. Such an identity is no more chosen, and bears no more moral import, than one's ethnicity. LGBT persons are people created in God's image, loved by God, and fully worthy of unstinting acceptance by their neighbors. To deny them this acceptance is to subject them to one of history's most pervasive and stubborn injustices. This is another message offered to our students.

WHAT MUST CHRISTIAN UNIVERSITIES DO?

Which of these messages is truly good news? How should Christian universities proceed in this context?

First, we must teach our students to have the courage of their convictions. Until God's Spirit changes our understanding of God's Word, despite the growing chorus to the contrary, we must be honest about our convictions and faithful to them. Doing anything less holds no honor or blessing. We must model for our students the way to hold biblical convictions with courage, humility, and grace: courage, because our convictions are increasingly out of step with our culture; humility, because in this life we see and know in part; and grace, because we simply cannot truly know another person's journey. The grace we wish to receive is the grace we must be willing to give.

Second, we must remind our students that what we believe about homosexuality is just one among many biblical truths that shape our lives and our interactions with our neighbors. It is good to remember that while believers are admonished to hold one another accountable for holy living, we are not called to impose our sense of moral rectitude on our neighbors. We are called to witness to them lovingly about our Lord Jesus Christ. Christians are called to be a winsome presence in their non-Christian societies through humility and service. We must not be drawn into an easy acceptance of the disordered loves of our age. But we must learn to live in this time and place as ambassadors of God's redeeming love.

Third, we must teach our students that the body of Christ is called to various kinds of ministries. Some may be called to a prophetic ministry—to speak the truth regardless of fear or favor. Many will be called to some form of pastoral ministry—caring for our neighbors regardless of who they are, how they behave, or what they believe. Those who hold one ministry must not dismiss or denigrate those called to other expressions of God's grace in this world.

Fourth, we must help our students learn to live godly lives in the presence of those who do not hold their convictions. This is what it means to be salt and light. We live alongside friends, neighbors, and loved ones for whom homosexuality is not an issue but a lived experience. Regardless of how it happens, whether by nature or by nurture, they hunger for personal and physical intimacy with members of the same sex. They are as driven to achieve this intimacy as are their heterosexual neighbors. This desire sets up a life trajectory that is fraught with questions and dangers. Three things make this journey intolerable. One is the merciless taunting, bullying, and violence of peers. Another is enforced silence—the inability to talk about this experience for fear of losing the only remnants of love and belonging that they have. A third is the bleak prospect of a life without the kind of intimacy they crave. These persons are our neighbors whom God has called us to love as we love ourselves. If we begin from this command, the Holy Spirit will show us how to be a redemptive presence in their lives.

LIFTING UP A VISION OF HOLINESS

Christian universities have both the responsibility and the privilege of drawing upon the rich wisdom of our spiritual heritage in our pursuit of understanding. At the heart of our faith is a passion to be holy—to bear in this world, even if only faintly, the image of God's goodness, loving-kindness, mercy, and righteousness.

Holiness is the birthright of Jesus' followers. Our pursuit of holiness causes us to find and address those issues that most define us and our time. This is the point at which holiness best emerges into meaning and significance. God's holiness is a fountain of well-being. It is the source of human flourishing.

Holiness does not begin with what is wrong in us or in our society. It begins with what is right about God—God's passionate love and impeccable goodness. Once this love and goodness permeate all of life, they fashion and shape us after the likeness of Christ. They do so organically, at the speed and in the way that is most true to our inner being, to the persons we are, and to the way we are best able to follow the one we come to love most—our Lord Jesus Christ.

This vision is what we are called to offer our students and our world.

25

TENSIONS BETWEEN *"WHAT SHOULD BE"* AND *"WHAT IS"*: A Response

SHERWOOD G. LINGENFELTER

I am grateful to the editors, Robert Priest and Dwight Baker, for inviting professional colleagues to write these thirteen critical reflections in response to my chapter. They embody the very best kind of academic scholarship and represent for me a first step toward the type of conversations I envisioned in writing the essay and presenting it at the annual meeting of the Evangelical Missiological Society. Graham Cole has best captured the essence of my objective, to stimulate a "think tank" approach for discussion of the very complex issues that surround *what is* the case—namely, that "devout Christians find themselves with persistent, life-long same-sex attraction" (Jenell Paris).

These reflections are a first step in what I hope will become a larger collective effort on the part of the church to dialogue together on these issues. The respondents include scholars with expertise in the study of the Old Testament (Daniel Carroll, John Goldingay), New Testament (Joshua Jipp), theology (Graham Cole, Steve Roy), anthropology (Jenell Paris, Michael Rynkiewich), ethics (Andrew Cameron), missiology (Phillip Marshall, Craig Ott, Michael Rynkiewich again), psychology (Stanton Jones), sociology (Kersten Priest), and university administration (David Wright). I rejoice that these responses have added much more to the conversation than I could have written. In that spirit I encourage an even broader dialogue that could include contributions from Christians in human biology, in human origins and cultural history, in economics and political science, in public policy and international relations, and in church history and global mission. So much is happening on these issues both on the public front in the United States and internationally in secular governments, church polity, and human rights organizations that we cannot make significant progress pastorally or theologically in considering these issues as the church of the Lord Jesus Christ unless we enlarge the conversation.

But even more important to me, these reflections have not included the wounded. I submitted an earlier draft of my chapter to some pastor friends, to two men who are gay, and to my daughter, Jennifer. A friend, who "came out" just before graduating with his M.Div. degree from Fuller Theological Seminary, agreed to send comments on the chapter to me. Since he does not have a voice here, I will try to capture the essence of two of his comments:

- The chapter focuses too much on the debate about Scripture and does not give enough attention to the kinds of pastoral response that are faithful to Scripture yet at the same time listen to and show love and encouragement toward gay people.
- Is it possible to approach these issues recognizing the humanity, decency, and value of LGBTQ people, that is, an approach without hate, condemnation, or pity, but rather one that sees their potential for contributing to the greater church and to God's mission of redemption?

Among my pastor friends, one is agonizing over how to love and support a son who has come out while attending a Christian university. This man, like me, has been reflecting on his pastoral and parental response, as a deeply committed follower of Jesus Christ. These are core issues that I have not addressed, but in their responses Cameron, Ott, and Wright provide readers with thoughtful insights.

LIVED EXPERIENCE: REFLECTION ON "WHAT IS"

Reading the responses of others to one's scholarship has the positive effect of helping a writer to see more clearly what has been communicated. Eight of the respondents note that I use the stories of my daughter Jennifer and of my friend's son Nicodemus to frame my essay with very specific reference to their lived experience. Jenell Paris affirms this strategy, noting that evangelicals prefer abstractions about *what should be* and are often unresponsive to *what is*. Her observation captures the essence of what I wish I had said more clearly in my chapter, and I intend to follow this theme throughout this concluding essay.

Marshall, Paris, Priest, and Rynkiewich each contribute new perspectives on the "what is" of LGBTQ lived experience. Paris and Rynkiewich remind us of the diversity of ways in which human beings deal culturally with issues of their sexuality. Marshall makes clear how such diversity stretches and tests young men and women deployed in global ministries. Priest introduces some of the basic biological and social tensions of what sexuality is and means for human beings. One of her most important contributions is the distinction between sexuality, which is biologically determined, and gender, which is culturally determined. Another is the significant variance that occurs around issues of sexual arousal and sexual attraction in the human body. All note appropriately that I have missed much relevant material on this subject, material that is critical to understanding the lived experience of LGBTQ men and women, and to thinking biblically and theologically about those experiences. Their insights illustrate why I believe it is so important to include in our conversations Christian researchers who are experts in the medical, biological, and psychological dimensions of these questions of sexuality and spiritual life.

Respondents Carroll, Cole, Jipp, and Roy also affirm the significant power of the stories and how they force us to consider issues we customarily would have dismissed. All also raise questions about what role experience *should* play in our theological reflection. Jipp and Roy worry about giving too much weight to experience in theological reflection, and Jipp invites readers into a deeper discussion of what Scripture says on this topic. To begin such a conversation, Jipp cites the story of Peter and Cornelius as a case study from Scripture that can be analyzed to see how the apostles and early Christians dealt with the question, "*What is* God doing with the Gentiles?"

The diverse points made in these essays about "lived experience" have enriched the conversation and expanded my understanding with perspectives that I could not have achieved alone. I think we together would agree that *what is* must become an essential piece of any conversation on this topic. The personal stories of the men and women who struggle with all forms of LGBTQ attraction cannot be ignored; rather, they give us a deeper understanding of the human questions that must be answered and of the critical moral, social, political, and theological issues that emerge from this human experience. At the same time, Cole and Ott argue, and I agree, we cannot and must not do theology or apologetics on the basis of our individual stories. Rather, our theology must speak to the questions that the stories raise in ways that articulate the whole message of God for all of us—including these people. Toward that end, we must consider not only *what should be* but also *what is*, and must ponder how we can respond as followers of the Lord Jesus Christ, fulfilling his command to love the Lord our God and to love our neighbors as ourselves.

THE CREATION NARRATIVE: *"WHAT SHOULD BE"* AND *"WHAT IS"*?

In writing my chapter I felt most inadequate in researching and summarizing what I found to be the debates among biblical scholars about the reading and interpretation of Scripture. It was not a surprise that Carroll, Cole, Goldingay, and Roy should cite my failure to give priority to Genesis 1 and 2 in my discussion of the biblical literature. In different ways they emphasize the creation narrative as having critical relevance for the question of *what should be* as a guide for our understanding of and response to LGBTQ behaviors.

Carroll points out that sexual differentiation, reproduction, and the marriage of male and female are grounded in the natural order. Goldingay speaks of God's creation ideal versus "the way things are in a stubborn world." Carroll and Roy note that the metaphor of marriage is used to describe the relationship between God and Israel and between Christ and the church. Goldingay and Roy cite Matthew, where Jesus specifically applies the creation narrative in his instructions to his disciples on marriage and divorce. These commentators are absolutely correct in their assessment of my chapter. I did not address the creation narrative except in one reference to the conservative Anglican response to gay marriage. I am thankful for the opportunity to come back to this topic.

First, these respondents' comments are absolutely relevant to the topic, and sexual reproduction is one of the key components of God's creation design or vision. Carroll notes that man and woman are to "be fruitful and multiply." The prophet Malachi, speaking for faithfulness in marriage, cites God's motive: "He was seeking godly offspring" (2:15 NIV). My quarrel is not with Scripture; rather it is with what I will term loosely as an *idealist/order of nature* view of creation versus a *critical realist* view.

Carroll uses the more typical language, speaking of creation as "pattern," "framework," and "order"; Goldingay speaks of God's creation "ideal" or "vision." The concepts of framework, order, and ideal imply a philosophy of research and interpretation that is seeking "certainties, coherences, and structures"[1] as the end result. Goldingay's use of "God's creation vision" implies a wider range of potentiality within it, and perhaps allows for "the ambiguities, the confusions, . . . and the ambivalences that arise in the midst of our . . . experiences as lived."[2]

So I return to my lived experience of reproduction, and the tension between *what should be* and *what is.* My wife, Judy, and I have two biological children, Jennifer and Joel. Joel has two biological children, Grace and Jacob. Of these four of our offspring, three suffer from biologically derived dysfunctions. Grace, our granddaughter, was born with a heart defect, the result of a malfunction of the chemical programming that forms the fetus, which was corrected through major heart surgery at three months of age. Jacob, our grandson, was born with genetic susceptibility to autoimmune disease for type 1 diabetes, which attacked his pancreas in full force at the age of ten, destroying his body's ability to produce insulin. Jennifer, our daughter, has lived since early adolescence with a malfunction of chemical programming in the brain that forms sexual attraction (whether it occurs in fetal formation, in childhood trauma, or in some other complex of variables is unknown).

So what is the point? Scripture states clearly that "God saw all that he had made, and it was very good" (Gen. 1:31 NIV). It does not state that the creation was perfect, or that it was without illness or pain. It does not state that all offspring would be perfectly formed or develop perfectly into adulthood, and geneticists and paleontologists will testify that illness, disease, and deformation are evident long before humans appeared on the earth. Many Christians are quick to attribute the problems in my offspring to "the Fall" and "sin." In my view this is bad science and worse theology.

I have hope that some theologians have already begun to expand our capacity to respond to current knowledge and are reimagining a theology of creation that reflects the eternity and complexity of the Creator God we worship. Such a theology will perhaps recognize that a "very good" creation includes such factors as disease, viruses, bacteria, dysfunctional sexual reproduction, and death, as well as including natural disasters such as hurricanes, earthquakes, tsunamis, and other natural events that are so destructive to local life.

The notion of "God's ideal," as opposed to "very good" creation, leads us to contradictions in our response to tensions between *what should be* and *what is*. For example, evangelicals place high value on the sanctity of life, and most would argue that we should do everything possible to preserve life for my grandchildren Grace and Jacob without reference to cost. But many of these same people would sentence Jennifer (or Nicodemus) to a lifetime of celibacy, and of social stigma, isolation, and despair, because of a brain chemistry that drives their same-sex attraction.

Goldingay makes note of our confusion on creation and sexual issues, citing different evangelical responses on four sexual issues that fall short of God's creation vision: "horrified by polygamy . . . take birth-control for granted . . . welcome divorced and remarried Christians into the fellowship of the church . . . are in a turmoil over same-sex relationships." Goldingay makes one additional observation that I found helpful for reflection on our possible pastoral response to LGBTQ people; he draws attention to how Jesus notes the difference between God's creation vision and the way Scripture makes allowance for human stubbornness. In this we find biblical precedent for how to deal with the tensions between *what should be* and *what is*.

SEXUAL IMMORALITY: *"WHAT SHOULD BE" AND "WHAT IS"?*

Carroll, Cole, Jones, and Goldingay all have identified some part of my chapter that fails to deal with some of the ethical and moral issues that have surfaced in the public LGBTQ agenda in the United States. I apologize to Jones for the fact that my chapter led him and perhaps others to conclude that I wish to suspend discussion on ethical and moral issues. Jones states, "Lingenfelter fails to establish a case justifying suspension of our moral teaching." Frankly, I am glad that I failed in this regard. That was never my intent in writing the chapter; and if I seem to be making a case to justify such a suspension, I repent of that here.

More specifically, my failures are documented as follows. Carroll notes that Old Testament legislation prohibits violations of the "divine ideals." He goes on to point out that same-sex behaviors of any kind are labeled "detestable." Jones notes correctly that the history of the church shows a very strong consensus on these issues, prohibiting all same-sex behaviors.

Cole points out that my paper does not wrestle with the differences between descriptive, prescriptive, proscriptive, and permissive passages. More importantly, I do not use argument to persuade for the proscriptive viewpoint, particularly in relationship to the differences between one who has same-sex attraction and another who identifies as LGBTQ. Cole is correct; I chose not to wrestle with these issues. I am looking to others for help, to those skilled in biblical and theological scholarship who would deliberate on these matters in a context with committed LGBTQ Christians, so they might represent their own case. I prefer that we reach some consensus on these questions by including *what is*—that is, Christians who have one of the many LGBTQ expressions of sexuality—in the conversation.

What is my position on sexual immorality? I personally believe that sexual immorality is destructive in all its forms and that God's love for humanity is at the root of prohibitions against it. I believe that by living in accordance with the standards that God provides for us in Scripture, most are enabled to live full and joyful lives as human beings. As those standards are currently interpreted by many evangelicals, however, that is not the case for LGBTQ people.

Cameron, Ott, and Wright, in distinctive ways, have helped me with new perspectives on what it means to be followers of Jesus in regard to these challenging issues. Cameron notes that the church has given Nicodemus the "thinnest of social or cultural grounds" to deal with his sexuality, and reminds us that we too are on "the same difficult journey, to discern and inhabit the true 'nature' God dreams of for his people." Ott points to our history in missions with polygamy and how 150 years later we are responding in a parallel way to legally married same-sex couples with potentially similar unintended spiritual consequences. Wright captures the political climate of our times and frames a message for students and the church that affirms our biblical convictions, places LGBTQ issues as just one of many challenges for faithful witness to our neighbors, and encourages living godly lives of prophetic and compassionate witness among and with those who have LGBTQ lived experience.

SCRIPTURE AND CULTURE: *"WHAT SHOULD BE" AND "WHAT IS"*?

Jones states that in my concluding section I attribute "traditional readings of Scripture" as a byproduct of "the church having allowed culture or politics" to set the agenda. This is a serious objection and is worthy of comment. Jones has misunderstood my point, which is to say that the church is always in danger of allowing culture and politics to set the agenda and that historically it has in fact often reflected its local culture and politics more than the teachings of Scripture. We should always be aware of this danger, and as the body of Christ we need to resist it as much as we are able. In the last century, the church reflected the widespread homophobia of the wider culture, rejecting LGBTQ persons as either criminals or mentally disturbed pariahs, and often treated them as outcastes. Such attitudes and actions are not the Gospel that Jesus taught. Yet a similar danger exists today: the church is under tremendous cultural and political pressure to accept the "gay script." That is why I have called for a fresh examination of these issues and for the framing of alternative scripts by people deeply committed to God, the Scriptures, and the church.

It is a given that humans have finite understanding, and that people's understanding is particularly shaped and limited by their own language and culture. In Romans 11:32 Paul notes that God has given Jews and Gentiles alike over to prisons of disobedience so God might have mercy upon us all. In my view this prison of disobedience is emotional, intellectual, social, cultural, and spiritual. So in one sense, Jones is correct; I do not believe that any theology or reading of Scripture is cultural-free, but I also argue that *redundancy* in biblical texts corrects much of that problem. Roy affirms the principle of *redundancy*, but then turns it against my openness to other interpretations, arguing that there is a uniformly and consistent negative portrayal of same-sex coupling in Scripture. While Goldingay notes that *redundancy* is far greater for the distortions of opposite-sex coupling, Roy's point is legitimate and must be taken seriously.

In my Anabaptist church heritage, our motto is "the Bible, the whole Bible, and nothing but the Bible." This is a wonderful principle, but also a seduction, and here I present my final *what is*—humans have never been able to receive, interpret, reflect, and live out the message of Scripture apart from the presuppositions and schemas of their languages and cultures. The reformers, in all of their diverse versions of reform, reflected their local languages and cultures, just as did the early church fathers and their church councils. In my global anthropological research with SIL International, in every context I have found local churches conformed to and reflecting local cultures. Andrew Walls captured this so well in his notion that any healthy church must be both fully indigenous and fully on pilgrimage.[3]

CONCLUSION

In conclusion, I am grateful for the *redundancy* represented in the thirteen responses to my chapter by these respected colleagues. I pray that their combined efforts will correct for readers the errors of my thinking and writing, and that by participating together in this scholarly exercise, we together will have obtained a deeper understanding of the *what is* of LGBTQ sexuality, and also of the *what should be* in our evangelical churches and mission communities as we seek together to live in obedience to our holy God, and to fulfill his mission to the lost and broken people of our time.

When I began this journey, I knew that I was wholly inadequate to address these questions. At this point I am more convinced of that truth, but I would like to be one of many called by our Lord to dialogue together, learning from one another and seeking the guidance of the Holy Spirit to minister to the LGBTQ men and women in our college, university, church, and mission communities.

NOTES

1. C. Jason Throop, *Suffering and Sentiment: Exploring the Vicissitudes of Experience and Pain in Yap* (Berkeley: Univ. of California Press, 2010), 3.
2. Ibid.
3. Andrew F. Walls, "The Gospel as Prisoner and Liberator of Culture," in *The Missionary Movement in Christian History: Studies in the Transmission of Faith* (Maryknoll, N.Y.: Orbis Books, 1996), 7–9.

BIBLIOGRAPHY

Alagodi, S. D. L. "Carey's Experiment in Communal Living at Serampore." In *Carey's Obligation and India's Renaissance*, edited by J. T. K. Daniel and R. E. Hedlund, 18–33. Serampore: Council of Serampore College, 1993.

Allender, Dan B. *The Wounded Heart*. Colorado Springs, Colo.: NavPress, 1990.

Alpert, Judith L., et al. "Final Conclusions of the American Psychological Association Working Group on Investigation of Memories of Child Abuse." *Psychology, Public Policy, and Law* 4, no. 4 (1998): 933–40. doi:10.1037//1076-8971.4.4.933.

Altman, Dennis. "Rupture or Continuity? The Internationalization of Gay Identities." *Social Text* 14, no. 3 (1996): 77–94.

American Board of Commissioners for Foreign Missions. *Annual Report of the Board for 1848*. Boston: T. R. Marvin, 1848.

American Board of Commissioners for Foreign Missions. *Annual Report of the Board for 1849*. Boston: T. R. Marvin, 1849.

American Board of Commissioners for Foreign Missions. *Annual Report of the Board for 1861*. Boston: T. R. Marvin & Son, 1861.

American Medical Association. *Memories of Childhood Abuse. Report #5-A-94 of the Council of Scientific Affairs*. Washington, D.C.: American Medical Association, 1994.

American Psychiatric Association. *Statement on Memories of Sexual Abuse*. Washington, D.C.: American Psychiatric Association, 1994.

American Psychological Association. *Report of the Task Force on Appropriate Therapeutic Responses to Sexual Orientation*. Washington, D.C.: American Psychological Association, 2009.

Anderson, John R. "Verbal and Propositional Representation of Sentences in Immediate and Long-Term Memory." *Journal of Verbal Learning and Verbal Behavior* 13 (1974): 149–62.

Anderson, John R., and Lael J. Schooler. "The Adaptive Nature of Memory." In *Handbook of Memory*, edited by Endel Tulving and Fergus I. M. Craik, 557–70. New York: Oxford Univ. Press, 2000.

———. "Reflections of the Environment in Memory." *Psychological Science* 2, no. 6 (November 1991): 396–408. doi:10.1111/j.1467-9280.1991.tb00174.x.

Anderson, Rufus. "Introductory Essay on the Marriage of Missionaries." In *Memoir of Mrs. Mary Mercy Ellis, Wife of Rev. William Ellis, Missionary to the South Seas*, by William Ellis, vii–xxii. Boston: Crocker & Brewster, 1836.

Appelbaum, Paul S., Lisa A. Uyehara, and Mark R. Elin, eds. *Trauma and Memory*. New York: Oxford Univ. Press, 1997.

Applewhite, Monica. "Address of Dr. Monica Applewhite to the Irish Bishops." March 10, 2009. www.safeguarding.ie/dr-monica-applewhite-irish-bishops/.

"At Evangelical Colleges, a Shifting Attitude toward Gay Students." *Indianapolis Recorder*, Thursday, April 4, 2013. www.indianapolisrecorder.com/religion/article_8771308a-9d5c-11e2-827f -001a4bcf887a.html.

Barr, R. Arnold. *My Lives*. New York: Ballantine, 1994.

Barth, Tom. "Crisis Management in the Catholic Church: Lessons for Public Administrators." *Public Administration Review*, September/October 2010, 780–91.

Bass, Ellen, and Laura Davis. *Courage to Heal: A Guide for Women Survivors of Child Sexual Abuse*. New York: Perennial Library, 1988.

Baumeister, Roy F. "Gender Differences in Erotic Plasticity: The Female Sex Drive as Socially Flexible and Responsive." *Psychological Bulletin* 126, no. 3 (2000): 347–74.

Beardsley, Howard, Lois Edmund, James Evinger, Nancy Poling, and Geoffrey Stearns. *Final Report of the Independent Commission of Inquiry, Presbyterian Church (U.S.A.)*. 2002. www.pcusa.org/resource/icireport/.

Beck, James. *Dorothy Carey: The Tragic and Untold Story of Mrs. William Carey*. Eugene, Ore.: Wipf & Stock, 1992.

Beidelman, T. O. "Altruism and Domesticity: Images of Missionizing Women among the Church Missionary Society in Nineteenth-Century East Africa." In *Gendered Missions: Women and Men in Missionary Discourse and Practice*, edited by Mary Taylor Huber and Nancy C. Lutkehaus, 113–43. Ann Arbor: Univ. of Michigan Press, 1999.

Bernstein, Daniel M., Cara Laney, Erin K. Morris, and Elizabeth F. Loftus. "False Beliefs about Fattening Foods Can Have Healthy Consequences." *Proceedings of the National Academy of Sciences of the United States of America* 102, no. 39 (2005): 13724–31.

Bernstein, Daniel M., and Elizabeth F. Loftus. "How to Tell If a Particular Memory Is True or False." *Perspectives on Psychological Science* 4, no. 4 (July 2009): 370–74. doi:10.1111/j.1745-6924.2009.01140.x.

Biola Queer Underground [Biola University]. www.thebiolaqueerunderground.com.

BJUnity [Bob Jones University]. www.bjunity.org.

Blaney, P. H. "Affect and Memory: A Review." *Psychological Bulletin* 99, no. 2 (March 1986): 229–46.

Blume, E. Sue. *Secret Survivors*. New York: Ballantine, 1991.

Bonk, Jonathan J., ed. *Family Accountability in Missions: Korean and Western Case Studies*. New Haven, Conn.: OMSC Publications, 2013.

Boserup, Ester. *Woman's Role in Economic Development.* London: Earthscan, 1970.

Braun, Kathryn A., Rhiannon Ellis, and Elizabeth F. Loftus. "Make My Memory: How Advertising Can Change Our Memories of the Past." *Psychology and Marketing* 19, no. 1 (2002): 1–23.

Brown, Roger, and James Kulik. "Flashbulb Memories." *Cognition* 5, no. 1 (January 1977): 73–99. doi:10.1016/0010-0277(77)90018-X.

Brownson, James V. *Bible, Gender, Sexuality: Reframing the Church's Debate on Same-Sex Relationships.* Grand Rapids: Eerdmans, 2013.

Butterfield, Rosaria. *The Secret Thoughts of an Unlikely Convert.* Pittsburgh: Crown & Covenant, 2012.

Cameron, Andrew J. B. *Joined-Up Life.* Nottingham, U.K.: InterVarsity Press; Eugene, Ore.: Wipf & Stock, 2011.

"Can a Memory Be Forgotten and Then Remembered?" www.apa.org/topics/trauma/memories.aspx.

Carey, Eustace. *Memoir of William Carey, D.D.: Late Missionary to Bengal; Professor of Oriental Languages in the College of Fort William, Calcutta.* London: Jackson and Walford, 1836.

Carey, S. Pearce. *William Carey, D.D., Fellow of Linnaean Society.* London: Hodder and Stoughton, 1924.

Carey, William. *An Enquiry into the Obligations of Christians to Use Means for the Conversion of the Heathens.* Leicester: Ann Ireland, 1792.

Carter, Terry G., ed. *The Journal and Selected Letters of William Carey.* Macon, Ga.: Smyth & Helwys, 2000.

Ceci, Stephen J., Mary Lyndia Crotteau Huffman, Elliott Smith, and E. F. Loftus. "Repeatedly Thinking about a Non-event: Source Misattributions among Preschoolers." *Consciousness and Cognition* 3, no. 3 (1994): 388–407.

Cedarville Out [Cedarville University]. www.facebook.com/CedarvilleOut?hc_location=timeline.

Center for Applied Research in the Apostolate. "2009 Survey of Allegations and Costs: A Summary Report for the Secretariat of Child and Youth Protection, United States Conference of Catholic Bishops, February 2010." In *2009 Annual Report on the Implementation of the "Charter for the Protection of Children and Young People."* Washington, D.C.: United States Conference of Catholic Bishops, 2010. www.usccb.org/issues-and-action/child-and-youth-protection/upload/annual-report-on-the-implementation-of-the-charter-for-the-protection-of-children-and-young-people-2009.pdf.

Chatterjee, Sunil K. *John Clark Marshman: A Trustworthy Friend of India.* Sheoraphuli: Sunil Kumar Chatterjee, 2001.

Chee, Yeon Kyung. "Elder Care in Korea: The Future Is Now." *Ageing International* 26 (2000): 27.

Child Safety and Protection Network. http://childsafetyprotectionnetwork.org.

Chivers, Meredith F. "Leading Comment: A Brief Review and Discussion of Sex Differences in the Specificity of Sexual Arousal." *Sexual and Relationship Therapy* 20, no. 4 (2005): 377–90.

Choe, Sang-Hun. "As Familes Change, Korea's Elderly Are Turning to Suicide." *New York Times,* Feburary 17, 2013. www.nytimes.com/2013/02/17/world/asia/in-korea-changes-in-society -and-family-dynamics-drive-rise-in-elderly-suicides.html?pagewanted=1&_r=2&hp&.

Choi, Young-Jun. "Transformations in Economic Security during Old Age in Korea: The Implications for Public-Pension Reform." *Aging and Society* 26 (2006): 549. doi: 10.1017 /S0144686X06004879.

Clancy, Susan A. *The Trauma Myth.* New York: Basic Books, 2009.

Clark, Walter. Africa Letters. Presbyterian Historical Society, Philadelphia, Pennsylvania.

Cohen, Fred, ed. *Law of Deprivation of Liberty.* St. Paul, Minn.: West, 1980.

College Stats. http://collegestats.org/colleges/Christian.

Colomb v. Roman Catholic Diocese of Burlington, No. 2:10-cv-254 (D. Vt. Sept. 28, 2012). www .leagle.com/decision/In%20FDCO%2020121031810.

Conn, Harvie. *Eternal Word and Changing Worlds: Theology, Anthropology, and Mission in Trialogue.* Phillipsburg, N.J.: P & R Publishing, 1992.

Conn, Jacob H. "Brief Psychotherapy of the Sex Offender." *Journal of Clinical Psychopathology* 10, no. 4 (1949): 347–72.

Corwin, David L., and Erna Olafson. "Videotaped Discovery of a Reportedly Unrecallable Memory of Child Sexual Abuse: Comparison with a Childhood Interview Videotaped 11 Years Before." *Child Maltreatment* 2, no. 2 (1997): 91–112.

Craik, Fergus I. M., and Robert S. Lockhart. "Levels of Processing: A Framework for Memory Research." *Journal of Verbal Learning and Verbal Behavior* 11, no. 6 (1972): 671–84.

Craik, Fergus I. M., and Endel Tulving. "Depth of Processing and the Retention of Words in Episodic Memory." *Journal of Experimental Psychology: General* 104, no. 3 (1975): 268–94. doi:10.1037/0096-3445.104.3.268.

Crouch, Andy. "Sex without Bodies." *Christianity Today,* July/August 2013, 74–75.

Darch, John. "Love and Death in the Mission Compound: The Hardships of Life in the Tropics for Victorian Missionaries and Their Families." *Anvil* 17, no. 1 (2000): 29–39.

Davidoff, Leonore, and Catherine Hall. *Family Fortunes: Men and Women of the English Middle Class, 1780–1850.* Chicago: Univ. of Chicago Press, 1987.

Davidson, Richard M. *Flame of Yahweh: Sexuality in the Old Testament.* Peabody, Mass.: Hendrickson, 2007.

Davis, Deborah, and Elizabeth L. Loftus. "The Scientific Status of 'Repressed' and 'Recovered' Memories of Sexual Abuse." In *Psychological Science in the Courtroom: Consensus and Controversy,* edited by Jennifer L. Skeem, Kevin S. Douglas, and Scott O. Lilienfeld, 55–79. New York: Guilford Press, 2009.

De Rivera, Joseph. "The Construction of False Memory Syndrome: The Experience of Retractors." *Psychological Inquiry* 8, no. 4 (1997): 271–92.

De Young, James B. *Homosexuality: Contemporary Claims Examined in Light of the Bible and Other Ancient Literature and Law.* Grand Rapids: Kregel, 2000.

Diamond, Lisa M. *Sexual Fluidity: Understanding Women's Love and Desire.* Cambridge, Mass.: Harvard Univ. Press, 2008.

Dinwiddie, Stephen, Andrew C. Heath, Michael P. Dunne, Kathleen K. Bucholz, Pamela A. F. Madden, Wendy S. Slutske, Laura J. Bierut, Dixie B. Statham, and Nicholas G. Martin. "Early Sexual Abuse and Lifetime Psychopathology: A Co-twin-control Study." *Psychological Medicine* 30, no. 1 (2000): 41–52.

Douglas, Mary. *Purity and Danger: An Analysis of Concepts of Pollution and Taboo.* New York: Praeger, 1966.

Drewery, Mary. *William Carey: A Biography.* Grand Rapids: Zondervan, 1979.

Dunaetz, David R. "Organizational Justice: Perceptions of Being Treated Fairly." In *Serving Jesus with Integrity: Ethics and Accountability in Mission,* edited by Dwight P. Baker and Douglas Hayward, 197–221. Pasadena, Calif.: William Carey Library, 2010.

Eich, Eric. "Searching for Mood Dependent Memory." *Psychological Science* 6, no. 2 (1995): 67–75.

Eitel, Keith E., ed. *Missions in Contexts of Violence.* Pasadena, Calif.: William Carey Library, 2008.

Eligon, John, and Laurie Goodstein. "Kansas City Bishop Convicted of Shielding Pedophile Priest." *New York Times,* September 6, 2012. www.nytimes.com/2012/09/07/us/kansas -city-bishop-convicted-of-shielding-pedophile-priest.html?_r=0.

Elliot, James. *The Journals of Jim Elliot,* edited by Elisabeth Elliot. Old Tappen, N.J.: Revell, 1978.

Evinger, James, Carolyn Whitfield, and Judith Wiley. *Final Report of the Independent Abuse Review Panel, Presbyterian Church (U.S.A.).* 2010. www.pcusa.org/resource /final-report-independent-abuse-review-panel-presby/.

Exodus International. http://exodusinternational.org.

Farlex. *Free Dictionary.* http://legal-dictionary.thefreedictionary.com/Probable+Cause+and +Reasonable+Suspicion.

Farrell, B. Hunter. "Broken Trust: Sexual Abuse in the Mission Community; A Case Study in Mission Accountability." In *Accountability in Missions: Korean and Western Case Studies,* edited by Jonathan J. Bonk, 206–15. Eugene, Ore.: Wipf & Stock, 2011.

Federal PROTECT Act of 2003, 18 U.S.C. § 2423(c). www.law.cornell.edu/uscode/text/18/2423.

15 U.S.C. § 1681 *et seq.* www.law.cornell.edu/uscode/text/15/1681.

Form, William. *On the Shoulders of Immigrants: A Family Portrait.* Columbus, Ohio: North Star Press, 1999.

Freeh Sporkin & Sullivan, LLP. "Report of the Special Investigative Counsel Regarding the Actions of the Pennsylvania State University Related to the Child Sexual Abuse Committed by Gerald A. Sandusky." July 12, 2012.

Freeman, Derek. *The Fateful Hoaxing of Margaret Mead: A Historical Analysis of Her Samoan Research.* Boulder, Colo.: Westview Press, 1999.

———. *Margaret Mead and Samoa: The Making and Unmaking of an Anthropological Myth.* Cambridge, Mass.: Harvard Univ. Press, 1983.

French, Lauren, Rachel Sutherland, and Maryanne Garry. "Discussion Affects Memory for True and False Childhood Events." *Applied Cognitive Psychology* 20, no. 5 (July 2006): 671–80. doi:10.1002/acp.1219.

Freud, Sigmund. "The Aetiology of Hysteria." In *The Standard Edition of the Complete Psychological Works of Sigmund Freud*, edited by Anna Freud and James Strachy, 187–221. London: Hogarth Press, 1962.

Freyd, Jennifer J. *Betrayal Trauma.* Cambridge: Harvard Univ. Press, 1997.

Friesen, James G. "Satanic Ritual Abuse Indicators." www.jamesgfriesen.com/PDF-Files/Satanic -Ritual-Abuse-Indicators.pdf.

———. *Uncovering the Mystery of MPD.* San Bernardino, Calif.: Here's Life, 1991.

Fullbright, Lori. "Victory Christian Staff Members Plead No Contest to Failing to Report Teen Rape." *WNOW News on 6*, March 22, 2013. http://wnow.worldnow.com/global/story .asp?s=21767011.

Gabel, Laurel K. "'I Never Regretted Coming to Africa': The Story of Harriet Ruggles Loomis." *Markers: Annual Journal of the Association for Gravestone Studies* 16 (1999): 140–73.

Gagnon, Robert A. J. "The Bible and Homosexual Practice: Key Issues." In *Homosexuality and the Bible: Two Views*, by Dan O. Via and Robert A. J. Gagnon, 41–92. Minneapolis: Fortress, 2003.

———. *The Bible and Homosexual Practice: Texts and Hermeneutics.* Nashville: Abingdon, 2001.

Gandhi, Leela. *Postcolonial Theory.* New York: Columbia Univ. Press, 1998.

Gardner, Laura Mae. "Missionary Families." In *Sorrow and Blood: Christian Mission in Contexts of Suffering, Persecution, and Martyrdom*, edited by William D. Taylor, Antonia van der Meer, and Reg Reimer, 369–73. Pasadena, Calif.: William Carey Library, 2012.

Garland, David E. *1 Corinthians.* Grand Rapids: Baker Academic, 2003.

Garry, Maryanne, Charles G. Manning, Elizabeth F. Loftus, and Steven J. Sherman. "Imagination Inflation: Imagining a Childhood Event Inflates Confidence that It Occurred." *Psychonomic Bulletin & Review* 3, no. 2 (1996): 208–14.

Garry, Maryanne, and Kimberley A. Wade. "Actually, a Picture Is Worth Less than 45 Words: Narratives Produce More False Memories than Photographs Do." *Psychonomic Bulletin & Review* 12, no. 2 (2005): 359–66.

George, Timothy. *Faithful Witness: The Life and Mission of William Carey.* Birmingham, Ala.: New Hope, 1991.

Geraerts, Elke, Michelle M. Arnold, D. Stephen Lindsay, Harald Merckelbach, Marko Jelicic, and Beatrijs J. A. Hauer. "Forgetting of Prior Remembering in Persons Reporting Recovered Memories of Childhood Sexual Abuse." *Psychological Science* 17, no. 11 (November 2006): 1002–8. doi:10.1111/j.1467-9280.2006.01819.x.

Geraerts, Elke, Daniel M. Bernstein, Harald Merckelbach, Christel Linders, Linsey Raymaekers, and Elizabeth F. Loftus. "Lasting False Beliefs and Their Behavioral Consequences." *Psychological Science* 19, no. 8 (August 2008): 749–53. doi:10.1111/j.1467-9280.2008.02151.x.

Geraerts, Elke, Jonathan W. Schooler, Harald Merckelbach, Marko Jelicic, Beatrijs J. A. Hauer, and Zara Ambadar. "The Reality of Recovered Memories: Corroborating Continuous and Discontinuous Memories of Childhood Sexual Abuse." *Psychological Science* 18, no. 7 (July 1, 2007): 564–68. doi:10.1111/j.1467-9280.2007.01940.x.

Gibson, James J. *Perception of the Visual World.* Boston: Houghton Mifflin, 1950.

Glaser, Barney G., and Anselm Strauss. *The Discovery of Grounded Theory: Strategies for Qualitative Research.* Chicago: Aldine Publishing Company, 1967.

Global Ministries in the United Methodist Church. "Final Report of Independent Panel." http://new.gbgm-umc.org/about/globalministries/childprotection/finalpanelreport/.

Godden, D. R., and A. D. Baddeley. "Context-Dependent Memory in Two Natural Environments: On Land and Underwater." *British Journal of Psychology* 66, no. 3 (1975): 325–31.

"Go Figure: Homosexuality." *Christianity Today*, September 2013, p. 14.

Goldingay, John. "Biblical Interpretation and Same-Sex Relationships." www.fuller.edu/sot/faculty/goldingay; click "Interpretation."

———. *Key Questions about Christian Faith: Old Testament Answers.* Grand Rapids: Brazos Press, 2010.

Goldingay, John E., Grant R. LeMarquand, George R. Sumner, and Daniel A. Westberg. "Same-Sex Marriage and Anglican Theology: A View from the Traditionalists." *Anglican Theological Review* 93, no. 1 (2011): 1–50.

Goode, William J. *World Revolution and Family Patterns.* New York: Free Press, 1963.

Goodman, Gail S., Simona Ghetti, Jodi A. Quas, Robin S. Edelstein, Kristen Weede Alexander, Allison D. Redlich, Ingrid M. Cordon, and David P. H. Jones. "A Prospective Study of Memory for Child Sexual Abuse: New Findings Relevant to the Repressed-Memory Controversy." *Psychological Science* 14, no. 2 (2003): 113–18.

Goodman, Gail S., Jodi A. Quas, and Christin M. Ogle. "Child Maltreatment and Memory." *Annual Review of Psychology* 61 (2010): 325–51.

Goodstein, Laurie, and Erik Eckholm. "Church Battles Efforts to Ease Sex Abuse Suit." *New York Times*, June 14, 2012. www.nytimes.com/2012/06/14/us/sex-abuse-statutes-of-limitation-stir-battle.html.

Goodwin, Donald W., Barbara Powell, David Bremer, Haskel Hoine, and John Stern. "Alcohol and Recall: State-Dependent Effects in Man." *Science* 163, no. 3873 (1969): 1358–60.

Goody, Jack. *Production and Reproduction: A Comparative Study of the Domestic Domain.* Cambridge: Cambridge Univ. Press, 1976.

Goody, Jack, and S. J. Tambiah. *Bridewealth and Dowry.* Cambridge: Cambridge Univ. Press, 1973.

GRACE (Basyle Tchividjian, Victor Vieth, Diane Langberg, Janet Brown, and Duncan Rankin). *Amended Final Report for the Investigatory Review of Child Abuse at New Tribes Fanda Missionary School.* 2010. www.bishop-accountability.org/reports/2010_08_28_GRACE_Fanda_Report.pdf.

GRACE: Godly Response to Abuse in the Christian Environment. http://netgrace.org/.

Gramick, Jeannine, and Pat Furey. *The Vatican and Homosexuality: Reactions to the "Letter to the Bishops of the Catholic Church on the Pastoral Care of Homosexual Persons."* New York: Crossroad, 1988.

Grimshaw, Patricia. *Paths of Duty: American Missionary Wives in Nineteenth-Century Hawaii.* Honolulu: Univ. of Hawaii Press, 1989.

Guest, Deryn, et al., *The Queer Bible Commentary.* London: SCM Press, 2006.

Hacking, Ian. *Rewriting the Soul.* Princeton, N.J.: Princeton Univ. Press, 1995.

Hallett, Martin. "Homosexuality: Handicap and Gift." In *Holiness and Sexuality: Homosexuality in a Biblical Context,* edited by David Peterson, 120–45. Milton Keynes: Paternoster Press, 2004.

Harrison, Dan. *Strongest in the Broken Places: A Story of Spiritual Recovery.* Edited by Maria Henderson. Downers Grove, Ill.: InterVarsity Press, 1990.

Hartley, L. P. *The Go-Between.* London: Hamish Hamilton, 1953.

Hastings, Adrian. "The Church's Response to African Marriage." *AFER* 13, no. 3 (July 1, 1971): 193–203.

Hayes, Richard. *The Moral Vision of the New Testament.* San Francisco: HarperSanFrancisco, 1996.

Heacock, Anthony. *Jonathan Loved David: Manly Love in the Bible and the Hermeneutics of Sex.* Sheffield, U.K.: Sheffield Phoenix Press, 2011.

Health and Human Services, ed. *Child Maltreatment 2009.* Washington, D.C.: U.S. Department of Health and Human Services, 2009.

Heaps, Christopher M., and Michael Nash. "Comparing Recollective Experience in True and False Autobiographical Memories." *Journal of Experimental Psychology: Learning, Memory, and Cognition* 27, no. 4 (2001): 920–30. doi:10.1037//0278-7393.27.4.920.

Heldt, Diane. "Regents: All University of Iowa Employees Should Have Sexual Harassment Training." *Gazette,* February 6, 2013. http://thegazette.com/2013/02/06/regents-all-university-of-iowa-employees-should-have-sexual-harassment-training/.

Herdt, Gilbert H. "Ritualized Homosexual Behavior in the Male Cults of Melanesia, 1862–1983: An Introduction." In *Rituals of Manhood: Male Initiation in Papua New Guinea,* edited by Gilbert H. Herdt, 1–81. Berkeley: Univ. of California Press, 1984.

———. *The Sambia: Ritual and Gender in New Guinea.* New York: Holt, Rinehart, and Winston, 1987.

———. "Semen Transactions in Sambia Culture." In *Rituals of Manhood: Male Initiation in Papua New Guinea,* edited by Gilbert H. Herdt, 167–210. Berkeley: Univ. of California Press, 1984.

Herman, Judith L., and Emily Schatzow. "Recovery and Verification of Memories of Childhood Sexual Trauma." *Psychoanalytic Psychology* 4, no. 1 (1987): 1–14. doi:10.1037/h0079126.

Hicks, Robert D. *In Pursuit of Satan.* New York: Prometheus, 1991.

Hill, Wesley. *Washed and Waiting.* Grand Rapids: Zondervan, 2010.

Hiney, Tom. *On the Missionary Trail.* New York: Grove Press, 2000.

Hofstede, Geert H., Gert Jan Hofstede, and Michael Minkov. *Cultures and Organizations: Software of the Mind.* 3rd ed. New York: McGraw-Hill, 2010.

Holmes, Emily A., Richard J. Brown, Warren Mansell, R. Pasco Fearon, Elaine C. M. Hunter, Frank Frasquilho, and David A. Oakley. "Are There Two Qualitatively Distinct Forms of Dissociation? A Review and Some Clinical Implications." *Clinical Psychology Review* 25, no. 1 (2005): 1–23.

Horne, Melvill. *A Collection of Letters Relative to Foreign Missions.* Andover [Mass.]: Ware, 1810. https://archive.org/details/acollectionlett00horngoog.

Howell, Nancy. *Surviving Fieldwork: A Report of the Advisory Panel on Health and Safety in Fieldwork, American Anthropological Association.* Washington, D.C.: American Anthropological Association, 1990.

HU Queer Press [Harding University], www.huqueerpress.com.

Hunter, James Davidson. *To Change the World.* New York: Oxford University Press, 2010.

Hunter, Jane. *The Gospel of Gentility: American Women Missionaries in Turn-of-the-Century China.* New Haven: Yale Univ. Press, 1984.

Hyman, Ira E., Troy H. Husband, and F. James Billings. "False Memories of Childhood Experiences." *Applied Cognitive Psychology* 9, no. 3 (1995): 181–97.

Iteanu, Andre. "The Concept of the Person and the Ritual System: An Orokaiva View." *Man* 25 (1990): 35–53.

Jackson, Peter A. "Gay Capitals in Global Gay History: Cities, Local Markets, and the Origins of Bangkok's Same-Sex Cultures." In *Postcolonial Urbanism: Southeast Asian Cities and Global Processes,* edited by Ryan Bishop, John Phillips, and Wei-Wei Yeo, 151–63. New York: Routledge, 2003.

Jacoby, Larry L., Jeffrey P. Toth, and Andrew P. Yonelinas. "Separating Conscious and Unconscious Influences of Memory: Measuring Recollection." *Journal of Experimental Psychology: General* 122, no. 2 (1993): 139–54. doi:10.1037//0096-3445.122.2.139.

Jenkins, Philip. *Beyond Tolerance.* New York: New York Univ. Press, 2001.

———. *Moral Panic.* New Haven: Yale Univ. Press, 1998.

———. *Mystics and Messiahs.* New York: Oxford Univ. Press, 2000.

———. *The New Anti-Catholicism.* New York: Oxford Univ. Press, 2003.

———. *The New Faces of Christianity: Believing the Bible in the Global South.* Oxford: Oxford Univ. Press, 2006.

———. *Pedophiles and Priests.* New York: Oxford Univ. Press, 1996.

Jewett, Paul K., and Marguerite Shuster. *Who We Are: Our Dignity as Human; A Neo-Evangelical Theology.* Grand Rapids: Eerdmans, 1996.

Jipp, Joshua W. "The Beginnings of a Theology of Luke-Acts: Divine Activity and Human Response." *Journal of Theological Interpretation* (forthcoming).

John Jay College of Criminal Justice, City University of New York. *The Causes and Context of Sexual Abuse of Minors by Catholic Priests in the United States, 1950–2010.* Washington, D.C.: United States Conference of Catholic Bishops, 2011. www.usccb.org/issues-and-action

/child-and-youth-protection/upload/The-Causes-and-Context-of-Sexual-Abuse-of-Minors-by-Catholic-Priests-in-the-United-States-1950-2010.pdf.

John Jay College of Criminal Justice, City University of New York. *Nature and Scope of Sexual Abuse of Minors by Catholic Priests and Deacons in the United States, 1950-2002.* Washington, D.C.: United States Conference of Catholic Bishops, 2004. www.usccb.org/issues-and-action/child-and-youth-protection/upload/The-Nature-and-Scope-of-Sexual-Abuse-of-Minors-by-Catholic-Priests-and-Deacons-in-the-United-States-1950-2002.pdf.

Johnson, Luke Timothy. "Scripture and Experience." *Commonweal*, June 11, 2007, 14-17. www.commonwealmagazine.org/homosexuality-church-1.

Johnson-Odim, Cheryl. "Actions Louder than Words: The Historical Task of Defining Feminist Consciousness in Colonial West Africa." In *Nation, Empire, Colony: Historicizing Gender and Race*, edited by Ruth Roach Pierson and Nupur Chaudhuri, 77-93. Bloomington: Indiana Univ. Press, 1998.

Jones, Stanton L. "The Loving Opposition." *Christianity Today*, July 9, 1993, 18-25.

———. "Same-Sex Science: The Social Sciences Cannot Settle the Moral Status of Homosexuality." *First Things* (February 2012): 27-33. www.firstthings.com/article/2012/01/same-sex-science.

Jones, Timothy Willem. "The Missionaries' Position: Polygamy and Divorce in the Anglican Communion, 1888-1988." *Journal of Religious History* 35, no. 3 (September 1, 2011): 393-408.

Josephides, Lisette. "Metaphors, Metathemes, and the Construction of Sociality: A Critique of the New Melanesian Ethnography." *Man* 26 (1991): 145-61.

Karpman, Benjamin. "A Case of Pedophilia Cured by Psychoanalysis." *Psychoanalytic Review* 37, no. 3 (1950): 235-76.

Keeping Our Promise to Protect. www.usccb.org/search.cfm?site=newusccb&proxystylesheet=newusccb_frontend&q=%22Keeping+our+promise+to+protect%22&btnG.x=22&btnG.y=18&lang=eng.

Kennedy, John W. "Missions: From Trauma to Truth." *Christianity Today*, April 27, 1998. www.christianitytoday.com/ct/1998/april27/8t5016.html.

Kessler, Ronald C., Amanda Sonnega, Evelyn Bromet, Michael Hughes, and Christopher B. Nelson. "Posttraumatic Stress Disorder in the National Comorbidity Survey." *Archives of General Psychiatry* 52, no. 12 (1995): 1048-60.

Kim, Dong-Hwa. "Ministry to the Elderly Parents of Missionaries." In *Worth Keeping: Global Perspectives on Best Practice in Missionary Retention*, edited by Rob Hay, Valerie Lim, Detlef Blocher, Jaap Ketelaar, and Sarah Hay, 366-67. Pasadena, Calif.: William Carey Library, 2007.

Kim, Erin Hye-Won, and Philip J. Cook. "The Continuing Importance of Children in Relieving Elder Poverty: Evidence from Korea." *Ageing and Society* 31 (2011): 969. doi: 10.1017/S0144686X10001030.

Kim, Sungmoon. "Trouble with Korean Confucianism: Scholar-Official between Ideal and Reality." *Journal of Comparative Philosophy* 8 (2009): 43. doi: 10.1007/s11712-009-9105-1.

Kinsey, Alfred C., Wardell B. Pomeroy, Clyde E. Martin, and P. H. Gebhard. *Sexual Behavior in the Human Female*. Philadelphia: W. B. Saunders, 1953.

Kinsey Institute. www.kinseyinstitute.org/research/ak-hhscale.html.

Klemens, Michael J., and Lynette H. Bikos. "Psychological Well-Being and Sociocultural Adaptation in College-Aged, Repatriated, Missionary Kids." *Mental Health, Religion, and Culture* 12, no. 7 (2009): 721–33.

Knauft, Bruce. *The Gebusi: Lives Transformed in a Rainforest World*. 3rd ed. New York: McGraw-Hill, 2012.

———. "Homosexuality in Melanesia." *Journal of Psychoanalytic Anthropology* 10 (1987): 155–91.

———. "Text and Social Practice: Narrative 'Longing' and Bisexuality among the Gebusi of New Guinea." *Ethos* 14 (1986): 252–58.

Kohls, Robert. *Learning to Think Korean*. Boston: Intercultural Press, 2001.

"Korea Must End the Suicide Epidemic." *Chosumilbo*, September 11, 2012. http://english.chosun.com/site/data/html_dir/2012/09/11/2012091101353.html.

Korean National Statistical Office. "Final Results of Birth Statistics in 2011." August 23, 2012. http://kostat.go.kr/portal/english/news/1/8/index.board?bmode=read&aSeq=260076.

Korean National Statistical Office. "Household Income and Expenditure Trends in the Third Quarter 2012." November 16, 2012. http://kostat.go.kr/portal/english/news/1/7/index.board?bmode=read&aSeq=269155.

Korean National Statistical Office. "Population Statistics." 2011. http://census.go.kr/hcensus/ui/html/data/data_020_010_Detail.jsp?p_bitmId=60482&q_menu=4&q_sub=2&q_pageNo=1&q_div=ALL.

Korean National Statistical Office. "2011 Life Tables for the Nation and Provinces." December 4, 2012. http://kostat.go.kr/portal/english/news/1/17/1/index.board?bmode=read&aSeq=273092&pageNo=&rowNum=10&amSeq=&sTarget=&sTxt=.

Korean National Statistical Office. "2012 Statistics on the Aged." September 27, 2012. http://kostat.go.kr/portal/english/news/1/8/index.board?bmode=read&aSeq=268470.

"Korean Parents Spend Too Much on Their Children." *Chosumilbo*, August 29, 2013. http://english.chosun.com/site/data/html_dir/2012/07/05/2012070501469.html.

Korean Statistical Information Services (KOSIS). "Impulse to Commit Suicide and Reasons (13 Years Old and Over)." http://kosis.kr/eng/; enter "Suicide" in search box.

Lacy, Joyce W., and Craig E. L. Stark. "The Neuroscience of Memory: Implications for the Courtroom." *Nature Reviews Neuroscience* 14, no. 9 (2013): 649–58.

Laney, Cara, Nicci B. Fowler, Kally J. Nelson, Daniel M. Bernstein, and Elizabeth F. Loftus. "The Persistence of False Beliefs." *Acta Psychologica* 129, no. 1 (September 2008): 190–97. doi:10.1016/j.actpsy.2008.05.010.

Laney, Cara, and Elizabeth F. Loftus. "Emotional Content of True and False Memories." *Memory* 16, no. 5 (January 2008): 500–516. doi:10.1080/09658210802065939.

Laney, Cara, Erin K. Morris, Daniel M. Bernstein, Briana M. Wakefield, and Elizabeth F. Loftus. "Asparagus, a Love Story." *Experimental Psychology* 55, no. 5 (January 1, 2008): 291–300. doi:10.1027/1618-3169.55.5.291.

Latourette, Kenneth Scott. *A History of the Expansion of Christianity.* Vol. 6. Grand Rapids: Zondervan, 1970.

Laurence, Jean-Roch, and Shelagh Freedman. "Research Brief: Number of Clients at Risk for Developing False Memories of Abuse: Addendum to Legualt and Laurence (2007)." *Crime Scene* 16, no. 1 (2009): 15–16.

LeDuc Media. www.worldlifeexpectancy.com.

Lee, Cameron. "Specifying Intrusive Demands and Their Outcomes in Congregational Ministry: A Report on the Ministry Demands Inventory." *Journal for the Scientific Study of Religion* 38, no. 4 (1999): 477–89.

Lee, Justin. *Torn: Rescuing the Gospel from the Gays-vs.-Christians Debate.* New York: Jericho Books, 2012.

Legault, Ellen, and Jean-Roch Laurence. "Recovered Memories of Childhood Sexual Abuse: Social Worker, Psychologist, and Psychiatrist Reports of Beliefs, Practices, and Cases." *Australian Journal of Clinical and Experimental Hypnosis* 35, no. 2 (2007): 111–33.

Levitan, Robert D., Neil A. Rector, Tess Sheldon, and Paula Goering. "Childhood Adversities Associated with Major Depression and/or Anxiety Disorders in a Community Sample of Ontario: Issues of Co-morbidity and Specificity." *Depression and Anxiety* 17, no. 1 (2003): 34–42.

Lief, Harold I., and Janet Fetkewicz. "Retractors of False Memories: The Evolution of Pseudo-memories." *Journal of Psychiatry and Law* 23 (1995): 411–35.

Liefeld, Olive Fleming. *Unfolding Destinies: The Untold Story of Peter Fleming and the Auca.* Edited by Verne Becker. Grand Rapids: Zondervan, 1990.

Lilienfeld, Scott O., Lorie A. Ritschel, Steven Jay Lynn, Robin L. Cautin, and Robert D. Latzman. "Why Many Clinical Psychologists Are Resistant to Evidence-Based Practice: Root Causes and Constructive Remedies." *Clinical Psychology Review* 33, no. 7 (November 2013): 883–900. doi:10.1016/j.cpr.2012.09.008.

Lindsay, D. Stephen, Lisa Hagen, J. Don Read, Kimberley A. Wade, and Maryanne Garry. "True Photographs and False Memories." *Psychological Science* 15, no. 3 (2004): 149–54.

Lingenfelter, Jennifer. "Reflections of a Gay Christian." *The SEMI*, June 29, 2012. http://infoguides .fuller.edu/lingenfelter/otherpapers.

Lingenfelter, Sherwood. "Reflections of a Father." *The SEMI* (June 29, 2012). http://infoguides .fuller.edu/lingenfelter/otherpapers.

Littauer, Fred and Florence. *Freeing Your Mind from Memories That Bind.* San Bernardino, Calif.: Here's Life, 1992; orig. 1988.

Loftus, Elizabeth F. "Make-Believe Memories." *American Psychologist* 58, no. 11 (2003): 867–73.

Loftus, Elizabeth F., and Deborah Davis. "Recovered Memories." *Annual Review of Clinical Psychology* 2 (2006): 469–98.

Loftus, Elizabeth F., and Melvin J. Guyer. "Who Abused Jane Doe? The Hazards of the Single Case History. Part I." *Skeptical Inquirer* 26, no. 3 (2002): 24–32.

Loftus, Elizabeth F., and Kathrine Ketcham. *The Myth of Repressed Memory: False Memories and Allegations of Sexual Abuse*. New York: St. Martin's Press, 1994.

Loftus, Elizabeth F., and John C. Palmer. "Reconstruction of Automobile Destruction: An Example of the Interaction between Language and Memory." *Journal of Verbal Learning and Verbal Behavior* 13 (October 1974): 585–89. doi:10.1016/S0022-5371(74)80011-3.

Loftus, Elizabeth F., and Laura A. Rosenwald. "Buried Memories, Shattered Lives." *American Bar Association Journal* 79, no. 11 (1993): 70–73.

Loomis, Chauncey L. Report, 1861. Presbyterian Historical Society, Philadelphia, Pennsylvania.

Love, Gregory S., and Kimberlee D. Norris. "Church Employees Arrested/Charged for Failure to Report Sexual Abuse." *Ministry Safe Blog*, September 25, 2012. http://blog.ministrysafe .com/2012/09/25/church-employees-arrestedcharged-for-failure-to-report-sexual-abuse/.

Malick, David E. "The Condemnation of Homosexuality in 1 Corinthians 6:9." *Bibliotheca Sacra* 150 (October–December 1993): 479–92.

Maran, Meredith. *My Lie: A True Story of False Memory*. San Francisco: Jossey-Bass, 2010.

Marie André du Sacré Cœur, Sister. *The House Stands Firm: Family Life in West Africa*. Milwaukee: Bruce Pub. Co., 1962.

Marin, Andrew. *Love Is an Orientation: Elevating the Conversation with the Gay Community*. Downers Grove, Ill.: IVP, 2009.

Marsh, Elizabeth J. "Retelling Is Not the Same as Recalling: Implications for Memory." *Current Directions in Psychological Science* 16, no. 1 (2007): 16–20.

Marshman, J. C. *The Life and Labours of Carey, Marshman, and Ward*. London: Alexander Strahan & Company, 1864.

Martin, Dale B. "*Arsenokoites* and *Malakos*: Meanings and Consequences." In *Biblical Ethics and Homosexuality: Listening to Scripture*, edited by Robert Brawley, 117–36. Louisville: Westminster John Knox, 1996.

Mbiti, John S. *African Religions and Philosophy*. New York: Praeger, 1970.

McNally, Richard J. "Explaining 'Memories' of Space Alien Abduction and Past Lives: An Experimental Psychopathology Approach." *Journal of Experimental Psychopathology* 3, no. 1 (2012): 2–16.

———. *Remembering Trauma*. Cambridge, Mass.: Harvard Univ. Press, 2003.

McNally, Richard J., and Elke Geraerts. "A New Solution to the Recovered Memory Debate." *Perspectives on Psychological Science* 4, no. 2 (2009): 126–34.

McNally, Richard J., Carol A. Perlman, Carel S. Ristuccia, and Susan A. Clancy. "Clinical Characteristics of Adults Reporting Repressed, Recovered, or Continuous Memories of Childhood Sexual Abuse." *Journal of Consulting and Clinical Psychology* 74, no. 2 (2006): 237–42.

McQueen, Georgianna. "Corisco Graveyard." *The African Repository* 39, no. 6 (June 1863): 183–84.

Mead, Margaret. *Coming of Age in Samoa: A Psychological Study of Primitive Youth for Western Civilization.* New York: Morrow, 1928.

———. *Sex and Temperament in Three Primitive Societies.* New York: W. Morrow, 1935.

Meadors, Marshall L., Edith M. Fresh, James S. Evinger, and Lauri B. Bracey. *Final Report of the Independent Panel for the Review of Child Abuse in Mission Settings.* New York: General Board of Ministries of the United Methodist Church, 2009. http://new.gbgm-umc.org /about/globalministries/childprotection/finalpanelreport/.

Meggitt, Mervyn J. "Male-Female Relationships in the Highlands of Australian New Guinea." *American Anthropologist* 66 (1964): 393–407.

Menkel, Peter. Diary. Papers. Presbyterian Historical Society, Philadelphia, Pennsylvania.

Meyer, David E., and Roger W. Schvaneveldt. "Facilitation in Recognizing Pairs of Words: Evidence of a Dependence between Retrieval Operations." *Journal of Experimental Psychology* 90, no. 2 (1971): 221–34.

Minh-ha, Trinh T. *Woman, Native, Other.* Bloomington: Indiana Univ. Press, 1989.

MK Safety Net. www.mksafetynet.net/.

Moena, Sylvia N. "Family Life in Soweto, Gauteng, South Africa." In *African Families at the Turn of the Twenty-First Century,* edited by Yaw Oheneba-Sakyi and Baffour K. Takyi, 249–71. Westport, Conn.: Praeger, 2006.

Moffat, John S. *The Lives of Robert and Mary Moffat.* 12th ed. London: T. Fisher Unwin, 1925.

Mohanty, Chandra Talpade. "Under Western Eyes: Feminist Scholarship and Colonial Discourse." In *Colonial Discourse and Postcolonial Theory: A Reader,* edited by Patrick Williams and Laura Chrisman, 196–220. New York: Columbia Univ. Press, 1994.

Mohr, Johann W., Robert E. Turner, and Marian B. Jerry. *Pedophilia and Exhibitionism: A Handbook.* Toronto: Univ. of Toronto Press, 1964.

Moore, Erasmus Darwin. *Life Scenes from Mission Fields: A Book of Facts, Incidents, and Results, the Most Material and Remarkable in Missionary Experience, Condensed and Arranged for Popular Use.* New York: Charles Scribner, 1857.

Moran, Lee. "Florida Missionary Sentenced to 58 Years in Prison for Sexually Abusing Indigenous Girls in Amazon." *New York Daily News,* January 30, 2014. www.nydailynews.com/news /crime/missionary-sentenced-sexually-abusing-girls-amazon-article-1.1596392.

Morgan, C. A., Steven Southwick, George Steffian, Gary A. Hazlett, and Elizabeth F. Loftus. "Misinformation Can Influence Memory for Recently Experienced, Highly Stressful Events." *International Journal of Law and Psychiatry* 36, no. 1 (2013): 11–17. doi:10.1016/j .ijlp.2012.11.002.

Mpolo, Masamba Ma. "Polygamy in Pastoral Perspectives." In *Families in Transition,* edited by Masamba Ma Mpolo and Cécile de Sweemer, 97–126. Geneva: WCC Publications, 1987.

Murphy, Jan. "Pa. Lawmakers Push for Extending Statute of Limitations for Child Sex Abuse Victims." *Penn Live,* Sept. 25, 2013, www.pennlive.com/midstate/index.ssf/2013/09/pa _lawmakers_push_for_extendin.html.

Murphy, Samuel Howell. Africa Letters—Gaboon and Corisco Mission. Presbyterian Historical Society, Philadelphia, Pennsylvania.

Nash, June. "Ethnology in a Revolutionary Setting." In *Ethnographic Fieldwork: An Anthropological Reader*, edited by Antonius C. G. M. Robben and Jeffrey A. Sluka, 223–32. Malden, Mass.: Blackwell, 2007.

Nassau, Robert Hamill. "Africa." In *Historical Sketches of the Missions under the Care of the Board of Foreign Missions of the Presbyterian Church*, 9–36. 3rd ed. Philadelphia: Women's Foreign Missionary Society of the Presbyterian Church, 1891.

———. *Corisco Days: The First Thirty Years of the West African Mission*. Philadelphia: Allen, Lane, and Scott, 1910.

———. *Crowned in Palm-Land: A Story of African Mission Life*. Philadelphia: J. B. Lippincott, 1874.

———. *My Ogowe: Being a Narrative of Daily Incidents during Sixteen Years in Equatorial West Africa*. New York: Neale Publishing Company, 1914.

———. "Some Causes of the Present Improved Health of Missionaries to Africa." *Missionary Review of the World* 6, no. 12 (1893): 926–29.

Nathan, Debbie. *Sybil Exposed*. New York: Free Press, 2012.

Nathan, Debbie, and Michael Snedeker. *Satan's Silence: Ritual Abuse and the Making of a Modern American Witch Hunt*. New York: Basic Books, 1995.

National Review Board. *A Ten Year Progress Report*. Washington, D.C.: United States Conference of Catholic Bishops, 2012. www.usccb.org/issues-and-action/child-and-youth-protection /upload/10-year-report-2012.pdf.

Neill, Stephen. *A History of Christian Missions*. London: Penguin Books, 1990.

Neisser, Ulric, and Nicole Harsch. "Phantom Flashbulbs: False Recollections of Hearing the News about Challenger." In *Affect and Accuracy in Recall*, edited by Eugene Winograd and Ulric Neisser, 9–31. New York: Cambridge Univ. Press, 1992.

Newcomb, Harvey. *Cyclopedia of Missions: Containing a Comprehensive View of Missionary Operations throughout the World; With Geographical Descriptions, and Accounts of the Social, Moral, and Religious Condition of the People*. New York: Charles Scribner, 1854.

Ngoa, Henri. "Qu'est-ce que la Polygamie Négro-Africaine?" *Flambeau* 45 (1975): 7–12.

Nissinen, Martti. *Homoeroticism in the Biblical World: A Historical Perspective*, trans. K. Stjerna. Minneapolis: Fortress, 1998.

Nugent, Robert, and Jeannine Gramick. *Building Bridges: Gay and Lesbian Reality and the Catholic Church*. Mystic, Conn.: Twenty-Third Publications, 1992.

Nussbaum, L. Martin, and Theresa Lynn Sidebotham. "Are Protestant Ministries a New Market? Lessons Learned from the Catholic Sexual Abuse Scandal." 2011. www.rothgerber.com /files/10436_AreProtestantMinistriesaNewMarketv3.pdf.

Oheneba-Sakyi, Yaw, and Baffour K. Takyi. "Introduction to the Study of African Families: A Framework for Analysis." In *African Families at the Turn of the Twenty-First Century*, edited by Yaw Oheneba-Sakyi and Baffour K. Takyi, 1–26. Westport, Conn.: Praeger, 2006.

OneGeorgeFox [George Fox University]. www.onegeorgefox.org.

OneTable [Fuller Theological Seminary]. www.onetablefuller.com.

OneWestmont [Westmont College]. http://westmontlgbt.wordpress.com/.

OneWheaton [Wheaton College]. www.onewheaton.com.

Ost, James, Alan Costall, and Ray Bull. "False Confessions and False Memories: A Model for Understanding Retractors' Experiences." *Journal of Forensic Psychiatry* 12, no. 3 (2001): 549–79.

Ost, James, Pär-Anders Granhag, Julie Udell, Emma Roos af Hjelmsäter. "Familiarity Breeds Distortion: The Effects of Media Exposure on False Reports Concerning Media Coverage of the Terrorist Attacks in London on 7 July 2005." *Memory* 16, no. 1 (January 2008): 76–85. doi:10.1080/09658210701723323.

O'Sullivan, Julia T., and Mark L. Howe. "Metamemory and Memory Construction." *Consciousness and Cognition* 4, no. 1 (March 1995): 104–10. doi:10.1006/ccog.1995.1011.

Otgaar, Henry, Ingrid Candel, and Harald Merckelbach. "Children's False Memories: Easier to Elicit for a Negative than for a Neutral Event." *Acta Psychologica* 128, no. 2 (2008): 350–54.

Ould, Peter. An Exercise in the Fundamentals of Orthodoxy: The Website of Peter Ould. www .peter-ould.net.

Owusu, Sam. "Towards a Theology of Marriage and Polygamy." *Direction* 36, no. 2 (September 1, 2007): 195.

Paris, Jenell Williams. *The End of Sexual Identity: Why Sex Is Too Important to Define Who We Are.* Downers Grove, Ill.: IVP Books, 2011.

Park, Keong-Suk, Voonchin Phua, James McNally, and Rongjun Sun. "Diversity and Structure of Intergenerational Relationships: Elderly Parent–Adult Child Relations in Korea." *Journal of Cross Cultural Gerontology* 20 (2005): 289. doi: 10.1007/s10823-006-9007-1.

Parrott, Gerrod, and Matthew P. Spackman. "Emotion and Memory." In *Handbook of Emotions*, edited by Michael Lewis and Jeanette M. Haviland-Jones, 476–90. 2nd ed. New York: Guilford Press, 2000.

Passantino, Bob and Gretchen. "The Hard Facts about Satanic Ritual Abuse." www.equip.org /articles/the-hard-facts-about-satanic-ritual-abuse/#christian-books-1.

Patihis, Lawrence, Lavina Y. Ho, Ian W. Tingen, Scott O. Lilienfeld, and Elizabeth F. Loftus. "Are the 'Memory Wars' Over? A Scientist-Practitioner Gap in Beliefs about Repressed Memory." *Psychological Science* 20, no. 10 (2013): 1–12.

———. "Are the 'Memory Wars' Over? A Scientist-Practitioner Gap in Beliefs about Repressed Memory." *Psychological Science* 25, no. 2 (2014): 519–30.

Paulme, Denise, ed. *Women of Tropical Africa.* Berkeley: Univ. of California Press, 1960.

Pendergrast, Mark. *Victims of Memory: Sex Abuse Accusations and Shattered Lives.* Hinesberg, Vt.: Upper Access Books, 1996.

Periodical Accounts Relative to the Baptist Missionary Society. Vol. 1. Clipstone [Eng.]: J.W. Morris, 1800.

Periodical Accounts Relative to the Baptist Missionary Society. Vol. 2. Clipstone [Eng.]: J.W. Morris, 1801.

Perner, Josef, and Ted Ruffman. "Episodic Memory and Autonoetic Consciousness: Developmental Evidence and a Theory of Childhood Amnesia." *Journal of Experimental Child Psychology* 59, no. 3 (1995): 516–48.

Peterson, David. "Holiness and God's Creation Purpose." In *Holiness and Sexuality: Homosexuality in a Biblical Context*, edited by David Peterson, 1–17. Milton Keynes: Paternoster Press, 2004.

Pew Research. "Gay Marriage around the World." www.pewforum.org/2013/12/19/gay -marriage-around-the-world-2013.

Pirolli, Peter L., and John R. Anderson. "The Role of Practice in Fact Retrieval." *Journal of Experimental Psychology: Learning, Memory, and Cognition* 11, no. 1 (1985): 136–53.

Pope, H. G., and J. I. Hudson. "Can Individuals 'Repress' Memories of Childhood Sexual Abuse? An Examination of the Evidence." *Psychiatric Annals* no. 25 (1995): 715–19.

Pope, Kenneth S., and Laura S. Brown. *Recovered Memories of Abuse.* Washington, D.C.: American Psychological Association, 1996.

Population Reference Bureau. "World Population Data Sheet 2012." www.prb.org.

Porter, Nancy Sikes. Diary. Papers. Ellington Historical Society, Ellington, Connecticut.

Priest, Robert J. "Etiology of Adult Missionary Kid (AMK) Life-Struggles." *Missiology: An International Review* 31, no. 2 (2003), 171–92.

Priest, Robert J., and Esther E. Cordill. "Christian Communities and 'Recovered Memories' of Abuse." *Christian Scholar's Review* 41, no. 4 (Summer 2012): 381–400.

———. "Response to Evinger and Darr's 'Determining the Truth of Abuse in Mission Communities.'" *Christian Scholar's Review* (forthcoming).

Quarry v. Doe 1, 272 P.3d 977 (Cal. 2012). http://scocal.stanford.edu/opinion/quarry-v-doe-i-34062.

Rainey, Dennis. "Missionary Marriages." Unpublished manuscript, February 2007.

Ramirez, Luis Felipe, and Julio E. Rubio. "Culture, Government, and Development in South Korea." *Asian Culture and History* 2, no. 1 (2010): 77.

Rankin, Jerry. *In the Secret Place.* Nashville, Tenn.: B&H Publishing, 2009.

Rankin, Russell. "Foreword." In *In the Secret Place*, by Jerry Rankin, ix–xi. Nashville, Tenn.: B&H Publishing, 2009.

Rankin, William. "Mrs. H. E. Loomis." In *Memorials of Foreign Missionaries of the Presbyterian Church U.S.A.*, 200–202. Philadelphia: Presbyterian Board of Publication, 1895.

Read, Kenneth E. "Morality and the Concept of the Person among the Gahuku-Gama." *Oceania* 25, no. 4 (1955): 233–82.

———. *The High Valley.* New York: Columbia Univ. Press, 1980.

Reading, Joseph Hankinson. *The Ogowe Band: A Narrative of African Travel.* Philadelphia: Reading & Company, 1890.

Rediger, G. Lloyd. *Ministry and Sexuality: Cases, Counseling, Care.* Minneapolis: Fortress Press, 1990.

Regnerus, Mark. *Forbidden Fruit: Sex and Religion in the Lives of American Teenagers.* New York: Oxford Univ. Press, 2007.

Robbins, Susan P. "Social and Cultural Forces Were Partially Responsible for Satanic Panic." In *Satanism,* edited by Tamara L. Roleff, 91–102. San Diego: Greenhaven Press, 2002.

Robert, Dana L. *American Women in Mission: A Social History of Their Thought and Practice.* Macon, Ga.: Mercer Univ. Press, 1997.

———. "The 'Christian Home' as a Cornerstone of Anglo-American Missionary Thought and Practice." In *Converting Colonialism: Visions and Realities in Mission History, 1706–1914,* edited by Dana L. Robert, 134–65. Grand Rapids: Eerdmans, 2008.

Roberts, Christopher. *Creation and Covenant.* New York: T&T Clark International, 2007.

Rogers, Jack. *Jesus, the Bible, and Homosexuality: Explode the Myths, Heal the Church.* Rev. ed. Louisville: Westminster John Knox, 2009.

Ross, Scott. *Abuse: The Hidden Secret; A Prevention Guide to Dealing with Child Abuse.* Video series. Sanford, Fl.: New Tribes Mission, 2003.

Roxburgh, Alan, and Scott M. Boren. *Introducing the Missional Church: What It Is, Why It Matters, How to Become One.* Grand Rapids: Baker Books, 2009.

Rubin, David C., and Adriel Boals. "People Who Expect to Enter Psychotherapy Are Prone to Believing that They Have Forgotten Memories of Childhood Trauma and Abuse." *Memory* 18, no. 5 (2010): 556–62.

Rucker, Derek D., and Richard E. Petty. "Effects of Accusations on the Accuser: The Moderating Role of Accuser Culpability." *Personality and Social Psychology Bulletin* 29, no. 10 (2003): 1259–71.

Rucker, Derek D., and Anthony R. Pratkanis. "Projection as an Interpersonal Influence Tactic: The Effects of the Pot Calling the Kettle Black." *Personality and Social Psychology Bulletin* 27, no. 11 (2001): 1494–1507.

Russell, Diana. *The Secret Trauma.* Rev. ed. New York: Basic Books, 1999.

"Same-Sex Relationships Are Still Criminalized in 76 Countries, according to the United Nations. Almost All Are in Africa and the Middle East." *The Week,* December 20, 2013, 14.

Saunders, B. E., L. Berliner, and R. D. Hanson, eds. *Child Physical and Sexual Abuse: Guidelines for Treatment (Revised Report: April 26, 2004).* Charleston, S.C.: National Crime Victims Research and Treatment Center, 2004.

Scanlon, Leslie. "Six Persons Named by Abuse Review Panel in Physical, Sexual Abuse Investigation." *The Presbyterian Outlook,* August 11, 2010. http://pres-outlook.org/2010/10/six-persons-named-by-abuse-review-panel-in-physical-sexual-abuse-investigation/.

Schacter, Daniel L. "Illusory Memories: A Cognitive Neuroscience Analysis." *Proceedings of the National Academy of Sciences of the United States of America* 93, no. 24 (November 26, 1996): 13527–33.

———. *Searching for Memory: The Brain, the Mind, and the Past.* New York: Basic Books, 1996.

———. *The Seven Sins of Memory.* New York: Houghton Mifflin, 2001.

Schacter, Daniel L., Joan Y. Chiao, and Jason P. Mitchell. "The Seven Sins of Memory." *Annals of the New York Academy of Sciences* 1001 (October 2003): 226–39. doi:10.1196/annals.1279.012.

Schacter, Daniel L., Scott A. Guerin, and Peggy L. St. Jacques. "Memory Distortion: An Adaptive Perspective." *Trends in Cognitive Sciences* 15, no. 10 (October 2011): 467–74. doi:10.1016/j .tics.2011.08.004.

Schattschneider, David. "William Carey, Modern Missions, and the Moravian Influence." *International Bulletin of Missionary Research* 22, no. 1 (January 1998): 8–12.

Schmolck, H., E. A. Buffalo, and Larry R. Squire. "Memory Distortions Develop over Time: Recollections of the O. J. Simpson Trial Verdict after 15 and 32 Months." *Psychological Science* 11, no. 1 (2000): 39–45.

Scroggs, Robin. *The New Testament and Homosexuality: Contextual Background for Contemporary Debate.* Philadelphia: Fortress, 1983.

Seaman, Paul Asbury, et al. *Far above the Plain.* Pasadena, Calif.: William Carey Library, 1996.

Secretariat of Child and Youth Protection for the National Review Board. *2011 Annual Report on the Implementation of the "Charter for the Protection of Children and Young People."* Washington, D.C.: United States Conference of Catholic Bishops, 2012. www.usccb.org /issues-and-action/child-and-youth-protection/upload/2011-annual-report.pdf.

———. *2012 Annual Report on the Implementation of the "Charter for the Protection of Children and Young People."* Washington, D.C.: United States Conference of Catholic Bishops, 2013. www.usccb.org/issues-and-action/child-and-youth-protection/reports-and-research.cfm.

Seglin, Jeffrey L. "Too Much Ado about Giving References." *New York Times,* February 21, 1999. www.nytimes.com/1999/02/21/business/the-right-thing-too-much-ado-about-giving -references.html.

Sharman, Stefanie J., Charles G. Manning, and Maryanne Garry. "Explain This: Explaining Childhood Events Inflates Confidence for Those Events." *Applied Cognitive Psychology* 19, no. 1 (January 2005): 67–74. doi:10.1002/acp.1041.

Sidebotham, Theresa Lynn. "Protecting Children and Organizations from Child Sexual Abuse: An Overview of Legal and Practical Issues." White paper. www.telioslaw.com.

Simons, Daniel J., Christopher F. Chabris, Tatiana Schnur, and Daniel T. Levin. "Evidence for Preserved Representations in Change Blindness." *Consciousness and Cognition* 11, no. 1 (March 2002): 78–97. doi:10.1006/ccog.2001.0533.

Simons, Daniel J., and Daniel T. Levin. "Failure to Detect Changes to People during a Real-World Interaction." *Psychonomic Bulletin and Review* 5, no. 4 (December 1998): 644–49. doi:10.3758/BF03208840.

Simpson, Paul. *Second Thoughts.* Nashville, Tenn.: Thomas Nelson, 1996.

Singer, Margaret Thaler, and Abraham Nievod. "New Age Therapies." In *Science and Pseudoscience in Clinical Psychology,* edited by Scott O. Lilienfeld, Steven J. Lynn, and Jeffrey M. Lohr, 176–204. New York: Guilford Press, 2003.

Sluka, Jeffrey A. "Reflections on Managing Danger in Fieldwork: Dangerous Anthropology in Belfast." In *Ethnographic Fieldwork: An Anthropological Reader*, edited by Antonius C. G. M. Robben and Jeffrey A. Sluka, 259–69. Malden, Mass.: Blackwell, 2007.

Smith, A. Christopher. "William Carey: Protestant Pioneer of the Modern Mission Era." In *Mission Legacies: Biographical Studies of Leaders of the Modern Missionary Movement*, edited by Gerald H. Anderson, Robert T. Coote, Norman A. Horner, and James M. Phillips, 245–54. Maryknoll, N.Y.: Orbis Books, 1994.

Smith, Christian. *American Evangelicalism: Embattled and Thriving*. Chicago: Univ. of Chicago Press, 1998.

Smith, George. *The Life of William Carey, D.D.: Shoemaker and Missionary*. Lexington: Feather Trail Press, 2010.

Soulforce. www.soulforce.org.

Spanos, Nicholas P. *Multiple Identities and False Memories*. Washington, D.C.: American Psychological Association, 1996.

Spivak, Gayatri Chakravorty. "Can the Subaltern Speak?" In *The Post-colonial Studies Reader*, edited by Bill Ashcroft, Gareth Griffiths, and Helen Tiffin, 28–37. New York: Routledge, 2006.

———. "French Feminism in an International Frame." In *In Other Worlds: Essays in Cultural Politics*, edited by Gayatri Chakravorty Spivak, 134–53. New York: Routledge, 1988.

SPU Haven Supporters [Seattle Pacific University]. www.supportspuhaven.wordpress.com.

Squire, Larry R., Craig E. L. Stark, and Robert E. Clark. "The Medial Temporal Lobe." *Annual Review of Neuroscience* 27 (January 2004): 279–306. doi:10.1146/annurev.neuro.27.070203.144130.

Squire, Larry R., and Stuart M. Zola. "Structure and Function of Declarative and Nondeclarative Memory Systems." *Proceedings of the National Academy of Sciences of the United States of America* 93, no. 24 (1996): 13515–22.

Stafford, Wess. *Too Small to Ignore: Why the Least of These Matters Most*. With Dean Merrill. Colorado Springs, Colo.: WaterBrook Press, 2007.

Starr, Douglas. "False Eyewitness." *Discover Magazine*, September 2012, 40. http://discovermagazine.com/2012/nov/04-eyewitness#.UTztRRlifNA.

Stearns, Geoffrey B., Pamela G. Dunn, Marcus R. Earle, Lois J. Edmund, and Chilton Knudsen. Final Report of the Independent Commission of Inquiry to the Board of Managers of the Christian and Missionary Alliance. 1997. www.mksafetynet.net/usa/reports/invcmareport.html.

Steffan, Melissa. "Missionary Group Fires Sex Abuse Investigator." *Christianity Today*, February 12, 2013. www.christianitytoday.com/gleanings/2013/february/missionary-group-fires-sex-abuse-investigator.html.

Strathern, Marilyn. *The Gender of the Gift: Problems with Women and Problems with Society in Melanesia*. Berkeley: Univ. of California Press, 1988.

Stuart, Elizabeth. *Gay and Lesbian Theologies: Repetitions with Critical Difference*. Burlington, Vt.: Ashgate, 2003.

Swartley, Willard M. *Homosexuality: Biblical Interpretation and Moral Discernment.* Scottdale, Pa.: Herald, 2003.

Talarico, Jennifer M., and David C. Rubin. "Confidence, Not Consistency, Characterizes Flashbulb Memories." *Psychological Science* 14, no. 5 (2003): 455–61.

Tanner, Marcus N., Jeffrey N. Wherry, and Anisa M. Zvonkovic. "Clergy Who Experience Trauma as a Result of Forced Termination." *Journal of Religion and Health* 52, no. 4 (December 2013): 1281–95. doi:10.1007/s10943-012-9571-3.

Tanner, Marcus N., Anisa M. Zvonkovic, and Charlie Adams. "Forced Termination of American Clergy: Its Effects and Connection to Negative Well-Being." *Review of Religious Research* 54, no. 1 (2012): 1–17. doi:10.1007/s13644-011-0041-2.

Taylor, William D., Antonia van der Meer, and Reg Reimer, eds. *Sorrow and Blood: Christian Mission in Contexts of Suffering, Persecution, and Martyrdom.* Pasadena, Calif.: William Carey Library, 2012.

Terry, Karen J., Margaret Leland Smith, Katarina Schuth, James R. Kelly, Brenda Vollman, and Christina Massey. *The Causes and Context of Sexual Abuse of Minors by Catholic Priests in the United States, 1950–2010: A Report Presented to the United States Conference of Catholic Bishops by the John Jay College Research Team.* Washington, D.C.: United States Conference of Catholic Bishops, 2011.

Throop, C. Jason. *Suffering and Sentiment: Exploring the Vicissitudes of Experience and Pain in Yap.* Berkeley: Univ. of California Press, 2010.

Tracy, Steven R. *Mending the Soul: Understanding and Healing Abuse.* Grand Rapids: Zondervan, 2005.

Trobisch, Ingrid Hult. Interview by Robert Shuster. September 27, 1988. Audiotape. Collection 400. Billy Graham Center Archives, Wheaton College, Wheaton, Illinois.

———. *On Our Way Rejoicing.* New York: Harper & Row, 1964.

———. Papers. Private Collection.

Trobisch, Walter. *A Baby Just Now.* Kehl/Rhein, West Germany: Editions Trobisch, 1969.

———. *The Complete Works of Walter Trobisch.* Downers Grove, Ill.: InterVarsity Press, 1987.

———. *I Loved a Girl.* New York: Harper & Row, 1965.

———. *I Married You.* New York: Harper & Row, 1971.

———. *Love Is a Feeling to Be Learned.* Kehl/Rhein, West Germany: Editions Trobisch, 1971.

———. *My Journey Homeward.* Ann Arbor, Mich.: Servant Books, 1986.

———. *My Wife Made Me a Polygamist.* Kehl/Rhein, West Germany: Editions Trobisch, 1971.

Trobisch, Walter, and David Trobisch. *The Adventures of Pumpelhoober in Africa, America, and Germany.* St. Louis: Concordia, 1971.

Trobisch, Walter, and Ingrid Trobisch. *The Joy of Being a Woman . . . and What a Man Can Do.* San Francisco: Harper & Row, 1975.

Tronson, Natalie C., and Jane R. Taylor. "Molecular Mechanisms of Memory Reconsolidation." *Nature Reviews: Neuroscience* 8, no. 4 (April 2007): 262–75. doi:10.1038/nrn2090.

Tucker, Ruth A. "William Carey's Less than Perfect Family Life." *Christian History* 11, no. 4 (1992).

Tulving, Endel, and Zena Pearlstone. "Availability Versus Accessibility of Information in Memory for Words." *Journal of Verbal Learning and Verbal Behavior* 5, no. 4 (1966): 381–91.

U.S. Equal Opportunity Commission. *EEOC Enforcement Guidance*, no. 915.002. April 25, 2012. www.eeoc.gov/laws/guidance/arrest_conviction.cfm.

Vähäkangas, Auli. *Christian Couples Coping with Childlessness: Narratives from Machame, Kilimanjaro.* Eugene, Ore.: Pickwick Press, 2009.

Via, Dan O. "The Bible, the Church, and Homosexuality." In *Homosexuality and the Bible: Two Views,* by Dan O. Via and Robert A. J. Gagnon, 1–39. Minneapolis: Fortress, 2003.

Via, Dan O., and Robert A. J. Gagnon. *Homosexuality and the Bible: Two Views.* Minneapolis: Fortress, 2003.

Wade, Jarrel. "Judge Rules against Victory Christian Ministers." *Tulsa World,* November 20, 2012. www.tulsaworld.com/news/crimewatch/judge-rules-against-victory-christian-ministers /article_88497413-9a6a-59d7-9521-22d975701e8c.html.

Waites, Elizabeth A. *Memory Quest.* New York: Norton, 1997.

Walker, William. Diary. Papers. Wisconsin Historical Society, Library-Archives Division, Madison, Wisconsin.

Walls, Andrew F. "The Gospel as Prisoner and Liberator of Culture." In *The Missionary Movement in Christian History: Studies in the Transmission of Faith,* by Andrew F. Walls, 3–15. Maryknoll, N.Y.: Orbis Books, 1996.

Watkins, Michael J., and Endel Tulving. "Episodic Memory: When Recognition Fails." *Journal of Experimental Psychology: General* 104, no. 1 (1975): 5–29.

WAVY. "Former Missionary Admits Sexual Abuse." www.youtube.com/watch?v=kT9j8WNAw1M.

Webb, William J. *Slaves, Women, and Homosexuals: Exploring the Hermeneutics of Cultural Analysis.* Downers Grove, Ill.: InterVarsity Press, 2001.

White, Mel. *Stranger at the Gate: To Be Gay and Christian in America.* New York: Plume, 1995.

Widom, Cathy Spatz. "Posttraumatic Stress Disorder in Abused and Neglected Children Grown Up." *American Journal of Psychiatry* 156, no. 8 (1999): 1223–29.

Williams, Joan. *Unbending Gender: Why Family and Work Conflict and What to Do about It.* New York: Oxford Univ. Press, 2001.

Williams, Leighton, and Mornay Williams. *Serampore Letters: Being the Unpublished Correspondence of William Carey and Others with John Williams, 1800–1816.* Memphis: General Books, 2010.

Williams, Linda Meyer. "Recall of Childhood Trauma: A Prospective Study of Women's Memories of Child Sexual Abuse." *Journal of Consulting and Clinical Psychology* 62 no. 6 (1994): 1167–76.

Williamson, Mabel. *Have We No Rights? A Frank Discussion of the "Rights" of Missionaries.* Chicago: Moody Press, 1957.

Willis, Terri, ed. *Parents as Partners.* Richmond, Va.: International Mission Board, 2003.

Winter, Ralph D. "William Carey's Major Novelty." In *Carey's Obligation and India's Renaissance*, edited by J. T. K. Daniel and R. E. Hedlund, 127–49. Serampore: Council of Serampore College, 1993.

Wold, Donald J. *Out of Order: Homosexuality in the Bible and the Ancient Near East.* Grand Rapids: Baker Books, 1998.

Woo, Hanki. "Hankukeui Kyuyangeul Ikneunda" (Discussion of Korean Culture), *Humanist* 5 (2007): 63.

World Health Organization. http://apps.who.int/gho/data/node.main.A997?lang=en.

———. www.who.int/countries/en.

Wrobbel, Karen A., and James E. Plueddemann. "Psychosocial Development in Adult Missionary Kids." *Journal of Psychology and Theology* 18 (1990): 363–74.

Yancey, Phillip. *Soul Survivor: How My Faith Survived the Church.* New York: Doubleday, 2001.

Yap, Mui Teng, Leng Leng Thang, and John W. Traphagan. "Introduction: Aging in Asia—Perennial Concerns on Support and Caring for the Old." *Journal of Cross Cultural Gerontology* 20 (2005): 259. doi 10.1007/s10823-006-9005-3.

Yarhouse, Mark A. *Homosexuality and the Christian.* Minneapolis: Bethany House, 2010.

Yehuda, Rachel. "Post-Traumatic Stress Disorder." *New England Journal of Medicine* 346, no. 2 (2002): 108–14.

Young, Mary. "The Devil Goes to Day Care: McMartin and the Making of a Moral Panic." *Journal of American Culture* 20, no. 1 (1997): 19–25.

Youngdale, Ingrid Trobisch, and Katrine Stewart. *On My Way Home.* Bolivar, Mo.: Quiet Waters Publications, 2002.

Yun, Ji-Whan. "The Myth of Confucian Capitalism in South Korea: Overworked Elderly and Underworked Youth." *Pacific Affairs* 83 (2010): 241.

Zerbst, Fritz. *The Office of Woman in the Church: A Study in Practical Theology.* St. Louis: Concordia Pub. House, 1955.

Zhu, Bi, Chuansheng Chen, Elizabeth F. Loftus, Qinghua He, Chunhui Chen, Xuemei Lei, Chongde Lin, and Qi Dong. "Brief Exposure to Misinformation Can Lead to Long-Term False Memories." *Applied Cognitive Psychology* 26 (2012): 301–7.

Zulu, Edwin. "Reverence for Ancestors in Africa: Interpretation of the Fifth Commandment from an African Perspective." *Scriptura: International Journal of Bible, Religion, and Theology in Southern Africa* 81 (2002): 479.

CONTRIBUTORS

Dwight P. Baker is senior associate editor of the *International Bulletin of Missionary Research*. Prior to retirement he also served as program director and then associate director of the Overseas Ministries Study Center, New Haven, Connecticut (2001–11). Previously he was director of the World Christian Foundations study program at the U.S. Center for World Mission, Pasadena, California (1994–2001). He is coeditor, with Douglas Hayward, of *Serving Jesus with Integrity: Ethics and Accountability in Mission* (William Carey Library, 2010) and co-associate editor of *Family Accountability in Missions: Korean and Western Case Studies* (OMSC Publications, 2013).

Andrew J. B. Cameron has been senior lecturer in ethics, social ethics, and philosophy at Moore Theological College, Newtown, N.S.W., Australia, since 2002. He began a new role as director of St. Mark's National Theological Centre in Canberra, A.C.T., Australia, in mid-2014. He is the author of *Joined-Up Life: A Christian Account of How Ethics Works* (InterVarsity Press; Wipf & Stock, 2011).

M. Daniel Carroll Rodas, a Guatemalan American, is distinguished professor of Old Testament at Denver Seminary, Denver, Colorado. He taught for thirteen years in Guatemala before coming to Denver and continues as an adjunct there. His teaching combines the Old Testament with his Majority World interests. Carroll founded a Spanish-speaking leadership training program at Denver Seminary and is a national spokesperson on immigration for the National Hispanic Christian Leadership Conference. His book *Christians at the Border: Immigration, the Church, and the Bible* (Baker Academic, 2008) has recently been issued in a second edition.

Mary Carol Cloutier has an M.Div. degree from Alliance Theological Seminary, Nyack, New York. After serving on staff with Allegheny Center Alliance Church, Pittsburgh, Pennsylvania, she transitioned to international ministries with the Christian and Missionary Alliance. Mary taught for six years at the Institut Biblique de Bethel in

Libreville, Gabon, Africa, training African church leaders and missionaries. She recently taught intercultural studies courses at Nyack College, Nyack, New York, and is a Ph.D. candidate in the Intercultural Studies program at Trinity Evangelical Divinity School, Deerfield, Illinois.

Graham A. Cole is currently Anglican professor of divinity at Beeson Divinity School, Samford University. He teaches theology and ethics. He has written several monographs in Christology and pneumatology as well as numerous academic articles for books and journals. His most recent monograph is *The God Who Became Human: A Biblical Theology of Incarnation* (InterVarsity Press, 2013).

David R. Dunaetz is assistant professor of psychology at Azusa Pacific University, Azusa, California. His research focuses on organizational processes in churches and missions. He recently completed an empirical study on pastoral attitudes that predict numerical church growth, which appeared in the *Great Commission Research Journal*. He and his wife spent seventeen years in evangelism and church planting in France, where they started two churches.

John Goldingay is David Allan Hubbard Professor of Old Testament at Fuller Theological Seminary, Pasadena, California, and priest-in-charge of St. Barnabas Episcopal Church, Pasadena. He worked in a parish and taught in seminary in England until moving to the United States. He was married to his wife Ann for 42 years until she died in 2009; he is now married to Kathleen Scott. He has written a number of books on the Old Testament, including the "Old Testament for Everyone" series (Westminster John Knox Press). He was a member of an Episcopalian task force on the theology of same-sex marriage, and his writings in this connection and on many other matters are posted at http://infoguides.fuller.edu/content.php?pid=190354&sid=1596614.

Donald Grigorenko is professor of intercultural studies, Cedarville University, Cedarville, Ohio. His doctoral research, carried out at Trinity Evangelical Divinity School, Deerfield, Illinois, focused on morality considered across cultures. He and his wife, Margaret, worked for nine years in a place of risk in South Asia.

Margaret Grigorenko is associate dean of education at Cedarville University, Cedarville, Ohio. She earned a Ph.D. in language, education, and society at Ohio State University and is involved in research focused on literacy and discourse analysis. She has taught in public, Christian, and international elementary, middle, and high schools in Colorado, Oregon, Nepal, Indiana, and Ohio. She and her husband, Don, have four grown children and four grandchildren.

Sunny Hong served as a mobilizer with Wycliffe Bible Translators for sixteen years. She currently serves as an interculturalist with SIL Asia Area in Manila. She is a Ph.D. candidate in intercultural studies at Biola University, La Mirada, California.

Philip Jenkins, author of *The Next Christendom: The Coming of Global Christianity* (3rd ed., Oxford, 2011), taught at Penn State University, 1980–2011. On the faculty of Baylor University, Waco, Texas, since 2012, he has worked extensively in the area of child abuse and sexual crime, and his book *Moral Panic* (Yale Univ. Press, 1998) remains the only systematic history of concepts of child abuse and molestation throughout American history. He has published on child abuse within the context of the Roman Catholic Church and on charges of abuse by cults and religious sects. His 2001 book *Beyond Tolerance* (NYU Press) explores the world of the manufacturers and traders of child pornography.

Joshua W. Jipp teaches New Testament at Trinity Evangelical Divinity School, Deerfield, Illinois. His recent scholarly publications include "Paul's Areopagus Speech of Acts 17:16–34 as both Critique and Propaganda," *Journal of Biblical Literature*, and the book *Divine Visitations and Hospitality to Strangers in Luke-Acts: An Interpretation of the Malta Episode in Acts 28:1–10* (Brill, 2013).

Stanton L. Jones is provost of Wheaton College, Wheaton, Illinois. His scholarly work focuses on psychology and Christianity (e.g., *Psychology: A Student Guide*, Crossway, 2014), Christian perspectives on psychotherapy theories (e.g., *Modern Psychotherapies*, with Richard Butman, InterVarsity Press, 2011), and human sexuality, where his writings have included the five-volume *God's Design for Sex* series (a resource series for Christian parents written with Brenna Jones, NavPress, 2007). His empirical research on Christian perspectives on homosexuality and sexual orientation change includes "A Longitudinal Study of Attempted Religiously-Mediated Sexual Orientation Change" (with Mark Yarhouse), *The Journal of Sex and Marital Therapy* (2011).

Sherwood G. Lingenfelter retired in 2011 as provost and professor in the School of Intercultural Studies at Fuller Theological Seminary, Pasadena, California; he had served previously at Biola University, La Mirada, California. He and his wife, Judith Lingenfelter, have served as consultants for Wycliffe/SIL over nearly four decades in Papua New Guinea, Borneo, Philippines, Africa, and Latin America. Lingenfelter currently mentors doctoral students at Fuller, serves on the SIL International Board, and continues research, writing, and lecturing on missiological topics.

Phillip Marshall is currently missiologist for Asia-Pacific for SIM, an international mission organization based in Charlotte, North Carolina. He has a D.Min. from Trinity Evangelical Divinity School. Previously he has taught cross-cultural studies and Old Testament at Morling Theological College, Sydney, Australia, facilitated SIM's global response to HIV/AIDS, been regional director for SIM in South America, and worked as a family physician.

Andrew D. McFarland is a Ph.D. student in intercultural studies, with a concentration in evangelization, at Asbury Theological Seminary, Wilmore, Kentucky. His interests are cross-cultural evangelism, discipleship, and church planting in the North American and Indian contexts. His research focuses on the significance of William Carey's interdependent missionary partnerships. He has served as a local pastor in the Missouri Conference of the United Methodist Church (2002–8), as a member of the Parkland Regional Youth Pastors Alliance (2002–5), and as an urban church planter (1996–99, 2009–10). He currently serves as the American representative for Bethany Mission Welfare Society in Vizianagaram, India.

Craig Ott is professor of mission and intercultural studies at Trinity Evangelical Divinity School, Deerfield, Illinois. He previously served as a church planter and theological educator in Germany for twenty-one years. His coauthored or coedited publications include *Missionary Methods: Research, Reflections, and Realities* (William Carey Library, 2013), *Global Church Planting* (Baker Academic, 2011), *Encountering Theology of Mission* (Baker Academic, 2010), and *Globalizing Theology* (Baker Academic, 2006).

Jenell Paris is professor of anthropology at Messiah College in Grantham, Pennsylvania. Her publications include *The End of Sexual Identity* (InterVarsity Press, 2011) and *Introducing Cultural Anthropology: A Christian Perspective* (with Brian Howell, Baker Academic, 2011).

Raymond Phinney earned a Ph.D. in experimental psychology and was a postdoctoral research fellow at Rutgers University's Center for Molecular and Behavioral Neuroscience and at the Medical College of Wisconsin. He has used single unit electrophysiology, functional MRI, optical imaging, and behavioral methods to study human attention, perception, and cognition. He has taught undergraduate and graduate courses in experimental methodology, perception, learning, emotion, and memory for over twenty years. He is currently associate professor and chair of undergraduate psychology at Wheaton College, Wheaton, Illinois.

Kersten Bayt Priest holds a B.A. in Bible, M.A. in anthropology, and Ph.D. in sociology. She has designed and taught courses on sexuality. Her publications have focused on issues of race, gender, and international resource brokering. Currently she advises Indiana Wesleyan University's social justice organization and researches issues of human trafficking.

Robert J. Priest is G. W. Aldeen Professor of International Studies and professor of mission and anthropology at Trinity Evangelical Divinity School, Deerfield, Illinois. His research and writings have focused on a wide variety of missiological topics, including short-term missions, the anthropology of conversion, culture and conscience, race and ethnicity, witch accusations, and adult children of missionaries. He has served on the board of the Evangelical Missiological Society (2003–11) and as president of the American Society of Missiology (2013–14).

Jerry Rankin was for twenty-three years a missionary in South and Southeast Asia and seventeen years president of the International Missionary Board of the Southern Baptist Convention. In September 2013 he received the Lifetime Achievement Award presented by Missio Nexus. He is the author of eight books. He currently serves as director of the Zwemer Center for Muslim Studies at Columbia International University, Columbia, South Carolina, and as adjunct professor at several universities and seminaries.

Steven C. Roy is associate professor of pastoral theology at Trinity Evangelical Divinity School, Deerfield, Illinois. He was a pastor for twelve years in Minnesota and Oregon prior to going to Trinity to complete his Ph.D. in systematic theology. He teaches in the areas of pastoral theology and practice, worship, homiletics, and ecclesiology. Roy has published two books, *How Much Does God Foreknow?* and *What God Thinks When We Fail: Finding Grace and True Success* (InterVarsity Press, 2006 and 2011).

Michael A. Rynkiewich did his undergraduate anthropology studies at Bethel University, St. Paul, Minnesota, and his graduate work in anthropology at the University of Minnesota (M.A. 1968, Ph.D. 1972). In addition, he earned an M.Div. at Asbury Theological Seminary in 1994 and is an ordained elder in the United Methodist Church. He has conducted fieldwork in the Marshall Islands (1969–70, 1980) and both fieldwork and missionary service in Papua New Guinea (1997–2002). He has taught at Macalester College (1971–81) and Asbury Theological Seminary (2002–12), and is now retired to the family farm in southwestern Indiana. He has published many articles and several books, the most recent being *Soul, Self, and Society: A Postmodern Anthropology for Mission in a Postcolonial World* (Cascade Books, 2011).

Theresa Lynn Dixon Sidebotham, owner of Telios Law PLLC, is a former MK/TCK. She and her husband, Bruce, both Wheaton College graduates, ministered as tentmaker missionaries in Indonesia for seven years and are parents to four MKs. Theresa serves ministries and missions by advising on a variety of issues, and was selected as a Colorado Super Lawyers Rising Star in the area of nonprofits in 2013 and 2014. For child sexual abuse issues, she has been involved in creating policies, monitoring investigations, giving counsel, and providing litigation defense for churches and missions. She and Brent Lindquist publish a missions blog, The Rock and the Hard Place, on legal and psychological issues.

Anneke Stasson (Ph.D., Boston University) is an independent scholar living in Boston. She has done extensive work on the relationship between Christianity and cultural conceptions of gender and family life. Most recently, her work on American evangelical gender roles appeared in *Religion and American Culture: A Journal of Interpretation*. Her dissertation, "Love, Sex, and Marriage in the Global Mission of Walter and Ingrid Trobisch," examined the way in which the Trobisches shaped a transcultural conversation about the meaning of Christian marriage during the mid-twentieth century.

David Wright has been president of Indiana Wesleyan University, Marion, Indiana, since July 2013. He has held numerous faculty and administrative posts in Christian higher education, most recently as provost at IWU and as dean of the School of Theology at Azusa Pacific University. He holds the M.A. in biblical studies from George Fox University and the Ph.D. in policy studies in higher education from the University of Kentucky. His most recent publication is *How God Makes the World a Better Place: A Wesleyan Primer on Faith, Work, and Economic Transformation* (Christian Library Press, 2013).

GENERAL INDEX

abduction, 39, 156–57, 171
Abraham, 46, 224
accountability
  in Christian lifestyle, 209, 256, 283
  and risk, 38, 80, 109
  and sexual abuse, 124–27,136
addiction, 208, 221, 262
affirming the consequent (logical
  fallacy), 192
Africa, 5, 11–13, 17–19, 26, 28, 53,
  79–81, 83, 85–86, 89–92, 262
  African, 76, 93
    fever, 81, 92
    gender roles and marriage, 10–12
    society, 8, 10
    women, 11–12
  rural, 6
agency, mission. *See under* mission
Alcoholics Anonymous, 152
alcoholism, 163
alienation, 93, 107, 216, 262, 266
All-Africa Conference, 18
alleged offender, 126, 128–29, 133–34,
  137–38
America, American. *See* United States
  of America.
American Medical Association, 157, 167
American Psychiatric Association, 167,
  211
American Psychological Association
  (APA), 157, 182, 193, 211–12
amnesia, 185
  childhood, 169–70

source, 188, 190, 193
Anderson, Rufus, 7
Anglican, 215, 242, 288
anthropology, anthropologist, 27, 93,
  206, 215–16, 224, 232, 234, 256,
  264–65, 268–70, 277, 285, 292
antimissionary spirit, 99
apologetics, 263, 288
arousal, 268–71, 287
arsenokoitai, 213
Asia, 71, 256
  Asian, 57, 72, 75, 256
  Central Asia, 28, 56
  East Asia, 28, 45, 75
  South Asia, 28–29
  Southeast Asia, 75
attraction, 206, 208, 210, 213, 216, 218,
  225, 243, 261, 269, 287, 289
Austria, 13, 17, 19–20

background checks, 124–25
Bangkok, 56, 278
Bangladesh, 58
baptism, 37, 87, 105, 208, 249, 262
Baptist Missionary Society (BMS), 98,
  100, 109–10
Baraka Mission, 80–82, 89, 91
Bass, Ellen, 152, 164
Beck, James, 103, 109
Beidelman, T. O., 93
Believe the Children, 152
Bengal, 98, 105
Bengali, 100

Benita Mission, 82, 85, 88
bestiality, 238–39
bias, 11, 129, 189, 192–93, 197, 212, 225
Bible, 7, 46, 54–55, 57, 64, 75, 86, 209,
    213, 221, 224, 226, 232, 238, 244,
    246, 253, 258, 282, 292
biblical
    interpretation, 224, 242, 247–48,
        250, 260, 265, 273–75, 277, 292
    mandate for missions, 46, 98
    understanding of humanity, 232,
        234
    values or principles, 50, 177, 223,
        258, 260–61, 263, 283
    view of sexuality and
        homosexuality, 224–25, 227,
        232–33, 236–37, 239, 242–43, 247,
        253–54, 260, 264, 274–75, 288
    reading, 55–56
    stories, 55
    study, 51
biography, proper role of, 273–74
Biola University, 209, 222, 227
biology (in sexual orientation), 212,
    215, 285
bisexual, 210, 212, 216–17, 243, 253–
    54, 269
Boserup, Ester, 10–11
Bovet, Theodor, 9, 11
Brownson, James, 215
Bugs Bunny at Disneyland
    (experiment), 171–73, 187
burial, 48, 79, 81, 84, 87–89, 92
Burnham, Gracie and Martin, 45–46

Calcutta, 102, 108–10
California, 135, 153–54, 244
calling, 4, 47, 49, 56, 68, 75, 80, 219,
    236, 254
    missionary. See missionary
Cameroon, 5–6, 15, 18
Cameroon Christian College, 15
Campus Crusade for Christ (Cru), 50
care for parents of missionaries, 60–61,
    63, 65, 68, 70–71, 74, 76
Carey, Dorothy, 98–100, 103–4, 107–8
    Christian care for, 108–9

Carey, Felix, 99, 103, 107–8
Carey, Jabez, 103, 107–9
Carey, Jonathan, 107–8
Carey, Peter, 103
Carey, William, 4, 99–110
    mission family strategy, 100, 102,
        105–6, 109–10
    vision for missionary families, 98
    work in India, 99, 111
Carey, William, Jr., 107–8
Ceci, Stephen, 156, 172
celibacy, celibate, 47, 79, 159–60, 210,
    215, 219–21, 232, 251, 258–59, 262,
    264, 271, 274, 290
cemetery, mission, 80–82, 87–88
chastity, 212, 219–20, 231–34, 242, 258
child protection, 124–25, 130
children of missionaries. See
    missionary kids
children's ministry, 67–68, 70, 73–74
child sacrifice, 238
Child Safety and Protection Network
    (CSPN), 120, 123, 125, 129
child safety policy, 124
child sexual abuse, 120, 122–24,
    126–27, 129, 131–34, 136–38, 143–
    46, 148–50, 152, 156–60, 163–65,
    167–70, 173–77, 192–93, 258
    characteristics of good investigation,
        127–28
    litigation, 122, 130, 134, 137–38
    prevention of abuse, 120, 123–28,
        130, 163
    reporting, 124, 126–28, 136, 151
    therapeutic attitudes toward,
        146–49, 152
Christian
    community, 39, 100, 219, 233–34, 271
    faith, 9, 19
    families, 7, 18, 86
    gay/lesbian. See LGBTQ
    home, 5–7, 13–15, 17, 20, 79, 93
    identity, 27
    parents, 65, 67, 70
    schools, 37, 167
    therapy. See therapy
Christian and Missionary Alliance, 119

Church Missionary Society, 93
claimants, 131–32
Clark, Maria (Jackson), 83–85, 87
Clark, Walter, 83–85, 87
clergy sexual abuse, 150–51, 156,
    158–60, 163–64
Cloutier, Mary, 4, 26
community
    Catholic, 219, 252
    Christian. *See* Christian
    evangelical, 211, 218, 271
    gay, 218, 256
    LGBTQ, 205, 221, 239
complementarian principle/
    perspective, 51, 223
conflict, 27, 41, 47–48, 158, 193
Confucianism, 60–61, 71, 76
conservative, 208, 211–12, 252, 281, 288
contingency plans, 41
conversion, convert, 9, 79, 81, 93, 101,
    105, 108–9, 220
Cook, Philip, 63
Cordill, Esther, 164
Corisco Mission, 80, 82–83, 85, 88–90
Cornelius, 249, 287
corroboration, corroborative studies,
    132, 137, 153, 157, 169–70, 177,
    194–95, 197
Council for Christian Colleges and
    Universities (CCCU), 218, 222
couple power, 5–6, 13–15, 17, 20
Courage to Heal, The, 152–53, 164
creation
    and sexuality, 237, 239
    ideal, 239, 244–46, 288–90
    mandate, 237
    narrative, 237, 288
    order of, 9, 239
    vision, 245, 289–90
criminology, 146–48
crisis management, 33, 46
cross-cultural perspective, 47, 278
cross-cultural witness, 47, 53, 59
cult, 151, 154, 238
    ritual abuse, 150
culturally appropriate practices, 40–41,
    72

cultural
    competence, 32
    context, 26, 40, 144, 158–59, 213–14,
        224, 236, 244, 257, 270
    expectations, 33, 72, 76
    scripts, 232, 264

David (biblical king), 55, 224, 226, 238,
    241, 242, 275
Davis, Laura, 152, 164
death, dying, 29–30, 35–37, 39, 57, 61,
    68, 70, 79–84, 86–88, 90, 92–94, 103,
    108, 110, 210, 215, 262, 289
De Bruyn-Kops, Jacob and Mary, 89
DeHeer, Cornelius and Anna, 82–83,
    88, 92
depression, 92, 100, 163, 167, 171
Dewsnap, Susanna, 91–92
Diamond, Lisa, 216
discipleship, 35, 221, 225, 227, 242
discrimination, 131, 225
disease, 27–28, 33, 48, 104, 289
diversity, 215–16, 260, 277, 287
division of labor, 7, 9–10, 12, 16, 20
divorce, 234, 244–46, 252, 262, 275,
    288, 290
Douglas, Mary, 270
dream interpretation, 175, 193
dysentery, 36, 86, 90–91, 103

East Java, 48, 55
ecology, 231, 234
education, 4, 42, 62, 66, 158, 222, 257, 264
elder care in Korea, 61–63, 74
England, 99–101, 104–5, 107–10, 220
English Baptist, 98
ethics, 206, 215, 253–54, 260, 285
ethnicity, 219, 257, 282
ethnocentrism, 3, 13
ethnography, 27–28, 271, 277–78
etiology of same-sex attraction, 210, 212
Europe, 6
    European, 11, 100, 104, 107, 109–10
evacuation, 30–31, 83, 88
Evangelical Missiological Society
    (EMS), 26, 273, 285
evangelism, 17, 48

Fa' afa' fine, 269
Fair Credit Reporting Act (FCRA), 125
false
  accusations, allegations, 155, 164–65, 170–71, 173–77
  claims, charges, 128, 133, 149
  memories. *See* recovered memory
Family Life Today, 50
family
  bonding, 51
  life, 5, 11, 13–14, 18, 50, 52–53, 84, 92, 110, 174
  in mission. *See* missionary
  planning, 8–10
  spiritual nurture of the, 54
fear, 14, 40, 108, 125, 146, 210, 283–84
feminism, 10–12, 152, 157, 269, 271
Fernandez, Ignatius, 105
fertility rate, 8–9, 62, 71, 76
filial piety, 4, 61, 71, 74–75
folk sexual categories, 268–69
forced termination of missionaries/ clergy, 174
Form of Agreement, 107
Foucault, Michel, 243
Fountain, John, 105–6
Freeman, Derek, 271
Freud, Sigmund, 152, 164
Friesen, James, 154
frogs in a pot, 32
Fuller, Andrew, 100, 110
Fuller Theological Seminary, 209, 222, 224, 227, 246, 286
funerals, 48, 61, 65, 68, 71

Gabon, Gaboon, 80-81, 83, 88-92
Gagnon, Robert, 213–15
Gardner, Laura Mae, 26, 40
Garland, David, 213–14
Gault, William Chambers, 82, 90
gay. *See* LGBTQ
Gay Christian Network, 221
gender, 11, 28, 128, 215–17, 225, 234, 238, 265, 268–69, 271, 277
  formation, 277
  identity, 11, 222
  roles, 7, 10–11, 216, 257, 269–70

generations, 6, 46, 57–59, 136, 211
Geraerts, Elke, 176
Gibeah, 237
Global Bible Translators (GBT), 60, 64–66, 68–72, 74–75
global
  flows, 278
  perspective, 223, 256, 265
globalization, 277–79
Global South, 279
Godly Response to Abuse in the Christian Environment (GRACE), 120
God's acts (or divine activity), 249–50
Goldingay, John, 215, 224, 226, 285, 288–90, 292
Good, Adolphus Clemens, 90
Goodman, Gail, 169
Gospel, 10, 25, 30, 35, 37, 43, 47, 52–53, 57, 70, 72–73, 79–82, 92, 94, 98, 101, 205–7, 210, 225, 227, 242–43, 260, 262, 277, 292
government, 38, 46, 62, 64, 106, 125, 135, 286
grace, 49–50, 57, 205, 226, 241, 253, 259, 263, 283
gravestones, 80, 82, 87
Great Commission, 50, 58
Greek, 213–14
Grigorenko, Donald and Margaret, 3–4, 94
guided imagery, 167, 175, 193
Guyer, Melvin, 166

Hallet, Martin, 220–21, 227, 233, 265
healing and reconciliation, 131, 133
Herdt, Gilbert, 278
heterosexual, 215–17, 219, 237, 242, 244, 246, 253–54, 257–58, 268, 271, 278, 284
hierarchy of sins, 225, 241, 252
HIV/AIDS, 211
holiness, 214, 226, 253, 283–84
homeschooling, 47, 51
homesickness, 92
homophobia, 222, 259, 292
homosexuality, 146–47, 149, 209–12, 214–17, 220, 225, 237–38, 246, 51–52, 254, 257–60, 262–64, 275, 281–83

and marriage, 262
hospitality, 14, 53, 238, 249
Howell, Nancy, 27
human sacrifice, 151
husbands, 3–4, 6–7, 9–11, 14–16, 18–
    19, 28, 31, 47, 50–51, 60, 71, 81,
    88–92, 94, 131
hyo, 61–64, 67, 74
hypnosis, 152, 167, 171, 175, 193

identity, identity formation, 27, 41, 52,
    195, 210, 212, 216–18, 226, 232,
    243, 249, 251, 253–54, 257, 261, 268,
    270, 276–77, 279, 281–82
idolatry, 225, 232, 241, 252
illness, 27, 39, 79, 83, 90–92, 103–4,
    211, 289
image of God, 13, 216, 218, 232, 251,
    282, 284
imagination inflation, 189, 192
immorality, 225, 251–53, 282, 290–91
imprisonment, 31
incarnational witness, 36, 53
incest, 147, 152, 167, 224, 238–39
India, 29, 54, 98–102, 105, 107, 110–11
    Indian, 29, 98, 101–2, 105–7, 109–10
Indonesia, 45, 54–57
initiation rites, 277
intercourse, male/male, 213–14
interdependence, as an approach to
    missions, 109–10
International Mission Board, 45, 51, 58
investigation, 120, 122, 126–34, 137–38,
    144, 157–58, 193, 195, 197, 259
investigative team, 129–30
Isaac (patriarch), 46, 224
Israel, 46, 54, 56, 214, 226, 236, 238,
    249–50, 288

Jackson, Peter, 278
Jacob (patriarch), 46, 89, 224, 289–90
Japan, 71
Jenkins, Philip, 120, 279
Jewett, Paul, 219, 225–26
John Jay Report, 151, 158, 160
Johnson-Odim, Cheryl, 12
Jonathan (Bible character), 238

Jones, Stanton, 211–12, 218, 285, 290–92
justice, 30, 32, 122, 128, 130–31,
    133–36, 138, 149, 173, 222 282

Kahng, Philip and Okja, 65, 68–70, 75
Kidderpore, 105
kidnapping, 28–29, 31, 39–40
killing, 26, 35–36, 154
Kim, Erin Hye-Won, 63
Kinsey, Alfred, 148, 269
Knauft, Bruce, 278
Korea, 60–66, 68, 70–72, 74–76
    Korean, 4, 60–66, 69–70, 73–74

Lavner, Lynne, 246
LeDuc Media, 27
Lee, John and Esther, 65, 68–69, 73–75
Lee, Justin, 216, 218–19, 221, 227, 265
LGBT, LGBTQ, 205–6, 210, 212–13, 215,
    217–18, 221–27, 232, 234, 239, 241–42,
    252–54, 257–58, 264, 266, 274–75, 277,
    279, 282, 286–88, 290–93
    children, 211
    Christians, 221, 239, 291
    community. See community
    evangelical youth, 208, 218, 220–22,
        226–27, 241, 266
Libamba, 15–19
Liberia, 83, 85, 88–89
limiting effects, 224, 241, 275
lines in the sand, 37–38
Lingenfelter, Jennifer, 209–10, 247, 258,
    273–74, 286, 289–90
Lingenfelter, Sherwood, 206–7, 234,
    236, 241, 244, 247, 251, 256–57,
    259–60, 264, 268, 271, 273, 276–77
Littauer, Fred and Florence, 154

lived experience, 27, 264, 273, 283,
    286–87, 289, 291
local language, 6–7, 33, 40, 52, 82, 292
Loftus, Elizabeth F., 136, 156, 166
loneliness/isolation, 6, 26, 56, 64, 74, 87,
    92–94, 127, 219–22, 232, 257, 282, 290
Loomis, Chauncey, 83–84
Loomis, Harriet (Ruggles), 82, 84
lust, 214, 232

Macquarrie, John, 242
Majority World, 72, 75–76
Malick, David, 213–14, 225
managing risk, 4, 29, 34, 39
Marin, Andrew, 219, 226–27, 242, 265
Marling, Arthur, 90
marriage, 3, 5–6, 9–14, 17–18, 37, 41,
    47, 50, 79, 89, 91–92, 215, 219–22,
    224–26, 232–34, 236–37, 243–46,
    251, 253, 258, 262, 265, 275, 279, 288
    covenant marriage, 246
Marshman, Joshua and Hannah, 106–8
Martin, Dale, 213
maternity, 79–80, 84, 89, 93
McMartin Preschool, 150, 164, 172
McNally, Richard, 176
McQueen, George and Georgianna, 84
Mead, Margaret, 269–71
memory
    distortion, 189, 194
    encoded, 184
    failures, 188
    reconstruction, 184, 186–87, 190–93
    retrieval, 184–86, 191–92
    storage, 184, 191
Menaul, John and wife, 82, 88
mental health, 98, 167, 182, 197
Michelle Remembers, 151–53
MinistrySafe, 125
misattribution, 188–90, 192–93
misinformation effect, 187, 191–92, 196
missiology, 5–6, 13–14, 17, 20, 111, 206,
    278–79, 285
mission
    agency, 33, 38, 42, 46, 58, 71, 76,
        119–20, 143, 145, 195, 206, 256–59
    field, 6–7, 20, 28, 47, 51–52, 54, 56,
        58, 75, 80, 82, 85–86, 90, 93, 182
missionary
    calling, 4, 19, 45, 47, 48–49, 59, 75, 80
    care, 60, 71, 205
    children, kids (MKs), 3, 31–32, 48,
        52, 57, 60, 74–75, 81–83, 107,
        119–20, 137, 175, 256
    community, 20, 100–101, 106–7, 206
    couples, 3, 6, 12–13, 50, 89

families, 3–4, 25, 39, 45, 53, 74, 86,
    98, 100–102, 105–6, 108–11, 258
    MK Safety Net, 119
    parents, 30, 42, 54, 59, 65, 68, 72, 80,
        93–94, 98
    core retention, 105
    salvation of, 72
    unity, 106
    widowers, 84, 89, 92
Moena, Sylvia, 12–13
Moody Bible Institute, 209
morality, 242–43, 251–52, 258, 261, 282
Moravians, 99–100, 109
mousetrap experiment, 171–72
multiple personality disorder (MPD),
    154–55
murder, 36, 39, 79, 104, 153, 170, 190,
    226
Murphy, Sophia Lord and Samuel
    Howell, 89
Muslim, 53, 56, 256

Naomi (Bible character), 238
Nash, June, 27
Nassau, Mary Latta, 82, 85–91
Nassau, Robert Hamill, 79–80, 84–94
Navigators, 14
Nepal, 4, 25, 27
network, 34, 40–41, 68, 119, 171, 221,
    278
New Testament, 55, 215, 237, 239, 245,
    252, 285
New Tribes Mission, 45, 119
Nixon, Gary, 222
Nouwen, Henri, 219
Nyquist, Ruth, 19

offspring, 46, 215, 288–89
Ogden, Phebe, 83–84, 92
Ogden, Thomas Spencer, 82–84
Ogowe River, 90
Old Testament, 55, 214, 236–38, 285, 290
    law, 214, 238
OneTable, 222
OneWheaton, 222
"open" celibate leaders, 220–21

opposite-sex attraction, 212, 217
organizational culture, 127
Orthodox (church), 252

Papua New Guinea, 65, 277
parental care ministry (PCM), 60, 64–76
parents
  nonbelieving, 67, 70, 72–74
  of missionaries, 4, 60, 68–69, 71–72,
    74–76
Park, Keong-Suk, 63
Paris, Jenell, 216–19, 225, 254, 257,
  285–87
pastoral response
  to LGBTQ people, 286, 290
  to victims of abuse, 132
Path She Trod, The, 91
Paul (apostle), 3–4, 25, 41, 47, 213–15,
  226, 231, 243, 248, 252, 260, 270,
  275, 292
pedophilia, pedophile, 143, 147–49,
  159, 163
Pentecostal, 252
perpetrator, 119, 127, 146, 164, 169, 195
persistence (in memory), 189
personhood, 11, 218, 265, 277
Peter (apostle), 249, 287
Peterson, David, 213–14
Philippines, 45–46, 65, 265
political pressure, 210, 225, 266, 292
polygamy, 8–10, 226, 238, 245, 262,
  265, 275, 279, 290–91
polygyny, 10
pornography, 124, 149, 208–9, 258, 262
Porter, Rollin and Nancy, 81–82, 94
posttraumatic stress disorder (PTSD),
  163, 167–68, 174, 189
prayer movement, 70, 72–73
Presbyterian, 80, 89
  Presbyterian Church USA, 119
privacy, 129–30, 133
privilege, 50, 52, 58, 82, 130–31, 137–
  38, 216, 284
procreation, 215–16, 233, 237, 245
promiscuity, 211, 220, 226
proscriptive passages, 243, 291

PROTECT Act of 2003, 127
Protestant, 3, 5, 7, 14, 105, 119, 124,
  163–64, 176, 209, 219, 232, 245, 252

queer, 210, 216, 220–21, 243, 253–54,
  278
Queer Underground, 222

Rainey, Dennis, 50
rape, 147, 159, 168, 170, 214, 237–38
Reading, Joseph Hankinson and Mark
  Slack, 90–92
Read, Kenneth, 277
reasonable suspicion, 126–27
recall (in memory), 168, 184–86
recovered memory, 120, 136–37, 152,
  154–57, 165, 173, 175–76, 183, 187,
  191, 194–95, 197
  false memory, 136, 155–57, 171, 173
redundancy, 224, 275, 292–93
repression, 67, 156, 164, 166, 168, 170,
  183, 192–93
  of memory, 136–37, 164–68, 170–71,
    173–75, 177
  of trauma, 166, 175
reproduction, 186, 268, 288–89
retirement, 58, 62–63, 71, 74
retractors, 156, 171
Reutlinger, Solomon and Louise, 82,
  87–88, 92
risk, 32, 34–35, 38
Robert, Dana, 6
Roman Catholic Church, 3, 99, 120,
  122–25, 127, 129, 134, 144–45, 151,
  156–60, 163–64, 176, 209, 219, 225,
  252, 271
  Catholic priests, 123, 143, 160, 163,
    219
  sexual abuse. See clergy sexual
    abuse
romantic love, 219, 232
Ruth (Bible character), 238
Ryland, John, 101, 107

safety, 42, 48, 68, 80, 124, 132
salvation, 46, 70, 72–74, 210, 279

same-sex
attraction, 205–6, 209–10, 212,
214–21, 223, 226–27, 241–43, 247,
258, 260–64, 266, 275–77, 285,
290–91
behavior, 211, 213–15, 221, 227,
277–78, 290
relationships, 224, 226, 236–38,
244–46, 256, 265, 274–76, 290
unions, 215, 236–37
Samoa, 269
Samoan youth, 270
Satan, 49, 154
satanic claim, cult, 151–52, 154,
171–72
Satanic Ritual Abuse (SRA), 150,
153–54, 157
Schacter, Daniel, 188
Scroggs, Robin, 213–14, 225
security, security advisor, 14, 33, 38–39,
41–43, 48, 63, 257
separation, 66, 86, 93, 127
Serampore, 105–8, 110
Covenant, 107
sexual
abuse
allegations, 123, 126–28, 137, 160,
164
of children. See child sexual abuse
identity, 208, 216–17, 233, 236, 263, 266
immorality, 225, 251–53, 290–91
intimacy, 217, 282
orientation, 205–6, 210–12, 216, 222,
251, 253, 266
taboo, 8
violence, 238
sexuality, 132, 145, 152, 160, 211, 215,
220–25, 233–34, 237, 239, 247–48,
254, 256–59, 261, 263, 264–65,
270–71, 274, 278–79, 287, 291
biblical theology of, 237, 239
sexualized coupling, 232–33
Shuster, Marguerite, 219, 225–26
sickness, 26, 29, 36, 64, 83, 92–93, 104
SIL, 65, 292
SIM, 258–59

singleness, 220, 232–34, 251, 258
Sluka, Jeffery, 27, 41–42
Smith, Christian, 271
Sneed, Charity (See also Charity
Menkel), 90
Sneed, Lavinia, 88–89, 92
Sodom, 214, 237–38
sorrow, grief, mourning, 37, 48, 67, 85,
87, 89, 91, 104, 136, 231
Soulforce, 221–22, 265
spilled punch at wedding experiment,
171–72
Strathern, Marilyn, 277
Stuart, Elizabeth, 225
suicide rate among Korean senior
citizens, 64, 74
survivors
of childhood abuse, 151–53, 155–57,
175, 177, 196
of concentration camps, 156

Tanner, Marcus, 174
Tcholliré, 6–13, 15–16
third-culture kid (TCK), 52
terrorist, 29, 31, 37, 45–46
theology, 37, 43, 94, 206, 237, 239, 241,
253, 265, 273, 277, 279, 285, 288–89
of couple power, 13
of marriage, 11
of risk and suffering, 34–35, 40
therapist, 146, 151–54, 156, 165–67,
170–71, 174–75, 182, 191–94, 196–97
therapy, 131–32, 136–37, 147, 149,
151–52, 155–57, 169–71, 174, 177,
182–83, 188, 191–92, 194, 195–97,
212–13
Christian, 154
group, 148
Thomas, John, 98, 102–3
Thurman, Tom and Gloria, 58
Tracy, Stephen, 168
training, 26, 31, 41, 51, 55–56, 70,
124–25, 128, 130, 144, 268
transgender, 217, 254, 265
Trobisch, Walter and Ingrid, 3, 5–6,
8–20, 94

Udney, George, 103
uncertainties, 33, 39, 86, 108, 157, 171,
    223
United Methodist Church
    General Board of Ministries, 119
United States of America, 32, 47, 57,
    87–90, 143, 151, 210, 219, 271
    American, 6, 30, 34–35, 42, 52, 57,
    88, 143, 146, 154, 281
unreached area, unreached peoples, 37,
    43, 48, 57, 82, 89
urbanization, 64, 277–78

Vähäkangas, Auli, 279
Via, Dan O., 214–15
Victims of Child Abuse Laws
    (VOCAL), 155
violence, 27, 29, 284

Walker, William, 89
Walker, Zeviah (Shumway), 81
West Africa, 5, 12–13, 256
Western, 10–12, 32, 35, 52, 75–76, 143,
    164–65, 220, 224, 238, 245,
    256–57, 260, 277, 279, 281
What is . . . What should be, 264,
    285–93

White, Mel, 221, 227
wideness of God's mercy, 226, 241, 275
widow, widower, widowhood, 65, 80,
    83–84, 88–89, 92, 106, 226, 234
Wilberforce, William, 99
Williams, Linda Meyer, 168–69
Williamson, Mabel, 26
wisdom, 41, 43, 80, 94, 147, 209, 242,
    265, 284
witness, 3, 37, 47–49, 51, 53, 58–59, 74,
    94, 128, 135, 195, 205, 237, 252,
    258, 264–65, 275, 283, 291
    wives, 8–10, 12, 28, 39, 50–51, 79, 89,
    94, 100, 131, 224, 241, 243, 245, 262
Wold, Donald, 214
work-family balance, 6, 19–20
World Evangelical Alliance, 26
World Health Organization, 27
wounded, emotionally, 131, 223, 253,
    256, 266, 286
Wycliffe Bible Translators, 4, 64, 71–72

Yancey, Philip, 219
Yarhouse, Mark, 206, 209, 212, 216–19

zeal, 47, 81–82, 92, 94, 99, 155
zero tolerance policy, 131, 133

SCRIPTURE INDEX

Genesis 1–2, 274, 288
Genesis 1:22, 237
Genesis 1:26–28, 237
Genesis 1:28, 46
Genesis 1:31, 289
Genesis 2, 237
Genesis 2:15, 288
Genesis 2:24, 9, 11, 14, 238, 243
Genesis 5:2, 237
Genesis 19, 214, 237–38
Exodus 20:12, 75
Leviticus 18, 239
Leviticus 18:2–3, 214, 239
Leviticus 18:7–18, 239
Leviticus 18:20, 239
Leviticus 18:21, 238
Leviticus 18:22, 213–14, 237–39
Leviticus 18:23, 239
Leviticus 18:24–29, 239
Leviticus 19:3, 75
Leviticus 19:15, 249
Leviticus 20:9, 75
Leviticus 20:13, 213–14, 238
Deuteronomy 5:16, 75
Deuteronomy 6:5, 54
Deuteronomy 10:17–19, 249
Deuteronomy 21:18–21, 75
Deuteronomy 27:16, 75
Judges 19, 237
1 Samuel 1, 238
1 Samuel 1:10–28, 73
1 Samuel 10:1, 238
1 Samuel 18:3–4, 238
1 Samuel 18:15–16, 238

1 Samuel 18:22, 238
1 Samuel 19:1, 238
2 Samuel 14:33, 238
2 Samuel 15:5, 238
2 Samuel 16:11–12, 226
2 Samuel 19:39, 238
2 Samuel 20:9, 238
1 Kings 5:1, 238
1 Chronicles 9:17, 249
Psalm 68:6, 91
Psalm 78:3–4, 56
Psalm 82:2, 249
Psalm 96:2–3, 46
Proverbs 5:18–20, 237
Proverbs 17:15, 173
Song of Songs, 237, 243
Jeremiah 1:5, 59
Ezekiel 16:49–50, 238
Ezekiel 22:7, 75
Matthew 5:14, 74
Matthew 5:15, 238
Matthew 5:17–20, 251
Matthew 15:5–8, 75
Matthew 19:1–9, 243–44
Matthew 19:4–6, 275
Mark 7:11–13, 75
Luke 2:25–35, 73
Luke 2:36–38, 73
Luke 24:47, 249
Acts 10, 249
Acts 10:1–11:18, 248
Acts 11:15–17, 249
Acts 11:17–18, 249
Acts 15, 252

Acts 15:14–18, 249
Romans 1, 214, 232, 275
Romans 1:24–27, 214, 237
Romans 1:30, 75
Romans 7, 232, 270
Romans 11:32, 292
Romans 12:9, 177
1 Corinthians 5:10–11, 225
1 Corinthians 6:9, 237, 252
1 Corinthians 6:9–10, 213, 225
1 Corinthians 6:9–11, 231
1 Corinthians 6:12–20, 243
1 Corinthians 6:15–18, 260
1 Corinthians 7:2–3, 8–9, 226
1 Corinthians 7:29–34, 41

1 Corinthians 14:24–25, 232
2 Corinthians 11:26, 3, 25
Ephesians 5, 243
Ephesians 5:22–33, 51, 243
Ephesians 6:1–3, 75
Colossians 3:20, 75
1 Timothy 1:8–10, 213
1 Timothy 1:10, 237
1 Timothy 5:8, 75
2 Timothy 3:2, 75
James 1:19–20, 242
1 Peter 3:15–16, 263
3 John 4, 59
Jude 7, 238